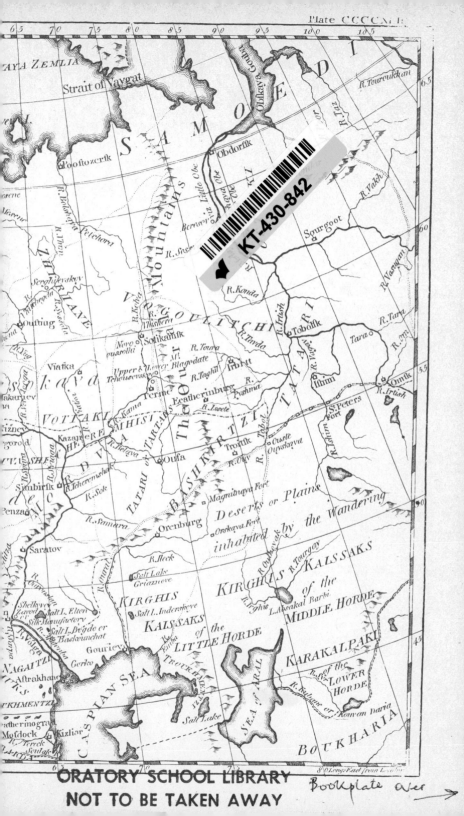

Catherine the Great

Also by Joan Haslip

Parnell: A Biography
Lady Hester Stanhope
Lucrezia Borgia
The Sultan: The Life of Abdul Hamid II
The Lonely Empress: A Biography of Elizabeth of Austria
The Imperial Adventurer

Novels

Out of Focus
Grandfather Steps
Portrait of Pamela

Catherine
the Great

Joan Haslip

Weidenfeld and Nicolson
London

For Henry MacIlhenny
in memory of lovely weeks at Glenveagh
where several of these chapters were written

Russia is no longer to be gazed at as a distant glimmering star, but as a great planet that has obtruded itself into our system, whose place is as yet undetermined, but whose motions must powerfully affect those of every other orb.

George Macartney, November 1765.
British Ambassador to St Petersburg

Contents

Illustrations

The endpapers show a late eighteenth-century map of Russia. *Reproduced by kind permission of the Mary Evans Picture Library.*

Foreword

This book makes no pretension to original scholarship or to the discovery of any startling new material. The two works of the Polish historian, Monsieur Waliszewski, written in the 1890s, are among the best documented and the most interesting of all the many books on Catherine II of Russia. I have drawn freely on both these works and on Mr Soloveytchik's excellent study of Potemkin. My own book is merely an attempt to depict the character and justify the actions of one of the most extraordinary women of her age. In writing I have relied chiefly on the despatches of the various foreign ambassadors attached to her court and apart from the many published diaries and memoirs, I wish to express my thanks to the directors of the Archives of the Quai d'Orsay and of the Public Record Office for giving me access to hitherto unpublished material. I also want to thank Prince Jean-Charles de Ligne for obtaining for me certain unpublished letters in his family archives. My gratitude is due to Countess Lodigensky for allowing me to reproduce the portrait of her ancestor, Count Bobrinsky and to Prince George Galitzine and to Monsieur George Kaftal for their kindness in reading my MS and correcting the Russian spelling of names, where I have tried to keep to the more familiar westernized form, e.g. Potemkin instead of Patiomkin etc.

Preface

When the Empress Catherine ascended the Russian throne in 1762, she was confronted with all the problems of a country still in the making, of which ninety per cent of the population was still illiterate. Peter the Great had died too soon to complete the wide, sweeping reforms which were to make his Empire into a modern European state, and little had been accomplished in the forty years which had elapsed since his death. His immediate successors, his widow Catherine and his grandson Peter II, had lived too short a time to leave their mark in history. Those who followed, his niece, the cruel and sadistic Anna Ivanovna, and her niece, the weak and shadowy Anna Leopoldovna, who had acted as regent during the brief reign of her own son, the Infant Ivan, left their country to be ruled by their brutal German favourites. While his daughter, the gay and luxury-loving Elisabeth, who was swept to power by a palace revolution, was more concerned in reigning than in governing. She glorified his memory by giving St Petersburg some of its most beautiful buildings, and gave Moscow its first university, while her generals brought her victorious armies to the gates of Berlin. But she was of too pious a nature to alienate the church, which under her reign recovered most of the privileges and property taken away by Peter, and she was too dependent on the nobility to enforce the compulsory state service, which Peter had exacted from the highest to the lowest in the land.

When Peter ascended the throne, the whole of his vast

country, stretching from the Arctic to the Pacific, had only one trading port with Europe, which was on the White Sea at Archangel. Sweden and Poland blocked the way to the Baltic, and the Black Sea was still a Turkish lake. It was only after his victories over Charles XII of Sweden that he could expand on the Baltic, construct a navy and build St Petersburg at the mouth of the River Neva. Peter realized that Russia could never become a part of Europe so long as Moscow with its Byzantine traditions remained the capital, and one of his greatest achievements was to make his unwilling subjects transfer themselves to the western limits of the Empire in one of the most inhospitable climates in the world. When he died at the age of fifty-two, he was both the most loved and most hated man in the country, adored by the army, detested by the nobility, execrated by the church.

Catherine, still less than Elisabeth, could afford to alienate the nobility which had put her on the throne. Though she lived in Peter's image and considered herself to be his natural heir, she nevertheless respected the traditions of the other Russias that the reforming Tzar had so ruthlessly discarded.

There was the mystical, mediaeval Russia of the old princes of Kiev; of St Vladimir who, in the tenth century, introduced Christianity into the country, and of his son, Jaroslav the Wise, whose court was a centre of culture and learning for the whole of eastern Europe, and whose daughter married Henry Capet and became Queen of France. The principality of Kiev and its sister republics flourished for two hundred years, till they were destroyed by the devastating hordes of Ghengis Khan. Other invaders followed – Lithuanians from the north and Poles from the west and Kiev became a Polish fief till the middle of the seventeenth century.

Out of the chaos emerged the Russia of the Grand Dukes of Muscovy, whose victories at Khazan and Astrakan freed their country of the Tartar domination. The most important of these princes was Ivan III, who by marrying Zoe Paleologue, the niece of the last Emperor of Constantinople, took upon himself the heritage of Byzantium; adopted the Double Eagle as his emblem and, under the title of Autocrat of all the

Russias, gathered under his rule the debris of the mediaeval principalities and republics. His grandson, Ivan IV, known as 'the Terrible', went a step further in calling himself 'Tzar' or Caesar. During his reign, merchant princes like the Stroganovs discovered Siberia and pushed on to the Pacific. Embassies were exchanged with western Europe and trade was established with England. In his ruthless war against the prejudices and obscurantism of the old Boyar families, Ivan IV may in many ways said to have been a precursor of Peter the Great, till in later years he degenerated into madness, leaving behind him the memory of a bloodthirsty tyrant.

After Ivan's death came what in Russia is known as 'the time of troubles', when a series of impostors, usurpers and foreign princes laid claim to the vacant throne. There was no peace until Michael Romanov, descended from one of Ivan's sisters, was elected Tzar in 1613 and was succeeded by his son, Alexis, who gave Russia its first legal code.

But whether under the rule of the Grand Dukes of Muscovy, of Alexis or of Peter the Great, the terrible abuses of serfdom remained an open sore which no reforms were ever able to heal. On the contrary, the more Russia evolved, the worse became the conditions of the serfs. Slavery, a state to which a man could be reduced by captivity or crime, had existed in old Russia as elsewhere in mediaeval Europe. But the wholesale transformation of free men into serfs had its origins in edicts introduced by rulers who believed they were acting for the good of their country. From the time when Russia began to expand under the rule of Moscow, it became clear that its survival depended on the efficient working of agriculture. There was a great shortage of land workers and this was aggravated by the vastness of the territory and the fact that the Russian peasant – a nomad by origin – always had the wish to move on to new and better pastures. The land owners secured the necessary labour either by offering better conditions than elsewhere, or merely by the process of kidnapping. But gradually the state intervened by a series of decrees spread over many years, which at first limited and then prohibited any freedom of movement for agricultural workers and, to a lesser degree, for other workers as well. Under the Dukes of Muscovy, the peasants still had the right to change their masters, should they so wish, every year at Michaelmas. But they had already lost this right by the time Peter came to the throne, and they were treated like criminals when they attempted to run away.

Peter's reforms, which imposed compulsory service on all, hit hardest at the peasants by binding them more closely to their masters by the Poll Tax, which the landlords had to collect and hand in to the state. He also introduced a passport system, by which a peasant could not cross the boundary of his master's estate without obtaining a written permission. Gradually the number of free peasants was being whittled down, and serfdom reached its lowest level under the reign of the Empress Anna and her lover, the rapacious Biron. Estates without men to work the land were useless, and rulers fell into the habit of rewarding their victorious generals and favourites with the gift of 'souls'. In this respect Catherine was more guilty than any of her predecessors. The enlightened German princess, who in her youth had dreamed of liberating the serfs, condemned with one stroke of her pen the free peasants of the Ukraine to the miseries of serfdom. The crown peasants, who till now had enjoyed a certain amount of liberty, were given away as presents to her favourites. The most worthless of her lovers received large estates and hundreds of serfs. With Orlov, Potemkin, and later with Zoubov, the numbers ran into thousands. Forgotten in the blaze of glory which surrounds her name is the fact that there were two million more serfs in Catherine's Russia than there had ever been before.

CHAPTER ONE

Sophia of Anhalt-Zerbst

Johanna Elisabeth of Anhalt-Zerbst was a woman with a grievance. Born of the princely house of Holstein-Gottorp, related to the royal families of Russia and of Sweden, her lack of dowry had condemned her to a narrow, restricted life as the wife of an obscure German princeling in the service of the King of Prussia. Christian August, who was over twenty-five years older than his wife, was an honest God-fearing Lutheran of limited brains and little ambition, content to spend the rest of his days as the military governor of Stettin, where his children played with the other children of the regiment and learned their catechism from the chaplain of the garrison church. But the pretty, worldly Johanna Elisabeth craved for wider horizons than the marshes of Eastern Pomerania and was for ever dragging her family on visits to the northern German courts, to Hamburg, Berlin and Kiel, ingratiating herself with the more important members of the family who, in spite of her wit and charm, never regarded her as anything more than a poor relation.

To add to her disappointments, her eldest child, born in Stettin in April 1729, was a daughter who, though precociously intelligent, in early years showed little promise of either beauty or feminine grace. Fortunately for Sophia, she had a sympathetic and affectionate governess, a French Huguenot by the name of Babette Cardel, who gave her the warmth and understanding denied her by her mother. But though Johanna Elisabeth was primarily interested in her sons, she gradually grew to realize that her neglected little daughter represented her one chance of ever playing a role on the world's stage.

A combination of circumstances and political events encouraged her ambitions. In 1741, a military *coup d'état* in Russia brought to the throne the last surviving daughter of Peter the Great. Elisabeth Petrovna, who was thirty-two when she assumed the Imperial crown, had in her youth been engaged to a brother of Johanna Elisabeth, a charming young man who, on the eve of their wedding, had succumbed to the then prevalent disease of smallpox. Sentimentalists asserted that the Princess's attachment to her handsome fiancé was one of the reasons why she had never married. The cynics were however nearer to the truth. Passionate and sensual, with the unbridled appetites she had inherited from her father and her mother, the Livonian peasant girl whom Peter had raised to the Imperial throne, Elisabeth Petrovna could find far more virile lovers among her own subjects than by choosing a princely consort from among the restricted circle of German royalties. Nevertheless, she still preserved a certain tenderness for the memory of the young Holstein Prince and her links with the family were strengthened by her elder sister Anne having married the reigning Duke. Anne died three months after giving birth to a son and one of Elisabeth's first acts on assuming the Imperial crown was to adopt her nephew, Peter Ulrich, as her heir. The thirteen-year-old boy who had also recently lost his father was brought from Kiel, where he had been subjected to the brutal discipline with which German princes saw fit to educate their children, and handed over to the care of a beautiful, capricious aunt, ruling over a licentious and extravagant court.

On a visit to Kiel in the summer of 1739, the ten-year-old Sophia had met her mother's cousin who was only a year older than herself. At the time she was surprised to see how everyone, beginning with her mother, went out of their way to charm the pale, lanky little boy who was overcome with shyness by these attentions. It was only later, from the gossip of relatives and ladies-in-waiting, that Sophia began to understand the reason for all this gracious condescension. Heir-apparent to the thrones of Sweden and Russia, Peter Ulrich was the greatest matrimonial prize in Europe, far beyond the aspirations of a little princess of Zerbst.

But Johanna Elisabeth was not a woman to miss an opportunity. She not only befriended her young cousin. She also cultivated his tutor, a harsh and unprepossessing Swede called Brümmer with whom she kept up an active correspondence during the following years. In these years, her daughter grew from an ugly, spotty child with 'an unpleasing expression', into an attractive little girl whom she was no longer ashamed to produce on their round of summer visits. Artists were now commissioned to paint Sophia's portrait and even a misogynist like Frederick, the young King of Prussia, was so favourably impressed by a picture executed by his court painter, Pesne, that the obscure little Princess began to figure in the King's political combinations.

She had none of her mother's pink and white prettiness but, although too thin for the current taste, she had a natural elegance and style. The little head poised proudly on the slender neck was crowned with a wealth of dark chestnut hair. The chin might be too long and pointed, but it was redeemed by the charming mouth with perfect teeth, and the most irresistible of smiles. The blue eyes were not large, but they sparkled with vivacity. As she described herself many years later: 'I was never beautiful but I pleased. That was my long suit.' Perhaps the most dominant trait in her character was this wish to please, which in her relationship with her mother, a difficult unreasoning woman of unpredictable moods, caused her to dissimulate, and this dissimulation gradually became so much a part of her nature that it was hard to tell where the actress took over from the woman. As a child she longed to be loved by her beautiful, domineering mother and suffered from her indifference, an indifference which must have been very apparent, for a Swedish diplomat, Count Gyllenburg, who met the Princesses of Zerbst in Hamburg, went so far as to accuse Johanna 'of underestimating her daughter who possessed far greater qualities than she was aware of and deserved a larger share of her attention' – hardly a remark calculated to please a vain, self-centred young woman whose indifference to her daughter was soon to be replaced by jealousy.

They had certain characteristics in common, but in Sophia's case her mother's superficial brilliance was tempered by her father's solid worth. Her mother's lady-in-waiting describes her as 'at once gay and impertinent, mischievous and unruly, but fundamentally serious-minded with an infinite capacity to assimilate and learn'. She was both the despair and delight of her teachers. The pedantic German professor and the strict Lutheran pastor complained of her as being inquisitive and argumentative, always wanting to know the whys and wherefores of everything. But her French governess succeeded in ruling her with gentle reasoning, inspiring her with a love of French literature and drama which remained with her all her life, so that when writing to Voltaire and Diderot, the Empress of all the Russias proudly signed herself 'the pupil of Babette Cardel'.

But there were certain traits in her pupil's character which even Babette Cardel ignored. There was a latent sensuality, a restless energy provoking unaccountable and uncontrolled urges, so that at night, after she had said her prayers and the lights were turned off in the little room under the clock tower of the castle of Stettin, Sophia would throw off her covers and, astride her pillow, go galloping up and down on her bed until she finally fell asleep from sheer exhaustion. Many years later the Empress Catherine recorded these details in her memoirs, where she frankly refers to her first sexual awakening through the attentions of a young uncle, Prince George Louis of Holstein. According to these memoirs, her mother not only appears to have been aware of these far from avuncular attentions but even went so far as to encourage them. One is inclined to doubt the truth of this statement. Johanna Elisabeth may have been sufficiently cynical to prefer having her daughter married to a Prince of Holstein rather than to having her remain a spinster, as a canoness of some minor order. But there was always Christian August to be reckoned with, who with his deep religious principles would never have countenanced the marriage. Sophia herself never seems to have contemplated the possibility. Her aims were already set far higher, for as a little girl at the court of Brunswick a chiromancer had foretold her a brilliant future, seeing no less than three crowns in her hand.

By 1743 the family prospects had improved. Johanna Elisabeth had the double satisfaction of an elder brother becoming the heir-apparent to the throne of Sweden in place of his cousin, Peter Ulrich, and her husband succeeding his brother as the reigning Prince of Anhalt-Zerbst – a principality of no importance, commanding very little revenue, but nevertheless preferable to garrison life in Stettin. No sooner was her husband installed at Zerbst than Johanna left for Berlin to pay homage to the King of Prussia who, for all his astuteness and deep-rooted distrust of women, appeared to be sufficiently impressed by her glib tongue and superficial culture to envisage her as a useful ally. Only a few weeks later Christian August, whose military talents appeared to be so negligible that Frederick openly referred to him as 'that idiot, Zerbst', was promoted to the rank of Field-Marshal in the Prussian army while his daughter's portrait was forwarded to the Prussian ambassador at the court of St Petersburg, where the Empress Elisabeth was searching for a bride for her fifteen-year-old nephew.

The rival powers each had their separate candidate. Frederick's arch-enemy, Maria-Theresa of Austria, who had the powerful Russian Chancellor, Count Bestuzhev-Ryumin, on her payroll, was in favour of a princess of Saxony. Frederick had a sister of marriageable age, but he was fond of his sister and, in his own words: 'Though an alliance between Saxony and Russia was contrary to the interests of Prussia, he nevertheless regarded it as inhuman to sacrifice a princess of the blood royal on the altar of political expediency.' It was easier to put forward a little princess of Zerbst whose clever, ambitious mother would always be devoted to his interests.

He already had a useful agent in the Imperial court in the shape of the Grand Duke's former tutor, Brümmer, who had now been elevated to the rank of Grand Marshal of the court of Holstein. But his duties were still the same and his title was no more than a sop to his pupil's vanity. For the unhappy Peter Ulrich, who had now become Peter Fedorovitch and had been forced to adopt the Orthodox faith and learn a language he detested, clung with a pathetic loyalty to his Baltic homeland and was far prouder of being Duke of Holstein than of being heir to all the Russias. This was hardly calculated to endear him to his aunt. Even more unpopular was his infatuation with everything that was Prussian and his exaggerated admiration for King Frederick. The Empress Elisabeth was adored by her people for having rescued her country from the 'Germanization' of her two immediate predecessors, her cousins Anna Ivanovna and Anna Leopoldovna. Dismissing their foreign advisers, she had made her court predominantly Russian and her nephew's Prussian cult made him all the more disliked. He was attractive neither physically nor mentally, and her one wish was to marry him off as soon as possible to some healthy young princess who might produce a more satisfactory heir. For all its unpopularity, Germany still remained the favourite breeding ground for eligible princesses and among their ranks Sophia of Anhalt-Zerbst was both the youngest and the most obscure. But two factors spoke in her favour. One was that her mother was the sister of the Empress's dead fiancé; the other was that her father had no pretensions to playing a political role and therefore need not be taken into consideration.

The letter which arrived in Zerbst from St Petersburg on 1 January 1744 was written by Count Brümmer and addressed to Her Highness, the Princess Johanna Elisabeth, marked 'Secret and Confidential'. It contained an invitation from the Tzarina Elisabeth Petrovna, asking the Princess and her daughter to come to Russia at the earliest possible date. No explanation was given as to why the Empress was suddenly so anxious to meet them or why Prince Christian was not included in the invitation. As a postscript, Brümmer allowed himself to add that Her Highness was sufficiently perceptive to grasp the motive underlying the Empress's desire to meet her daughter, 'of whom there had been so many flattering reports'.

This letter made a very different impact on husband and wife.

Johanna's delighted response was counterbalanced by a distinct coldness on the part of Christian August, who disliked the clandestine nature of the invitation and resented the slight to himself. He was genuinely fond of his daughter and, in the past century, the experiences of German princesses married in Russia had been far from enviable. But on the same day and only a few hours later came a special courier from Berlin bringing a letter from King Frederick, again addressed to Johanna rather than to her husband, and making it quite clear that His Majesty had a hand in the matter and that it was in the interests of Prussia for her to accept the Empress's invitation. He wrote that he had always held her in particular esteem 'and that nothing would give him greater pleasure than to be instrumental in helping her daughter to make a brilliant marriage'.

As a loyal vassal, Christian August had no choice but to submit to the inevitable, though with considerable heart-searching as to whether in the event of his daughter becoming a Russian Grand Duchess, she would still be allowed to retain her own religion. His faith meant a lot to Christian August and in spite of many moral lapses in the future, of sacrifices made to political interests and of lip-service rendered to the religion of her adopted country, the future Empress Catherine never entirely forgot the religious homilies delivered by her father, nor the deep-rooted principles of her Lutheran upbringing. As for Johanna Elisabeth, she was far too concerned with herself and the role she was going to play to give much thought to the apprehensions of either her husband or her daughter. Sophia was taken into her confidence under strict orders not to divulge a word to her governess. The fact that her daughter had no difficulty in maintaining this promise shows a control and self-discipline unusual for her years.

In her memoirs written so many years later, the Empress Catherine draws a singularly unflattering picture of herself as a child, making her appear both calculating and self-satisfied and already dominated by her ambitions. She appears to have forgotten the doubts and fears, the terrible homesickness which must have assailed a little girl on leaving her home, her friends, her beloved governess. However much she may have been dazzled by her brilliant prospects, there must have been a certain moment of terror at the thought of going off into the unknown – to that vast, mysterious country of ice and snow where the sun was said to shine for only three months of the year.

Following Brümmer's instructions, the Princesses of Zerbst travelled *incognito* with a small suite and limited luggage. An entirely new wardrobe, suited to the Russian climate, was to be provided for them on arrival. This was a delicate attention on the part of the Empress who knew that the revenues of Zerbst could not run to the luxurious standards of the Russian court, where Elisabeth herself was said to possess nearly fifteen thousand dresses. Sophia, who was later to outvie the most extravagant of her predecessors, arrived in Russia with 'three dresses, a dozen chemises and as many handkerchiefs and stockings'.

Prince Christian accompanied his family on the initial stages of their journey. Sophia scored her first triumph at a court dinner in Berlin which her mother had done her best to prevent her from attending. Johanna may have feared that the thin, pale little girl, worn out by the emotions of the journey, might not come up to Frederick's expectations, or there may also have been an element of jealousy involved. The King, however, refused the excuse that Sophia had nothing to wear and sent round an elaborate court dress belonging to one of his sisters. Johanna Elisabeth, who regarded herself as *persona grata* at the Prussian court, now saw herself relegated to the Queen's table, while her fourteen-year-old daughter sat in the place of honour beside the King, who put himself out to charm and fascinate. So well did he succeed that soon the little girl was chatting away as if she had known him all her life, her pale face flushed with excitement, her blue eyes sparkling. It was the first and last time that these two, who were later to become partners in one of the most heinous political crimes of the century, were ever to meet. Frederick was so delighted with his young guest that he wrote in all sincerity to the Empress: 'The little Princess of Zerbst combines the gaiety and spontaneity natural to her age with intelligence and wit surprising in one so young.'

But Sophia was no more than a lonely, pathetic little girl sobbing in her father's arms when he said goodbye to her at Stettin. It was even harder for Christian August to bid farewell to a child whom he feared he might never see again and whose future he viewed with apprehension. His parting present was a volume of Heineccius dealing with the dogma of the Greek Orthodox religion. This was accompanied by a *pro memoria* of his own composition laying down a line of conduct to be adopted at the Russian court. Written in the bastardized, Frenchified German fashionable in court circles, it contained extremely sensible advice, warning his daughter against the faults to which he knew her mother to be so unfortunately prone. She was to avoid becoming too intimate with any member of her entourage or indulging in any form of intrigue. She was to abstain from taking any part in politics or attempting to interfere in the government of her adopted country. Above all, she was to submit to her husband's wishes and be a good and obedient wife. Perhaps it was well that Christian August died before he saw his daughter disregard every word of his advice.

The journey took six weeks and from Stettin to Konigsberg the two Princesses, calling themselves the Countesses of Reinbeck, travelled in heavy old-fashioned coaches which were constantly breaking down on the bad roads. The cold was intense and the Empress Catherine recalls in her memoirs that by evening her feet were so swollen with chilblains that she had to be carried out of the coach. The inns in the towns and villages were often little better than stables, where the inn-keeper and his guests huddled for warmth round the only stove, disputing their places with dogs and chickens, and the proud Johanna Elisabeth had often to submit to the familiarities of her fellow travellers. From Memel to the frontier there were neither inns nor posthouses and the travellers had to hire their horses from the peasants. Johanna's ebullient spirits had given way to a ceaseless nagging from which her daughter's only escape was in pretending to be asleep.

At Riga, it was like waking from a bad dream. Their *incognito* was discarded together with the shabby, creaking coaches. As a relative to the heir-apparent Johanna was received with royal honours. The flags waved, the bands played and the bells of the burnished, onion-shaped steeples rang out in welcome. The civil and military authorities were waiting at the city gates. A gala carriage, escorted by a detachment of cavalry, drove them to the castle, where a magnificent suite of rooms had been placed at their disposal. The gentlemen and ladies in attendance included some of the greatest names in Russia – Naryshkins, Dolgoroukis and Troubetskoys, members of the old Boyar families whom Peter the Great had harnessed to the service of the state. The meanest lackey had more gold embroidery on his livery than a field-marshal in Prussia, while the ladies had finer jewels than any in the treasury at Zerbst. In her simple dress with her pale little face and unpowdered hair, Sophia appeared like Cinderella. But she was a Cinderella with her head held high, her bright blue eyes taking in every detail of the scene. Her mother was the one who seemed to have lost her head, writing somewhat fatuously to her husband: 'To think that all these honours should be for poor little me, who am so unaccustomed to such attentions. I wake to the sound of trumpets, I dine to the sound of flutes and the guards beat their drums every time I walk in and out of the gates.' Johanna was to have a rude awakening. The bells and trumpets were not for her but for her daughter. It was for Sophia that the Naryshkins and Dolgoroukis had travelled all the way to Riga and that the Empress had sent one of the Imperial sledges with a squadron of cavalry and a host of servants to escort them to St Petersburg.

It was a sledge straight out of a Russian fairy-tale, with gold and scarlet trappings, lined in sable, quilted in satin and stuffed with the softest down, where they could sleep as comfortably as in the most luxurious of beds. Drawn by twelve horses, they travelled smoothly and swiftly along the hard, frozen roads through a snow-covered landscape of vast forests, marshes and ice-bound lakes, where the only sound was the crackling of ice, the soft pad of an animal in the snow and the tinkling of the sleigh bells. Following them were the servants, grooms and cooks, lackeys and maids, to minister to their slightest needs. 'There is even a Tartar whose only duty is to prepare us coffee.' Johanna Elisabeth did not omit a single detail in her letters home.

Travelling in the opposite direction, they came across a train of sledges guarded by police. Barred and shuttered, with neither bells nor lights, they appeared sinister and anonymous. It was a convoy of prisoners being taken to some unknown destination. 'Who are they?' questioned Sophia, curious and inquisitive as always, but all she received was an evasive and embarrassed reply. No one told her it was a convoy bearing the four-year-old Tzar, Ivan the Sixth, his father Anthony Ulrich of Brunswick and his mother the ex-regent Anna Leopoldovna, who had ruled for six months before a palace revolution deposed 'the German brood' in favour of Elisabeth. The child who was guilty of no other crime than to be of royal blood was now fated to spend the rest of his short life incarcerated in a prison cell. Sophia was told only that they were prisoners of state and all unconsciously Sophia of Anhalt-Zerbst already identified herself with the Russian state, in the same way as she already thought of St Petersburg as her capital from the moment she saw its slender spires emerging from the mists of the Neva delta in the pale twilight of a winter's day.

Unreal and fantastic, conjured out of the marshes, St Petersburg was still a city in the making, re-echoing to the hammer of the stonemasons, hiding behind its sumptuous façade the wooden hovels of the original Finnish settlers. But the first impression was magnificent, with the lighted quays reflecting in the frozen Neva, shining on the Baroque carvings of Rastrelli's palaces; Russia's window on to Europe, imposed by Peter the Great on his unwilling subjects at the cost of thousands of lives lost in the marshes and millions of roubles sunk in its foundations. Peter had realized his dreams. St Petersburg now boasted as many inhabitants as Moscow and had become a haven for foreign merchants, a paradise for foreign adventurers.

Sophia fell in love with St Petersburg at first sight, but now there was no time to linger. The Empress was in Moscow where the Princesses were summoned to arrive on the eve of the Grand Duke's anniversary. There was barely time to re-stock her wardrobe with dresses such as Sophia had never dreamt of possessing, but unfortunately there was still time for her mother to indulge in her fatal passion for intrigue.

The French and Prussian ambassadors, the Marquis de la Chétardie and Count Mardefeldt, had deliberately abstained from accompanying the Empress to Moscow in order to pay their respects to the Princesses of Zerbst with whom they were already acquainted and through whom they hoped to derive substantial benefits for their respective countries. Though outwardly allied in the unnatural system of alliances resulting from the war of the Austrian Succession, the two ambassadors were only acting in the interests of their own courts and were at daggers drawn with the Russian Chancellor, Count Bestuzhev, who was heavily subsidized by both England and Austria. King Frederick of Prussia, who still cherished illusions of Johanna Elisabeth's diplomatic talents, wrote to his ambassador that 'the Princess of Zerbst will provide yet another string for the bow with which we will destroy Count Bestuzhev'. Small wonder if Johanna Elisabeth was in her element, seeing herself generously rewarded by Frederick and *persona grata* at the Prussian court. Weaving her extravagant day-dreams, she had nearly forgotten her daughter's existence. But in Moscow, she was to be rudely awakened to the fact that she was merely tolerated on account of being Sophia's mother.

The four-hundred-odd-miles between Petersburg and Moscow were covered in less than four days. Drawn by relays of a team of sixteen horses they travelled at an incredible speed, eating and sleeping in their sledge. On one occasion two of the horses broke their reins and crashed into a peasant's hut. Only the courage of the coachman and a postilion, both of whom were badly wounded, succeeded in saving the life of the future Empress Catherine.

It was eight o'clock in the evening of 9 February when the caravan of sledges drove through the gates of Moscow, which was brightly illuminated in honour of the Grand Duke's birth-day. The lights of flaring torches and Chinese lanterns gleamed on the golden steeples and bronze Byzantine doorways of the fortress palace of the old Dukes of Muscovy. Stone mansions built by foreign architects alternated with the wooden shuttered houses of the East. Luxury and squalor flourished side by side. This was Moscow, the city of a thousand churches, of a hundred cults and deep-rooted superstitions, a city whose rulers in the Middle Ages had resisted the Mongol hordes of Genghis Khan, and whose people still remained opposed to all foreign influences, suspicious of all that was new – a people who were never wholly to accept the German-born Princess who, even in the apotheosis of her glory, would always remain to them the foreign usurper.

CHAPTER TWO

The Empress and her Court

It had been so easy for Elisabeth to win the hearts of the Muscovites. Superbly beautiful, built on a heroic scale, the daughter of Peter the Great represented to her people the incarnation of the Russian spirit. She was the beloved 'Matouchka' who had rescued them from the German influence of her predecessors. Elisabeth's virtues, her superstitious piety, her large-hearted generosity, her spontaneity and warmth were as Russian as her faults – the extravagance and indolence, the recklessness and gluttony, which ended in destroying the beauty on which she set so much store, and the mind which, however lazy and uncultivated, was naturally intelligent and intuitive. No one who saw her could resist her smile or those laughing blue eyes which invited one to share her mirth, drawing one into the charmed circle of balls and masquerades through which she danced away her life.

'Is she never serious?' was the continual complaint of the ambassadors attached to her court when they were kept waiting week after week for the Empress to summon sufficient energy to affix her signature to a treaty or receive some distinguished visitor. But Peter's daughter had inherited from her father her sound judgment of men. Her Chancellor, Bestuzhev-Ryumin, descended from a Scotsman by the name of Best and one of the most brilliant politicians of his day, remained in power throughout her reign in spite of her personal dislike for him. Her earthiness and common-sense came from her peasant mother, who must have had exceptional qualities to attract and to hold the most difficult and unfaithful of men, so that Peter not only ended in marrying her, but in making her Tzarina in her own right under the name of Catherine I. Though kind and clement by the standards of the day, having made a vow on her accession never to sign a death warrant, Elisabeth could, on occasion when her jealousy was aroused, be as cruel and capricious as any of her predecessors, whether it was her father Peter, who had had his own son murdered for opposing his reforms, or her cousin, the sadistic and perverted Empress Anna, who had humiliated her enemies by submitting them to every indignity in serving as her buffoons.

But both Elisabeth's crimes and follies were forgotten in the radiance of her presence and, forty years later, the Empress Catherine could still recall the effect her glorious vision made on the fifteen-year-old Sophia of Anhalt-Zerbst. Sophia and her mother had arrived tired and exhausted at the Annenburg Palace which was then the Imperial residence. They had not even had time to change their clothes before the Grand Duke was announced, having in his curiosity disregarded every rule of etiquette. Sophia was shocked by the appearance of this puny, unattractive boy for, in her imagination, she had glossed over his defects. Wishful thinking had coloured the picture, so that she had come to think of Peter as being both elegant and handsome. But no word of disappointment transpires in her memoirs. All we hear of is the glorious Empress whom the ambitious little girl hoped one day to emulate and outvie. She writes:

No one could see Elisabeth for the first time without being overwhelmed by her beauty and her majesty. She was very tall and very stout without it being in the least bit disfiguring, or in any way impeding the grace of her movements. Her hooped dress was of glittering cloth of silver trimmed with gold. Her unpowdered hair glistened with diamonds and one black feather curled against her rosy cheek.

The Empress was all smiles and condescension, treating Johanna Elisabeth as a close relation, bestowing tender looks on her daughter, who seemed so very much a child in her dress of pink and silver moiré which only served to accentuate her thinness and immaturity. That same night the Empress wrote to the King of Prussia that she was delighted with his choice, and the following day she bestowed on the two Princesses the coveted Order of St Catherine.

For a fortnight Sophia and her mother basked in the Imperial favour. 'We live like Queens,' wrote Johanna to her husband. 'Sophia is commended on all sides. The Empress cherishes her, the Grand Duke loves her. I think everything is settled.' Poor Johanna Elisabeth was still living in a dream-world, dazzled by all the wealth and luxury, and the flattering but dangerous attentions of the French and Prussian ambassadors.

The daughter she should have been cherishing and protecting was left to her own resources, to form her own judgments and plan her line of conduct in a court which was full of pitfalls. With her sharp intelligence, it was not long before Sophia had taken the measure of her future husband and found him lacking in every quality she respected and admired. The brutality of his education, coupled with his pathetic loneliness, had made of Peter a braggart and a coward, recounting the most fantastic tales of his prowess in battle during his father's lifetime at a time when according to her calculations he could not have been more than nine years old.

The Grand Duke was delighted with his gay little cousin, though it could hardly have been flattering for her to be told that he was madly in love with a certain young Countess Lopoukine, whose beautiful mother had incurred Elisabeth's jealousy and, rightly or wrongly, had been accused of being involved in a conspiracy against the throne. Though already far gone with child, Eudoxia Lapoukine was condemned to be publicly knouted, to have her tongue cut off and sent into exile to Siberia. Her daughter shared in her disgrace and the Grand Duke, more out of dislike for his aunt than out of love for his Dulcinea, publicly espoused her cause. Humiliated and angry at having already a rival, Sophia swallowed her pride and won Peter's confidence by her sympathy and kindness. She saw how little could be expected of this weak and boastful boy, who was so extraordinarily backward for his age. But her common-sense told her that it was imperative to be on good terms both with the Empress and with the Grand Duke. With unusual candour she writes in her memoirs: 'I cared very little for the Grand Duke but I cared a lot about becoming an Empress.'

Her ambition sustained her through the long, unhappy years to come, during which she had to battle for her position, her future and even at times for her personal safety. Instead of joining with her mother in opposing the powerful Chancellor, who was angry at having his candidate set aside in her favour, Sophia went out of her way to conciliate and charm him. She was obedient and docile with the Empress, who one day would treat her like a beloved daughter and the following day ignore her existence. There was no one in the royal entourage whom she dared to call her friend. The Mistress of her Household seemed little more than a governess. Amidst all this luxury she felt she was back at school. There were three masters to instruct her, one to teach her the dogma of the Orthodox faith, another to teach her the Russian language, and a third, a famous French ballet master, to make her proficient both in the local Russian dances and in the complicated figures of the quadrilles and minuets. The choice of these three subjects was indicative of what the Empress regarded as the top priorities. In spite of her increasing corpulence, Elisabeth was an accomplished and tireless dancer, capable of holding the centre of a ballroom from dusk to dawn and often changing her dress as much as four times during the evening.

Sophia took her lessons to heart. She was determined to be the perfect pupil and in spite of her German blood become as Russian as Elisabeth. She was dismayed to see how Peter made no attempt to understand or like the people whom she would one day be called upon to rule. She trembled for him when he made mock of the Greek Orthodox religion and derided the Russian language. Every day she despised him more, just as every day she became more alienated from her mother, more self-reliant and at the same time more lonely in this alien world of smiling courtiers with cold, appraising eyes. They were men and women who, for all their jewel-embroidered clothes, were as obsequious in front of the reigning deity as the humblest *moujik* prostrating himself in the gutter when one of the Imperial carriages went by.

Even the luxury was only on the surface. Rubbish, now covered by a pall of snow, was piled against the palace gates; the royal apartments were built for outward magnificence rather than for comfort and the most primitive necessities were lacking. There was a great shortage of furniture in Russia at the time and the richest nobles, even the Empress herself, travelled from one palace to another with their own personal furniture which, usually being French and rather fragile, got broken in transit. In spite of the conservatories filled with exotic plants, the huge stoves and flaring braziers, the rooms were subject to icy draughts penetrating through the damask-covered walls and through the cold, uncarpeted corridors.

In her eagerness to master the Russian language, and being as yet unused to the Russian climate, Sophia would get up in the middle of the night and, while everyone else was asleep, would sit in her dressing-gown with bare feet, forcing herself to learn by heart the complicated syntax of the Russian grammar. The result was that she fell ill with a serious attack of pleurisy barely a fortnight after she had arrived in the country. The Empress was absent from Moscow on a pilgrimage to one of her favourite convents, but she had no sooner heard of Sophia's illness than she hurried back to Moscow where she found the little Princess lying at death's door with her mother and the doctors at loggerheads. Johanna's first reaction to her daughter's illness had been one of irritation at having to renounce the delightful company of her new friends in order to look after a sick child. As Sophia's fever increased, the irritation gave way to panic. Johanna was convinced her daughter had caught the dreaded smallpox and would either die or be so disfigured that she would be sent back in ignominy to Germany. The doctors recommended the fashionable remedy of bleeding the patient, to which the Princess was bitterly opposed, her brother Charles Louis having died after he had been bled. Elisabeth arrived to find Sophia unconscious, her mother and the doctors squabbling

1 Peter the Great of Russia. Painted by Jean-Marc Nattier.

2 The Empress Elisabeth of Russia – a portrait painted by F. Rokotov.

3 A portrait of Catherine in 1748, whilst Grand Duchess, painted by Groot.

4 Count Bestuzhev-Ryumin, the influential Russian chancellor. Engraving by N. Maslov.

5 Peter III with Catherine and their son Paul in 1756.

6 Sir Charles Hanbury-Williams, English diplomat to the Russian court. Painted by J. G. Eccardt.

at the bedside. From that moment the Empress took an intense dislike to her Holstein relative which events in the next few weeks only served to aggravate. The doctors were ordered to bleed the patient and the mother was ordered from the room. Sophia recovered consciousness in the arms of the weeping Empress and throughout the following weeks, while she lay between life and death, Elisabeth rarely left her bedside and even Peter was sufficiently concerned to inquire every day after her health.

It took her a long time to convalesce but the cool calculation, which was such an essential part of her character, never seems to have deserted her for a moment. There is a story told how, at a critical stage of her illness, her mother wanted to call in a Lutheran pastor and Sophia, with all the vehemence she could command, insisted on seeing her religious instructor, Simon Todorski. It seems almost unnatural for a sick, fifteen-year-old girl to have had sufficient presence of mind to make the very remark most calculated to please the Empress. Nor does it win our sympathy to hear of her lying in bed with her eyes closed, pretending to be asleep and listening all the time to the low-voiced chatter of her maids: 'This way', she writes, 'I learned a great deal of what was going on in the outside world.'

It was many weeks before Sophia was sufficiently recovered to appear at court. Her first appearance was on her fifteenth birthday, 21 April 1744, and no one who saw her that day could fail to be moved by her pathetically thin figure, her drawn little face on which the rouge ordered by the Empress only served to accentuate the fragility. She herself writes, 'I had grown during my illness and my hair had fallen out a lot. When I looked at myself in the glass, I was horrified at my own ugliness. I did not recognize my own face.' But the story of the little Princess who had fallen ill working at night to master the Russian language made her popular not only with Elisabeth but with her subjects.

The two people who should have been the closest to her were the very ones who seemed to be the most indifferent. Her mother had the heartlessness as well as the stupidity to ask her, when she was still convalescent, to hand over to her a beautiful piece of blue and silver brocade which had been a present from her paternal uncle. The brocades produced in Zerbst were among the finest in Europe and Sophia had particularly prized this present. But her mother was determined to have it. She was excessively vain and had had the imprudence to fall in love with young Count Betskoy, a natural son of Prince Troubetskoy. She was so infatuated that her one idea was to make herself as beautiful as possible in the eyes of her handsome lover and, however unwilling, her daughter had no choice but to comply with her demand. The Empress had no sooner heard of this incident than she sent Sophia a whole pile of brocades to refurnish her wardrobe, including one in blue and silver, even lovelier than the one she had given away. Johanna's selfishness made her fall still lower in the Empress's esteem, and certain indiscretions came to light which soon turned her dislike into real hatred.

Sophia had not only her mother's jealousy to contend with. There was also the Grand Duke's growing resentment at the way in which she was being held up to him as a good example. What he resented even more were the rich presents she was always receiving from his aunt, and in order to placate him, Sophia had to spend a lot of her pin money in buying him valuable gifts. But in their mutual loneliness this boy and girl who had so little in common were drawn together, not out of affection, for both were convinced the other did not care, but chiefly out of necessity; he because he relied on her superior judgment, later nicknaming her 'Madame La Ressource', she because he represented for her the one chance of ever achieving her ambition.

But there was a moment when her mother's stupidity and indiscretion came near to ruining Sophia's future. Bestuzhev's spies had intercepted the French ambassador's secret correspondence with Versailles. The Marquis de la Chétardie was in his second term of office and no longer enjoyed the same privileged position he had had in the past when he had helped to place Elisabeth upon the throne. A born intriguer, he had asked to return to Russia on a private mission from his king, rather than as an accredited ambassador, and he carried with

him two letters of credentials, one addressed merely to the
Tzarina Elisabeth Petrovna, the other to her Imperial Majesty
Elisabeth Petrovna, Autocrat of all the Russias, the coveted
title which Louis xv had not yet consented to recognize and
which was only to be offered as the price of Russia's alliance
with France in her continuing struggle against England and
Austria. But Bestuzhev was more interested in English gold
than in courtesy titles. Letters between the ambassador and
the 'Cabinet noir de Versailles', the secret diplomacy which
Louis xv maintained without the knowledge of his ministers,
had been intercepted by Bestuzhev's spies, and the decoded
correspondence discovered certain nefarious intrigues in which
both La Chétardie and his Prussian colleague were involved,
and in which the Princess Johanna Elisabeth was called a
Prussian agent. What particularly hurt the Empress's vanity
was the ambassador's slighting remarks on her moral and
physical decline. To excuse himself in having so far failed in
his mission, he described Elisabeth as being 'frivolous and
indolent, running to fat and no longer having sufficient energy
to rule the country'.

These unpleasant revelations were made known to the
Empress when she and her court were in retreat at the Monastery of St Sergius and the Trinity at a time when fasting made
her particularly irritable. Travelling in her suite were the Grand
Duke and the two Princesses of Zerbst, and she had no sooner
received the news than Johanna Elisabeth was summoned to her
presence, from where she emerged an hour later, trembling
and in tears. Sophia and Peter were playing games in the
monastery cloister when they were brought to order by the
Empress's physician, the celebrated Dr Lestocq, who had
enjoyed Elisabeth's confidence since her earliest youth and had
played a leading part in the coup d'état which brought her to
the throne. He was considered to be one of the most powerful
men in the Empire, but now he was afraid the French ambassador's disgrace might end by involving all the other foreigners
in the country, and being afraid he spoke brusquely and
unkindly to Sophia, telling her that this was not the time or
place for games and she would soon be packing her bags and

accompanying her mother back to Germany. One can picture the consternation with which the young girl heard the news which spelled the end of all her hopes and dreams.

Angry scenes and recriminations re-echoed through the monastery's vaulted cells – a somewhat unsuitable background for all those worldly intrigues. If Sophia prayed that night it was to the universal God of Lutherans and Greeks, begging him not to allow the Empress to send her back to Germany. Luckily Elisabeth was sufficiently fond of her not to hold her responsible for her mother's blunders. When Bestuzhev reminded her that the Princess of Saxony was still available, she ignored the suggestion by replying that she had already fixed the date for the official betrothal between her nephew, Peter Feodorovitch, and the Princess Sophia of Anhalt-Zerbst. Her one idea was to hurry on the marriage as quickly as possible, so as to produce an heir which would make the Romanov dynasty secure and, at the same time, get rid of Johanna Elisabeth. As for poor Christian August, there was never any intention of inviting him to the wedding though his wife continued to encourage him in the hope that he would still be asked. Sophia must have secretly resented this offence to her family. She was fond of her father and often found herself longing for his advice in the weeks which preceded her conversion. His letters urging her to consult her own conscience and not to be influenced by material considerations in a decision which concerned her spiritual welfare, were not calculated to assuage her doubts or allay the sense of panic of those last two weeks before she would be called upon to abjure the faith of her ancestors in front of the Empress and the whole court.

Fortunately, the teacher chosen by the Empress to become her religious instructor spoke perfect German, and having served during the two preceding reigns, was versed in the art of persuading Lutheran princesses that the differences between their two faiths were superficial rather than fundamental. Simon Todorski was a subtle and accomplished theologian, more like a sophisticated French abbé than a Greek Orthodox priest. The age-old traditions and superstitions, the mysterious rites and mysticism which made the Greek Church the most conservative and at the same time the most comforting of religions, were presented to Sophia as having evolved from the needs of a primitive people, who found in the incense-laden splendour of their churches, in the jewelled ikons and gold-embroidered robes of their priests, the chanted liturgies and gleaming candles, escape from the misery of their life on earth.

Persuaded by Todorski's brilliant rhetoric, Sophia was ready to revere him as one 'of the most saintly men she had ever known' and to write to her father that 'there was no fundamental difference between the Orthodox and the Lutheran faiths'. Whether from a sense of duty or from opportunism, Sophia was doing her best to assimilate the rites and dogmas of a church for which her clear, rational mind had neither sympathy nor understanding. She envied Elisabeth her simple, peasant faith which made her as credulous and as superstitious as the humblest of her subjects. Sophia wanted to accept what she could not understand, and in the days preceding her con-version she appears to have suffered from a genuine religious crisis. Even her mother noted that 'the child had something on her mind, though no doubt the exhaustion was brought about by all those days of fasting'.

In later life we hear the Empress Catherine referring with considerable cynicism to the conversion of her two German daughters-in-law, saying that 'it should take no longer than two weeks to become familiar with the ABC of the Orthodox church. As for conviction, that could come later.' But the worldly Catherine was a very different person from the im-mature Sophia who was now facing the greatest and the most irrevocable decision of her life.

On the morning of 28 June 1744 she was brought into Elisabeth's room to be dressed by her in person. The Empress paid her the compliment of having ordered her a red and silver gown, the exact replica of her own. The slim young girl, with her unpowdered hair held by a white ribbon, and the opulently beautiful Empress ablaze with diamonds must have made a fascinating contrast as, hand in hand, they led the long cortège, which passed through the length of the royal apartments into the Imperial chapel. There was not a woman at court who had not aspired to be a sponsor or godmother to the new convert, but Elisabeth had deliberately avoided arousing jealousy by choosing an eighty-year-old abbess renowned for her sanctity.

It must have been a terrible ordeal for someone who as yet could speak only a few words of Russian, to stand up in public and abjure the faith of her fathers on the grounds that it no longer satisfied her spiritual needs. But Sophia's clear young voice never faltered for a moment, nor did she forget a word when she professed her new faith in a long creed carefully learned by heart and recited, as she herself somewhat complacently remarks, 'without a single fault'. Even her mother felt proud of her daughter, looking so modest and at the same time so dignified. 'I confess I thought her beautiful,' wrote Johanna Elisabeth of the child she had so often decried as an 'ugly duckling'. The impressionable Elisabeth wept from emotion and the courtiers thought fit to follow her example. Even the Archbishop of Novgorod, who had been bitterly opposed to the marriage, was now moved to tears as he anointed Sophia with the holy oil and baptized her in her new faith as Catherine Alexievna. From that moment Sophia of Anhalt-Zerbst passed out of history and the Grand Duchess Catherine Alexievna took her first steps on the long and lonely road to power.

CHAPTER THREE

Betrothal and Wedding

The title of Grand Duchess on the day of her betrothal, an allowance of thirty thousand roubles, a continual shower of jewels – it seemed as if the Tzarina would never tire of indulging her future niece. Having always chosen handsome and virile young men for her lovers, she may have wanted to compensate Catherine for Peter's physical and mental inadequacy. No one was more aware of the Grand Duke's shortcomings than his aunt. But she was too indolent to make the necessary effort to get rid of the bullying tutors and hard-drinking Holstein officers in whose company he was rapidly deteriorating. Catherine, whose one desire was to please both aunt and nephew, needed all her powers of dissimulation to pretend that she was fond of Peter. She even ended in convincing herself and a friendly relationship developed which in time might have grown into affection.

With the Empress she was still the adoring little girl. Elisabeth's morals and irregular way of life might not provide a very edifying example, but she was far more artistic and intelligent than she is usually given credit for, and it was from her that Catherine learnt to appreciate the beautiful in art and architecture. Peter the Great laid the foundations of St Petersburg but it was his daughter who helped to make it one of the most beautiful cities of Europe. Under her patronage the 'great Rastrelli' adapted the mellowness of Italian Baroque, the tender frivolities of the Rococo, to the pale northern landscape, lighting brick and plaster with vivid colour, turquoise and orange, emerald and pistachio green which shone like jewels in a setting of ice and snow. Elisabeth's greatest gift to her country was Bartolomeo Rastrelli, who reflected in his buildings the majesty, the plenitude and warmth of his Imperial patron, just as Catherine's clear, incisive mind was later to be reflected in the Neo-classical façades and cool symmetry of Cameron's galleries at Tzarskoye Selo and at Pavlovsk.

In her later dislike of her aunt, Catherine would never admit all that she and Russia owed to Elisabeth. The National Ballet, emerging from the stylized Italian and French ballet, was developed in her reign. Her lover, Alexis Razumovsky, the Ukrainian chorister who had attracted her notice when she was still a young princess, was far more than just a handsome peasant. He was a generous and discerning patron of the arts, in particular of Russian drama and opera. Musicians and singers from all over Europe were welcomed to Elisabeth's court and paid princely salaries for their performances. Unlike her aunt, Catherine was totally unmusical. She herself admitted that the only tune she recognized was the barking of her dogs, and she wasted many hours in trying to learn to play the clavichord, the cover of which was more often used as a toboggan when she and her maids-of-honour indulged in high-spirited romps, by placing piles of cushions on a sofa and sliding down on the lid. Fortunately for Catherine, the dances of the day did not require a sense of rhythm and, thanks to the lessons of the famous French ballet master, Laudet, she soon became as proficient a dancer as the Empress.

Elisabeth revelled in masquerades. Today she would be called a transvestite, for nothing pleased her more than to assume male attire. Tall and powerfully built, with superb legs and feet, she looked her best on these occasions, and her favourite entertainment was to make all the gentlemen of her court dress up in hoops and corsets, with which she usually provided them, while the ladies had to wear breeches. Very few appreciated these evenings. Elderly gouty politicians struggled with their immense hoops. Dashing cavalry officers, blushing from discomfiture, wielded their fans like sabres as they manoeuvred a minuet. The ladies, who were usually short and plump with bandy legs, were very near tears at the end of an evening and those who could excuse themselves from attending on the grounds of sickness were accounted lucky. Elisabeth and Catherine, who was still so slim and frail that she must have made an enchanting little page, were probably among the only ones who enjoyed themselves, exchanging mutual and spontaneous compliments on each other's appearance. But at one of these parties the little Grand Duchess nearly broke an arm when she became caught up in the hoops of a huge major general and fell flat on the floor underneath his skirts. This was all very far from the elegance of Versailles which Elisabeth was at such pains to emulate.

The most dangerous and corrupting of all the entertainments at the Russian court was the passion for gambling for enormous stakes. Sums which, in Zerbst, would amount to a year's revenue, were lost every night at the faro tables. The Countess Roumiantsev, who had been appointed Mistress of the Grand Duchess's Household, was among the worst offenders and was constantly borrowing from her young charge. Totally absorbed in themselves, neither the Empress nor the Princess Johanna made any attempt to curb Catherine's growing enthusiasm for gambling. Elisabeth might have done some good, but it is doubtful whether any maternal advice would have been accepted for Catherine was finding it increasingly difficult to live on good terms with her mother.

One cannot wholly accept the account given in her memoirs, in which Johanna Elisabeth is represented as a jealous termagant and she herself as the sweetest and most forgiving of daughters. One must remember that the Princess of Zerbst was an attractive woman of only thirty-two, who by the standards of the day was a good wife and a reasonable mother. She appears to have had sufficient wit and charm to have been a social success on her rare visits to Paris and, in later years, Voltaire wrote to the Empress Catherine of his friendship and admiration for her mother. The Princess had pinned all her hopes on this Russian visit, seeing herself as the architect of a Prusso-Russian alliance. Instead of which, she was in sad disgrace and only tolerated because she was Catherine's mother.

She was openly humiliated on the night of the betrothal when she was not admitted to dine with the Empress and the young couple. Refusing to eat with the other ladies, she was served in solitary state. But what she minded most of all were the laws of protocol by which her daughter now took precedence over her at court ceremonies. She admitted that Sophia, as she still insisted on calling Catherine, had the grace to blush on these occasions. But wounded pride made her bitter and irascible and her daughter was the chief victim of her bad temper. What made the situation even worse was that she was on bad terms with the Grand Duke Peter who had admired her so much in his childhood and who had now taken a violent dislike to her; this came to a head on a journey to Kiev in the late summer of 1744.

Elisabeth was going through one of her religious periods when she spent hours every day in prayer, making the rounds of her favourite monasteries and convents. Wherever she went, she was always accompanied by two bishops and an abbot. These periods were very trying both for ministers and foreign ambassadors, as no politics were allowed to interrupt her devotions. Only a few of the courtiers were sufficiently religious to appreciate the uncomfortable and exhausting pilgrimages, mostly done on foot, and the prolonged fastings. The Empress, who was by nature the greediest of women, took her fasting so seriously that not even milk or eggs were allowed to be served at table. Disliking fish, she lived during these periods almost entirely on mushrooms and preserves.

The eight-hundred-kilometre journey to Kiev was the longest and most ambitious of all the Imperial pilgrimages. The party included over two hundred members of the court, numberless indoor and outdoor servants including grooms and huntsmen. It was characteristic of Elisabeth to stop for hours in prayer at a wayside shrine, and the following morning be off on a hunting expedition. The nobles whose houses she honoured with a visit were put to enormous expense, redecorating rooms, laying out gardens and hiring opera companies for one night's entertainment.

The Grand Duke, Catherine and her mother followed in the Empress's wake. They were not included in the hunting expeditions and travelled by a different route, the Grand Duke travelling with his tutors, the Princesses with their ladies. Peter soon left those whom Catherine called 'the pedagogues' to join his fiancée and there were high-spirited games between the two young people, which ended in Peter upsetting Johanna's reticule and sending her powder and rouge flying in the air. This enraged the Princess and, forgetting that she was addressing the heir to all the Russias, she called her future son-in-law 'an uneducated lout'. Realizing that her mother had gone too far, Catherine sprang to his defence, only to be berated in her turn and soundly cuffed on the ears.

She must have been relieved when Peter stormed out of the carriage in a rage and her mother relapsed into sulks. From out of the carriage window was a whole new world to discover – a world of which until now she had only had a glimpse on occasional trips in the neighbourhood of Moscow. Her arrival in Russia coincided with the one year in three which the Empress spent in the former capital. With her observant eyes, Catherine had already noted the squalor underlying the splendour, the utter misery of the poor. She had noted the chaos and confusion in the administration, the venality of the courtiers. But on this journey to Kiev she came for the first time into direct contact with the serfs – those millions of human beings who were bought and sold like cattle or given in gift by the Empress to one of her favourites. Born in bondage, a man might be the most talented of artists, the most popular of opera singers whom a benevolent master had sent to study abroad and allowed to perform in European capitals. But he still remained as much his master's chattel as his carriage or his horse. The freedom of the artist depended entirely on the nobleman's goodwill.

Catherine saw men and women tilling the fields with the foreman carrying a whip, and all the generous impulses of youth, all her Lutheran training, revolted against the system.

[33]

Both her liberalism and humanity were sincere but the tragedy of her life, making a mock of all her claims to greatness, was that she never succeeded in breaking down the system, and at the end of her reign there were two million more serfs in Russia than at the beginning.

It was during this journey to Kiev that Catherine came under the spell of Russia, awed by the strangeness and vastness of a land where a church, a village or large commercial town was reduced to the same dimensions by the immensity of the plains. The plains gave way to forests where millions of insects plagued horses and travellers, till at last they reached the fertile corn-fields of the Ukraine and saw the bulbous golden domes of Kiev, rising from a rocky bluff above the River Dnieper.

Kiev the Holy, where St Andrew preached the first gospel of Christianity and where the Petchersky Monastery still preserves the most sacred of all Russian relics, the miracle-working Virgin, said to have been painted by St Luke. What did a rational little German Princess understand of the symbolism and mysticism of medieval Kiev? All that Catherine noted in her dry, matter-of-fact way was that she 'had never in her life been so impressed, as by the Petchersky Monastery, where every shrine and niche was of solid gold and encrusted with precious stones'.

She saw with astonishment the corpulent Elisabeth carrying a heavy cross and walking barefoot into the city like the humblest of pilgrims, while soldiers held back the crowds, who clawed and fought with one another in their efforts to touch the hem of her dress. The leading members of the clergy were at the city gates and every monk and nun emerged from their monasteries and convents to join in the great 'Hosanna' of welcome. The crowds were immense and the heat was intense but Elisabeth was weeping ecstatic tears of joy. Alexis Razumovsky was almost as emotional. A Ukrainian by birth, he had inspired the Empress with the desire to undertake this pilgrimage and the fortnight in Kiev was the apotheosis of his career. Elisabeth's energy was incredible. She insisted on visiting every church and monastery on foot, never flagging during the endless round of festivities, assisting at every performance of the historical dramas and primitive religious allegories which both she and Razumovsky loved, but which were not always to the taste of the sophisticated little Grand Duchess.

For Catherine, the magic of Kiev lay not in the holy shrines, but in the muddy waters of the Dnieper, and the old commercial district of Podol sprawling along its banks. She was fascinated by people and by history, rather than by sacred images, and she never tired of watching the strange mixture of races converging in the streets, Turks and Poles, Greeks and Armenians, bartering their wares; half-naked anchorites with matted beards and manacles on their wrists; monks and mendicant friars rubbing shoulders with Jewish merchants and Cossacks from the Kuban. A richly dressed delegation of Polish noblemen come to pay homage to the Tzarina; a Georgian prince on horseback followed by an armed retinue, their scabbards studded with diamonds, all combining to form a pageant far more enthralling than any religious allegory.

Was the modest little Grand Duchess, who passed almost unnoticed in the shadow of the magnificent Tzarina, already envisaging the day when, escorted by a fleet of galleys, she would go sailing down the Dnieper to the shores of the Black Sea to claim a land that once had been Byzantium and was Russia's natural heritage?

The return to Moscow was an anti-climax. Elisabeth had been in a radiant mood throughout her romantic pilgrimage with Razumovsky but was now irritable and suspicious, finding fault with what she had formerly condoned. Catherine was taken to task for her extravagance and debts by a woman who, since she came to the throne, had never opened an account book. All unconsciously, the Tzarina's distrust of the Princess of Zerbst rebounded on her daughter and there were certain people in the Imperial entourage only too ready to insinuate that the young Grand Duchess was showing signs of being both proud and wilful. Nevertheless, plans were going ahead for the wedding early in the new year, when Peter Feodorovitch fell ill with measles. This was only a fore-runner of the tragedy to come. He had barely recovered from his illness, having grown considerably taller but, as Catherine remarked, 'unfortunately as childish as ever', when the court set out on the winter's trek back to St Petersburg.

It was a journey which in the bitter cold of December must have given rise to the most appalling problems, and which could only have been possible in a country of slave-labour. There were over four hundred kilometres of road to keep clear and smooth for the Imperial sledges to travel as fast as Her Majesty commanded. Barrels of pitch and tar and flaming braziers had to be kept refuelled all along the route to light the royal way. Thousands of horses had to be requisitioned for transport and trains of sledges loaded with provisions. Though contemporary travellers pay tribute to the cleanliness and efficiency of the Russian post-inns, they must at their best have been extremely primitive, and it was at one of these inns at Khotilovo, half-way between Moscow and St Petersburg, that the Grand Duke and the Princesses of Zerbst were spending the night when the former was seized by a violent attack of fever. The following morning, the terrified Princesses were informed that His Imperial Highness was afflicted by smallpox. A message was despatched to the Empress who had already reached St Petersburg, and Catherine and her mother, neither of whom had ever had smallpox, proceeded on their journey, leaving their two unfortunate ladies-in-waiting to nurse the invalid.

Their journey to the capital must have been fraught with anxiety. Catherine was in tears, partly out of remorse and compassion for Peter and partly for herself, in which terror of contagion combined with apprehension for the future. If Peter died, she would either be sent back to Germany, or even worse as a Grand Duchess of Russia condemned to spend the rest of her life in a nunnery. In the middle of the night, on the outskirts of Novgorod, they heard the bells of the Imperial sleigh. It was Elisabeth who, having heard the news, was on her way back to Khotilovo. Despite the lateness of the hour, she broke her journey and called on Catherine to give her the latest news, and the two women wept together for a boy neither of them loved.

On this occasion, Elisabeth showed a strength and willpower

worthy of Peter's daughter. Sacrificing her vanity and disregarding danger, the beautiful, spoiled sybarite spent two months in a primitive inn in a small, smelly sickroom, nursing a boy who had never shown her the slightest sign of affection but who had to live to prevent the hated Brunswick brood, the descendants of the half-witted Ivan, from succeeding to her father's throne.

Back at St Petersburg, Catherine lived through anxious days, attending services for the Grand Duke's recovery, writing him long, loving letters in Russian, of which every word was dictated by her teacher and to which she only added her signature. This was deliberately done to please the Tzarina, who never seems to have recognized the absurdity of Catherine writing letters in a language she only partly understood to a boy who would so much rather have received a few lines in his native German.

By the beginning of February, Peter was sufficiently recovered for his aunt to bring him back to St Petersburg where his fiancée was awaiting his arrival with nervous apprehension. They had prepared her for a shock, a disfigurement which they assured her was only temporary. Peter had never been good-looking but there had been a certain distinction in the long pale face with the pointed features. Now the nose was swollen, the eyes watered, the face had become red and bloated, pitted with pock-marks. Elisabeth had arranged for the first meeting between the young couple to take place at night in a dimly lit room in the Winter Palace, and the Grand Duke's valet and barber had been instructed to dress him to the greatest advantage. Their efforts only seemed to have made things worse. The elaborate curled wig, the laces and embroideries, served to accentuate the appalling disfigurement of which no one was more conscious than Peter himself.

Catherine entered the room, young, fresh, exquisitely pretty in her pastel-coloured satins and 'butterfly bows'. Peter took a step towards her, saying in a low voice 'Do you recognize me?', pathetically hoping for some word of reassurance. And it was at this crucial moment that Catherine failed him and, in failing him, added to the misery of the eighteen years to come.

If only she had come forward spontaneously to give him a warm, compassionate embrace, making him feel she loved him, that his appearance was of no account. But for once her powers of dissimulation appear to have deserted her. Hesitating, filled with revulsion, every nerve in her body recoiling from his touch, she forced herself to embrace him and to mutter a few words of congratulation on his recovery. Then she ran out of the room in tears and, according to her attendants, fainted on reaching her apartments. As she herself wrote many years later: 'He had become quite hideous.'

What Catherine did not realize at the time was that the smallpox had not only disfigured him physically; it had also attacked his brain – a brain too weak to stand up to prolonged bouts of fever in the space of a few weeks. Peter had always been shy and backward for his age. But he was not without flashes of intuition and intelligence, and at times was capable of acts of kindness. A gradual mental deterioration dates from this time – the vicious cruelty and addiction to drink which characterized his later years can all be traced back to that fatal illness of the winter of 1745.

Painfully aware of Catherine's physical and moral superiority, he retaliated in offending her pride by extolling the virtues of the coarse, vulgar women whom he professed to admire. His inferiority complex was such that he only felt at ease with ugly women, preferably those with some physical defect such as a hunch-back, a squint or a hare-lip. Catherine on her side was too young to understand his twisted mentality and too sorry for herself to feel pity for his infirmities. She was still very much the little Lutheran princess, hard and unsympathetic to the frailties of others. She was horrified when her mother, humiliated and rebuffed by the Empress and no longer allowed to share her daughter's apartments, found consolation with a lover, by whom she was rumoured to be pregnant. And it was many months before she learnt the true nature of the relationship between the Empress and Razumovsky. Catherine makes a point of stressing her innocence in her memoirs. But what of the amorous Holstein uncle who had paid court to a child of twelve with the full knowledge of the mother? Surely he must have woken the latent sensuality which she already gave signs of as a small child. After a year spent in the most licentious court of Europe, surrounded by idle, profligate young men all aspiring to royal favour, Catherine can hardly have been quite as innocent as she would have us believe. She was above all lonely and unhappy, and the person she missed most of all was her father, the only person who had ever really loved her. But she was far too insecure and too frightened of the Empress to ask her to invite him to her wedding. The official reason given was that the presence of a Lutheran Prince, a Prussian Field-Marshal, as father of the bride would have a bad effect on the Russian people.

Elisabeth had played the Good Samaritan too long and now she reverted to her life of frivolity and dissipation. Neither Catherine nor the Grand Duke was ever included in the intimate supper parties at which Alexis Razumovsky acted as host. But they and the rest of the court accompanied Elisabeth in June to Peterhof, the summer house built by her father on the shores of the Gulf of Finland and which, embellished with waterfalls, cascades and fountains, was among the most delightful of royal residences. Catherine must have refound her natural gaiety at those alfresco fêtes, where she relates how she and her maids of honour succeeded in escaping from the supervision of the older ladies-in-waiting to go boating on the canals or take walks along the sea shore in the opal-coloured twilight of the northern nights. These amusements were very harmless, but they were sufficient to bring her a scolding from her guardians, whose duty it was to see that the young Grand Duchess never deviated from the paths of virtue.

By July the court was back in St Petersburg to prepare for the royal wedding in which Elisabeth intended to impress the world with the wealth and elegance of the Russian court. Rastrelli and his assistants were kept working night and day to complete the new façade of the Summer Palace, court officials were given a year's salary in advance to equip themselves and their lackeys with the latest European fashions. Russian ambassadors abroad were ordered to study the ceremonial and rules of precedence in usage at the Western courts. In spite of the setbacks and disappointments she had suffered at the hands of France, Elisabeth had an unbounded admiration for everything that was French. Versailles was her Mecca and the Dauphin's recent wedding provided a model to copy and, if possible, outdo. French carpenters, decorators and painters, cooks, modistes and tailors were enticed to Russia at enormous salaries and the royal wedding of 21 August, 1745, provided a spectacle in which the Western elegance of France vied with the barbaric splendour of the East. One foreign ambassador described it as 'the most splendid show' he had ever seen. But the smiling bride in her gown of glittering silver cloth, the summer sun reflected on her jewelled crown, had spent the preceding evening crying into her mother's lap like any other frightened little girl. After so many weeks of jealousies and misunderstandings, Johanna had at last got close to her child and, faced with this wild outburst of tears, must have felt a terrible remorse.

But on the following morning Catherine had her first taste of glory, as the Empress placed on her unpowdered head a small Imperial crown and covered her with jewels out of the Imperial treasury. Peter's suit was made of the same cloth of silver as her gown. He also dripped with diamonds from his sword hilt to his shoe buckles. But as his future mother-in-law remarked with unnecessary sarcasm, 'He was not half as pretty as the bride.'

Johanna Elisabeth was not even allowed a place in the gilded coach in which the Empress and the young couple drove from the Winter Palace to the Kazan Cathedral. Only one of Catherine's Holstein uncles, the Prince Bishop of Lubeck, was invited to the wedding and he was so dull and insignificant that he might just as well have been forgotten.

We can envisage Catherine on her wedding day looking very much as she appears in her portrait – with a calm, composed little face and a set, tight smile. The whole day from beginning to end must have been a terrifying experience for a bride who knew how little she could expect from the nervous, twitching figure at her side. Her head was aching from the weight of the jewelled crown, her body was sweating under her heavy silver gown, but never for a moment did she forget to smile or omit a gracious nod. First came the interminable wedding service, the cheering crowds in the street, followed by a banquet of no less than fifty courses held in the long gallery of the Winter Palace. This banquet was followed by a ball, a lifeless, joyless affair at which only the highest in the land, weighed down with years and honours, were privileged to dance a polonaise with the sixteen-year-old bride. Even the irrepressible Johanna Elisabeth, still writing long letters to impress her relatives in Germany, could not disguise the sadness of this loveless wedding. 'The Ball lasted for less than an hour as the Empress was determined to get the bride to bed.' The Princess describes in detail the procession to the bridal chamber, 'where everything was so much quieter and more discreet than at our German courts. There was none of the jolliness and bawdiness usually associated with the unrobing ceremony! The Empress removed the crown. I ceded to the Princess of Hesse the honour of passing the chemise [even now, the poor Princess had to delude her relatives that she was still in favour and in a position to confer favours on others], the Mistress of the Wardrobe handed the bride the dressing gown' – part of the superb trousseau ordered in Paris. Then the ladies retired. Not even the mother was allowed to stay behind to murmur a few reassuring words. And the little bride was left alone, waiting for her husband in her enormous bed hung with puce-coloured velvet, embossed with silver.

From the mother's letters we pass to the memoirs of the bride. Nothing was forgotten in the space of forty years. 'Everyone had gone and I remained alone for over two hours, not knowing what I had to do, whether to get up or to remain in bed. At last the newly appointed woman of the bedchamber appeared and gaily told me that the Grand Duke was waiting to be served with supper, and would come as soon as he had finished.' One can imagine Catherine's rage, the tears of humiliation she was at such pains to hide, at having this insulting message conveyed to her by a woman who was little more than a servant. Ambitious little German princesses were brought up to be docile and obedient, but Catherine was not a docile character, and it must have required a superhuman effort to greet her husband with a loving smile when he finally staggered into her room, slightly tipsy, smelling of spirits and tobacco. She had been taught to accept unquestioningly whatever might be her husband's tastes and habits, but whatever she may have feared and anticipated, she had never envisaged his getting into bed, lying beside her and finding nothing better to say than to chortle 'How it would amuse my servants to see us here in bed together!' We do not know whether it was with relief, frustration or anger that Catherine moved over to her side of the bed and finally fell asleep.

CHAPTER FOUR

The Years of Hardship

I might have been fond of my husband, had he only wanted or
known how to be pleasant. But I came to a terrible conclusion about
him within the first days of my marriage. I said to myself: 'If you
love this man, you will be the most miserable creature on this earth.
Someone of your character will only be satisfied if you receive some
affection in return. This man hardly looks at you, and pays more
attention to every other woman than to you. You are too proud to
complain. So, put a curb on your feelings with respect to this gentleman and think of yourself, Madame.

So wrote Catherine in memoirs intended to justify her
conduct to posterity, assuring us that she would have given
herself 'heart and soul to a husband' who really loved her.
But whether this would have applied to someone as unattractive
as Peter Fedorovitch is open to doubt.

After a year of marriage, when there was still no sign of an
heir, Elisabeth began to accuse Catherine of not making
sufficient efforts to attract her husband who was still so young
and immature. But the little bride who, all consciously, was
longing to be raped by a strong, virile male, was herself too
inexperienced and perhaps too much of an egotist to give
Peter Feodorovitch the encouragement he needed.

The Grand Duke was still a virgin – a state in which he and
Catherine remained for the next nine years, still sharing the
same bed, which as the years went by became ever more odious
and intolerable to the young wife. The Empress, who refused
to believe that a Romanov could be impotent, placed all the

blame on his German wife. Only a few of the Grand Duke's intimates knew that His Imperial Highness was suffering from a slight physical defect requiring only a small operation, which any doctor or Rabbi could perform, but which he was too much of a coward to undergo. Meanwhile, he posed in front of his wife as a womanizer and a debauchee whom she alone was unable to attract. And it took her a long time to realize that Peter's talk was bluff and that his orgies consisted of little more than drinking beer with his Holstein guards and indulging in injudicious flirtations with her maids-of-honour. He was really at his happiest playing with his toy soldiers, making her bed into a battlefield, bawling out his orders as if he were on a parade ground and thereby preventing her from sleeping.

No one was a more unwilling virgin than Catherine who, at sixteen, was ripe for marriage and eager for love. Only fear of the Empress and of being sent back to Germany prevented her from encouraging the idle young courtiers who were so ready to initiate the pretty little Grand Duchess in all the amorous arts and mysteries. One of the Grand Duke's chamberlains, a certain Count Zachary Tchernichev, was banished from court and sent as minister to Ratisbon on the grounds of having attempted to seduce the Grand Duchess. Two other members of the same family, also in Peter's service, came under suspicion and one of them, called Andrew, who was the Grand Duke's particular favourite, was exiled to an obscure garrison town on the Volga for no other reason than that Catherine had been sufficiently unwise to let it be known that she shared her husband's predilection for the handsome young officer.

Soon she found that she had only to favour one of her attendants for him or her to be immediately removed from her service. This applied not only to her maids-of-honour and gentlemen-in-waiting, but also to her servants. It was demoralizing for a girl, so eager for affection, so avid for popularity, to feel that her smiles and favours were to be avoided. She blamed Bestuzhev rather than the Empress for inflicting these petty persecutions, for Elisabeth, who was becoming more indolent with age, dissipated her energies in her devotions and frivolities and left the Chancellor to run her Empire. Bestuzhev could never forget that Catherine had been Frederick's candidate. As Russia's relations with Prussia took a turn for the worse, so Catherine became tarred with her mother's brush and was suspected of being a Prussian agent. The secret police knew of her having been approached by King Frederick and by her uncle, who was now heir-apparent to the throne of Sweden and married to Frederick's sister. Both had offered to supply her with money and a cypher code with which to report the day-to-day events at the Russian court. But she had been too wise and too frightened to comply.

In the past weeks Catherine and her mother had come together and this sudden show of affection was viewed with suspicion by Elisabeth's entourage. Catherine was sad to have her mother go. For all her selfishness and blunders she was still her mother, the one person she could confide in without fear of having every word repeated and misunderstood. But her departure was irrevocable, and at a last interview with the Empress, in which Johanna humbled herself by falling on her knees and begging to be forgiven, Elisabeth gave no other answer than to say: 'It was a pity she had not been more humble in the beginning.'

But the Grand Duchess's mother was allowed to depart with honour, and the Princess of Anhalt-Zerbst left Russia laden with presents, which included a personal gift from the Empress of sixty thousand roubles with which to pay her more pressing creditors. After her departure it transpired that her debts amounted to over double that amount and Catherine, whose pride had suffered from her mother's humiliation, took upon herself the payment of her creditors – a brave gesture on the part of one who was already herself heavily in debt. This accounted for her permanent state of insolvency when, in the later years of the reign, her credit was so low that she was forced to resort to the dangerous practice of accepting bribes from foreign ambassadors.

On arrival in Riga, Johanna Elisabeth found a letter from the Empress requesting her to inform the King of Prussia that his ambassador, Count Mardefeldt, was no longer *persona grata* at the Russian court. The high-handed tone of this letter showed Frederick how much he had overrated Johanna's superficial talents and he never forgave her for her failure. Over ten years later, after her husband had died and the Princess was acting as regent for her young son, Frederick had no compunction in overrunning her estates and incorporating the principality of Zerbst into the kingdom of Prussia. Johanna and her son were forced to find refuge in Paris, where she died in reduced circumstances only two years before her daughter's accession to the Imperial throne.

Prince Christian August himself died a year after his daughter's wedding. In the last months of his life Catherine's letters to her parents were so heavily censored that they were reduced to the merest formula. But her grief over his death was deep and sincere. In his quiet, undemonstrative fashion, he had given her the only real, disinterested affection she had ever known. After only a week of mourning, she had to appear again at court, being informed that a Grand Duchess of Russia was not permitted to mourn for more than a week a father who was not a reigning sovereign.

In boredom and despair, Catherine threw herself with a frenzied gaiety into the puerile dissipations of the court. She devoted hours to her toilette, following the Empress's example in changing dresses eight or ten times a day. Conscious that she was becoming prettier year by year, she became inordinately vain of her appearance. And as she grew prettier, so the Empress's beauty began to fade. The lovely features coarsened, the double chin was becoming more pronounced, the radiant colouring more dependent on artifice and rouge. Always jealous of her beauty, Elisabeth began to notice that the thin little Cinderella was growing into a pretty young woman, with a figure which pleased and manners which enchanted. She herself was reaching an age when she was no longer satisfied with the good-natured, middle-aged Razumovsky, who behaved more like a husband than a lover, and was looking round for stronger and more virile candidates among the younger courtiers, whom Catherine was attracting into her orbit. At first, the Empress's jealousy was unavowed, but there began an era of petty persecutions, slights and unjustified reprimands. Ignoring the fact that she was the first to set an example of vanity and extravagance, Elisabeth accused the little Grand Duchess of being excessively vain, of taking so long over her toilette in the morning that she was often late for mass, and of being so proud and conceited that she considered herself superior to everyone else at court. According to the Empress, she had very little to be conceited about, having not even been able to produce a child. This was the most unjust and painful of all accusations, and Catherine, who did everything to please Elisabeth, even to displaying an exaggerated piety which enraged her husband, could not understand what she could have done to fall so suddenly from favour.

The Grand Duke was a constant source of irritation to his aunt, and on one occasion she went so far as to threaten him with the fate of her half-brother, Alexis, whom her father had disinherited and put to death for conspiring against the crown. In this case, the Grand Duke was guilty of little more than indiscretion. He was particularly fond of playing with puppets and staging performances which, according to his wife, 'were the most boring and insipid of entertainments' but which she was nevertheless forced to attend. These performances took place in a large room with a locked door at one end leading directly to the Empress's private apartments. One evening Peter took it into his head to drill some holes in the door so that he could spy on his aunt's activities. His curiosity was rewarded by the sight of the Empress, uncorsetted and in deshabille, supping with a few chosen intimates, including Alexis Razumovsky wearing slippers and dressing-gown. Instead of keeping this indiscretion to himself, Peter invited several of his friends to witness this unedifying spectacle. Only Catherine was too sensible to participate in an amusement which could easily land them in Siberia, and she begged her husband to desist from provoking his aunt's anger. One of his entourage was indiscreet and repercussions followed swiftly. The Empress came storming into their apartments, accusing her nephew of being 'a wretched, ungrateful brute' whom she had elevated to the throne but whom, if necessary, she would have no hesitation in disowning. The example of the unfortunate Alexis was now given as a warning, a threat so terrible that both Peter and Catherine were stunned into silence. Elisabeth, when in a rage, used the language of a fishwife, and Catherine saw her Olympian deity reverting to her mother's peasant origins. It was small comfort to be told that the Empress was aware that she had abstained from abetting her husband in his outrageous behaviour. There was neither warmth nor affection in Elisabeth's manner – only a grudging respect for an intelligence which aroused her suspicions. And Catherine, who wanted so desperately to be loved, saw that there was now no one at the Russian court whom she could call a friend.

Fortunately at this time there arrived in St Petersburg an old acquaintance from her childhood – that same Swedish diplomat who, in Hamburg, had been the first to recognize the latent quality of greatness in a callow little girl of twelve. On re-meeting the Grand Duchess Catherine, Count Gyllenburg's first reaction was one of disappointment at finding that she had become a smart young woman of fashion, wholly interested in herself and her appearance. He had the courage to tell her that she was in danger of losing her personality if she continued to lead such a futile and frivolous life, and that she would always be unhappy unless she had some resources in herself. He advised her to cultivate her mind and go in for serious reading. Neither foreign nor Russian books were easily procurable at the time. But, encouraged by Gyllenburg, Catherine read whatever came into her hands. It was a curious mixture, ranging from Plutarch's *Lives* to the letters of Madame de Sévigné, from Montesquieu's *Esprit des Lois* to the novels of Mademoiselle de Scudéry. She plodded through a long history of Germany and was fascinated by Brantôme. A life of Henry IV of France came her way and he instantly became her hero – a monarch after her own heart, on whom in many ways she later tried to model herself. The religious fervour she displayed in public, her scrupulous adherence to feast and fast days, were no more sincere than the religious sentiments of a king who declared '*Paris vaut bien une Messe.*'

It was only later that Catherine discovered Voltaire who became the great literary influence in her life. The person who first taught her to appreciate his genius was none other than the Empress's new favourite, the twenty-three-year-old Ivan Shuvalov, a member of the powerful Shuvalov family who ranked with the Vorontsovs among Bestuzhev's bitterest antagonists. In spite of her insatiable sexual appetites, Elisabeth always displayed a certain perception in the choice of her official favourites. She may, on occasion, have shared her bed with a handsome young guardsman on duty at the palace, but the names of the lovers who have come down in history – Dr Lestocq, the Marquis de la Chétardie, Alexis Razumovsky and young Ivan Shuvalov, were all men of a certain merit. The Empress herself was highly artistic but practically illiterate, rarely opening a book other than the Gospels printed in large type. But the new favourite was one of the most cultured men of his day, widely travelled, a patron of the arts and the friend and correspondent of Voltaire, whom he commissioned to write the history of Peter the Great for what was then equivalent to two thousand pounds.

This handsome commission won for Elisabeth the title of 'the Semiramis of the north', given her by that prince of sycophants, Voltaire, who gave the same name to her successor. Catherine, when writing in her memoirs that Ivan Shuvalov attempted to make her overt advances which she was intelligent enough to repel, never admits that it was Elisabeth's young lover who introduced her to the works of Voltaire, nor does she ever want to be reminded that the name given her by Voltaire had been inspired by her predecessor.

Study and reading was not sufficient to satisfy a woman of her temperament. She writes that, in the first years of her marriage, her loneliness was such that she was in danger of becoming a hypochondriac and suffered from terrible migraines. Today, she would have frankly admitted to have been suffering from sexual frustrations. Her craving for violent exercise, such as riding and particularly riding astride, which she only dared to do in secret, all stemmed from the same source and we are reminded of the little girl at Stettin galloping on her pillow in bed after the lights had been put out.

As soon as the snows had melted in those cold northern springs, Catherine, accompanied by an old groom, would ride out into the countryside along the winding canals of the Neva delta, and for a few happy hours escape from the stifling atmosphere of the court. Elisabeth, who was herself an accomplished horsewoman, disapproved of her riding, which she considered to be unconducive to child-bearing, and Catherine was never included in the hunting parties either of the Empress or of the Grand Duke.

As the months and years went by the young Grand Duchess was made to feel more and more that she had failed in her duties. She would never have dared to tell Elisabeth the truth, how her nights were spent in humouring a retarded adolescent playing with the toys procured for him by her maids, or how he was becoming so addicted to drink that he usually staggered into her bed reeking of liquor. She was still loyal to the husband who seemed to delight in making her life as unpleasant as possible. At one time, he chose to train a pack of hounds in their conjugal bedroom, locking them up in her dressing-room where the stench was unspeakable, and often beating them so mercilessly that their cries were pitiful to hear. She writes, 'I do not know who was the more unhappy, the dogs or I.' One of his few redeeming qualities was a passion for music, which unfortunately she did not share. He had a certain aptitude for the violin, but he had a completely untrained ear and it must have been agony for his wife to listen to his 'screeching' for hours on end.

Later, she often wondered how she ever survived those years of misery and degradation in the company of a man whom she could see was becoming ever more abnormal. One day she came into his room to find him hanging a rat and conducting, in the presence of his equerries, a solemn court martial, condemning the miserable creature who had been found guilty of nibbling at one of his cardboard fortresses. Catherine laughed at him for his absurdity, but at heart she was so revolted that for days she could not see him without feeling sick. But though she was now convinced that her husband was mad, she still did not dare to speak of him to Elisabeth.

By nature, Peter was not entirely bad. He was loyal and generous to his father's old servants who had accompanied him from Holstein. But in her determination to 'Russianize' her nephew, Elisabeth, advised by Bestuzhev, ended in dismissing all his Holstein entourage including Count Brümmer, who was blamed for having encouraged his Prussian sentiments. Peter saw his hated tutor leave without regret, but he wept bitterly when his father's old valet, the one person who really loved him, was included in the purge. He was still allowed to retain his Holstein guard, and in Catherine's early years of marriage these boorish soldiers were her husband's favourite companions from whom he learnt the barrack-room language which caused such offence at court.

There was a certain pathos about a Duke of Holstein who was not even allowed to visit his country, which was run in his absence by a Council of State. There were times when he tried to interest himself in the administration, but he was so incapable that in the end he usually had to enlist the help of his clever wife, who thereby learnt her first lesson in politics.

It is strange that a man as intelligent as Bestuzhev and a woman as intuitive as Elisabeth should have been so foolish in their treatment both of Peter and his wife. In order to remind Catherine of her marital duties, Elisabeth appointed as her new Mistress of the Household one of her own relatives – a certain Countess Choglokov, young, pretty, devoted to her husband and her children, and generally recognized as being one of the most virtuous women at court. The Empress appears to have been so naïve as to believe that the picture of Marie Choglokov's matrimonial happiness might set Catherine a good example. She seems to have forgotten that by now the Grand Duchess was a fully grown young woman of twenty, who resented any form of supervision and found Marie Choglokov's stupidity infuriating, and her curiosity insufferable. One of the Countess's duties was to report on the comings and goings of the young court, a role for which she was totally unsuited.

Terrorized by the Empress, she never left Catherine for a moment, making her life a misery with her perpetual nagging, vetoing the most innocent amusements and suspecting anyone with whom she was on friendly terms. Fortunately, it was not long before Catherine had taken the measure of the Choglokov couple and found them sufficiently stupid to be managed. The husband, who had been appointed as Chamberlain to the Grand Ducal court, was a petty little man who made a great show of his devotion to his wife, but was in private a lecherous libertine who even went so far as to make advances to the Grand Duchess, by which she was quick to profit. Nevertheless, for seven years she had to endure the company of this vain, mediocre couple, forever frustrating her wishes and contradicting her orders, driving her to seek the solitude of her own room, to study books which made strange reading for a twenty-year-old princess. But even the heaviest tomes of Montesquieu and Beccaria were preferable to the continual nagging of the insufferable Choglokovs.

These were the years which forged her character, from which she emerged hard, disciplined and controlled, having learnt to curb her temper and her pride. In spite of being an egotist at heart, she was easy to live with and easy to serve, never inordinately severe and, for a woman of her autocratic disposition, surprisingly indulgent, for the *leitmotiv* of her character was an overwhelming desire to love and to be loved. Women fell under her spell as much as men, for underlying her engaging femininity was a masculine strength which gave her the courage to present a bland and smiling mask in the face of the greatest tribulations.

Worst of all was the monotony of her life, the endless round of balls and entertainments; the constant peregrinations across the country, to which the restless Elisabeth submitted the court at all times of the year and where all but the Empress lived in the greatest misery and discomfort. There were occasions when even Catherine had to change into gala dress, shivering in front of a smoking kitchen stove and live in a tent where she was ankle-deep in water. Apart from the religious pilgrimages, which were a constant feature of court life, there were visits to the Baltic ports and dockyards, where Peter's daughter was at her happiest in the uniform of an admiral of the fleet, and where on one occasion the high winds swept the royal tents into the sea. Every three years there was the Imperial visit to Moscow, where both the Empress and the court lived in wooden, badly ventilated palaces, in constant danger of being burnt alive, for Moscow had the highest percentage of fires of any city in the world. On one occasion, when fire broke out in the Annenburg Palace, the whole vast edifice and its contents of valuable furniture and tapestries, including a large part of the Empress's wardrobe, burnt in the space of a few hours. Catherine recalls in her laconic fashion that she saw 'thousands of rats scurrying down the stairs like an evacuating army'.

She hated these visits to Moscow. She was to hate them all her life in the same way as she hated the inhabitants, with their slothful ways and oriental fatalism. 'There was not a nobleman in Moscow' who would not have liked to see St Petersburg sink back into the marshes so long as he was able to continue to live near his estates, where he could rule as a petty tyrant, maltreating his servants, martyrizing his serfs whom he punished by torture and condemned for the most trivial offences.

Forty years later Catherine was still inveighing against the Muscovites who lived in luxury and in squalor, 'the great ladies blazing with diamonds, driving out of courtyards piled high with filth, their lackeys wearing dirty liveries rich with gold lace'. What she resented most was that this corrupt aristocracy, whom she despised, had been powerful enough to prevent her from carrying out her plans for reform or to realize her ambitions to better the conditions among the serfs.

In Elisabeth's reign she was still an onlooker, still hoping the time would come when the Muscovites would acclaim her as warmly as they now acclaimed the Tzarina. All her love and admiration for Elisabeth had gone, and she noted with a cold, clear eye the famous beauty fading, the growing addiction to strong liquor, the obsessive fears and superstitions which were clouding her mind and distorting her judgment. Bestuzhev had only to hint of a conspiracy in favour of the boy

Tzar, incarcerated at Schlusselburg, and the Empress, who had formerly been so loyal to her friends, was now ready to sacrifice any one of them on the merest suspicion. In this way, the Chancellor proceeded to get rid of Count Lestocq, whose influence over the Empress had always been a thorn in his flesh. A few indiscreet letters had fallen into his possession, and the man who had been Elisabeth's physician since her earliest childhood, and later the lover of her youth, was accused of being in the pay of France and placed under arrest. 'She did not even have the courage to defend an innocent,' wrote Catherine in disgust. But how many times in the future would her own destiny compel her to yield to political expediency and allow the instruments of power to remove all obstacles from her path.

In all his arrogance and bluntness, the royal physician had always been on her side, warning her of dangers, watching over her interests and even at times protecting her from Elisabeth's anger. Now that Lestocq had gone she suddenly felt afraid both for herself and her weakling of a husband – a childless couple representing the only hope for a Romanov succession.

In 1751 Elisabeth had her first serious illness, violent and protracted colic with high fever, which was probably brought on by over-eating but was sufficiently dangerous to give cause for concern. Attention was now for the first time focused on the heir, of whom it was rumoured that, though he was always falling in love, pursuing his courtship with a passionate ardour, none of the objects of his affection were ever brought to bed. Peter's wife had noted his persistent refusal to go to the baths, a custom which in Russia, as in Turkey, derived from Byzantium and was one of the few native habits of which she thoroughly approved. Not even the Empress's threats could force Peter Feodorovitch to the bath house, nor did he ever allow himself to be examined by a doctor, partly out of nervousness, partly out of shame at his infirmity. Even the Empress had at long last to recognize the truth and accept the fact that the pretty, seductive Grand Duchess was not to blame for the childless marriage. In her alarm for the succession, Elisabeth accepted

Bestuzhev's suggestion 'that it might be wiser to relax the supervision at the Grand Ducal court'.

Was it by accident or design that, in the early spring of 1752, two new chamberlains were appointed to the young court, both good-looking and both belonging to the most distinguished of the old Boyar families. The older and by far the more intelligent was Leon Naryshkin, who, for all his charm, always persisted in playing the buffoon and by never aspiring to be more than an entertainer succeeded in winning and in retaining Catherine's lifelong friendship. Serge Saltykof was of a very different character – a spoilt young libertine, a born seducer, who delighted in courting risks, but who was adept at avoiding danger. There was a time when even the Empress was said to have fallen to his charm and offered him the role of Imperial favourite, an honour he had the courage to decline. After a brief absence from court he returned and, after a whirlwind courtship, married the prettiest of Elisabeth's maids-of-honour. But this was two years ago. Saltykof was already tired of married life and in search of new adventures. The fascinating Grand Duchess, who was still reputed to be a virgin, had an irresistible appeal for a man of his type.

At twenty-three, Catherine had all the arts and graces of an *allumeuse*. She was a woman who still curbed her natural inclinations through fear and derived what satisfaction she could from arousing the passions of her admirers. But now the situation had changed. The dreaded Choglokovs were suddenly amenable. Both Naryshkin and Saltykof went out of their way to cultivate their friendship and Catherine, who had hitherto avoided their company, now accepted their invitations with alacrity, certain of finding the two new chamberlains.

There were evening parties at their house in town and picnics on their island in the Neva delta. Even Peter appeared to be delighted with the two young officers, who succeeded in winning his confidence and in weaning him away from his Holstein grenadiers. When the court moved out to Peterhof for the summer, the atmosphere became even more relaxed. Marie Choglokov, who was expecting her seventh child, was confined to her couch, and Catherine went out riding every day accompanied by her two young cavaliers, with Naryshkin playing the role of the discreetest and most evasive of chaperons. As they galloped along the shingle beaches of the Gulf of Finland or followed the canals which meandered through the birch woods, Saltykof lost no opportunity in pursuing a courtship more ardent and more insistent than Catherine had ever experienced. She was so new to love, so malleable in his hands, though she prided herself on having at first resisted his advances by reminding him of his duties to his young wife. 'I held out all during the spring and early summer,' she declares. But her protests sound unconvincing and by August Saltykof could boast of having trespassed on forbidden ground and found the defences down. 'He was as beautiful as the day,' writes Catherine. 'No one at court could equal him.' But there was little tenderness or romance in her first love-affair which ended in bitterness and disillusion. Saltykof was a professional seducer rather than a lover. Nor was he very discreet. Rumours got around and both he and Naryshkin were advised to spend a few months on their country estates.

But this time there was no question of banishment, and Catherine recalls a curious conversation she had with Countess Choglokov in the early spring of 1753, when she had already been Saltykof's mistress for the past nine months. She writes of how Marie Choglokov came one evening to her room and, after a long preamble on the joys and vicissitudes of married life, the conjugal duties in which she herself had never failed, she went on to say that there were certain exceptions and certain situations where one's first duty was to one's country rather than to one's husband, and that Catherine was one of these exceptions. The Grand Duchess listened in astonishment to what was practically an invitation to adultery. At first she thought it was a trap to provoke some indiscretion on her part. But the Countess's obvious embarrassment showed she was sincere and that someone had deliberately ordered her to speak in this manner.

Marie Choglokov went on to say that 'she had noticed the Grand Duchess was paying particular attention to one person, whom she guessed to be either Serge Saltykof or Leon Naryshkin, and she was inclined to think it was the latter'. At which Catherine cried out unwittingly, 'Oh no, it's not him.' The Countess having gained her point, replied, 'Well, then, it's Saltykof', and she added with a smile, 'You will see that also I am a good patriot and will make no kind of difficulties for you.'

This conversation took place when Saltykof's enthusiasm was already on the wane. During one enchanted summer Catherine had believed herself to be loved and in love. But Serge was prudent by nature and nervous of becoming too involved. He had not reckoned on being made into an instrument of state, or of having every one of his assignations reported by the secret police. Catherine, when she was provocative and unattainable, had been far more attractive to him than now, when she was ardently and possessively in love. Saltykof was the first but not the last of Catherine's lovers to be put off by the eagerness and aggressiveness of her love-making.

CHAPTER FIVE

Begetting an Heir

Meanwhile the court had moved to Moscow and, on the journey, Catherine had her first miscarriage. Two months later she was joined by Saltykof, but he was no longer so assiduous in his courtship: his wife's presence gave him a valid excuse to exercise discretion. Nevertheless, in the summer of 1753, Catherine had a second miscarriage which terminated a three months' pregnancy, and there is no doubt that Serge Saltykof was responsible for both these pregnancies. But the paternity of the infant Paul, born in the September of 1754, is a matter which is still open to question. Physically and mentally, Paul Petrovitch resembled the Grand Duke Peter. There was the same streak of abnormality – the kind, even noble instincts allied to the cruelty and viciousness of the weak – characteristics which in turn were inherited by his second son, the Grand Duke Constantine.

A curious story is related by the French agent, Champeaux, one of the many spies in the service of the '*Cabinet noir de Versailles*', who related that 'Serge Saltykof, with the assistance of Leon Naryshkin, persuaded the Grand Duke Peter to submit to an operation which cured him of his infirmity, a service for which the Empress was so grateful that she rewarded Catherine's lover with a large diamond.' A pretty, impecunious widow was then hired to initiate the Grand Duke in the pleasures he had till now been unable to enjoy – after which Peter and Catherine were given to understand that whatever might be their personal inclinations, the nation expected a

Romanov heir. Champeaux's account tails off in a mass of inconsequential and inaccurate detail. But on the whole one is inclined to believe it. In his new-found manhood, Peter would have wanted to prove himself to a wife who so openly despised him, and Catherine, however unwilling, would not have dared to refuse.

It must have been agonizing for a young woman, still passionately in love, to have to submit to the coarse and fumbling love-making of a husband who physically revolted her. It was even more humiliating to know that her lover, in order to ingratiate himself with the Empress, had been largely instrumental in forcing her into bed with her husband. There is little doubt that Paul was Peter's son, though in her loathing of Peter, Catherine goes so far as to suggest in her memoirs that Serge Saltykof was the father. By denying Peter as the father of her son, she exonerated herself in front of her grandchildren of having forgiven the murderers of their grandfather.

The Empress also appears to have had some doubts as to the paternity of Catherine's son, for during the months of pregnancy when every care was taken to protect the Grand Duchess from having yet another miscarriage, Serge Saltykof still remained attached to Peter's household. But the magic had vanished, the ardent lover had become the prudent courtier. Disillusioned but still in love, Catherine became morbid and depressed. Her sexual experiences with Peter had a terrible effect on her nerves, and her return to St Petersburg on the eve of her confinement only tended to make her still more unhappy, for the apartments allotted to her in the Summer Palace adjoined those of the Empress and meant the end of any kind of liberty. The large, draughty rooms with only one door, and the windows giving out on to the fetid waters of the Fontanka Canal were hardly the ideal place for a confinement. In her demoralized condition, Catherine interpreted as cruelty what was largely due to carelessness. Rastrelli's architectural triumph, with its vaulted galleries and mirrored halls, was built for *grandezza* rather than for comfort and, in this respect, Elisabeth was probably no better off than her niece.

Catherine's description of her confinement makes pathetic

reading. It is one of the few occasions on which she, who usually hated to be pitied, talks with bitterness of her shameful treatment. When her son was born after a long and painful labour, Elisabeth, who was quite hysterical with joy, carried him off to her apartments, while no one bothered to remove the young mother from what she calls her 'couch of misery' back to her own bed on the other side of the room. For over three hours she remained alone with a lady-in-waiting who did not dare to change her sheets or as much as give her a glass of water without permission from the midwife, who was busy with the baby. The Grand Duke, who had made a brief appearance with his aunt, was receiving the congratulations of his friends in toasts of champagne. Most of her household had followed the Empress and were fawning in admiration round the baby's cradle. Free drink was being distributed to the populace who were celebrating in the streets, and the church bells were pealing all over the town. But in a cold, almost unfurnished room, the young Grand Duchess was shedding bitter tears, waiting for the congratulations which never came. Of Serge there was not a sign. Two weeks later she was told that he had gone on a mission to the King of Sweden to announce the birth of the Grand Duke Paul – a name which had been imposed on her child without her even being consulted.

Three days passed and she was left to weep and moan, suffering from rheumatic cramps without being given anything to alleviate the pain. Countess Shuvalov, who had taken over the duties of Marie Choglokov, was so taken up with the festivities at court that she paid her only the most perfunctory visits – 'not that I minded,' writes Catherine, 'for she was the most boring and tiresome of women. But I wanted to have some news of my son.' All that she heard was of the Empress's adulation for the baby Paul; of how he slept in her room, where she insisted on attending him herself, seeing to his slightest needs. Catherine had not dared to ask for details for fear it might be interpreted as casting aspersions on the Empress's care of her child. But what she heard from the gossip of her servants was hardly reassuring. Her son was being cossetted by a lot of old women whom Elisabeth revered for their sanctity rather than for their capabilities; he was living in a stifling atmosphere, smothered under a mass of fur and quilted satin. The Empress's passion for the child gave rise to the rumour that she had substituted Catherine's baby with one of her own. But it was probably no more than the frustrated mother-love of an essentially feminine woman who was meant to be normally married with a large family of her own.

Catherine resented this appropriation of her natural rights. But her resentment was brought on by pride rather than by maternal affection. However passionate and over-sexed, she was at heart a far colder woman than Elisabeth and her memoirs are those of a complete egocentric. One is unpleasantly reminded of her mother when she writes how, on the day of the christening which she was still too weak to attend, the Empress came into her room bringing her on a golden plate the gift of a hundred thousand roubles and a velvet jewel case containing what she describes as 'a very meagre necklace made up of small stones with matching earrings and a few rings, such as I would have been ashamed to give a maid'. She was grateful for the money for, as usual, she was full of debts. But it was hardly flattering to be given such shabby jewels when she felt that 'all Russia should have been ransacked for gems worthy to compensate for the misery of the past months'.

The poor quality of the gift from the Empress who, in the past, had showered her with jewels worth hundreds and thousands of roubles, proved that Catherine was no longer of primary importance. She had produced an heir for which she was being adequately paid. But the hopes of Russia were now centred in the Grand Duke Paul. Peter's only attempt to assert himself was to complain that he had not yet received his share of the money, and the exchequer at the time was so empty that Catherine was asked as a favour to return the money, which would be reimbursed at a later date. It did not improve her relations with her husband when she heard she had been made a victim of his cupidity.

Forty days passed before she had a glimpse of her child. 'I thought him very handsome,' was her only comment. But how could she be expected to feel affection for a son whom she was only allowed to carry in her arms on one occasion. This was at the official *levée* of 1 November 1754, when she received the congratulations of the court and the foreign ambassadors. All the finest furniture in the palace was moved into her apartment for this one day, and mother and child presented a charming picture, lying on a bed hung with rose-pink velvet, embroidered in silver, receiving the homage of princes and field-marshals, ministers and ambassadors.

Two weeks later, the court moved over to the Winter Palace. The baby Paul remained with the Empress, and Catherine shut herself up in her rooms, rendered odious for her by their proximity to those of the Grand Duke who, in his present state of euphoria, was always trying to invade her privacy, either in order to assert his conjugal rights or to flirt with one of her maids-of-honour, of whom the ugliest, Elisabeth Vorontsov, niece to the Vice-Chancellor, was the current favourite. Catherine was in such a state of gloom and despondency that her one desire was to be left alone. She became even more unhappy when she heard that Serge Saltykof was in St Petersburg without even having troubled to let her know he was back, and that he was shortly to leave for Hamburg, where he had been appointed Russian Minister. She was still very much in love and wanted at all costs to see him. But the crowning humiliation was when she sat up till three in the morning for a lover who never came. His excuses were not convincing – and Catherine made no attempt to dissimulate her feelings when she wrote: 'I kept on questioning Narishkin, till it became as clear as daylight that Serge had not come, because he had lost all interest in me and had no regard either for me or for all I had suffered solely on his account.' (Here again she hints that Saltykof was the father of her child.) 'To tell the truth, I was very hurt and wrote him a letter in which I complained bitterly of his behaviour. He replied by coming to see me,' and, she added, with a disarming frankness, 'It was not difficult to make me forgive him, for I was still very much taken with him. It was he who persuaded me to show myself again in public.' A few days later Serge Saltykof left for Hamburg and, as a crowning insult, she heard of him parading his triumphs and discussing her with other women both in Dresden and in Stockholm.

Nevertheless, she acted on his advice and she appeared at court for the first time since her confinement on the night of the Grand Duke's birthday, 10 February. Ten years had passed since the fourteen-year-old Sophia of Anhalt-Zerbst had arrived in Moscow as an obscure little German princess, dazzled by the fairy-tale opulence of the Russian court. Now she was an experienced woman of twenty-four, tempered by adversity, made cynical by disillusion, no longer willing to accept the slights and humiliations she had suffered in the past, or to fall on her knees before the Empress and beg the forgiveness of her 'beloved Matouchka' (little mother).

She appeared resplendent in a blue velvet gown embroidered in gold, prettier and more charming than ever with a smile for her friends, a look of cold disdain for her enemies – a woman whom both statesmen and diplomats realized could no longer be ignored, to whom Count Bestuzhev was beginning to make over-tures and to whom foreign diplomats referred in their despatches.

In the spring of 1755, she ventured for the first time into the political arena and she learned her first lessons in diplomacy from the new British ambassador but lately arrived in St Petersburg. As the pupil of Sir Charles Hanbury-Williams, Catherine was gradually to discard the last of the moral principles and advice given her by her father.

A worldly and unscrupulous politician who had only taken up diplomacy in middle age, Sir Charles was a man with a good brain and a witty tongue, whose inflated idea of his talents and passion for intrigue was always getting him into trouble. As His Britannic Majesty's envoy, first in Berlin and then in Dresden, he succeeded in antagonizing in turn both King Frederick and the Saxon Prime Minister, Count Brühl. In spite of having been a failure in both places, political influence at home got him appointed to St Petersburg. Here he was welcomed with open arms 'as a cultured and civilized representative of the West', added to which was the rumour of his being supplied with a limitless fund of gold. From Count

Bestuzhev downwards, there was not a man at court who was not head over heels in debt. Having had his political training under Walpole, Williams was convinced that 'every man had his price' and his dealings with Count Bestuzhev confirmed him in this opinion.

His mission was to conclude a treaty of subsidies with Russia by which, in return for British gold, Russia would supply troops for the defence of Hanover. The question had already come up in 1749 but had hung fire owing to the enormous sums demanded by the Russians. But fear of Prussia's belligerent intentions, Frederick's appointment of an English ex-Jacobite as ambassador to France, had revived King George II's fear for the future of his electorate and made him a convert to the policy of subsidizing Russia. On Williams's arrival in St Petersburg there was still a considerable difference between Britain's offer and Russia's exorbitant demands, with Bestuzhev insisting at the same time that the thirty thousand Russian troops involved were not to be used in the general Franco-British conflict, but only in defence of Hanover itself.

The ambassador's task was to combine a treaty of subsidies with the renewal of the defensive alliance made between Britain and Russia as far back as 1742. He was also to press for a commercial treaty by which British merchants resident in St Petersburg were to be consulted on all matters concerning their interests. To conclude the successful negotiation of this treaty, the Chancellor's friendship was essential and the ambassador was empowered to offer him a bribe of no less than ten thousand pounds or, if necessary, to grant him a regular pension. Bestuzhev's enemy, the Vice-Chancellor Vorontsov, and the Empress's favourite, Ivan Shuvalov, without whose help Elisabeth could scarcely be persuaded to affix her signature to a document, were all to be approached with an open purse in hand. Both the Vice-Chancellor and the favourite were known to be pro-French. But the French had neither the means nor the intention of paying out as heavily as England and there had been no official ambassador at the Russian court since the hurried departure of the Marquis de la Chétardie.

No one knew how to bribe more tactfully than Sir Charles Hanbury-Williams, whose opinions of the Russians are summed up in a letter to the Foreign Office: 'It is persons and passions which govern at the Russian court. Without keys to both, a minister might be two or three years in St Petersburg before he can do His Majesty any service.'

The man who wrote these lines had already proved the weakness of the leading protagonists. His mistake lay in underestimating Elisabeth, whom he dismissed as an ageing voluptuary, dominated by her favourite and too lazy to see to any business which required the slightest concentration. At the same time he tended to overestimate the importance of the Grand Duchess Catherine, being as dazzled by her brilliance as he was impressed by her erudition. In order to gain her as an ally, he was ready to pander to her frailties, her desperate need of money and her longing for a new lover. As a middle-aged widower in delicate health, he did not aspire to the position himself, but he had in his suite a handsome young Polish count called Stanislaus Poniatowski, related through his mother to the powerful Czartoryski family and already, in his early twenties, recognized to be one of the most fascinating men of his day, widely travelled, as much at home in the salons of Paris as in the clubs of London. Poniatowski was not only a charming companion but also the perfect political appendage for a diplomat as supple and as unscrupulous as Sir Charles.

At a summer fête held in the gardens of Oranienbaum to celebrate the Grand Duke's name day, Catherine found herself sitting at supper next to the new British ambassador. Both were charmed with one another's company. 'We had a delightful and entertaining conversation,' writes Catherine. 'It was not difficult to talk to Chevalier Williams for he was extremely witty and had a great knowledge of the world, having visited most of the European capitals.' She was flattered when she was told that 'he had enjoyed his evening as much as I had and was loud in my praises. I never have any difficulty in getting on with people whose mind works on the same level as my own.' That evening saw the beginning of a friendship by which a Grand Duchess of Russia was to be placed on the payroll of the British government.

Would the English ambassador have succeeded so well with Catherine had it not been for the assistance of Poniatowski, and would Poniatowski ever have aspired to become the Grand Duchess's lover had it not been for the encouragement of Hanbury-Williams? The young Pole was no more than a romantic weakling, propelled by ambition to play the game of power politics for which, by temperament, he was wholly unsuited. None of the three were disinterested in their relations. Williams was working for his country, Catherine for herself and Poniatowski for his family.

The family were the Czartoryski, one of the greatest and most powerful of Polish families. Of his two uncles, Prince Michael and Prince Augustus, the one was Grand Chancellor of Lithuania, the other was Palatine of Red Russia, both of which were Poland's frontier provinces. Stanislas's mother, Constance, had fallen in love with the heroic Count Poniatowski, who had campaigned against Russia in the armies of Charles XII and, after the Swedish king's defeat, had returned penniless to his country. Poniatowski had had to change his politics on marrying into a family which represented the pro-Russian party in Poland. The Czartoryski hoped, with the help of their powerful neighbour, to shake off the rule of the Saxon King, August II, and establish a native dynasty in a country sunk in anarchy and confusion through individualism run riot. From the hereditary princes to the simplest of landed gentry, all had the right to take part in the government of Poland and, as members of the Diet, exercise the famous *Liberum Veto*, by which a single individual could obstruct any attempt at legislation or reform. The Polish throne was elective and, in their jealousy of one another, and in particular of the Czartoryski, the only family with sufficient patriotism to think of their country rather than themselves, the Polish nobility preferred to submit to the weak rule of a foreign king rather than sacrifice one iota of their privileges. Their nephew's friendship with the new English ambassador to Russia, Sir Charles's offer to include him in his embassy, were welcomed by the Czartoryskis as a means of establishing a diplomatic footing at St Petersburg.

Young Stanislaus had spent most of his life abroad and his charm of manner and witty conversation had won him universal praise. Women liked him as much as men. In Paris, the celebrated Madame Geoffrin had welcomed him to her salon and treated him like a son. French politicians asserted that he was better informed on their country's politics than themselves. In London he was almost as popular as in Paris, and the uncles who knew him so little heard him commended on all sides. They were flattered when Sir Charles spoke with enthusiasm of their nephew's diplomatic talents, though no one would have been more shocked than the bigoted and pious Constance Poniatowski, had she known that the cynical ambassador looked upon her son as a potential lover either for the ageing Empress or the young Grand Duchess. There were rumours even more damaging regarding the equivocal nature of the relationship between the fifty-year-old ambassador and his twenty-two-year-old protégé. What his uncles ignored was that, underlying the brilliant exterior, was a nature at once timid and insecure and that, having lived most of his life abroad, Stanislaus Poniatowski had little knowledge either of his country or of his people. He himself was fully aware of his defects and his self-portrait, written in the fashionable manner of the day, dissects his failings with a surgeon's knife:

An excellent education enables me to conceal my mental and bodily defects, so that many people may perhaps expect more from me than I am really able to give. I have sufficient wit to take part in any conversation, but not enough to converse long and in detail on any one subject. I have a natural penchant for the arts. My indolence, however, prevents me from going as far as I should like to go, either in the arts or sciences. I work either overmuch or not at all. I can judge very well of affairs. I can see at once the faults of a plan or the faults of those who propose it, but I am very much in need of good counsel in order to carry out any plans of my own.

The honesty of the self-analysis is disarming, but it was an evil day for Poland when this cultured dilettante came under the spell of a woman as fascinating and as unscrupulous as the

Grand Duchess. They were introduced by the English ambassador on the night of the summer fête at Oranienbaum, and Williams was quick to note how Catherine's eyes were fastened on the young Pole, whose distinction and grace made him stand out among the dancers. A less admiring observer once described the Grand Duchess's predatory look as 'fixed and glassy like that of a wild beast tracking down its prey'. But when Poniatowski met her for the first time, he described the Grand Duchess's eyes as 'the bluest and merriest in the world, subjugating all who came within her orbit'.

Nevertheless, several months were to elapse before he plucked up sufficient courage to avail himself of his opportunities. The Romanovs had a sinister reputation abroad and the cautious Stanislaus had no wish to spend the rest of his life in Siberia, even for the sake of the most ravishing of Grand Duchesses.

This time it was Catherine who found herself in the role of the seducer. For at twenty-two, Poniatowski was still a self-professed virgin; it needed all the persuasion of the English ambassador and the intrigues of the ever-complaisant Naryshkin to get him to bed with a woman he professed to adore and to whom we owe a vivid description of Catherine at the age of twenty-six.

She had but lately recovered from her first pregnancy, a time when any woman who has a claim to beauty is at her loveliest. She had dark hair, a dazzling skin, a Greek nose and a mouth which invited kisses. Her hands and feet were perfect, her voice was soft and agreeable, and her laugh the quintessence of gaiety. Her temperament was mercurial. One moment she would be revelling in the wildest and most childish of games; a little later she would be seated at her desk, coping with the most complicated affairs of finance and politics.

Yet still he hesitated, and it was autumn by the time he had even got so far as to address her a *billet doux*. It was only by a ruse that Leon Naryshkin got him into such a compromising situation that he had either to bring dishonour on himself or risk dishonouring the Grand Duchess. All unknowingly he was conducted to the entrance of her private apartments, where he found the door half open and Catherine waiting for him, wearing as he recalls 'a simple white gown trimmed with lace and pink ribbons, and looking so enticing as to make one forget the very existence of Siberia'. That night, Catherine had the satisfaction of initiating the tenderest and, at the same time, the most ardent of lovers in the erotic arts she had learned from his predecessor.

CHAPTER SIX

Poniatowski

Many years later, as Empress of Russia, Catherine wrote to Potemkin, 'Poniatowski was loving and beloved from 1755 to 1758, and the liaison would have lasted for ever if he himself had not got bored by it. I remarked this on the day of his departure from Tzarskoye Selo, and I was more distressed than I can tell you. I don't think I ever cried so much in my life.' These lines have more the ring of truth than the literary effusions in which Poniatowski dwells on his unhappy passion for the woman who was to reward him with a crown of which, one by one, she later plucked out the gems. But in the winter and spring of 1755 to 1756, before politics intruded into their romance, the two lovers lived in an enchanted world of secret assignations, of moonlit drives along the frozen Neva, and whispered words exchanged in the shadows of the palace gardens. Disguised in male attire, enveloped in a fur-lined cape, Catherine would slip out of her apartments to join Poniatowski waiting at the gate. Naryshkin and his sister-in-law, Anna, who was one of her favourite ladies-in-waiting, organized gay, informal suppers in their family palace. The lovers grew bolder as winter turned to spring and they would drive directly to Poniatowski's lodgings. The risks they ran were enormous, but all went well until the night of 6 July 1756, when an event occurred which caused too great a scandal to be ignored.

The court was in residence at Peterhof. Poniatowski was lodging with Hanbury-Williams in a *datcha* in the neighbourhood. The Grand Ducal couple were at 'Mon Plaisir', a small pavilion in the gardens of Peterhof giving out on the sea. Poniatowski, who had grown careless in the past months, went that evening to visit his royal mistress without giving her prior notice. Disguised with a blond wig and a mask, he travelled in a small, closed carriage driven by a trusted servant. But the clear white northern nights do not favour romantic assignations, and by bad luck he ran into a crowd of drunken revellers led by the Grand Duke and his mistress. His coachman, when questioned as to his passenger's identity, replied that he was a tailor attached to the Grand Duchess's household, and he was allowed to proceed. All would have gone well had not Elisabeth Vorontsov annoyed the Grand Duke by making lewd and appraising remarks on the tailor's elegant appearance. And, on his return home, Stanislaus was attacked by three men on horseback who dragged him forcibly out of his carriage and brought him straight to the Grand Duke. The hour was late and Peter, who was dead drunk and in the foulest mood, tore off his mask and wig, asking him with brutal frankness as to whether he 'had been fucking his wife'. Horrified by such language, the chivalrous young Pole persisted in his denial and was locked up for several hours in a guardroom before he was released and allowed to go home, exposed in full daylight to the curious eyes of every passer-by.

Within twenty-four hours this episode was known to the whole court, and Stanislaus Poniatowski, who had never been sympathetic either to the Empress or to the reigning favourite, was requested to leave the country. The British ambassador was powerless to intervene, and Catherine's only hope of postponing her lover's departure was to placate her husband and win him over to her side. Pocketing her pride, she made friendly overtures to Peter's mistress, and Elisabeth Vorontsov, who was a coarse but good-natured girl, was only too delighted to have the proud Grand Duchess as a suppliant.

In his memoirs, Poniatowski recounts a curious incident which occurred at Peterhof only a few nights after his unfortunate escapade. There was a court ball and he was dancing with Elisabeth Vorontsov, when she whispered in his ear that he was to meet her later in the rose garden by the pavilion of

'Mon Plaisir'. He arrived there, full of nervous trepidation, becoming even more apprehensive when Elisabeth brought him to the Grand Duke who this time, however, was in the best and most benevolent of moods, only scolding him for having been such a fool as not to have confided in him before as 'it would have saved so much talk and trouble'. Stanislaus could hardly believe his ears when he heard the Grand Duke say 'Now that we are all good friends, there is only one person missing to complete our party,' and without any further ceremony he went off to his wife's room, pulled her out of bed, leaving her barely time to slip on a négligée, and without either petticoats or stockings, brought her back with him, flinging her into Poniatowski's arms saying, 'Here she is, my friend, and I hope you are both pleased with me.'

The fastidious Pole, who was not used to such rough and ready manners, was profoundly embarrassed. But Catherine never lost her head for a moment. She accepted the situation in the gayest of spirits, remaining sufficiently imperturbable to demand of her husband a written declaration that he and Elisabeth Vorontsov would do all in their power to persuade the Vice-Chancellor to put pressure on the Polish government to facilitate Poniatowski's return. By now Peter was sufficiently drunk to put his signature to any declaration, and the rest of the night was spent in rollicking games which Catherine, much to Poniatowski's surprise, appeared to enjoy quite as much as her husband.

These intimate and ill-assorted foursomes continued up to the day of his departure which, for all her efforts, Catherine was unable to postpone for more than a few weeks. Poniatowski does not appear to have made much effort on his own behalf. One suspects that he was too sensitive and finely tuned to enjoy the equivocal situation of his 'adorable Grand Duchess' sitting down to supper with her husband's mistress who, though belonging to one of the oldest families in Russia, looked and behaved 'like a servant girl in a house of ill-fame'. Such conditions were scarcely conducive to romance and Catherine's ardour and physical demands were beginning to tell on her lover's health. He was sad to leave for his was the temperament which 'thrives on sweet despair', but the family had plans for his future in Poland where he was to seek re-election to the Diet, and it was still 'the Family' rather than his mistress who had the first claim on his loyalty.

Catherine wept bitter tears when they said goodbye, for Stanislaus was the first man with whom she had experienced both the tenderness and rapture of a romantic passion and the courtship of a cultured European. She was frank enough to admit 'When I want something, I want it desperately,' and now she wanted Stanislaus with a fierce determination which led her to sacrifice the last morals and principles she had preserved of a well brought up Lutheran princess. She succeeded in getting her lover back to St Petersburg by the end of the year and in having him appointed by an unwilling king as accredited envoy of his country. But in order to accomplish this, she launched into a world of political intrigue, putting herself in the hands of the cunning and venal Bestuzhev who, in view of the Grand Duke's growing unpopularity, was beginning to have a certain regard for Catherine as the mother of the infant Paul.

In those crucial months of Poniatowski's absence, Catherine made a friendship far more vital to her political future than the handsome Pole. In her secret correspondence with Sir Charles Hanbury-Williams, written as one man to another with the ambassador addressing her as 'Monsieur', she reveals herself for the first time as a woman who will stop at nothing to achieve her aim, so that even her longing for Poniatowski, referred to as 'the friend', fades before the urgency of the situation.

Throughout those early months of 1756 the Empress's health had been rapidly deteriorating. The courtiers spoke in whispers of fainting fits which left her for many hours unconscious; of dropsy and a shortness of breath which made it difficult for her to move from her bedroom to her private chapel. She, who had been so radiant and so gay, was now beset by fears, as frightened of assassination as she was frightened of disease, resorting in turn to prayers and to old women's spells and incantations. We find Catherine informing the

English ambassador, 'She offers up her prayers tomorrow but how can devotion and witchcraft work side by side? There is short shrift for those who have water on the belly, and I know at first hand that her cough has returned with a great shortness of breath.'

There is no word of pity for the woman she had once revered, but who in the past twelve years had inflicted too many slights and humiliations to be forgiven, and who so long as she lived retained the power to disinherit both her and her husband in favour of their child. She dreaded being supplanted by her son, but consoled herself with the thought

that the little certainty which the Empress can build on the destiny of a child of two years old, in addition to her timorous disposition, will, I am daring enough to hope, prove safeguards during her life-time . . . It will be my fault if my enemies gain the upper hand for, be assured, I have already laid my plans and shall either perish or reign.

The English ambassador was the only one at hand with the money to supply her needs. 'Make me Empress,' she exhorts him, 'and I will give you comfort.' For Hanbury-Williams was in as great a need of comfort as herself. His mission, which had begun under such favourable auspices, was now beset with difficulties. The Treaty of Westminster, in which King George II of England and his brother-in-law, the King of Prussia, mutually agreed to 'protect their respective territories against all foreign incursions', had burst like a bombshell on the political horizon, bringing about a complete reversal in the system of European alliances. France and Austria's immediate reaction was to sink their differences and sign a treaty in which Saxony and later Russia were to join. But for the moment there was too much confusion in St Petersburg to settle on any definite policy. The pro-French Shuvalovs, together with the Vice-Chancellor Vorontsov, pressed for the exchange of ambassadors with France. But Bestuzhev was still in power, and the corner-stone of his foreign policy till now had been friendship with England and Austria directed against France and Prussia. He wrote:

The English alliance is the oldest that Russia has with any European power and is based firstly on the necessity of their mutual protection against the combination of Sweden, Denmark, Prussia, Poland and France, and secondly upon their common welfare particularly in regard to commerce; the net result of which is an annual balance of five hundred thousand roubles in favour of Russia.

His greatest political triumph had been when his secret police succeeded in intercepting the indiscreet despatches of the Marquis de la Chétardie and the proud ambassador was ignominiously escorted across the frontier. Since then, there had been no official relations with France, and even the efforts of the Shuvalovs had failed to make Elisabeth Petrovna forget or forgive the behaviour of the only ambassador she had not only loved but trusted.

But now the Chancellor's policy lay in ruins. Austria was pressing for Russia's adherence to the Treaty of Versailles. An exchange of ambassadors with France appeared to be inevitable, which would be as detrimental to British interests as it would be disastrous to the Chancellor's prestige. United by a common policy, while disliking one another cordially as men and more than a little jealous of each other's influence with the Grand Duchess, both Bestuzhev and Hanbury-Williams combined in convincing Catherine and her husband, whose hero-worship of the King of Prussia made him a ready convert to their plans, that the appointment of a French ambassador would place them at the mercy of the Shuvalovs. Catherine did not need convincing. 'One more minister means one more intriguer,' was her comment. In Sweden, a Parliamentary cabal financed by France had reduced her uncle, the King of Sweden, to the position of a puppet, and brought the Queen, a sister of the King of Prussia, to public trial for misdemeanours against the state. With the help of France, the Shuvalovs might yet succeed in disinheriting Peter and sending them both back to Holstein, while one of them was made regent for her infant son.

Catherine knew she was playing a dangerous game in accepting bribes from the English ambassador. The Chancellor was in the secret, and so were many others, 'too many for her safety'. For they were men who would be ready to speak at the first threat of torture and the first stroke of the knout. There was an Italian jeweller, a certain Bernardi, whose profession brought him into contact with all the leading families, and whose name appears constantly in her correspondence, together with that of the English consul, a Baron Wolff, who kept an account of the money transmitted to her from the English Embassy. It never struck her that, in accepting bribes from a foreign power, she was running close to treason, for she always believed she was acting solely in the interests of Russia and that her destiny was irretrievably linked to that of her new country. Her plans were made and her hopes were high during that August month of crisis when the Empress was believed to be dying. Then Elisabeth made one of her semi-miraculous recoveries and the courtiers no longer paid homage to the young court.

Even so, Catherine never lost her head. In a letter to Hanbury-Williams, she writes, 'I would like to feel fear, but I cannot. The invisible hand which has led me for thirteen years along a very rough road will never allow me to give way. Of that I am firmly and perhaps foolishly convinced.' The men on whom she relied, Poniatowski, Williams, even Bestuzhev, were all weaker than her. But fortunately her enemies were even weaker than her friends, and in that maze of intrigue and counter-intrigue which gathered round the throne, she was the only one who never for a moment deviated from her aims and ambitions. While Bestuzhev was gradually coming round to the idea of her sharing her husband's throne and participating in the running of the country, or in the event of Peter proving intractable, setting her up as regent for her infant son, she herself never contemplated sharing a throne. She would 'either perish or be Empress in my own right', with all the privileges and prerogatives of power.

The Grand Duchess is romantic and passionate, but unless I am very much mistaken, that high forehead and those glittering eyes predict a long and terrific destiny. She is affable and forthcoming with all, but when she comes near me, I instinctively recoil. I do not know why, but there is something about her which frightens me.

So wrote the celebrated Chevalier D'Eon, the cleverest and most unscrupulous of all the French agents who, over the years, had succeeded in infiltrating themselves into the social life of St Petersburg and who worked for the *'Cabinet noir of Versailles'*. In the past year the principal agent in Russia had been a certain Chevalier Douglas, alias MacKenzie, self-confessed Jacobite and ex-Jesuit, whose job was to report on the military, financial and commercial state of the Empire, to obtain precise information on the English ambassador's intrigues, the fluctuating credit of the various ministers and the Empress's precarious health. But it required a far more subtle character than Douglas to negotiate the resumption of diplomatic relations. This delicate task was entrusted to the Chevalier D'Eon, who, in spite of his youth, was regarded as having the requisite talents to make his way at a court where so much depended on personality, a certain degree of effrontery and a complete lack of morals.

Both men and women fell under the charm of this fascinating, amorphous creature who began his career as a brilliant diplomatist and one of the deadliest swordsmen of his day, and ended it in London as a penurious spinster, mocked at and reviled. According to the testimony of his contemporaries, he was finally proved to have been a woman but there was very little of a woman in the young gallant who charmed the Empress Elisabeth sufficiently to be offered a post at her court – an offer he politely declined for he was one of the many who believed 'in always keeping one's back to Siberia'. Bestuzhev considered this young Frenchman to be so dangerous that, at one time, he contemplated having him murdered. But Catherine, whom D'Eon instinctively judged to be a dangerous enemy for France, makes no mention of him in her memoirs. With that curious lack of intuition which proclaimed her Teutonic blood, she never realized that the witty little Frenchman, who flitted like a gaily painted butterfly through the drawing rooms of St Petersburg, would do her more harm in the next two years than the most powerful of ministers.

By the end of the year, Poniatowski was back in St Petersburg as the official representative of his country, appointed by an unwilling king, accredited to a court he had left six months before in disgrace, and looked upon with jealousy and dislike by the Russian Chancellor who was mainly responsible for his return. The Austrian ambassador had formally protested against the appointment; his mother, Constance Czartoryski, had refused to give her consent to a mission undertaken at the wish of an amorous Grand Duchess, and even his ambitious uncles hesitated for fear of seeing their nephew's honour compromised in a country where diplomatic status did not always preserve one from Siberia.

But Catherine's iron will and unflagging efforts had succeeded in overcoming every obstacle, undeterred by the fact that Europe was again at war, the King of Saxony and Poland virtually a prisoner, with Frederick of Prussia's armies over-running his country in preparation for a triumphal march into Austria, and that Russia, as Austria's ally, was about to mobilize.

Her supreme egotism transpires in her letters to Hanbury-Williams. In order to get her lover back she was ready to bribe, flatter and coerce, to play off the Chancellor against the ambassador, two men bound together by their common interests but both possessively jealous of her favours, for the old statesman and the middle-aged ambassador were more than a little in love with her. In the next months, the latter had become not only her banker but her friend, giving her sound and often disinterested advice. It must have been hard for him to write 'Poniatowski's return is what you have most at heart. This can only be secured by means of the Chancellor.' Besthuzhev was a man whose venality he despised, who had been for years on the payroll of the British government, and who now, when the whole system of alliances had changed and there was no longer any question of Russian soldiers defending Hanover, was nevertheless still anxious to secure a pension from the King of England.

The Chancellor's influence was declining. After making Catherine's early years in Russia miserable by his spying and constant supervision, he now looked upon her as the only hope for the future, the one person who, in the event of the

Empress's death, could save both him and Russia from his enemies. Catherine, for her part, admired Count Bestuzhev as the only Russian politician who thought like a patriot and had kept the country at peace for the last fifteen years. But both Bestuzhev and Williams were dangerous associates for a young Grand Duchess who was expressly forbidden to take any part in politics and who was even frowned on when she was found to be assisting the Grand Duke in the administration of Holstein. By now, however, Catherine was sufficiently infatuated by Poniatowski to throw all caution to the winds. And in the late autumn of 1756 Count Bestuzhev had still sufficient power to carry out her wishes and write to the Saxon Prime Minister, Count Brühl, that:

in the present critical and delicate state of affairs, I find it all the more necessary that an envoy extraordinary should be sent here without delay from the kingdom of Poland whose presence would draw closer the ties of friendship between the two courts and, as I have found no one more pleasing to my court than Count Poniatowski, I suggest him to you.

The suggestion was little short of an order, with which Count Brühl, as Catherine had foreseen, would have no choice but to comply.

The Empress's reaction to Poniatowski's appointment shows that, in spite of her illness, she had not lost her sense of humour. When Bestuzhev announced the news, she questioned in a mocking tone 'Why are they sending him? Everyone will think he is my lover.' But although the Shuvalovs used all their arts of persuasion in trying to prevent the Pole's return, Elisabeth refused to humiliate the old Chancellor by going against his decision. The whole of St Petersburg knew Poniatowski to be Catherine's lover. But Elisabeth was tolerant of human frailties, and when her jealousy was not aroused, she could still feel affection and even pity for the vital full-blooded young woman married to the nephew she openly referred to as 'that little monster'.

Catherine deserved no pity from Elisabeth. There is something almost indecent in the cold-blooded tone of the letters in which she gives the English ambassador day-to-day accounts of the Empress's physical and moral decay. She openly admits, 'It is my dream to see her die.' Even the sensitive Stanislaus was on occasion sufficiently hard-hearted as to write of the Empress 'You madden us! Die as quickly as you can,' which makes one suspect that Catherine's lover already saw himself in the role of Prince Consort with Peter dethroned, divorced and sent back to Holstein.

But Elisabeth refused to oblige them. Her magnificent constitution enabled her to rally from one stroke after another. One moment she was dying, the next she was out hunting blackcock. One hears of a royal visit where, in spite of the difficulty of lacing up her corset and her constant breathlessness, she nevertheless insisted on appearing at a state banquet, superbly dressed, covered with diamonds and with that radiant smile which no illness could destroy. For all her infirmities she showed more enthusiasm for war against Prussia than the majority of her court. According to Catherine, 'she even talked of commanding her armies in person, taking the Grand Duke with her and leaving me here with my son. However, the Grand Duke will not readily consent.' The Empress still felt the blood of Peter the Great boiling in her veins, but her heir was a braggart and a coward whose idea of war was confined to fighting with tin soldiers against cardboard fortresses.

The Russian army under Elisabeth's father had defeated Charles XII of Sweden, the greatest military genius of his day. But the generals had grown fat and slothful during the long years of peace. Equipment and supplies were mishandled by corrupt administrators, and the soldiers were mostly raw, untrained recruits. Field-Marshal Apraxin owed his position as Commander-in-Chief to his seniority and to his friendship with Bestuzhev rather than to his talents. He was good-natured and lazy and showed no eagerness to embark on a winter campaign with an untrained and ill-equipped army. Ignoring the orders of the Grand Council he refused to move from his headquarters in Riga before the spring, by which time Saxony had capitulated to Prussia and Frederick's armies had overrun Bohemia.

Personal considerations may also have contributed to Apraxin's dilatory tactics. The Empress's health was so precarious and the Grand Duke's pro-Prussian sentiments were so well known that it was clear that the war would end as soon as he came to the throne. In these circumstances, even the most energetic of generals might be forgiven for not risking his political future. Also the Grand Duchess's position was ambiguous. Her friendship with the English ambassador, who was now working not only for England but for Prussia, gave the impression that she shared her husband's politics. People remembered that Frederick had arranged her marriage, that her mother had been a Prussian agent and even Frederick himself was under the illusion that he could count on the friendship of Sophia of Anhalt-Zerbst. He was sadly mistaken, for Catherine on the contrary longed for a glorious Russian victory which would restore the old Chancellor's rapidly declining prestige and prevent the triumph of her enemies. She even went so far as to write, at Bestuzhev's request, a personal letter to Field-Marshal Apraxim, begging him 'to attack the Prussians without delay and throw their armies back into their proper dominions', a letter which was later used against her and said to have been a cover-up for her secret intrigues with Hanbury-Williams and with Frederick. But no one was happier than Catherine when, in August 1757, came the news of the defeat of the Prussian armies at Grossjägersdorf, for her only loyalty was to Russia, the country she had made her own from the moment she first saw the gilded spires of St Petersburg emerging out of the winter mists of the Neva delta. She loved her adopted country with a passion which transcended all other passions in her life; for Russia's sake even the most charming of her lovers was destined to be sacrificed.

CHAPTER SEVEN

Apprenticeship
in Intrigue

By the time Poniatowski returned to St Petersburg Catherine
was already so deeply immersed in political intrigue that,
from the day of his arrival, the young Pole found himself
regarded by the French agents as enemy number one. Both
Douglas and D'Eon were spying on his every movement,
so that he did not even dare to visit or correspond with his
old friend Hanbury-Williams, who, while applauding his
caution, was nevertheless hurt by his behaviour. Stanislaus
was no hero, as his tragic career was later to prove, and only
his infatuation for Catherine gave him the courage to remain
at his post. Caught up in a maelstrom of politics, he must
have regretted the comparative anonymity of his earlier visit,
the rapture of those stolen meetings when their love was still
a precious secret known only to a few. Their liaison was now
public property, with the Grand Duke playing so openly the
role of a complaisant husband that he professed to be over-
joyed at his arrival. But Peter's moods were unpredictable and
relations between husband and wife deteriorated badly during
the year. The Grand Duchess was again pregnant and her
husband was heard to say in public, 'Heaven knows how it is
that my wife becomes pregnant, though I suppose I shall have
to accept the child as my own.' This dangerous and indiscreet
remark was promptly brought back to Catherine who sent
her husband the message that, 'he had no right to make that
kind of remark, unless he was prepared to swear on oath that
he had not slept with his wife in the last year.' Whatever may

have been the facts, Peter was far too frightened of his aunt to arouse her anger by making such a statement.

When the Grand Duchess gave birth to a baby daughter at the end of the year 1757, her husband was the first to appear at her bedside, dressed in the full uniform of a Holstein general. Though barely recovered from her labours, Catherine had sufficient presence of mind to whisper to him 'to go and change into Russian uniform before the arrival of the Empress'.

Ignoring the gossip of the court, Elisabeth was sufficiently magnanimous to acknowledge the newborn baby as a Romanov, bestowing on her the name of Peter's mother, Anne of Holstein, and presenting a gift of sixty thousand roubles both to the Grand Duke and to the Duchess. The mother was again deprived of her child who was immediately taken away to the Empress's apartments, while she was left abandoned to the care of a single lady-in-waiting. But this time Catherine makes no claim to pity. In her memoirs she frankly asserts that her principal concern was to ensure her own comfort and see that she was suitably entertained during the weeks of convalescence. An enormous screen was placed between her bed and an adjoining anteroom, giving out on a small passage, through which she was able to introduce her friends in secret. As soon as there was a threat of them being disturbed, they would vanish behind the screen. In this way she was able to have many a gay and informal supper party, and her attendants would be amazed at the large quantities of food the young mother was able to consume at all hours of the day.

Poniatowski appears to have been the life and soul of these parties. Fatherhood hung lightly on his shoulders and neither he nor Catherine gave much thought to the baby Anne, who from her birth appears to have been a frail and sickly child. But Poniatowski's days in St Petersburg were numbered. Throughout the whole of 1757 one finds Elisabeth's French and Austrian allies clamouring for his recall. Neither the bribes of the English ambassador nor the efforts of the ageing Chancellor had been able to prevent the resumption of diplomatic relations with France. And in June of 1757, the Marquis de l'Hôpital arrived in St Petersburg at the head of an enormous and dazzling retinue calculated to impress the splendour-loving Russians. The Chevalier Douglas was recalled and Jean Geneviève Auguste Marie D'Eon officially nominated to the post of first secretary.

'I am sending you our dear little D'Eon who, I am sure, will please you,' wrote Cardinal de Bernis to the new ambassador, and the delicate and somewhat lethargic Marquis had every reason to be pleased with the secretary who took most of the work off his hands and handled the negotiations so successfully that Russia consented to accept the onerous terms by which, in the event of a war with Turkey, her ally would give her no other help than to act as mediator, for King Louis refused to renounce his country's traditional friendship with the Turks.

Meanwhile, Sir Charles Hanbury-Williams was being pressed to ask for his own recall. No one was more eager to see him go than Bestuzhev who had filled his coffers at England's expense but who, in order to save himself, was anxious to be rid of a man who had so much incriminating evidence against him. Since Poniatowski's return, there had been a considerable falling off in the correspondence between Catherine and the devoted ambassador. Disappointed and frustrated by the failure of his mission, his health impaired by the rigours of the Russian winter, Hanbury-Williams was beginning to realize that the declarations of undying friendship made to him by his adorable Grand Duchess were not quite so sincere as they had sounded. She ignored his warning to beware of the treachery of Bestuzhev and turned a deaf ear to his offers of the King of Prussia's friendship now that she had developed an independent policy of her own in which the English ambassador was not so much her mentor as her banker. His departure came when she was in the greatest need both of his friendship and his money, and the tears she wept at his departure were sufficiently genuine to please his vanity and to make him hope that one day he would be recalled as minister to her court.

But by the time that Catherine came to power, the brilliant ambassador had degenerated into an embittered invalid, broken in mind and body. And the Empress of Russia had too many claims on her gratitude to give much thought to the English diplomat who had given her her first lessons in power politics. His departure left her terribly short of funds, for Hanbury-Williams had also extended credit to her husband, even paying with her consent a large bill for jewellery given by Peter to his mistress. It was the best way of keeping the avaricious Grand Duke in a good mood. But now the source of gold had dried up, and Catherine's relations with her husband suffered in consequence. French agents were at hand to supply his needs, and certain Holsteiners in his service were paid to make mischief between the young couple, leading Peter to believe that all his troubles with his aunt originated with the Grand Duchess and that, by allowing her to meddle in the affairs of Holstein, he was doing a disservice both to himself and to his country.

Peter had always relied on his wife to cover up his blunders and get him out of difficulties, but at heart he resented her airs of intellectual superiority, her reluctance to attend his parties when women of low moral character were present. If forced to be present, she would appear in her simplest dress with no jewels and leave before supper was served, which he looked upon as an insult to himself and to his friends. Matters became worse when Elisabeth Vorontsov, encouraged by her ambitious uncle, began to give herself the airs of the reigning favourite. Officially, she was still one of the Grand Duchess's maids-of-honour and Catherine threatened to complain officially of her impertinence. Two months after the birth of the child he had officially recognized as his own, the Grand Ducal couple were on such bad terms that Alexander Shuvalov was able to persuade Peter to go to the Empress and 'ask her forgiveness for his bad behaviour' which was 'entirely due to his having followed his wife's advice'.

Meanwhile, the French and Austrian governments were putting pressure on Warsaw for the King to recall an envoy who, according to them, was serving the Grand Duchess rather than his country. Russian allies spoke openly of treachery. Apraxin had failed to follow up his victory at Grossjägersdorf and, faced with enormous losses and a starving army, had beat a retreat when a bold offensive would have brought him to the gates of Konigsberg. It was in vain that both Bestuzhev and Catherine wrote to him imploring letters, begging him to exploit his victories. Long before the letters could reach him, the veteran Field-Marshal had been dismissed and banished to his estates to await Her Majesty's pleasure. The letters came into the possession of the secret police and served as yet another proof of the Grand Duchess interfering in matters which were no concern of hers. The Austrian envoy, Count Esterhazy, went so far as to accuse both the Chancellor and the Grand Duchess of having been largely responsible for the failure of the campaign and of pursuing an independent policy in opposition to the court. The Chevalier D'Eon had succeeded in obtaining information regarding Bestuzhev's plans for the succession and his ambassador assured the Empress that, if the Chancellor's house was searched, there would be sufficient evidence to have him tried for high treason.

The Empress was a sick woman who was terrified of dying. Any mention of the succession was sufficient to arouse her suspicions. In November 1757 the Marquis de l'Hôpital was writing to Versailles, 'Should the Empress die, a palace revolution will follow shortly, for the Grand Duke will never be allowed to reign.' A week later, he was informing his government that 'if the Empress lived for another few years, she intended to change the succession and disinherit her nephew in favour of Paul Petrovitch'. This was Elisabeth's dearest wish, but she never envisaged Catherine as regent and the fact that the old Chancellor was already counting on her death and intriguing with the young court was the determining factor which brought about his downfall.

It was towards the end of carnival in 1758 and Catherine, fully recovered from her confinement, was once more appearing in public, presenting a brave face to what she sensed to be impending danger. She felt it in the atmosphere, in the way some of her oldest friends tried to avoid her company; the embarrassment of those who only a few weeks before had begged her favours. The season of balls was drawing to a close, and she who so loved to dance was finding every party an ordeal. The Empress was cold and distant and the courtiers took their cue from her. Poniatowski, who had already received his letters of recall, was finding ways of putting off his departure, but he was so politically suspect that they only met with difficulty, and it was at considerable risk to himself that, on the Sunday morning of 15 February, he sent round a note telling her of the Chancellor's arrest which, although it had taken place in the very palace where Catherine was living at the time, had been kept secret from the young court. The old man had been summoned by the Empress from a bed of sickness, and had been formally arrested and stripped of all his orders and decorations in the Council Hall where he had presided for so many years.

But what struck terror in Catherine's heart was the news that among those arrested were the Italian jeweller, Bernardi, and her Russian teacher, Adadourov, both of whom in the past months had acted as go-between in her dealings both with the Chancellor and the English ambassador. 'I was thunderstruck,' she writes, 'for on reading the note, I saw all too clearly that I was far more involved than I had thought, and a host of ideas, one more unpleasant than the other, came into my mind.'

But still she kept her head, dressing with her usual care and attending mass in the court chapel where 'it seemed as if most of the people present looked as gloomy as I did. No one mentioned anything to me and I for my part said nothing to anyone.' That afternoon, there was a double marriage at court and one of the bridegrooms was Catherine's old friend, Leon Naryshkin. The Empress was not present and the Grand Duchess sat enthroned at the wedding feast. For all her apparent gaiety, she was conscious that people were avoiding mentioning in front of her the one subject which was on everybody's lips. Finally she could stand it no longer and summoning Marshal Troubetskoy, who was a member of the commission appointed to look into the Chancellor's affairs, she asked him point-blank as to whether they were making progress. 'If there were more crimes than criminals, or criminals than crimes.' The tone was flippant, the question was asked with a smile. But there was a certain embarrassment in the

Marshal's reply 'that they were still searching for the crimes'. The only comfort Catherine could derive was from the knowledge that the Chancellor's arrest was unpopular among all sections of the people and in particular among the army. All knew it to have been instigated by the hated Shuvalovs, the uncles of the Empress's favourite, and that they in turn had acted under pressure from foreign powers.

On the following morning, after a sleepless night, the Grand Duchess received a short note in which Bestuzhev, in spite of being under close arrest, managed to inform her that he had had the time to burn all his papers. These papers must have included the plan he had already made for the succession which, had it been found, would have incriminated Catherine to the hilt. She in turn replied that she had done the same thing. In one great holocaust she destroyed all her papers including her account books containing the various receipts from the banker, Baron Wolff. The whole of her correspondence with Hanbury-Williams, for she had always insisted on his returning her letters, now went up in flames. Fortunately for posterity the ambassador had had the forethought to copy them before doing so.

Never had Catherine felt so friendless and alone as in the weeks following on Bestuzhev's arrest. The commission, which dragged on for many months, was unable to find any concrete evidence of treason. But his conduct from the beginning of the war had been sufficiently suspect to earn him, if not the death penalty, imprisonment for life. In view of his past services, the Empress commuted his sentence to exile in one of his country estates. Field-Marshal Apraxin was spared the humiliation of an interrogation by succumbing to a fit of apoplexy before his trial. But the harshness of the sentences reserved for Catherine's associates, all of whom were banished for life to distant parts of the interior, showed that she herself was not exempt from guilt.

To add to her griefs, Poniatowski was so beset by fears for his own safety that only her tearful scenes prevented him from obeying his orders and leaving at the earliest opportunity. Feigning illness, he stayed on in the capital where his slightest

move was suspect and where he could no longer rely for protection either on the Grand Duke or his mistress, both of whom
had become Catherine's bitterest enemies. Recovered from
her confinement, Catherine was more passionate and more
ardent than ever. But Stanislaus was tired and exhausted. The
young man who had been at his happiest when conning epigrams in Madame Geoffrin's Parisian drawing-room was
unable to cope with the atmosphere of nefarious intrigue and
political skulduggery which his enchanting young mistress
accepted as part of her daily life. He left without regret when
he was finally expelled from Russia in the summer of 1758,
and Catherine writes that she never cried so much in all her
life as when they said goodbye, and she observed that 'he was
not sorry to go'.

The spring of 1758 was the most unhappy period of her life,
during which she came to the fateful decision that there could
no longer be any question of a friendly partnership between
herself and her husband. 'She would either perish with him or
through him or, acting on her own, save herself, her children
and perhaps the state, for Peter as Emperor could bring
nothing but disaster to his country.' Her fortunes were at
their lowest ebb. She was a suspect of whom no one mentioned
the crimes but whom nobody dared to uphold and whom even
her friends avoided. The Grand Duke persecuted her, the
Empress ignored her. Finding her situation to be untenable,
she staked her whole future on one colossal gamble, writing to
Elisabeth a letter in which she thanked her for all the favours
she had conferred on her in the past and begged her forgiveness
for having all unwittingly incurred her disapproval. She described the misery of her life at court, where she was hated by
the Grand Duke and not allowed to see her children, although
they lived under the same roof. In all humility she asked to be
sent back to her home in Zerbst where she could spend the
rest of her life 'praying to God for the Empress, the Grand Duke,
her children and all those who had been kind to her in the
past'. It was a pathetic, humble letter, worded in such a way
as to move the warm-hearted and vulnerable Elisabeth, the
letter of a consummate actress who never in her blackest hours

envisaged a return to Zerbst, where anyway she had no home to go to, for King Frederick had overrun her brother's estates and her mother was a refugee in Paris. But the pale little face and red-rimmed eyes were sufficiently convincing to move young Ivan Shuvalov, who had never shared his uncles' enmity and distrust of a woman he had always secretly admired, and now he offered to convey her letter to the Empress. Later that evening he returned to tell her that it had been read and that Her Majesty would grant her an audience as soon as her health allowed. Catherine had now to face up to the ordeal of waiting for an ill, capricious woman to decide her fate.

For a month she waited, all during the weeks of Lent which were spent in fasting and in prayer. Her strict observance of the rites of the Orthodox church was one of the things which endeared her most to her future subjects. But the fasting was too much for her nerves which were already at breaking-point, and she retired to her bed, weeping all day in a darkened room and in such a state of despair that her attendants feared for her life. There was no doubt that her illness was genuine, for even the strongest spirit would have given way under the stress of the past months. But still she refused to accept defeat. One of her maids was a niece of the Empress's confessor who, as guardian of the Imperial conscience, was one of the most important men in the country. She now declared her soul to be in danger and, after refusing to be visited by a doctor, she asked to see a priest. One of her maids was a niece of the Empress's confessor who, like most of the clergy, was on Catherine's side. The maid had but to ask him than he came, and was so move by her tears that he offered to act as intermediary between her and the Empress, depicting the young Grand Duchess's plight in such a heart-rending way as to arouse Elisabeth's pity, so that she finally decided to grant the long-awaited interview on the following night. The Empress who suffered from insomnia rarely went to bed till dawn.

Catherine had no sooner received this message than her spirits revived. On the evening of 13 April, she got out of bed, dressed in one of her simplest gowns, leaving her hair unpowdered and her cheeks unrouged and, after partaking of a hearty meal, lay down to rest on a couch waiting for her summons. She appears to have had sufficient peace of mind to fall asleep and was calm and refreshed when Alexander Shuvalov came to fetch her. She had hoped to find Elisabeth alone, but on the way to the royal apartments she ran into her husband who had also been summoned by his aunt. Their greeting was cold and formal, for they had not met for many weeks and no sooner were they ushered into the Empress's presence than Catherine, ignoring both Shuvalov and her husband, fell on her knees before her and, with the tears streaming down her cheeks, pleaded that life in the past months had been so intolerable and, having incurred Her Majesty's displeasure, she had no longer any wish to remain in Russia and begged to be sent back to Zerbst. Through her tears she noted with a surprising exactitude every detail of the room, the three doors, the large screen behind which she sensed the presence of Ivan Shuvalov, and between the doors two tables laid out with the Empress's golden toilet articles, including two bowls, one of which contained some letters. The room was dimly lit, for Elisabeth no longer cared to expose her ravaged beauty to too bright a light. But Catherine's sharp eyes noted she looked tired and drawn, and that her expression was sad rather than angry.

She addressed her gently, rather as one chides a child. 'How can I send you away? There are your children to be considered.' But Catherine, still weeping, cried 'My children are in your hands and thereby fortunate. I only pray you will never, never abandon them.' 'But how can you go back to Zerbst? Where would you go to? Your brother is in difficulties with the King of Prussia. Your mother is a refugee in Paris.' Catherine was quick to seize her opportunity. 'My mother has been persecuted by King Frederick for being too good a friend of Russia.' This was not strictly true, but in the past years her correspondence with her mother had been so limited that she may not have known that Johanna Elisabeth had been persecuted for being in the pay of France.

Elisabeth pursued. 'But what reason can I give my people

[91]

for sending you away?' 'Your Majesty may say what you wish. You can tell them how I happened to incur your royal displeasure, or why I am hated by my husband.' The Empress helped Catherine to her feet. It began to look as if the accused was turning into the accuser with Elisabeth protesting 'I would never have kept you by me for so many years if I had not loved you as my own child. God is witness as to how tenderly I nursed you when you fell ill so soon after your arrival.'

Meanwhile, the Grand Duke was biting his nails and champing with rage at being ignored, complaining loudly to Alexander Shuvalov of his wife's wickedness and pride. Elisabeth was suddenly reminded of Catherine's guilt, of the numerous occasions when her family had given offence. 'Your pride is insufferable. There have been times when you were so taken up with yourself that you barely bothered to curtsey when I came into a room. You imagine that no one is so brilliant as yourself and that everyone else at court is ignorant and uneducated.' The accusations might be just but they hardly constituted crimes. And now the Grand Duke began to inveigh with bitterness and vehemence against his wife who was obstinate and cruel and stopped at nothing to get her own way. Catherine took up the challenge. 'It is you who have made me hard, when I see how little you appreciate all I have done to help you. If I am cruel, it is only towards those who surround you and give you bad advice, leading you to commit injustices which make you hated by the people.'

Elisabeth was shocked to see how bitterly her niece and nephew hated one another. The tears had dried on Catherine's cheeks, the mouth was set in a thin, hard line. Her glittering eyes had the look which D'Eon once described as that of 'a wild beast'. It was now that Elisabeth began to realize that these two would never reign together, that one would end by destroying the other. She disliked and despised her nephew. But Peter was still a Romanov, and Catherine was no more than a little princess of Zerbst who, in her pride, had dared to challenge the succession, give orders to her Field-Marshal and intrigue with the Grand Chancellor. With rising indignation she turned on Catherine. 'How dared you meddle with affairs which did not concern you? I would never have allowed myself to act in such a way during the reign of the Empress Anna. How could you presume to give orders to my Field-Marshal Apraxin, as if you and Bestuzhev were running the Empire?'

Catherine faltered. The papers she had noticed in the golden bowl must be those very letters. But she defended herself with courage. 'I disobeyed your Majesty for which I beg forgiveness. But all I did was to write to Apraxin as a friend and as a patriot, begging him to go over to the offensive and not to dishonour his Empress and his country. These very letters are a proof of my good faith.' 'But Bestuzhev says there are many others.' Elisabeth now adopted the tone of an inquisition. 'If Bestuzhev says so, then he lies.' Catherine's answer came loud and clear. 'If he lies, then he will be put to the torture.' The Empress was directly threatening her through Bestuzhev. But Catherine knew that Elisabeth, who was averse to torture, would never subject the aged Chancellor to such a punishment, and she said with a certain defiance, 'Your Majesty has the power to do what you think best, but you will find that I never wrote more than three letters to Marshal Apraxim.'

Elisabeth, who was visibly impressed by the frankness of her replies, kept pacing slowly up and down the room, as if trying to come to some decision. The Grand Duke, who was visibly mortified to see his wife defending herself so cleverly, began shouting abuse, casting aspersions on her morals and enumerating her infidelities. Catherine countered by telling the Empress that all these accusations were only made in order to justify his own misconduct with Elisabeth Vorontsov, and that there was nothing he wanted more than to have his lawful wife repudiated, so that he could marry his mistress. No one till now had ever dared to tell the Empress that Elisabeth Vorontsov aspired to the Imperial crown. The revelation came as a shock. Ignoring her nephew, she went up to Catherine and whispered to her, 'There are many things I have to say to you. I cannot talk now, for I do not want to make things worse between you. But we will meet again, and next time we will be alone.' The sweetness of the voice, the gentleness of the manner coming at the end of a gruelling interview took Catherine unaware. She was so moved she could hardly speak and in between her tears she sobbed 'I, too, have so much I want to say. I long to open out my heart to you.' By her generosity and fairness, Elisabeth had succeeded in breaking down the barriers which had grown up between them over the years. Catherine had saved herself by her intelligence, but at heart she knew that it was Elisabeth who had triumphed and who had shown the elements of greatness in knowing how to forgive.

Peter's daughter loved her country and her people and, while recognizing the Grand Duchess to be guilty, had condoned her measureless ambition because she had sensed in it a quality which went beyond egotism and pride, and which, when the time came, would be wholly identified with the greatness of Russia.

It was three o'clock in the morning when Catherine returned to her apartments and she had not yet retired to bed before Alexander Shuvalov was announced, bringing a message from the Empress which told her not to grieve and promising her another meeting. This message brought by the man who, as head of the secret police and controller of the Grand Ducal household, had spied on her and persecuted her for the past years, was in every sense a victory. But there was no jubilation in the victory. So long as Elisabeth Petrovna remained on the throne, Catherine would never again dare to challenge her authority. And whatever might be their private sentiments, the Grand Ducal couple would have to live under the same roof on terms of outward amity. Many weeks elapsed before Catherine was accorded a second interview, and meanwhile she had to content herself with small signs of Imperial favour. The Empress condescended to drink her health on her birthday in April, and the Grand Duke was forced to imitate his aunt for fear of incurring her disapproval. Vorontsov and Shuvalov treated her with an added respect. But all depended on that second meeting, which did not take place till the end of May.

History has left no record of an interview so vital to Catherine's future, for it was now at the most crucial moment of her life that she chose to end her memoirs, and we are left to speculate as to the questions to which the Empress required an answer. With no one present to bear witness against her in the future, Catherine may have been forced to speak the truth regarding the nature of her relations with her husband, the parentage of her son Paul, the extent of her intrigue with Hanbury-Williams and the culpability of Bestuzhev. She was speaking to a woman who understood the frailties of human nature, and who in her day had also had to lie in order to survive. But Catherine's confessions hardly fitted into the picture of the noble, long-suffering young woman she is so anxious to present to posterity, which may explain the closing chapter of her memoirs on the eve of a meeting which rebounded to Elisabeth's credit rather than to her own.

CHAPTER EIGHT

Orlov

The Empress appears to have been satisfied with Catherine's defence and she was officially back in favour. She was even given the privilege of visiting her children once a month – a privilege which seems to have given her but little pleasure for the five-year-old Paul, a pretty, lively child, looked upon his mother as a stranger and Catherine, who was fond of children, was hurt by his indifference. Her little daughter, who had been sickly from birth, died within a few weeks of Poniatowski's departure, and the double grief of losing both her lover and their child brought Catherine to the verge of melancholia. After years of enforced virginity, the experience of the past few years had taught her 'it was impossible for her to live without love'. Stanislaus may not have been the most satisfying of lovers, but he had always treated her with tenderness and affection. The feeling that he was getting tired of her and that he was glad to go was a terrible blow to her pride. 'I sensed he was bored', she wrote, 'and it nearly broke my heart.' Exhausted would have been the better word, for Catherine may have exhausted her lovers, but she never bored them.

'I never cried so much as in that year' – tears of loneliness and despair, of sexual frustration and thwarted ambition. There were several aspiring claimants anxious to take Poniatowski's place, beginning with the young favourite who, according to the French ambassador, 'was afire to be the lover of the Grand Duchess, while still fulfilling his duties with the Empress'. But even if she had succumbed to the attractions of

Ivan Shuvalov, Catherine would have been far too frightened
to embark on an attachment which would have landed her in
a nunnery. Another aspiring suitor was the handsome Cyril
Razumovsky, younger brother to the ex-favourite, whom
Elisabeth had sent to Berlin to study under the celebrated
Euler. On his return, he had been given the important post
of Grand Hetman of the Ukraine and Colonel of the Ismailovsky
Regiment. The Razumovsky brothers had always been on
Catherine's side and Cyril had been in love with her for the
past year, a sentiment she professed to ignore till he confessed
it to her many years later. A woman as sexually aware as
Catherine, whose memoirs are sprinkled with the names of
the men whom she fancied to be in love with her, would have
been sure to notice the tender glances of one of the best-looking
young men at court. But it would have been neither politic
nor wise to involve herself with someone so near to the throne.
'It was better to keep him as a friend who, when the time came,
would rally his troops to her support.' She had learnt her
lesson and Poniatowski's successor would be chosen from among
the ranks of the young subalterns who were too unimportant
to arouse any jealousy at court.

The war was now in its third year. 1759, a year so glorious
for England's conquests overseas, brought little comfort to
her European ally. The losses sustained by Frederick against
the Russians at Zorndorf and at Künersdorf had reduced his
armies to a fraction of their strength, and Sir Robert Keith,
the British ambassador to St Petersburg (for Russia and
England continued to maintain diplomatic relations) was
instructed to mediate for peace. But all Elisabeth's remaining
energies and the strength she could summon in her poor,
debilitated body, were dedicated to victory. On New Year's
Day 1760, when she was in such pain that she could hardly
sleep and her legs were so swollen that she could barely drag
herself from one room to another, she still had the courage to
tell the Austrian ambassador, 'I will sell half my diamonds
and half my clothes in order to continue this war in conjunction
with my allies.'

No one prayed more fervently for her death than the agnostic

King of Prussia. He believed that the Grand Duke Peter's first act on his accession would be to recall his armies and sign a peace. The heir to the Russian throne was Frederick's most useful ally in keeping the British ambassador informed of the latest moves of the Russian high command. Keith, who had been formerly posted in Berlin, was a personal friend of Frederick's and all the couriers for England stopped at Potsdam on the way. Peter's scandalous behaviour was common knowledge and the loathing and contempt in which he was held by the army was such that even Keith was heard to say that 'he must be mad to behave in this way'. The French and Austrian ambassadors' complaints to the Chancellor made no impression for, in view of the Empress's precarious health, Vorontsov had no intention of jeopardizing his future by telling her of the Grand Duke's treachery.

Only Catherine was sufficiently courageous to show her disapproval by openly disociating herself from her husband and his friends. Her relations with the British ambassador were limited to the barest formalities and her circle was no longer confined to superficial courtiers and flirtatious maids-of-honour who helped to keep the Grand Duke amused. Now she sought out the company of older women who told her of the customs and traditions of the country, and of provincial governors who supplied her with facts and figures regarding the provinces over which they ruled. The conversation in her drawing-room no longer centred on Parisian culture but as to what was happening in Tver and Novgorod and Kiev, and the uneasy peace which reigned on the Turkish frontier. Bestuzhev was in exile, but one of his disciples, a brilliant young diplomat named Nikita Panin, was back from the embassy in Sweden and, although on bad terms with Michael Vorontsov, had been chosen by the Empress to be tutor to the Grand Duke Paul, yet another proof of Elisabeth's extraordinary intuition in choosing the right men independently of her ministers.

A politician of the new school, educated abroad, liberal in his outlook, Panin was inevitably drawn into Catherine's orbit. Like Bestuzhev, he foresaw the chaos that would follow at the Empress's death, but he went a step further than his former chief in considering it necessary to get rid of Peter and to set up a regency for his son presided over by the Grand Duchess. It was not in Catherine's interests to enlighten him as to the extent of her ambitions, for his very moderation was invaluable at a time when one dangerous gesture, one indiscreet remark, would jeopardize the whole of her future.

Of a very different character was the sixteen-year-old Princess Dashkov to whom Panin was so attached that some said she was his daughter, others his mistress. She was a wild little firebrand of a girl, precociously brilliant and inordinately conceited. Born Catherine Vorontsov, a younger sister to Peter's mistress and the Grand Duke's god-daughter, she was the very antithesis of her coarse-grained sister. The Grand Duchess first met her in 1758. She was only fifteen at the time but was already recognized as one of the leading personalities of the capital. An early marriage to Prince Dashkof took her for two years to Moscow. But she was too restless to settle down to life in a provincial town, and when her husband was sent abroad with his regiment, she returned to St Petersburg to complete her worldly education under the sophisticated Count Panin.

Both her sister and the Grand Duke treated her with affection, but the romantic young princess was irresistibly drawn to the unhappy and neglected Grand Duchess. In one of his brighter moments, Peter warned her that it was far wiser to be friends with a fool like him than go courting his clever wife 'who would squeeze all the juice out of a lemon and then throw it away', a warning the princess must later have had cause to remember. Catherine, on her side, was touched by the ardent and spontaneous admiration shown her by an adoring girl who, in spite of her intellectual maturity, was in many ways still a child. It flattered her pride to wean her away from her husband's circle and have Elisabeth Vorontsov's sister and the Chancellor's niece become her adoring slave. At last she had found a friend who was totally disinterested and indifferent to public opinion. What Catherine did not reckon with was the fact that the little princess was at heart a prude with strict moral principles and a fierce intolerance of the frailties in others. In spite of current gossip, she was probably never more than Count Panin's platonic love. Unconsciously, she was probably a lesbian, for there was an element of hysteria in her hero-worship of Catherine, which Catherine for her part interpreted as a young girl's '*schwärmerei*'. The Grand Duchess encouraged these emotional transports, partly out of sympathy, partly out of opportunism. The princess had powerful connections in Moscow. Her husband was one of the most popular officers in the Preobrajensky Guards and she was intimate with Count Panin, the new governor of the Grand Duke Paul.

But in the summer of 1759, an influence came into Catherine's life before which all others faded into insignificance. Among the prisoners captured at Zorndorf had been King Frederick's favourite adjutant who, as a privileged prisoner-of-war, was allowed to circulate freely in the capital accompanied by a military escort, a handsome young guards officer who had distinguished himself in battle and, after being wounded three times at Zorndorf, had led a dashing cavalry charge to victory. In recognition of his bravery Gregory Orlov had been given charge of the most important of the prisoners. He was barely twenty-four, the second of five brothers, all of them endowed with an exceptional physique, great personal courage and a whole-hearted devotion to each other, the regiment and their country. They came from a simple family. Their grandfather had been no more than a ranker in the Strelitz, the rebellious palace archers whom Peter the Great had exterminated with a savagery which has left a permanent stain on his memory. The elder Orlov's cool courage saved him from sharing the fate of his companions. On his way to the execution block, his path was obstructed by the still-bleeding head of one of his fellow archers. Kicking it aside, he continued on his way. This contempt for death so impressed the Tzar that he spared his life and posted him to an infantry regiment where his outstanding qualities soon raised him to the rank of officer.

His five grandsons were worthy descendants, recklessly brave, indifferent to danger; wild in peacetime, whoring, gaming and drinking with the greatest debauchees in town, but superb in battle and idolized by their soldiers. Of the five brothers, Alexis, the third one, was by far the most outstanding: being more ambitious and more unscrupulous than the others but also more intelligent. His beauty was marred by a sabre cut which gave him a somewhat baleful expression and earned him the name of 'the scarred one'. It was he who was later to carry out the murky deeds which were necessary to consolidate Catherine's throne; acts which may not have been done directly at her orders but to which she gave her tacit consent and for which he always accepted full responsibility, thereby earning her life-long gratitude.

But Gregory Orlov was of the stuff of legends, chivalrous, dashing and romantic with the physique of a young god. His first exploit, on arriving in the capital, was to win the love of the beautiful Elena Kourakin, mistress to his commanding officer, General Peter Shuvalov. And only the General's timely death saved him from the gallows. He disliked the job of guarding a Prussian officer and was disgusted to find the Grand Duke treating the enemy as an honoured guest. While his prisoner was being wined and dined at Peter's table, he was left kicking his heels in the ante-chamber as if he were his servant rather than his guard.

There is a story told of how the bored and lonely Grand Duchess was looking one day out of the window when she caught sight of the good-looking lieutenant waiting below in the courtyard, and fell in love with him at first sight. They had plenty of opportunities to meet. It was easy for Catherine to invite the young officer to eat with her household. It was a graceful and patriotic way to show her admiration for one of the heroes of Zorndorf and her contempt for her husband's pro-Prussian sympathies. Gregory Orlov was not timid. His success with the Princess Kourakin had given him sufficient courage to aspire to a Grand Duchess who was known to be both ardent and accessible. In any other country except Russia it would have been unthinkable for an ordinary lieutenant to set his sights so high. But there were plenty of precedents in the annals of the Romanovs. The great Tzar Peter had made a Livonian peasant girl first his mistress then his wife and, in the end, Tzarina of all the Russias. The Empress Anna had picked out the son of a German grocer and made him Duke of Courland and Elisabeth had given her heart, and, some said, married a sweet-voiced shepherd from the Ukraine. All that we know for certain is that Catherine and Gregory Orlov were lovers by the end of 1759. They loved in secret and even intimates like the Razumovskys and Dashkova were kept in ignorance of a situation which they would have criticized and justly resented at a time when both their own and Catherine's future was in jeopardy, when the Grand Duke was no longer the good-natured buffoon throwing her into Poniatowski's arms, but a jealous rival consumed with hate and envy, longing to humble and repudiate her in public.

In Gregory Orlov, Catherine found what unconsciously she had always been looking for, a primitive strength, a natural life force, sweeping all obstacles aside and taking her by storm. He was not a seducer like Saltykof or a sentimentalist like Poniatowski. He was at once brutal, tender and strong, simple and uncomplicated. There is no clearer evidence of Catherine's guiding star and of her extraordinary good fortune than that it was her love for Orlov, the devotion of the Orlov brothers and their popularity in the army, which finally brought her to the throne.

But Elisabeth's death in the last days of 1761 took Catherine completely unawares, when she was six months gone with child and in no shape to lead a revolution. For over four years she had been plotting and scheming in the event of the Empress's demise. Time after time she had assured Sir Charles Hanbury-Williams 'that her enemies would not find her unprepared', but the subtlest of intriguers, the most intelligent of women, had made no allowances for the tricks that could be played by fate. The Empress had so often been on the brink of death and every time her magnificent constitution had enabled her to rally. But every time she became weaker and the pains grew worse. At one moment she was longing to die, at the next she was dragging herself out of bed to attend a *Te Deum* for another Russian victory. Her armies had raided Berlin and advanced deep into Frederick's hereditary lands. Brilliant young leaders had emerged like General Roumiantsev whose victories were to add to the glory of Catherine's reign. But there was no gratitude among Russia's allies, for both France and Austria viewed with a growing dismay the pride and pretensions of a vast, barbaric Empire encroaching on Europe.

Now there was mourning among the generals and consternation in the barracks at the news that their beloved 'Matouchka' was dying and that the hated Holsteiner would succeed. Elisabeth's last public appearance had been amongst her soldiers. She had gone to the theatre with the little Grand Duke Paul and, depressed by the emptiness of the auditorium, had invited the palace guards to assist at the performance. Whether it was a spontaneous gesture on the part of a dying woman wanting for the last time to be with the soldiers who twenty years ago had raised her to the throne; or whether it was an attempt to stage a demonstration of loyalty which would enable her to announce a change in the succession and the establishment of a regency for the young Duke – whatever may have been the reason, it failed. The soldiers filling the pit only saw her from afar as a radiant vision. They did not see the ravages of illness beneath the rouge, the swollen legs beneath the silver gown. They only saw the enchanting, all-embracing smile. Whoever said that 'Matouchka' was ill must be lying. She was here among them, a warm and living presence, and they cheered and shouted: 'Vivat! Vivat! Elisabeth Petrovna!'

There was panic at court and in the chancellories. In the royal apartments, Ivan Shuvalov, the pampered favourite, was crying like a child, for in the past weeks the Empress had turned for comfort to her former lover, and only seemed at peace when Alexis Razumovsky was sitting by her bed, soothing her pain with the soft lullabies of the Ukrainian peasants.

By order of the Empress, the Grand Ducal couple were to be kept in ignorance of her condition until the last moment. Elisabeth knew that her heir would immediately communicate the joyful news to his friend, the King of Prussia. Peter saw so little of his aunt that, though living under the same roof, he knew less of what was happening in the Imperial sickroom than anyone else at court. Catherine's condition prevented her from appearing much in public. Though the fashion for loose sacques and hooped skirts helped her to conceal her pregnancy, she feared the scrutiny of hundreds of prying eyes, quick to observe the slightest change in shape. So she stayed at home on the excuse that it mortified her to see the Grand Duke in public with his mistress, to whom he accorded almost royal honours. This excuse won her the sympathy and pity of every chivalrous young man at court.

She still received visits both official and unofficial. Everyone was welcome, even the new French ambassador, the twenty-seven-year-old Baron de Breteuil, appointed by King Louis in the hopes that his good looks might win him favour with the Grand Duchess and counterbalance the intrigues of his English colleague, Sir Robert Keith, who was on good terms with the Grand Duke. But King Louis and his ministers failed to take into account that the newly married ambassador was passionately fond of his wife whom he had insisted on bringing with him to Russia, and he had no intention of paying court to the Grand Duchess who, for her part, was far too occupied in other directions and only interested in him as a possible source of income.

Money had become more than ever essential to her. Her finances were at their lowest ebb and she hoped against hope that France might supplement her income in order to gain her goodwill. But the French were more ready to produce a virile young ambassador than to open their money-bags. They had lost too much in Russia in the past; so long as Elisabeth lived, the young Grand Duchess's fortunes were too precarious to be a good investment. Catherine had a bitter deception when her mother died in Paris so deeply in debt that her personal effects had to be sold by public auction, and King Louis made no effort to spare her this humiliation. She was deeply grieved at her mother's death, all the more so because she had been able to do so little to help her in the last years. And now she even failed in her attempts to persuade Baron de Breteuil to get his government to intervene.

Help came from an unexpected quarter, with Ivan Shuvalov prevailing on the Empress to settle the debts of a Princess who, in her lifetime, had done very little to deserve her generosity.

The favourite's timely intercession was later to assure him an honourable position at Catherine's court. But it was to take over twenty years and an ambassador as charming and as gifted as the Count de Ségur to make her feel any sympathy towards France.

No foreign diplomat took part in the conspiracies and plots which were being hatched in the privacy of the Grand Duchess's boudoir. There was no one coherent plan and most of the conspirators ignored the existence of the others. Catherine's powers of dissimulation came into full play. Each one of her adherents was made to feel that he or she was the only person on whom she could rely for help. Her relations with the Orlovs, and particularly with Gregory, were carefully concealed from Dashkova and Panin. The adoring little Princess would have been miserable to know that the Grand Duchess's most intimate confidante was not her, but another young married woman, Countess Prascovia Bruce, born a Roumiantsev and sister to the general whose victories had added lustre to the last campaign. She was a woman after Catherine's heart, gay, witty, totally amoral, and at the same time amazingly discreet. It was in her little house on the Vasily Ostrov that Catherine met her lover when it became too dangerous for them to have their assignations in the palace. Prascovia Bruce and her trusted maid were the only ones in the secret of the unwanted pregnancy which was tying Catherine hand and foot at a time when action was imperative.

CHAPTER NINE

The Tide of Events

It was late on a winter's evening towards the end of December 1761, and the Grand Duchess had already retired for the night, when she heard raised voices in the ante-chamber. Brushing aside the restraining arm of a soldier on guard, disregarding the protests of a lady-in-waiting, Princess Dashkova entered, or rather erupted into her room, in such a state of agitation that, forgetting her condition, Catherine jumped out of bed. But the Princess was far too excited to notice the rounded belly beneath the heavily pleated gown, and in a shrill voice cried out 'There's not a moment to lose. We must act now before it is too late. The Empress is dying. It is a matter of a day, perhaps hours. What plans have you made and how can your friends protect you?' The young woman was shivering with cold and feverish from nerves. Catherine was touched by her obvious devotion and insisted on her visitor getting into her bed and warming herself, before committing herself to an answer. 'I have no plans and can undertake nothing. All I can do is to trust in God, who will help me to bear with fortitude whatever may be my lot.' They were noble words spoken in a tone of gentle resignation by a woman who had never felt less noble, and was railing at the trick of fate which had paralysed all her plans.

The little Princess, who was longing to man the barricades in defence of her beloved Grand Duchess, was somewhat disconcerted by such noble resignation, and interrupted with impatience: 'If you can do nothing, then your friends will have to act in your defence. I will be the first to sacrifice myself on your behalf.' Catherine took fright lest this irresponsible girl might end in exposing them all by her foolhardiness, and she begged her not to court danger for her sake, 'for there was nothing one could do'. But the impetuous Dashkova was burning for action, longing to suffer 'if suffer I must', and assuring her that she would never have any reason to regret her devotion. These words brought tears to Catherine's eyes, and embracing her young friend she begged her to leave, for if she was found in her room at this hour of the night it would only mean trouble for them both. And with many flurried apologies Princess Dashkova left as suddenly as she had come, little suspecting that the handsome officer who passed her in the palace courtyard was the Grand Duchess's lover on his way to fetch his prisoner from supper at the Grand Duke's. Nor would she have been edified to know that Catherine had already called for Prascovia Bruce to give her a letter to Gregory Orlov, telling him of her nocturnal visitor and warning him and his associates against any possible indiscretions on the part of the impetuous Princess.

Two days later, the Empress had another stroke; this time, all four doctors in attendance agreed that there was no hope of recovery. The Grand Duke and Duchess were summoned to her bedchamber, where they found the two Razumovsky brothers, Alexander Shuvalov and his nephew Ivan, and the Chancellor Vorontsov who, to the very end, had conspired to prevent the dying woman from carrying out her last wishes and changing the succession. The ante-chambers and corridors were crowded with weeping and praying courtiers, and for once the sorrow and the piety were genuine, for Elisabeth had been greatly loved and was going to be bitterly regretted. She remained lucid to the end. When the priests administered the last sacraments, she insisted on them repeating twice the beautiful Orthodox prayer for the dying. Then she blessed everyone in turn, and according to custom asked of each one their forgiveness. Catherine, who could not control her tears, was carried away in a state of collapse. Was it grief and remorse, or merely a physical nausea brought on by the heat in the close, overcrowded room?

Elisabeth was dying and she was barely fifty-two, a woman who had loved life and wasted it with reckless abandon, destroying both her beauty and her health by refusing to restrict either her passions or her appetites. But for all her shortcomings, she had been a good ruler, keeping her country at peace for the first fifteen years of her reign, trying in her own fashion to preserve her father's heritage, reviving the glory of his army and, while remaining Russian to the core, giving to her court the gloss of Western civilization. Under her reign, Russia had become a European power, ready to take her place at the conference tables which dictated the peace of the world – a power to be reckoned with and feared in the future.

It was four o'clock in the afternoon of 25 December, Christmas Day, 1761, when the Grand Marshal, Prince Troubetskoy, with the tears pouring down his cheeks, came out of the Empress's bedroom to announce the death of Her Imperial Majesty Elisabeth Petrovna, Tzarina of all the Russias, and the accession of the Emperor Peter III.

Peter turned to the assembled crowd. His eyes were shining, and his face was twitching with nerves. This was the moment he had been waiting for over so many years. He hated the country he was being called upon to rule, he hated and despised the people. But he was obsessed by the desire to reign, to assert his royal will on all those who, with the Empress's consent, had kept him under a shameful tutelage. There was not a single tear, not a shadow of regret for the aunt he had feared and hated, and the courtiers who now slavishly acclaimed him showed in their eyes their horror and disgust.

When one considers the hatred with which the Grand Duke is regarded by all sections of the population, how he commits one foolish mistake after another, then one is convinced that the Empress's death will be followed by revolution. On the other hand, when one considers the laziness and cowardice of those in power, the cringing civility of the average courtier, then one begins to wonder whether anything will happen at all.

So wrote the Baron de Breteuil, a few weeks before Elisabeth's death, and the ambassador's prognostications were correct. In spite of the gloomy faces in the street, the threatening rumours in the barracks, Peter III ascended the throne without a single minister resigning or a single shot being fired.

The first to swear allegiance was his wife who, according to an eye witness, prostrated herself in front of her husband, professing to be ready to obey him as the chief servant of his Empire. The Empress Catherine was later to deny the truth of this story, but the very vehemence of her denial lends substance to the tale. As a consummate actress it would have cost her nothing to play a role calculated to placate the new Emperor, but her greatest act was reserved for the Russian people.

Following tradition, the body of the late Empress, embalmed and dressed in gala robes, was exposed in public ten days before the funeral. It was laid out in state on a catafalque in the Kazan Cathedral, with the palace guards and ladies of the court keeping a continuous vigil. All day long the people from the highest noble to the humblest peasant, from the city and the surrounding countryside, came in their hundreds and thousands to pay their last respects to the Empress they had loved as a mother and worshipped as a divinity.

Not one of them could fail to notice the veiled woman in black, kneeling at the foot of the bier and apparently so lost in prayer that she seemed unaware of their presence. It was the new Empress, sharing the mourning of the Russian people, kneeling on the cold stone and prostrating herself in prayer like the most fervent of Orthodox believers. She was there every day and almost all day, a heroic effort for even the healthiest of women, but doubly so for one who was already six months gone with child and physically nauseated by the smell of candle grease and incense and the stench of the unwashed crowds. But never for a moment did she falter, thereby winning the love and respect of her future subjects, and dissociating herself from her husband; for Peter not only publicly insulted the memory of his aunt by refusing to say a prayer at her bier, but on the few occasions when he did appear, he did nothing but joke with the ladies on duty, forcing them to laugh, or reprimanding a soldier on guard for some trifling offence, and even at times going so far as to ridicule the priests.

His behaviour at the state funeral was so scandalous as to give rise to comment. Even his friend, Sir Robert Keith, came to the conclusion 'that the Emperor's reign could not last for long'. Walking behind the hearse, with his long black train carried by the highest dignitaries of the Empire, most of them elderly gentlemen grown grey in the service of the state, Peter deliberately made mock of the ceremony by lagging behind till the hearse was some way ahead, and then running to catch up with it. This threw the whole solemn procession into confusion, with the elderly courtiers puffing and panting behind him, and finally letting go of the train which flapped grotesquely in the wind, making Peter appear more like a mummer than an emperor.

But all his foolish antics, his drunken orgies and indecorous behaviour during the time of mourning were as nothing compared with the way in which he flouted the sentiments of every patriotic Russian by concluding a peace with Prussia in the first days of his reign. On the very night of the Empress's death he was already drafting despatches to the generals in the field, ordering them to lay down arms and even to relinquish their positions when fighting beside their Austrian allies. The conquests so hardly won were to be given up. Not a single Russian soldier was to remain on German soil, all in order to win favour with his friend and idol, the King of Prussia, to whom his letters read more like those of a faithful vassal, a little duke of Holstein, than a victorious emperor. No thought was given to his people, the families who had lost fathers, husbands, sons and brothers. No thought was given to his allies or to his own honour and self-respect. Even the time-server, Michael Vorontsov, was ashamed to meet the ministers of France and Austria. At a dinner-party given by the Chancellor, at which the Emperor was present, Peter went deliberately out of his way to provoke a quarrel with the French ambassador by drinking a toast to the King of Prussia, saying in a loud and aggressive voice that he wanted peace in spite of his allies. What appeared to be a drunken threat became a reality when, on 25 February 1762, Russia signed a secret peace treaty with Prussia. Frederick, who had been beaten to his knees, was given back all his territories, but he had little admiration for his generous friend whom he described as 'a Don Quixote of whom I am the Dulcinea'.

In some ways, Don Quixote was a fair description, for Peter was not wholly bad. He was weak and degenerate, vitiated by a deplorable education and deplorable companions, but at heart he was still the frightened and lonely child, pathetically unsure of himself, swaggering and drinking to give himself courage. He was still capable of noble, even generous impulses. None of Elisabeth's favourites were persecuted or dispossessed, while those she had exiled, like her French doctor Lestocq, the notorious Biron, lover to the Empress Anna, and the veteran Field-Marshal Munnich, guilty of no other crime than his German origin, were recalled and given back their titles and estates. These men, most of them of foreign origin, were loud in praise of the new Emperor, and embittered by their experience, urged him to show more severity to his enemies. According to the somewhat biased memoirs of a Saxon diplomat, Peter suffered from being too clement. When he was warned of the danger of such a course, he is said to have replied, 'Would you have me commence my reign by shedding blood?' Even Catherine, who had little good to say of her husband, never went so far as to accuse him of physical violence. He appears to have gone no further than to delight in thwarting her simplest wishes, humiliating her in public by treating his mistress as a reigning princess and forcing her to confer on Elisabeth Vorontsov the Order of St Catherine, which was usually only given to those of princely birth. But he had to be very drunk before he found the courage to openly repudiate his wife and announce his intention of declaring his son to be a bastard and of marrying his mistress, words which Catherine took care should be repeated in every barrack-room in St Petersburg, thereby winning her the sympathy of every patriotic soldier.

But not all the decrees which came tumbling out of Peter's

muddled mind were foolish, for some of his German advisers were capable and intelligent. He abolished the dreaded secret chancellory, while a *Ukaze* emancipating the nobles from all military and civil duties to the state won him popularity with a class whose one desire was to gain power without responsibility. Catherine was quick to realize the harm which Peter was causing both to himself and his successors by putting the great landowners in an even stronger position than before, giving them unchallenged authority over their serfs and increasing their privileges by diminishing their duties. She could hardly hide her contempt for an emperor who, on the advice of a favourite *aide-de-camp*, was placing himself at the mercy of his nobles. When Prince Dashkof came to her with tears of joy, saying that her husband deserved to have a gold statue put up to him for having given freedom to the nobility, she who was usually so self-controlled snapped back, 'I did not realize before that you were a serf.'

Fortunately, the majority of the army officers were not rich princes like young Dashkof. They were simple, patriotic men, angry and humiliated by the peace with Prussia and on the verge of mutiny when Peter, acting as Duke of Holstein rather than as Emperor of Russia, picked a quarrel with Denmark on account of Schleswig, and threatened a war in order to regain for Holstein an obscure German province. Even King Frederick tried to dissuade him from an action which would enrage the whole of his general staff. But Peter carried his love for Holstein even further by appointing his uncle, Prince George of Holstein, as Commander-in-Chief of the Russian army and announcing his intention of remodelling it on the Prussian pattern. As a foretaste of what was to come, the élite regiment of the Preobrajensky were given new uniforms copied from those of King Frederick's guards.

Not content with having antagonized the army, Peter now began to attack the clergy, the dominating force of Russian life, who exercised a mystical hold over millions of voiceless people, to whom the words of their bishops reflected the words of God. Peter had always hated the Orthodox religion which had been imposed upon him by his aunt. What little faith he had was strictly Lutheran and one of his first acts on coming to the throne was to turn Elisabeth's private chapel into a Lutheran church. Imitating his grandfather, who had forced the Boyars to cut their beards and dress in Western clothes, he now ordered the clergy to cut off their beards, discard their rich vestments and adopt the short dress of the Lutheran pastor. All images other than those of Christ and the Virgin were to be removed from the churches. And as the crowning blow, the church lands were to be confiscated and the clergy were to become salaried state officials. These edicts aroused such a storm of protest from all classes of the people that his ministers begged the Emperor to desist from carrying out a measure which could lead to revolution. But Peter was drunk with power, seeing himself in the light of a liberal reformer, a second Peter the Great.

Meanwhile, Catherine remained quietly in the background, still ostensibly in mourning for the late Empress. The time of her confinement was drawing near and it required all her imagination and resourcefulness to devise a scheme by which she could give birth to a child without her husband being aware of it, while living under the same roof. She had always been able to count on the devotion of her servants and on this occasion, one of them, named Skourine, showed such a spirit of self-sacrifice as to deserve the rich rewards which were later showered on him by his grateful Empress. Peter had a passion for pyrotechnics, but what pleased him even more than fireworks was the sight of a building in flames. It was a pleasure he had plenty of opportunity of indulging in in Moscow, where hundreds of wooden houses were destroyed every year by fire. But they were less frequent in St Petersburg, where brick and stone were rapidly replacing wood.

To oblige his mistress, Skourine set fire to his house on the night of 11 April, and Catherine gave birth to Orlov's son in her apartments in the new Winter Palace while Peter was at the other side of the city gloating over the destruction of poor Skourine's house. The baby, whom Prascovia Bruce smuggled out of the palace wrapped in a beaver skin, was later given the name of Bobrinsky – a derivation from the Russian for beaver.

For the time being, Catherine had other things to do than to give much thought to her newborn son. The time was at hand when the various threads in the conspiracy had to be drawn together and the conspirators made known to one another, when Princess Dashkova and the Orlovs, Panin and Cyril Razumovsky were to join forces in forming what the princess described in later years as 'a disconcerted plan, dreamt of rather than studied by a group of ill-assorted individuals with little sympathy or understanding for one another'. But there was no need for a concerted plan. The whole country was seething with discontent and the poor, mad Emperor was every day adding another nail to his coffin.

On the night of 12 June 1762, the Emperor Peter held a banquet in the Summer Palace to celebrate the ratification of the peace treaty with Prussia. Frederick's ambassador sat on his right hand, viewed with dour looks by the Russian generals present, while the French ambassador was subjected to continual quips and jibes on the part of his host. This was the occasion so often quoted when Peter publicly insulted Catherine in front of his five hundred guests. Three toasts were drunk, each of them accompanied by a salvo of cannon fire from the square below. The first was to the Imperial family, during which the Empress remained seated. Peter, who was already the worse for drink, ordered the adjutant, who was standing behind his chair, to go to the Empress and ask her why she had not risen to drink the toast. Catherine replied with great dignity that 'she had not thought it necessary, as the family consisted of the Emperor, her son and herself'. This sensible answer made Peter apoplectic with rage and, losing all control, he shouted at the adjutant to go and tell the Empress that his uncles, the Princes of Holstein, were members of the Imperial family and that she was a '*doura*' (idiot). Suspecting that the officer would never dare to repeat such an insult, he yelled at Catherine from across the table '*Doura, doura*'. The guests were stunned with horror. Several hands went instinctively to their sword hilts. Only Peter appeared completely unaware of the enormity of his offence. Catherine burst into tears, but within a few moments had recovered sufficiently to turn to Count

Stroganov who was in attendance, requesting him with a pitiful little smile to tell her something amusing. At the same time everyone noted the look of cold, unadulterated hatred she gave her husband.

According to Catherine, it was now that she began to listen to the various plans and propositions which had been put forward during the past months. This is the version she gives when writing to Poniatowski a detailed account of the events which led to the *coup d'état* for, in spite of her infatuation for Orlov, she still found the time to keep up a tender and affectionate correspondence with her former lover. Poniatowski must have known better than anyone that Catherine had been planning and plotting to usurp her husband's throne as long ago as 1758, when she openly confessed both to him and to Hanbury-Williams that she was 'longing for Elisabeth to die and that her death would not find her unprepared'. But the account given to Poniatowski, who was her only link with the Western world, was the one which she wished to go down in history. It was her first attempt at public relations in which she was later to excel, and was deliberately written for him to pass on to his friends abroad, to be read and believed in the clubs of London and the salons of Paris. According to her, she was forced to act when she heard that the Emperor was planning to have her arrested, which he would already have done had he not been prevented from doing so by his uncle, Prince George of Holstein, who feared that her arrest would spark off a revolution in the army.

The projected campaign against Denmark had brought the general discontent to boiling-point and, as a crowning folly, the Emperor announced that he was taking command of the army in person. Two days after the banquet he set out for Oranienbaum, which had been transformed into an army camp. Here he spent hours every day drilling his troops, much in the same way as he had formerly drilled his toy soldiers on the matrimonial bed, refusing to listen to the advice and warnings of his ministers who had remained behind in the capital.

Catherine had been ordered to take up residence at Peterhof, where the Emperor planned to join her in time to celebrate his name day on 29 June. She asserts that her husband intended to have her arrested on the evening following the festivities. This is hard to believe, because Peter was a coward, who throughout his married life had been frightened of his wife; any action he intended to take would have been carried out after his departure for Denmark on the grounds that it was dangerous to leave the Empress at liberty in his absence.

Catherine spent five days alone in St Petersburg, sufficient time in which to co-ordinate her plans and give and receive the last instructions, for in many instances it was the Orlovs, rather than she, who commanded. When she left for Peterhof, the little Grand Duke Paul remained behind in the capital in the charge of his tutor, Count Panin, for neither she nor the Orlovs had any intention of her being proclaimed regent for her son. At Peterhof she stayed not at the palace but at the pavilion of 'Mon Plaisir', a hundred yards nearer to the sea with terraces giving out on to the Gulf of Finland and a secluded beach where messengers could land by boat without having to pass by the palace sentries.

The Empress's days were spent in a state of nervous and suppressed excitement lest one false move, one rash remark, might place them all in peril. The Orlovs were making headway in the capital, winning over fresh recruits so that when the time came there were from thirty to forty officers and over ten thousand men in the secret. Cyril Razumovsky, the most powerful of all Catherine's adherents and Colonel-in-Chief of the Ismailovsky Guards, had won over the whole of his regiment. Being the President of the Academy of Arts and Sciences, he had also mobilized the printing press in preparation for the issue of a manifesto. Dashkova, who looked upon herself as the heart and soul of the conspiracy, was buzzing and flapping her wings like an excited dragonfly, not realizing that, in the Empress's eyes, her greatest assets were her friendship with Panin and her husband's popularity in the Guards. All these rival personalities had to be soothed, placated and charmed, but at heart Catherine relied solely on the Orlovs and her own lucky star.

CHAPTER TEN

Vivat! Vivat!

In the account given to Poniatowski Catherine omits the fact that she saw her husband for the last time on the evening of 19 June when he invited her to attend a theatrical performance at Oranienbaum. Would even someone as erratic and unpredictable as Peter have invited his wife to a theatrical entertainment where it amused him to show off his talents as a producer, if he was seriously contemplating getting rid of her? He may have threatened to do so and on occasion boasted of it in public to his mistress, but Peter's threats were very different from his actions.

It suited Catherine to believe and later to publicize these threats. The Orlovs were pressing for action, and the arrest of one of their associates, a certain Captain Passek charged with having slandered the Emperor, brought matters to a head. Any further delay was dangerous and, on the evening of 27 June, Gregory Orlov notified Princess Dashkova that the Empress would be proclaimed on the following day. In her letter to Poniatowski, Catherine writes:

It was six o'clock in the morning of 28 June and I was fast asleep when Alexis Orlov came into my room and woke me up by telling me in the calmest manner that I must get dressed and come with him to St Petersburg, where the army was ready to proclaim me as their Empress. I asked for details. He replied that Passek, one of his associates, had been arrested. I leapt out of bed and dressed as quickly as I could, without even bothering to arrange my hair or powder my face. A carriage was waiting below with an officer disguised as a footman on the box and a second one sitting beside the driver.

We had got within a few miles of the capital when we ran into Gregory Orlov and Prince Bariatinsky, who had come out to meet us. The latter gave me his seat in the carriage, as our horses were on the verge of collapse, and we drove straight to the Ismailovsky Barracks where twelve men and a drummer boy gave the alarm. The soldiers came running out of their quarters, some of them still half-dressed, others fastening their sword belts – all of them shouting with joy and hailing me as a saviour, kissing my hands, my feet, even the hem of my dress. Two of them brought with them a priest carrying a cross, and one and all swore me allegiance. The Colonel-in-Chief, Cyril Razumovsky, produced a gala coach, in which he and the Orlovs accompanied me to the Semeonowsky Barracks. By now news of my arrival was spreading through the town, and the streets and quays were a solid mass of cheering people, soldiers and civilians all shouting 'Vivat! Vivat!'

Catherine's account of these stirring events is factual and laconic. Certain details are deliberately omitted – of how Alexis Orlov had forgotten to procure a relay of horses so that, when their own collapsed only a few miles out of Peterhof, the Empress of Russia had to proceed to the conquest of her capital driven by two sorry nags procured from a local peasant. Only the fortuitous arrival of Gregory Orlov prevented her from arriving at the Ismailovsky Barracks in this condition. Another detail she would have scorned to mention was the fact that she was still wearing her house-slippers, for no comic element must be allowed to detract from the solemnity of the occasion which must in every way compare with the *coup d'état* of 1741 which had placed the Empress Elisabeth on the throne.

But the daughter of Peter the Great had had all the cards in her hands. Her magnificent appearance, her Romanov and above all her Russian blood, made her into a natural heroine. She was not just a little German upstart, profiting by her husband's unpopularity and the general discontent to steal a throne. Catherine had need of all her courage and *sangfroid*, her firm belief in her own destiny, to help her to forget that she was born Sophia of Anhalt-Zerbst. She may have dressed that morning in a hurry, but every move had been carefully planned; the plain black dress still worn out of filial respect for the late Empress; the unbound hair falling about her shoulders which only served to accentuate her youthful femininity, rendering her far more appealing than if she had been wearing the most elaborate of court gowns.

There was a fresh outburst of cheering when the procession, now swelled by hundreds of civilians, approached the precincts of the Cathedral of Our Lady of Kazan. The cheering grew to a crescendo when the two elite regiments of the Preobrajensky and the Horseguards appeared almost simultaneously to offer their allegiance, the former protesting that they had been kept in barracks by their officers whom they had managed to overwhelm and now brought along as prisoners. This situation had been caused by the fact that the conspirators were so disorganized that some of the officers who happened to be on duty that day had not been initiated into the secret and were quelling what they believed to be a mutiny. But no sooner did they see the Empress than they joined in the general cheering and swore their allegiance. Everyone seemed to be laughing and crying at the same time in what Catherine describes as a 'delirium of joy'.

It was nine o'clock in the morning, only three hours since she had set out from Peterhof, and already she was kneeling by the high altar of the Kazan Cathedral, blessed by the archbishop and publicly acclaimed as Catherine II, Autocrat of all the Russias. In this short time she had accomplished what she had set out to do from the beginning. The prayers which were being said for her and for her son, the Tzarevitch Paul Petrovitch, spoke of him only as heir to the throne. But even in these first hours of triumph, she never lost her head. The time had come for her to produce her son and to conciliate Panin, the only statesman among the ranks of the conspirators.

Bishops and priests now lent dignity to the procession which was gradually becoming an Imperial cortège, and the young woman who held her head so proudly and smiled so happily at the crowds appeared convinced that she was God's annointed with a divine right to rule. But the mood changed when she

appeared on the balcony of the new Winter Palace, holding
by the hand the eight-year-old Paul. Though late on a summer's
morning, the little Tzarevitch appears to have been in his
nightgown, his cheeks still flushed with sleep. On seeing the
child, the crowd broke into a frenzy of cheering, surging forward on a wave of adulation, adulation not so much for the
mother as for the child. Behind Paul stood his tutor, Nikita
Panin, with his benign smile and watchful eyes, a man whom
Catherine knew she would never be able to get rid of, for only
by managing Panin could she succeed in managing her son.

Back in the palace, senators and courtiers, the heads of the
various colleges of state and the members of the Holy Synod,
were all fighting for precedence, struggling up Rastrelli's great
marble staircase to pay homage to the new divinity. Among
them was a small, agitated figure, who until now appears to
have been forgotten by her beloved Empress. Princess Dashkova
had been unable to fight her way through the tightly packed
crowds and was in danger of being trampled underfoot when
some soldiers fortunately recognized her and lifted her up in
their arms, passing her from one to the other till she was carried
into the palace and landed at the Empress's feet, breathless,
tousled, but triumphant. The greeting between the two friends
was heartfelt and sincere and Dashkova had the honour of
standing beside the Empress when a manifesto fresh from the
printing presses of the Academy of Science was read to the
assembled crowd.

It was a skilful document, composed by Catherine with
the assistance of an obscure Chancellory official who was later
to become one of the most efficient of her secretaries. Teplow
was one of those shadowy figures who never sought the limelight, but who in the years to come was to have far greater
influence over his mistress than many of the more spectacular
members of her entourage. In the manifesto, Catherine declared
to the Russian people that circumstances had compelled her to
rescue them from the dangers that were threatening them on
every side:

Our Orthodox church is being menaced by the adoption of
foreign rites, our military prestige raised so high by our victorious

army, is being degraded by the conclusion of a dishonourable peace. All the respected traditions of our fatherland are being trampled underfoot. So we, being conscious that it is the honest desire of all our loyal subjects and having God and justice on our side, have ascended the throne as Catherine II, Autocrat of all the Russias.

'Autocrat' was a brave word to use for a woman whose husband, the legal Emperor, might even now be marching on his capital. All precautions had been taken to prevent the news of the *coup d'état* from reaching Peter until the situation in St Petersburg had been consolidated. There was still a large army in Pomerania, who had given their oath of allegiance to the Emperor, while the troops destined for the Danish campaign were concentrated at Narva, only a few miles from Peterhof. Fourteen hundred well trained and loyal Holsteiners guarded the Emperor at Oranienbaum, and in his suite was the famous veteran, Field-Marshal Munnich, whom he had recalled from exile and who was now his devoted henchman. The capital had acclaimed Catherine, but as yet she had only four regiments at her disposal, all of them belonging to the privileged Guards who were envied and disliked by the rest of the army. If Peter showed sufficient energy and decision, the events of 28 June might be no more than an adventuress's presumptuous dream, for which the Orlovs would be publicly hanged and Catherine immured in a nunnery for life.

But with that imperturbability which was one of her greatest assets, Catherine, having proclaimed herself as Empress and changed into the uniform of a Colonel of the Guards, set out to review her fourteen thousand men, as if she had the whole of the Russian Empire at her command. At first she hardly recognized them for by common accord they had all discarded the hated Prussian uniforms introduced by Peter and taken out of store their old Russian ones. It was on this occasion that a twenty-two-year-old subaltern from the Horse Guards rode boldly out of the ranks to point out to the Empress that her uniform was lacking a sword knot and gallantly presented his own. His superior officers frowned at the impertinence of young Potemkin. But his proud and independent bearing pleased the Empress, who accepted his gift with an appraising smile. She asked him his name and later made further enquiries, and neither his face nor his name was ever forgotten.

But the Orlov brothers were the heroes of the day. Catherine was so lost in admiration of their courage, their common-sense and gift for leadership, that even when writing to Poniatowski, she could not resist singing the praises of those wonderful brothers who showed such devotion both to her and to their country that 'it would take a whole book in which to describe their feats of bravery and their generous deeds'. But when it came to deciding matters of statecraft, the only one she could rely on was Panin, and on his advice she now moved to the old Winter Palace where Elisabeth had lived and died. From here she sent messages to announce her accession to her naval and military chiefs in Livonia and Pomerania. There was no time for formal *Ukazi* and Catherine wrote out her Imperial commands in her own hand, still not knowing whether they were already marching against her on the Emperor's orders. At four o'clock in the afternoon, a delegation consisting of Chancellor Vorontsov, Marshal Troubetskoy and Alexander Shuvalov brought her the first news from Peterhof, where the Emperor had arrived to find her gone and, immediately suspecting the worst, had sent them post-haste to the capital to bring her back by force. But the time-server Vorontsov was quick to see which way the wind was blowing, and within an hour he and his companions, who knew no loyalty other than to themselves, had given allegiance to the Empress.

Peter was in a festive mood when he and his court set out that morning from Oranienbaum. His companions included Elisabeth Vorontsov and sixteen of the gayest and most flirtatious of the young maids-of-honour. What with games and picnics on the way, it was long past noon when the company arrived at the Pavilion of 'Mon Plaisir' to find no welcome and no wife, no preparations for the festivities of the following day, only some barking dogs and squeaking parrots and a horde of frightened servants who only knew that the Empress had left early that morning. Everyone from the Chancellor to his niece knew that this sudden departure had an ominous meaning, but Peter could only storm and rage against the wife who had dared to disobey his orders, crying like a spoilt child to find no preparations for his party. His counsellors advised immediate action, but for the moment the Emperor appeared to be incapable of coming to any decision and precious time was wasted before he allowed a delegation to leave for St Petersburg.

The first news of the *coup d'état* was brought to him by one of his Holsteiners returning after twenty-four hours' leave in the capital. On hearing that the Guards had gone over to the Empress, Field-Marshal Munnich's immediate reaction was for the Emperor to summon his troops from Narva and march directly on St Petersburg. The Prussian ambassador, who happened to be of the party, suggested that His Majesty should strengthen the defences of Peterhof and await the arrival of the bulk of his army from Pomerania. But Munnich declared that Peterhof was indefensible and it would be wiser to proceed to the naval base of Cronstadt. Peter, however, was in such a hysterical state of nerves that he could do nothing but compose one manifesto after another, all of which he destroyed as soon as he had written them. Precious time was wasted, till one of the Holsteiners, who appears to have been under no illusions as to his master's courage, said quite frankly that 'the best thing he could do would be to flee the country and return in safety to his own town of Kiel'.

This ignominious suggestion made Peter refind his manhood and remember that he was a Romanov. Orders were given to proceed by yacht to Cronstadt. It was already late in the evening and Field-Marshal Munnich and General Goudovitch, his loyal *aide-de-camp*, looked on aghast when the Emperor insisted on taking along with him his mistress and the sixteen maids-of-honour. Cronstadt was not reached until one in the morning. It was a clear summer night, almost as light as day. A sentinel on the ramparts called out 'Who goes there?' 'The Emperor,' replied Goudovitch. 'There is no longer an Emperor, only an Empress. Move on or we fire.' The words rang short and sharp across the water. Catherine's admiral was already in charge. Both Field-Marshal and *aide-de-camp* implored Peter to stay the course. If he anchored beneath the ramparts, no one would dare to fire. 'I swear it on my life,' cried the old veteran, who needed all his iron discipline to refrain from insulting his monarch. But Peter was hiding in the hold of the ship trembling with fear, clinging to his mistress who was screaming hysterically. In a last attempt to bring him to his senses, the Field-Marshal told him it was madness to return to Peterhof, that there was still a chance of going to Revel where he could board a ship and rejoin his troops in Pomerania. 'Do this and I swear that within a month you will be back in your palace at St Petersburg.' But Peter kept whimpering that he wanted to go back to Oranienbaum and open negotiations with his wife. 'Then we are lost,' said the old Marshal, whose honour compelled him to remain loyal to this deflated puppet whom he had believed to be an Emperor.

Meanwhile Catherine and her little army were on their way to Peterhof. Astride a white horse she rode at the head of her troops, wearing the green uniform of a Preobrajensky grenadier, a sable bonnet crowned with oak leaves on her head, and her long hair floating down her back. Her soldiers saw her as a living incarnation of the goddess of victory, and from Cyril Razumovsky, Hetman of the Ukraine, to the youngest of ensigns, there was not one who was not prepared to die for her sake.

The Orlovs had gone on ahead to clear the Holsteiners out of Oranienbaum and secure the palace of Peterhof before the Empress's arrival. Princess Dashkof, who in the past hours had never left Catherine's side, now had her moment of glory, riding beside her beloved Empress, wearing an identical uniform and looking, as she somewhat complacently remarks, 'like a fifteen-year-old boy'. With her ineffable conceit she saw herself that morning in the role of a king-maker. But her presumption and possessiveness were soon to lose her the friendship she valued so highly. Prince Dashkova's popularity with his regiment, her youth and spirit, won her a large measure of applause, too much for Catherine's taste, though today nothing was allowed to cloud the idyllic nature of their relationship. They even shared a bed in the little inn when they stopped to rest for a few hours on the way, but both young women were far too excited to sleep. While Dashkova was conjuring up visions of the future with herself as the power behind the throne and her husband as Commander-in-Chief of the Russian army, Catherine was beset by uneasy fears of what tomorrow might hold. There was still no news of Peter's movements. When she left the city, the Senate was making preparations to resist a naval attack from either Cronstadt or Reval. The Orlovs might even now be fighting against reinforcements of troops brought in from Narva, and her beautiful Gregory might be maimed or killed. The early morning, however, brought reassuring news with the arrival of the Vice-Chancellor, Prince Alexander Galitzine, bearing a message from the Emperor in which Peter frankly admitted that he had treated his wife with cruelty and neglect and asked her forgiveness by promising to make amends and offering to share his throne.

After all these years, it was pathetic to see how little Peter understood the character of the girl he had married and whom eighteen years of loneliness and misery had turned into a hard, self-centred woman, who admired nothing so much as courage and despised nothing so much as weakness. By the time she arrived at Peterhof, the palace was surrounded by her Guards, the Holsteiners had been disbanded and the Orlovs had taken the Emperor prisoner at Oranienbaum and brought him back to Peterhof. It was the morning of 29 June, the feast of Peter and Paul, but there were no triumphal arches in the park, no salvos of cannon nor pealing bells to celebrate the Emperor's name day, only the heavy silence of defeat. Before leaving Oranienbaum, Peter had been forced to sign an act of abdication. He was in such a state of collapse that he did not even appear to know what he was signing; even the Orlovs turned away from the spectacle of a moral disintegration they were ashamed to witness.

CHAPTER ELEVEN

Securing the Throne

Catherine may have been unscrupulous, but she was rarely cruel. By nature she was kind-hearted and on occasion could be both generous and forgiving, and now she had no wish to gloat over her husband's humiliation. Nor did she trust herself to see him, fearing that pity might get the upper hand and remind her of the shy, stammering boy who had befriended her on her arrival in Russia. She would have liked to have sent him back to his native Holstein to live in liberty at Kiel. But she knew she could not afford to be merciful. So long as Peter lived, there would always be a faction of malcontents conspiring to bring him back. She had no more wish to put him behind bars than Elisabeth had when she was forced to incarcerate the infant Tzar, Ivan VI, who still lived on in the fortress of Schlusselburg, a prisoner without a name.

Catherine, the little German usurper, could not afford to be more generous than Elisabeth, and beyond giving orders to assure that he should be allowed all his creature comforts, she left the ex-Emperor to the care of her loyal henchmen. In one of her letters to Poniatowski which so often deviate from the truth, Catherine asserts that Peter abdicated of his own free-will, '*en plein liberté*', with fifteen hundred loyal Holsteiners still at his command, and that he left for Peterhof in his own carriage, accompanied by Elisabeth Vorontsov and his faithful *aide-de-camp*. It was only after his arrival at Peterhof, which was completely surrounded by her troops, 'that she had deemed it wiser to place him under guard, in order to protect him from the insults of her over-zealous soldiery'. A specially chosen escort of officers and soldiers, under the command of Alexis Orlov, had escorted him that same evening to his country estate of Ropscha situated about twenty-seven *versts* from Peterhof, 'a secluded but very pleasant place, which he had always liked'. Catherine is at great pains to stress the fact that his escort was picked from men, 'known to be *doux et raisonable*', by which she probably means 'courteous and well-behaved' in contrast to the majority of her wild, undisciplined troops.

Everything was done to make his confinement as pleasant as possible. She writes: 'He was given everything except his liberty, his wishes were immediately complied with. His French valet, his violin, his favourite little negro called Narcisse and his pet dog Mopsy, were all sent to him.' She regretted that she had been unable to comply with his wish by allowing Elisabeth Vorontsov to share his captivity, 'but it would have caused too great a scandal and would certainly not have pleased her family'. If the Chancellor stayed on at his post, and for the time being Catherine had no intention of changing her ministers, he would be the last to wish such a thing.

Catherine sounds so sweet and reasonable in her letter to Poniatowski. There is no mention of the humiliations to which the ex-Emperor was subjected on his arrival at Peterhof. Years later, Nikita Panin recalled that he 'regarded it as the greatest misfortune of his life to have been obliged to see Peter under these conditions'. On arrival, the ex-Emperor had been taken to the quarters he occupied as Grand Duke, where he was stripped of his decorations, his Russian uniform and sword. He had submitted to these indignities without a word of protest, standing trembling and abject, without making the slightest attempt to resist. The only time he spoke was when he implored his guards not to separate him from his mistress. It was Panin's painful duty to inform him that Ropscha was to be only a temporary residence while suitable quarters were being prepared for him at Schlusselburg. A braver man than Peter might have quailed at the prospect of being incarcerated in the grim fortress from where no prisoner had ever been known to escape.

Peter had once gone to Schlusselburg to visit another royal prisoner, the unfortunate Ivan, who had spent most of the twenty-two years of his life shut up in a dank cell where the sun rarely penetrated through the casements. On this occasion, the Emperor had been so moved by the spectacle of a Romanov dressed almost in rags, subjected to the brutal treatment of his drunken jailors, themselves demoralized by the boredom of their lives, that he had given orders to alleviate his treatment. But Peter's orders were rarely carried out and it is doubtful whether the unfortunate Ivan ever benefited by his visit. Now Ivan was to be moved to another fortress to make way for an even more dangerous prisoner, and Peter collapsed in a dead faint when he heard the name of his final destination.

Having settled her husband's immediate future while secretly praying that his delicate health would soon remove him from the scene, Catherine returned in triumph to St Petersburg. She made her state entry into the capital on the morning of Sunday, 30 June, still dressed in uniform and still riding at the head of her troops. Detachments of artillery and infantry from Narva were included in the cortège and every house was crowded to the roof-tops with cheering people, hanging out of windows, clinging on to balconies and trees in order to have a better view of the young woman whom they acclaimed as though she were the elect of God and Peter the foreign usurper. There was not a single sullen look, not a single dissenting voice, in that sea of happy faces. A revolution had been accomplished at the price of a few pillaged houses and a few wounded Holsteiners.

The members of the Holy Synod, the leading hierarchy of the church, all wearing their richest garments and holding aloft their jewelled ikons, had come out to bless her at the city gates, as she had so often seen them bless Elisabeth on the return from one of her pilgrimages. All the church bells pealed out in welcome, mingling with the drums and trombones of the military bands which to Catherine was the sweetest music she had ever heard. No wonder she looked beautiful that morning with her flushed cheeks, her blue and glittering eyes, riding through the streets of St Petersburg on her way to conquer an empire and win the admiration of the world.

But among those who had been closest to her and who had plotted and schemed to put her on the throne were some who were already disillusioned. Catherine Dashkova was among the first to be disappointed, for no honours or money could repay a woman who, with a conceit bordering on paranoia, regarded herself as the heroine of the day. Added to this was a high moral sense, a fundamental innocence, which till now had led her to ignore the Empress's relationship with Gregory Orlov, a man whom the Princess considered to be so far beneath her both in breeding and intelligence that the knowledge came as a terrible shock.

One evening at Peterhof, she entered the Empress's apartments and found the young lieutenant, who had been slightly wounded in a skirmish with the Holsteiners, lying full length on a couch, looking at some papers stamped with the Chancellory seals. Infuriated at seeing him so obviously at his ease, tampering with what she believed to be documents of state, she asked him in her coldest and most arrogant manner, 'by what right he was reading papers which were no concern of his'. The young man smiled a lazy, insolent smile which only served to enrage her further. Orlov disliked this fierce little firebrand who traded on her name and position to give orders to his soldiers. He could not understand how an attractive man like Dashkof could have married a woman whom he regarded as devoid of all feminine charms, being built like a sturdy boy with no bosom, a short neck and full red cheeks. He replied that he was reading these papers at the Empress's special request. Whereupon she said 'I doubt it. They could have waited until Her Majesty had appointed someone who was qualified to read them, and neither you nor I are sufficiently experienced in these matters.' With these words, she flounced out of the room having made an enemy of one who was about to become the most important man in Russia.

Her eyes were opened when returning later she found Orlov still reclining on the couch and the Empress sitting beside him looking happy and relaxed, with a table laid for dinner drawn up beside the couch. Catherine welcomed her young friend with effusion and invited her to stay to dinner. But all pleasure went when the Princess noted the solicitude with which the Empress treated the young officer, hanging on his slightest word, laughing at his feeblest jokes, making no secret of her infatuation for a man whose beauty in the Princess's eyes was that of a handsome and dangerous animal. She looked so dejected that Catherine asked her what was the matter, and she excused herself on the grounds that she was feeling tired after a sequence of sleepless nights, whereupon she was dismissed with a great show of affection. It never struck Catherine that this nineteen-year-old girl, already married and a mother and the reputed mistress of her husband's uncle, the cynical Panin, could be a moral prude. Her own Lutheran principles had long since been discarded at a court where Elisabeth set an example of unbridled licentiousness. Now she was at last free to follow her normal inclinations and give free range to her desires which for so many years had been forcibly repressed. With his superb physique, his physical potency, Gregory Orlov dominated her as no man had ever dominated her before and, like many strong and self-willed women, Catherine needed to be physically subjugated.

Dashkova's school-girlish adoration counted for nothing beside a smile from the reigning favourite, and it was a bad day for the impetuous Princess when she quarrelled with the Orlovs, for Gregory and his brothers were a single unit, utterly devoted to each other's interests. Her jealousy only served to embitter those first glorious days, when Catherine was ready to treat her as a favoured friend. She should have remembered that her family was in a delicate position, with her sister and her father dependent on the Empress's magnanimity. Even her uncle, the Chancellor, was in doubt as to whether he would be allowed to remain at his post. But her overweaning pride would not let her rest, and no sooner was she back in St Petersburg than she began to behave as if she were a mouthpiece of the Empress, strutting about in uniform, giving orders and generally making herself objectionable.

She was furious to find guards posted outside her father's

house, a natural precaution as her sister Elisabeth had been brought there from Peterhof and, while awaiting the Empress's decision, was virtually a prisoner-of-state. The Princess was particularly incensed on account of the guards having been placed there on the orders of a certain Captain Kakavinsky, who was a friend of the Orlovs. She not only took it upon herself to have them removed, but sent them back to the Winter Palace which she declared to be inadequately protected.

Kakavinsky naturally complained of the Princess's high-handed behaviour and the Empress summoned her young friend to tell her gently but firmly that it was none of her business to give orders to the soldiers, and it was time for her to put away her uniform and to take up her duties as a lady-in-waiting. To soften her words, the Empress presented her with the Order of St Catherine. Instead of receiving this honour on her knees and thanking Her Majesty for her gracious condescension, Dashkova went on arguing. With a defiance which bordered on rudeness, she gave back the ribbon saying, 'I implore Your Majesty not to give me this decoration, which as an ornament I do not prize and as a reward is of no value to me, whose services, however they may appear in the eyes of some individuals, never have and never can be bought.' Catherine listened with patience and forbearance, though she was already beginning to realize that this impetuous girl was going to cause her a lot of trouble. Embracing her with every show of affection, she placed the order round her shoulders saying, 'at least let friendship have some rights and may I not in this instance have the pleasure of giving a dear young friend a memento of my gratitude.' Her gentle, persuasive manner succeeded in reducing the Princess to tears, and she fell on her knees swearing eternal devotion to her Empress.

But Catherine had more important matters to see to than to cope with Dashkova's jealous scenes. If she humoured her it was largely for the sake of Panin, the one man whose judgment she could rely on and whose caution and wisdom protected her from the hasty decisions of the Orlovs, or rather of Alexis who directed the family's policy and was in his own way as invaluable to Catherine as Panin. Panin had received the ex-Emperor's abdication, but Alexis was now in charge of the prisoner at Ropscha, providing the Empress with daily bulletins of his state of health.

On the first day, Peter had been so stunned by the suddenness and swiftness of events, that in the words of his friend and ally, the King of Prussia, he gave up his throne as quietly 'as a child who had been sent off to bed'. But the reaction set in when he began to realize the horror of his future, and he wept and screamed in hysterical and frustrated rage. Two days after his abdication, Catherine received the joyful tidings that her husband was feeling so ill that he had asked for his own doctor. The Empress's one wish was for Peter to die a natural death in which case she was ready to mourn him as a loving widow. But the colic subsided under his doctor's care, and the only reports which came through from Ropscha stated that the prisoner suffered from bad headaches caused by excessive drinking.

By leaving her husband to the mercy of the Orlovs Catherine became an accessory to crime. She knew that Alexis was bold, unscrupulous and wildly ambitious and would stop at nothing to achieve his aims, which were no less than to see his brother become Imperial consort. The Orlovs' arrogance was already giving offence at court. Members of the old families like the Dolgouroukis and Galitzines could not forgive a low-born adventurer for treating the Empress in public as his mistress. But it was his male arrogance which Catherine found the most irresistible of all her lover's traits, so she waited passively for news from Ropscha, knowing that the Orlovs would not keep her long in doubt.

On the day following her accession, she was already in the Senate presiding over her first Council of State. Michael Vorontsov was reinstated in his position as Chancellor, but at the same time his former enemy, Count Bestuzhev, was re-called from exile. The old statesman was welcomed with honour and given back all his estates as well as a handsome pension. But he was disappointed in his hopes of regaining power, for Catherine was too familiar with his ambition and intrigues to want him interfering in her government.

On 6 July, barely a week after the *coup d'état*, she received the news she was waiting to hear. The ex-Emperor had died in circumstances so mysterious that even the most servile of courtiers could not believe the jailers to be innocent. For it appeared as if this pleasant and secluded country house had been deliberately chosen because it was a place where there were no witnesses, no peasants tilling the fields outside the gates, no village within miles. Earlier in the day, Peter's faithful valet had been abducted and driven across the frontier, and all that we know of what took place at Ropscha comes from a short, incoherent letter addressed to the Empress by Alexis Orlov and delivered to her in the evening. According to the testimony of Princess Dashkova, who in such circumstances could always be relied upon to be a loyal friend, Catherine was so shocked and horrified by the contents of this letter that she burst into a flood of tears. Yet Alexis Orlov had only acted according to her wishes, proving once more his gallantry and devotion in accepting full responsibility for a deed which at heart he knew would be welcomed by his Imperial mistress. If Catherine was shocked, it was probably at herself, as to how quickly she had assimilated the standards of the country she was going to rule.

The note, which was no more than a drunken scrawl and written in what appears to be a fit of remorse, reads:

Matouchka! Merciful sovereign! How can I explain – how can I describe what has happened. You will not believe me but before God I am telling the truth. Matouchka, I am ready to die. But I myself cannot tell you how it came about. We are lost if you do not forgive us, Matouchka. He is no longer in this world but no one intended it so. For how could any of us have ventured to raise our hands against our former sovereign. Nevertheless it happened. He started a quarrel with Prince Bariatinsky at dinner and, before we could separate them, he was dead. We ourselves cannot remember what we did. But we are all equally guilty and deserve to die. Have mercy on me, if only for my brother's sake. I have confessed my guilt and there is nothing further for me to tell. Forgive me or order me to be executed at once. The sun will no longer shine for me if you are angry and my soul will be lost forever.

Was it a premeditated crime? Or had it been committed in a drunken brawl by a group of wild, reckless young men, too impatient to wait for a slow death by poison, which would have been the easier to explain? The marks on the throat, the blackened face, all pointed to death by strangling. Even the hands appeared to have been battered, for when the body according to time-honoured custom was brought back to St Petersburg and laid out in state in the Alexander Nevsky Monastery, the hands holding the cross instead of being bare were covered by heavy gauntlets. But the doctors who carried out the autopsy by order of the Empress were told only to look out for symptoms of poisoning and therefore declared that His Imperial Majesty had died from natural causes, probably caused by a severe colic. It was not their business to notice signs of a struggle which had not been brought to their notice.

According to Princess Dashkof, Catherine received the news on the evening of 6 July and her tears and commiseration convinced her young friend that she was innocent of having connived at the assassination, though in her usual tactless manner the Princess could not refrain from saying, 'it is a death too sudden, Madam, for your glory and for mine', words which in the circumstances can hardly have been appreciated. Nor did she improve matters by saying later, in front of a large gathering, that she trusted that, 'from now on Alexis Orlov would realize that she and he were not meant to breathe the same air, and that she had pride enough to believe he would not dare in future to approach her even as an acquaintance'.

Catherine was fully aware that the only way of exonerating herself was in punishing Peter's murderers, which was the one thing she had neither the inclination nor the power to do. There is a telling phrase in her letter to Poniatowski, 'I am compelled to do a thousand strange things – one wonders what will happen next.' The strangest of all was for a well-brought-up Lutheran princess to condone her husband's assassination. Alexis Orlov's letter was kept a secret from all but a chosen few, Cyril Razumovsky on whose love and loyalty she knew she could count, and Nikita Panin whom she had to consult on the wording in which to announce her husband's death. The note was then locked in a casket where it remained for over thirty years till after her death, when it was opened by her son, the Emperor Paul.

Catherine soon dried the tears which had convinced Dashkova of her innocence, and for the rest of the evening appears to have been in a particularly happy mood. On the following morning, the ex-Emperor's death was publicly announced in a manifesto composed by Panin which read that 'His Majesty had died from a severe colic, causing a haemorrhage which had then gone to the brain.' Catherine appeared in black, pale but dry-eyed, to receive the condolence of the Senate. There were a few raised eyebrows, a few whispers on a death which in the circumstances was regarded as inevitable, but the majority heard the news with indifference and even Peter's friend and ally, the King of Prussia, appears to have been totally unmoved by his end, writing to a friend a partial defence of the little German Princess whom he had helped to put upon the throne:

The Empress was ignorant of the fact and learnt of it with indignation which was not feigned. She correctly foresaw the judgment which all the world now passes on her. As an inexperienced young woman, she thought that once she was crowned all would be well, and that so pusillanimous an enemy as her husband was not dangerous. The Orlovs, more audacious and clear-sighted, foreseeing that the ex-Emperor might be made into a rallying point against them, had him put out of the way. She has reaped the fruits of their crime and has been obliged, in order to secure their support, not only to share but even to retain about her person the authors of that crime.

In her letter to Poniatowski, Catherine admits that 'the Orlovs are an extremely determined family and loved by the common soldiers, and I am under great obligations to them'. Alexis Orlov had committed the nefarious deed, but now she counted on Panin to make the deed acceptable to public opinion. It was on her minister's advice that the coffin was laid out on a catafalque in the monastery of Alexander Nevsky so that the people could pay their last respects. But it was

Catherine herself who had ordered the body to be dressed in the pale blue uniform of a general of the Holstein cavalry rather than in the uniform of a Russian field-marshal. The crowds came dutifully to render up their prayers, but few tears were shed for the man who had never known how to win their love, and few stopped to notice the blackened face half-hidden by a huge hat, the high collar which hid the strangle marks on the throat.

Would foreign opinion be so easily satisfied? Not all the European monarchs were as cynical as Frederick of Prussia. Would the pious Queen-Empress Maria-Theresa acknowledge as a 'sister' a woman tainted with her husband's murder? Would Louis 'the well-beloved' offer his friendship to one who fraternized with an Emperor's assassins? Catherine's letter to Poniatowski, the most cosmopolitan and civilized of all her friends, serves as her defence. And she relied on her former lover to accept her explanations and to publicize them to the world. Peter's death is ascribed 'to a divine providence which decreed that he should succumb from an attack of dysentery brought about by fear and an excessive bout of drinking. In the last few days, his sufferings had been increased by severe colics causing a haemorrhage. The doctors were unable to save him and he died receiving the last sacraments from a Lutheran pastor.' 'I feared', writes Catherine, 'that the officers on duty might have poisoned him, so greatly was he hated. Therefore I ordered an autopsy but there was no trace of poison in the stomach which was quite healthy. Only the lower bowels were greatly inflamed. His heart was small and in a very bad condition.' She made no attempt to feign regret in writing to a man who knew how much she loathed her husband. Her account is factual and concise. Written in August, over six weeks after the event, it already belonged to past history. She wrote and maybe believed that a divine providence had placed her on the throne 'for nothing short of a miracle could have brought about such a fortuitous result!' But for the time being she was a tool of the Orlovs rather than the mistress of her own destiny.

CHAPTER TWELVE

Power and Glory

Catherine had only been a day upon the throne when she ordered her secretaries to bring her every morning a full report of the despatches and ministerial agenda which had come in the previous day. Both Elisabeth and her nephew Peter had shown such a marked aversion to reading that even the shortest extracts of governmental reports were often too burdensome for them to read. But Catherine loved work for its own sake, she was never so happy as with a pen in her hand and her energy and powers of concentration far exceeded that of any of her ministers. One wonders how she was able to tolerate the supineness of a Michael Vorontsov or the indolence of a Panin. It was not until the second half of her reign that Catherine found in the Ukrainian Bezborodko a secretary, and afterwards a minister, as industrious as herself.

For the moment she had to satisfy herself with Panin, who with his lucid intelligence and European outlook towered above his colleagues. While retaining Vorontsov as Chancellor, she nominated a younger man to be head of the College of Foreign Affairs. And for the first fourteen years of her reign, Russia's external policy reflected the views of Panin, who favoured what became known as the 'northern system', an alignment of all the non-Catholic countries, but including Poland, under the leadership of Russia, against the Catholic coalition of France, Austria and Spain. Panin believed that the combined might of Russia, Sweden, Prussia, Saxony, Poland and England would be sufficiently strong to maintain the balance of power and keep Europe permanently at peace. Those who had hoped that the Empress's dislike of her husband and her disapproval of his pro-Prussian sentiments would bring about a change in policy and the return to the old Austrian alliance, were disappointed to find her initial dislike gradually being tempered by expediency. In the first week of her reign, she issued a manifesto branding Frederick of Prussia as 'enemy number one'. But this manifesto was issued at a time when she was still in the hands of her officers, smarting from the humiliation of a dishonourable peace. With her sound common-sense, a quality she shared with Panin, she knew that the Empire was in no condition for her to indulge in histrionics.

The Seven Years' War combined with Elisabeth's reckless extravagance had emptied the Treasury; the soldiers had been without pay for the past eight months; the fortresses on the frontiers were in a state of disrepair and there was a dangerous rise in the price of grain which had nearly doubled in the past months, after a terrible fire had destroyed many of the wooden warehouses in the mercantile quarter of St Petersburg and large quantities of wheat and other cereals had gone up in flames and many merchants were ruined. In spite of promises no concrete help was given them, till Catherine took action and ordered the construction of stone warehouses with money provided from her private funds.

The prevailing corruption which extended through every walk of Russian life was condemned in her first *Ukaze*. Such cases of extortion as came to her notice were swiftly punished. But how could Catherine hope to be obeyed, when in many cases the governors and officials appointed to carry out her orders were even more corrupt than the merchants and usurers they were supposed to condemn? How could she protect the helpless victims of shameless extortion in regions hundreds and thousands of miles from the capital?

Russia's frontiers extended from the frozen tundras of the Arctic to the Turkish frontier; from Riga to Kamchatka. A country of limitless horizons, of steppe, forest and lakes as large as seas, it was sparsely inhabited by barely twenty-two million people of whom over ninety per cent were serfs bought and sold like cattle, tied to their masters' land with no life or freedom of their own. What did Catherine know of her subjects, of the Finns and Laps, the Kirghizes and Kalmucks, the Tartars and the Poles, who inhabited her great and unhomogeneous Empire? What did she know of Russia other than the pageantry of cities prepared for an Imperial visit; a country glimpsed out of the window of a carriage or a sledge on the four-hundred-mile drive to Moscow, a journey accomplished by Elisabeth in less than four days, whereas it would take several weeks or months to reach the frontier beyond the Urals.

There were times when even Catherine's courage failed her and she quailed before the immensity of her task. The French ambassador, who was certainly no friend, heard her repeating not in boastful pride but in humility and fear, 'mine is such a vast and such a limitless empire'. It was the vastness which must have appalled her and the knowledge that she would never really know her country or even begin to understand the people. Yet in the end she succeeded in realizing the deams of Peter the Great and making Russia into a European power, so that kings and princes who despised her on her accession were forced to accept her as an equal and even on occasion to submit to her arbitration.

The qualities which enabled her to succeed were essentially German; a tremendous energy and power of concentration, common-sense and self-control allied to an iron will. But so great was her art of dissimulation, her talent as an actress, that she succeeded in convincing both herself and her subjects that she was as Russian as themselves. Her munificence was Oriental rather than European, for though her Treasury was empty, her loyal servants, beginning with the Orlovs, were rewarded with a generosity which would have appalled her German kindred. All five brothers were created Counts and decorated with the highest orders of the Empire. They received the lion's share of the half a million roubles which were distributed among the heroes of the *coup d'état*. The Princess Dashkova was awarded no less than twenty-four thousand roubles which went to pay her husband's debts. The Prince was recalled from abroad and appointed to be one of Her Majesty's *aides-de-camp* and the young couple had the honour of being lodged in the Winter Palace. But all these marks of Imperial favour counted as nothing for a young woman devoured by jealousy of the Orlovs.

No one was forgotten in Catherine's rewards to her friends. Even the youngest of subalterns figured in the list drawn up in her own hand. Inserted at the end was the name of Cornet Potemkin, promoted by two ranks in his regiment and awarded the gift of ten thousand roubles. Catherine had not forgotten the tall, bold-eyed young man who at her first review had ridden out of the cavalry ranks to offer her his sword knot. He is even mentioned in the famous letter to Poniatowski, where he figures as 'a seventeen-year-old subaltern in the Horse Guards who directed everything with courage, discernment and activity'. His deeds are not specified, but he is known to have been one of the officers '*doux et raisonable*' who was chosen to escort the unfortunate Emperor Peter from Oranienbaum to Peterhof. The extent of the Empress's interest in this obscure young officer can be judged by the exaggerated reward for his services.

In her generosity to her friends, Catherine was being forced to hand over not only land but 'souls'. It was all part of the serf system which she had bitterly condemned and with the high hopes of youth had sworn that, should she ever come to the throne, her first duty would be to reform and if possible abolish. But in Russia a man's power and position depended on the number of his serfs. In the first months of her reign, Catherine condemned to serfdom no less than eighteen thousand peasants formerly attached to crown lands where they had enjoyed a certain amount of freedom.

After decrying the custom of treating human beings like chattels to be bought and sold, she now gave the Orlovs and their friends the *droit de seigneur* over thousands of men and women. They could gamble away a whole family in one night at cards, exchange an agricultural worker for a prize shooting-dog or sell his daughter by public auction. Gregory Orlov and his companions were neither cruel nor lacking in human sentiment, it was the system itself which degraded alike the proprietor and the serf. With the exception of a few high-minded noblemen, who treated their peasants with a paternal kindness and even on occasion gave them their freedom, the majority stood by their privileges and resisted any attempt at reform. Even Dashkova, who was so fond of quoting the French encyclopaedists and in parading her liberal principles, displayed little charity in her treatment of her peasants. Worst of all was the condition of the industrial serfs purchased to work in the mines, where their treatment was so appalling and the rate of mortality so high that few of them ever reached middle age; their only hope of survival was to escape to the unknown deserts beyond the Urals which were peopled by nomad and often savage tribes.

In August 1762, when Catherine had barely been a month upon the throne, she bravely took the first step towards reforming a system she privately abhorred by decreeing that in future no serf could be taken away from the land to work in the mines, other than at his own free-will and on the payment of an agreed wage. But she soon saw that it needed more than courage to break down the impregnable wall of prejudice and ignorance, not only among the educated classes but among the serfs themselves who, with the dawning of understanding and a gradual realization of their own strength, turned against their oppressors.

When the Empress's *Ukaze* was proclaimed in the Siberian mines, the workers became so excited at the prospect of voluntary labour that they laid down tools and went on strike. With the Empire's economy threatening to come to a standstill, Catherine had no other choice but to send in troops to suppress what was gradually growing into a full-scale revolt. At the same time, she briefed the general in command to investigate working conditions in the mines and ascertain the reasons for the discontent. She is said to have read the report with compassion, and even went so far as to draw up a plan to alleviate the lot of the industrial serf, but in the end she allowed the local governors and officials to convince her that it was too early to attempt reform among a savage, primitive people, who could only be kept in order by the knout. Catherine was a woman quick to forget what she could not remedy. The condition of the industrial serf remained unchanged, an open sore in the heart of Russia. And a few years later the terrible rebellion known as the Pugachefschina swept like a forest fire from the Urals to the Volga, threatening the very existence of Moscow.

Meanwhile there were pleasanter things to think of. The preparations for the forthcoming coronation in Moscow took priority over all other matters. One of Peter's many blunders had been to underestimate the importance of the solemn act of consecration in a city which a large majority of Russians still regarded as their capital. He had made no plans for his coronation up to the day he died. And once more his foolish conduct only served to benefit his successor, who knew she could never feel secure till she had been acclaimed as Empress by the conservative and traditionalist Muscovites. As Breteuil remarked with his customary cynicism, 'till then she lives in fear of losing what she had the audacity to take'.

On the very day on which the ex-Emperor's death was publicly announced Catherine proclaimed the date of her coronation and the impoverished Treasury was called upon to produce fifty thousand roubles towards the expenses, while no less than six hundred thousand roubles from the Empress's privy purse were sent under special guard to Moscow for Catherine to distribute as largesse among the population. For the next few months, Moscow became the seat of government and a number of Colleges were moved from the handsome brick palaces on the Neva back to the vermin-infested offices of the Kremlin. Also the Senate preceded the Empress to Moscow, thereby giving the inhabitants the illusion that their city was about to recover its former importance. Catherine, who wanted so desperately to please, spared no effort to win the affection of the Muscovites, setting out to impress them by her splendour and by the magnificence of her gifts to religious institutions, displaying her fervent devotion to the church which dominated their lives.

On 13 September she made her state entry into Moscow, driving in a gilded coach through streets strewn with fir branches, past houses decorated with carpets and precious Chinese silks. The coronation itself took place in the fifteenth-century Uspensky Cathedral in the heart of the Kremlin, a church small in dimension compared with the great cathedral in St Petersburg but far richer in history and tradition, with the high altar bearing the mediaeval cross brought by Sophia Paleologue from the ruins of Christian Constantinople. The heavy-lidded Madonnas staring out of golden ikons, the massive columns and dimly frescoed walls breathed the very spirit of Byzantium and the young woman crowned and anointed by the Metropolitan of Novgorod, attended by twenty bishops and thirty archimandrites, saw herself as a successor of the Paleologues rather than of the Dukes of Muscovy.

The daughter of the last Byzantine Emperor had introduced into Russia the civilizing influence of Byzantium and Catherine intended to revive the glories of the Eastern Empire. It was a dream she had cherished ever since the days when she had travelled down to Kiev as an unloved, obscure little German Grand Duchess. In Elisabeth's life-time she was already confiding in her diary her plans for making the Russian Empire the greatest in the world by joining the Caspian to the Black Sea and linking them both by a system of riverways to the Baltic and the White Sea. Thereby Russia would get control of the whole Eastern commerce using the old silk routes from China and India. The young Empress, who on the day of her coronation spoke of the need of peace, was already contemplating the necessity for war.

Catherine's coronation robes were as splendid as those of any Byzantine Empress. The finest jewels in the Imperial Treasury glittered in her crown, no less than four thousand skins of ermine lined her train, and she impressed all who beheld her by the dignity of her bearing, the sweetness of her smile. Her magnetism was such that she conveyed the illusion of beauty when she was in reality barely pretty with her long face and aggressive chin. She carried herself superbly with her head held high, so that she was often described as tall, when she was only of medium height. Men spoke of the grace and elegance of her movements, but her French secretary, who saw her every day, said that she had a mincing walk and a stiff, unsupple body.

Court painters, so ready to flatter their royal sitters, depict Catherine in the year of her coronation as a solid young German matron with a tight-lipped smile and cold, hard eyes. Successive pregnancies had thickened the delicate little figure with the tiny waist, and there was already a considerable difference between the measurements of Catherine's wedding-dress and coronation robes. The portraits make her eyes look dark, but both D'Eon who disliked her and Poniatowski who loved her describe them as 'a glittering blue'. Like all great actresses, Catherine could assume beauty, youth and majesty at will, and even the foreign ambassadors so apt to criticize succumbed to the magic of her smile. The fact of her husband having died in mysterious circumstances, of his guards, or rather his murderers, having gone unpunished, was already being regarded as an inevitable necessity.

Alexis Orlov had shared in his brother's triumph and was now a Count and Admiral of the Empire. When he reappeared at court, Princess Dashkova was the only one who dared to turn her back and was reproved for her temerity by her uncle, the Chancellor. As Catherine's personal *aide-de-camp*, Gregory Gregorievitch was always at her side, resplendent in the scarlet uniform of the Household Guards, wearing in his button-hole the proud insignia of the Empress's portrait set in diamonds. His beauty in those early days appears to have been unchallenged. Men and women agreed as to the perfection of his classic features, the grace of his movements. Some, like Princess Dashkova, complained of his arrogance, but it was the arrogance of youth and insecurity, the embarrassment of a man who found himself in a position for which he was totally unprepared. Writing to King Frederick, the Prussian ambassador noted:

There may be artisans and even lackeys who can boast of having sat at the same table with the reigning favourite. But in Russia one is used to favouritism, the rapid rise to power of men of the humblest birth. Therefore one can but rejoice at the choice of a young man who is pleasant and polite in his manners, shows neither vanity or pride, who still keeps up with his old friends and even makes a point of singling them out in a crowd – a man who makes no attempt to

interfere in public affairs, except occasionally to recommend a
friend.

This description was written in 1762 and would hardly
have applied to the Orlov of later years. It was Alexis's ambition for the family and Catherine's ambition for her lover which
turned a gay and gallant young soldier into a moody, discontented, human-being, chafing against the golden chains
which bound him to a life he would never have chosen for
himself. Being simple and primitive and very much in love
with Catherine, he naturally wanted to marry her, not so
much because he coveted the role of Prince Consort, as
because he wanted to dominate her completely. He resented
the fact that her working hours, which extended from twelve to
fifteen hours a day, left her too little time to satisfy a passion
which should have filled her life. He was jealous of men like
Cyril Razumovsky and Nikita Panin who, with their superior
education, were often called upon to advise on matters of which
he was completely ignorant. On these occasions he asserted himself by being deliberately rude to Catherine in their presence
and reminding her of the debt she owed both to him and to his
family.

The Empress had not yet left for Moscow when one evening
at supper in the Winter Palace Gregory boasted in public of
his influence with the army, 'of how easily he had put Catherine
on the throne and how easily he could depose her in a month'.
No one except Orlov would have dared to speak in this fashion,
and Catherine was near to tears when Razumovsky gently
interposed 'no doubt you are right, my friend, but long before
the month was past we would have you hanging by the neck'.
Cyril Razumovsky had been in love with Catherine in the days
when she was still a young Grand Duchess. As Hetman of the
semi-autonomous province of the Ukraine and one of the
richest men in the country, his support had been as invaluable
as that of the Orlovs. But he was too independent and too
powerful for the taste of a budding autocrat, and Catherine,
who prided herself on her loyalty towards her friends, showed
little gratitude in her treatment of Cyril Razumovsky. Two
years later, when he claimed for his heirs the hereditary

Hetmanship of the Ukraine, she not only refused him, but forced him to resign by eliminating the post of Hetman and making the Ukraine into a province of the Empire directly governed from St Petersburg.

Cyril Razumovsky was only one of the many who deplored the growing power of the Orlovs. All petitions and favours passed through their hands. Those who wished to make their way at court had to attend the favourite's *levée*, where he was treated like a royal prince. A Prince Sheremetief or a Dolgorouki objected at having to escort the Empress's carriage on horseback when the ex-subaltern was sitting inside. Catherine was aware that the more eminent and cultured members of the nobility avoided the society of the Orlovs, and she admitted when writing to Poniatowski 'the men who surround me are devoid of education, but I am indebted to them for the situation I now hold. They are courageous and honest and I know they will never betray me.'

She took immense pains to educate her lover, who when she first met him could not even speak French, the language spoken by all cultivated Russians. She loved teaching for there was a strong element of the German pedagogue in her character and there was nothing she regarded so rewarding as to 'train a virgin mind'. Gregory possessed little brain but considerable intuition, and Catherine succeeded in transforming the simple soldier into a *grand seigneur*. The magnificent Prince Orlov of later years had little in common with the high-spirited young subaltern who was more at home in the taverns than at court and would as readily jump into the bed of the ostler's wife as that of the beautiful Princess Kourakin. Catherine created a legend but she destroyed the man. Orlov's tragic end, the gradual clouding of his mind, the tragic dementia of his last year can be attributed to a life for which he was totally unsuited and which was a continual strain on his limited faculties.

But in 1762 Gregory Orlov was omnipotent. The Empress worshipped him as the man who had placed her on the throne and had given her the fullest satisfaction in bed. Her gratitude was boundless and her generosity was such as to arouse the jealousy of all those who thought they had as great a claim on her gratitude. Princess Dashkova was inevitably the first to complain, having counted on acting as the Empress's *alter ego*. She had envisaged herself driving in the royal coach, sitting at the high table at the coronation banquets. But the Orlovs, who were in charge of the arrangements, ordered all precedence to depend on military rank and, as the wife of a mere colonel, the Princess was relegated to a subordinate place. Both Panin and her uncle, the Chancellor, begged her to hold her tongue. But she was not even satisfied when Catherine tried to compensate her by promoting her husband to the rank of general.

The young Prince was a great favourite both with the Empress and the Orlovs and was teasingly referred to by Catherine as 'her little field-marshal'. He was far more popular than his wife who was regarded as a potential trouble-maker. Her greatest fault was in advertising herself abroad as the heroine of the *coup d'état*. The legend of a nineteen-year-old changing the course of history appealed to the imagination of the French. Ivan Shuvalov was decried by Catherine as 'the basest of men' for having praised the Princess when writing to Voltaire. In a letter to Poniatowski, she begged him to correct the error and to let the great man know 'that Princess Dashkof played only a minor part in the events. She was in bad odour on account of her family and was neither liked nor trusted by the leaders, who told her as little as they could. Admittedly she has brains, but her character is spoilt by her wilfulness and conceit.' These lines show little gratitude or sympathy for the friend who had risked so much for her sake. But Catherine could not tolerate having another woman take even a share of the limelight, particularly with someone as important as Voltaire, whom she was anxious to win to her side. The most famous man in Europe and the greatest publicist of his age, who had already introduced Russia to the West with his history of Peter the Great, was to be flattered and persuaded by the generosity of her gifts to circulate throughout the world the image of the enlightened Empress.

CHAPTER THIRTEEN

A Royal Death

Catherine's concern with her image abroad appears very early in her reign. It was part of her fundamental insecurity and explains her friendly and at times almost familiar relations with the foreign envoys, the affectionate correspondence she kept up with Stanislaus Poniatowski, when she was already heart and soul given up to Gregory Orlov. The Polish nobility had many ties with Vienna and with Paris, where Marie Lecynska's marriage to the French King brought many of her compatriots to France.

Catherine counted on the compliance of her former lover to paint her in glowing colours to his friends and acquaintances abroad. The last thing she wanted was for Stanislas to appear in St Petersburg, as he was threatening to do, never suspecting that his 'beloved Sophie' had changed in her feelings towards him. His love had thrived on absence and he had forgotten how glad at the time he had been to get away. Now he kept imploring her to let him join her, to which she replied 'for you to arrive under the present circumstances would be dangerous for you and painful for me. I am overwhelmed with work, and I could spare you but little time ... I promise I will always remember you and do what I can for you and your family. But things are very critical at present.' Stanislaus must at all costs be kept away from St Petersburg, where he had always been unpopular at court, and where he was now hated by the Orlovs. Her love-affair with the handsome Pole had caused so much scandal at the time that his arrival would immediately give rise to the rumour that she was planning to marry him, which was just what Stanislaus was hoping she would do.

News travelled slowly between St Petersburg and Warsaw and Stanislaus knew nothing of his successor till his suspicions were aroused by Catherine's letter writing of the Orlov brothers with exaggerated warmth and admiration. Even so he would never have believed that his cultivated, sophisticated Sophia could have lost both her heart and head to a roistering, low-born lieutenant, who could not even speak French. If Gregory Orlov had not come into her life, Catherine might well have ended in marrying Poniatowski, after making him King of Poland. It would have been an easy way of extending her influence westwards without arousing the jealousy of her powerful neighbours. Yet such was her infatuation for Gregory Gregorievitch that, during her first winter in Moscow, she gave serious thought to becoming what Panin slightingly referred to as 'Madame Orlov'.

Her enthusiastic reception in Moscow gave her a false sense of security. Always eager to advertise her triumphs one finds her writing to her envoy in Warsaw, Count Kayserling, that it was impossible to describe the joy with which she was received: 'I have only to show myself at a window and there is a fresh outburst of cheering.' But the honeymoon atmosphere did not last for long. The Muscovite nobility might vie with one another in the oriental lavishness of their entertainment; the beggars might bless her name as they grovelled for her largesse in the mud of the unpaved streets. But it was all part of a performance where the chief actors were already grumbling at their parts. The greatest shock to her security was that most of the grumbling and seditious talk emanated from the palace guards, and in particular from the Ismailovsky Regiment which had been the first to acclaim her. On the whole it consisted of little more than loose and drunken talk on the part of a few disgruntled officers. But they had been sufficiently unwise to question why the Tzarevitch Paul had not been crowned instead of his mother. Some had gone even further and talked of restoring Ivan VI. In the midst of her triumphs,

Catherine was forced to recall the existence of the unnamed prisoner in Schlusselburg and to realize that she could never feel secure so long as he remained alive.

There was no question of any conspiracy or plot, but the Empress was sufficiently alarmed to appoint a commission to investigate the matter. Not satisfied with their findings, she sent the case up to the Senate, who, noting her anxiety, sentenced those who had called her a usurper to death and the others, who had merely criticized, to exile. This punishment, which was out of all proportion to the crime, gave Catherine the opportunity to show magnanimity and commute the death penalty to imprisonment and exile.

Catherine took every opportunity of appearing to be a fervent Orthodox, following the example of Elisabeth of fasting on holy days, praying at all the city shrines and making the annual pilgrimage to the monastery of St Sergius and the Trinity. But she never really conquered her dislike of Moscow, or felt at ease in the mediaeval palace of the Kremlin. Only a few weeks after her arrival she woke one morning to hear that the triumphal arches carrying her image had been torn down during the night. Many times she would drive through the streets and a voice would suddenly call out from the crowd, 'we want Paul Petrovitch for Tzar'. To make matters worse, the eight-year-old Tzarevitch fell seriously ill and was unable to appear at the festivities. This naturally gave rise to rumours, and Catherine knew that, should he die, her enemies would not hesitate to say that she had poisoned her son. Paul recovered to remain throughout her reign her rival and at the same time her justification.

She, who loved children and later took time from the cares of state to write charming and affectionate letters to the pupils of the Smolny Institute, and in her old age spent hours in playing blindman's buff with her grandsons, never succeeded in winning the affection of her son. The child who ran crying into his nurse's arms when she paid him the weekly visits permitted by Elisabeth, always retained his initial distrust of the mother who wooed him as she wooed all those who came within her orbit. The smiles she gave him were no warmer than the smiles she bestowed on her adoring servants. Later when he

7 Ivan Shuvalov.

8 Serge Saltykof, Catherine's first lover.

9 Count Gregory Orlov. Painted by F. Rokotov.

10 Bobrinsky – Catherine's natural son by Gregory Orlov.

11 The Princess Dashkof. Etching by G. Skorodumov.

12 The Coronation of Catherine II. Engraving by A. Kulpaschnikov, according to tradition, from an original drawing by Catherine's court painter.

13 Peterhof – about 20 miles west of St Petersburg, which figured in the coup that brought Catherine to the throne. A contemporary engraving.

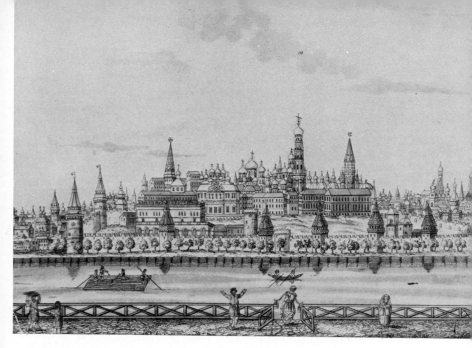

14 An eighteenth-century drawing of the Kremlin by Dufeld.

15 A view of the old Winter Palace, St Petersburg. Engraving by Makhaev.

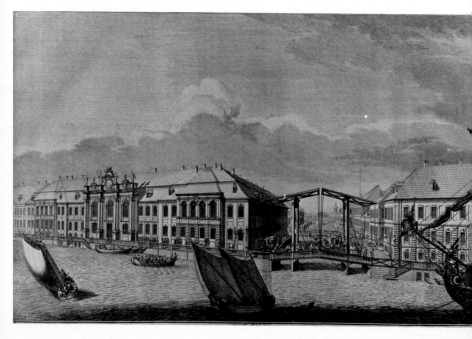

learnt the facts of his father's death, the initial distrust turned to jealousy and fear. Paul was a blond, pretty little boy, who could easily have passed for the son of Serge Saltykof, but grown to puberty he became Peter's son with the same puny body, grimacing face and ungainly walk. Catherine saw the tastes and mannerisms which had been so odious to her reflected in a child she was supposed to love, and her initial affection froze into dislike.

In the first year of her reign, Paul was still a delicate, lonely little boy who missed his great aunt, the large, beautiful woman who had shown him such tenderness and warmth and indulged his every whim. He rarely saw his mother unaccompanied by Orlov, and all the jealousy, of which an only child is capable, vented itself on this glorious figure who claimed the attention which he felt should have been given to him. It was not in Orlov's nature to take trouble in winning over Catherine's son. Living in the house of a devoted secretary was a lusty baby who, should he ever succeed in marrying Catherine, would be legally recognized to be their child.

There appears to have been a moment when Catherine contemplated marrying her lover. Twenty years at the court of Russia had not yet entirely destroyed the principles of her youth. She had not yet fallen under the influence of the man who, in corrupting her morals, was to change her whole mode of life. She was still sufficiently young and naïve to envisage Orlov as her partner for life. This winter she was again with child, in a clinging, feminine mood, favourable to Orlov's plans. She always maintained that she was faithful by nature, that she would even have remained faithful to her husband had he ever shown her the slightest sign of affection. But 'she needed to be loved and could not live one hour without a man'.

In those first months she felt so terribly alone, placed on a pinnacle of power to which her own ambition had brought her, and she was obsessed with the fear of losing her lover unless she gave in to his wishes. The Orlovs played on these fears. Gregory declared he would prefer to go back to be a subaltern in the army than act the role of 'a male Pompadour'; Alexis persistently reminded her of services she would have preferred to forget. Backing their claims was the old intriguer Count Bestuzhev who thereby hoped to win his way back to power. But while Catherine hesitated, an event occurred which showed even the Orlovs that they could not defy the gods. They found their position challenged by their old comrades in the Guards, the very men with whom formerly they had been so popular. Their rise had been too rapid to be accepted by those who had run the same risks and shown the same devotion to their Empress.

The marriage rumour spread through Moscow, to be treated at first with laughter and disbelief, but as it grew in substance, the reaction changed to one of consternation and anger. The Empress was on a pilgrimage to Rostov when she received the news of a plot to kill the Orlovs. It was all the more serious as the would-be assassin was an officer in their own regiment, a certain Captain Khitrovo who had been among the forty heroes rewarded for their services in the *coup d'état*. There were suggestions that other and more important people were involved, including Count Panin and Princess Dashkof. But on examination, Khitrovo proudly denied having any accomplices. He insisted

that he had acted of his own free-will and would have no hesitation in killing either Alexis or Gregory, though he looked upon the former as the more dangerous and regarded the latter merely as a presumptuous fool. All he wanted was to prevent a marriage which would be disastrous for the Empress and for Russia. He was all in favour of her marrying again, providing she chose a consort worthy of her fame.

The interrogation was allowed to lapse when it became ·clear that the commissioners themselves were on the side of Khitrovo. Far from being a criminal, he had saved his sovereign from jeopardizing her whole future. Public sympathy was so obviously on the side of the accused that even the Orlovs did ·not dare to have him brought to trial, and Khitrovo suffered no further punishment than exile to his country estates. But there were other and deeper repercussions. The very fact that someone so close to the Empress as Princess Dashkova should have her name associated in a conspiracy against the Imperial favourite, showed the extent of the discontent. The Orlovs went so far as to demand that the Princess should be interrogated, though Catherine would have preferred to hush up the affair as quietly and as quickly as possible. But nothing concerning Dashkova could ever remain a secret.

In reply to her examiners, the little Princess declared that she knew nothing about the plot, but even if she did, she would still have refused to speak. And with characteristic bravura she added 'that if the Empress wanted to lay her head upon a scaffold in reward for having placed a crown upon her own, then she was quite prepared to die'. It was the kind of remark that Catherine found impossible to forgive, and the Princess made sure that it was repeated all over Moscow. Driven to exasperation and prompted by the Orlovs, the Empress wrote to Prince Dashkov, asking him to exercise some authority over his wife: 'it is my earnest desire not to be obliged to forget the services of Princess Dashkova, by her forgetfulness of what she owes herself. Remind her of this, my Prince, as she gives herself, I understand, the indiscreet liberty of menacing me in her conversation.' Not wishing to antagonize the powerful Dashkof family, the Empress consented to act as godmother to the Princess's baby boy born in the spring of 1763. But no enquiries were made as to her health, either before or after the birth, and shortly afterwards she retired to a country house outside the city, where she was at liberty to air her grievances against the Orlovs.

The Khitrovo affair put an end to all talk of marriage. But Catherine remained faithful to Gregory Gregorievitch for another ten years, putting up with his moodiness, his jealous scenes, his flagrant infidelities, covering him with honours in compensation for having failed to give him the one thing he wanted. In face of a disapproving Senate, she made him Grand Master of Artillery, Member of the Grand Council and finally a Prince of the Empire, and he accepted riches and honours alike with a bored indifference. For ten years he was the most important man in Russia and it is to his credit that, being conscious of his inadequacy, he made very few attempts to interfere in affairs of state. In 1771 he had an hour of glory when, against Catherine's wishes, he volunteered to restore order in the plague-ridden city of Moscow, where the terror-stricken population were murdering one another in the streets and a venerable archbishop was torn to pieces by a mob grown mad from fear. With the reckless courage he had shown as a young subaltern at Zorndorf, Orlov succeeded in bringing order and sanity back to Moscow. The plague was halted and the Imperial favourite was the hero of the day. Gold medals were struck in his honour and Catherine erected in the gardens of Tzarskoye Selo a triumphal arch in gratitude to 'Orlov who delivered Moscow from the plague'.

The ten years of her life with Orlov completed the Empress's Russian education. The Princess of Anhalt-Zerbst learnt to accept things which would have shocked her only a few years ago. Gregory's grandfather had been one of the archers (the Strelitz) who had seen his comrades butchered before his eyes, when Peter the Great determined to stamp out mutiny by executing the ring-leaders with his own hands. Now Gregory helped Catherine to understand that Peter's elimination of the mutinous palace guards had been as necessary to Russia as her husband's death and so many other deeds which in the course of years were to add both shame and glory to her name.

The Empress returned to her capital on the anniversary of her succession and the tumultuous welcome at St Petersburg compensated for the disillusions she had experienced in Moscow. Two of the subversive guards regiments had been left behind, thereby forfeiting their privilege of acting as her escort. Disgruntled members of the old nobility had retired to their country estates, others like the veteran Field-Marshal Munnich had made their peace and were back in Imperial favour, for Catherine was ready to be reconciled with all who were prepared to serve her.

But the rumours which Catherine had hoped to stifle in Moscow were revived in St Petersburg. Hardly a month went by without Ivan's name being mentioned in the police reports of seditious talk and anonymous letters. In Schlusselburg, only a few miles distant from the capital, the child now grown to manhood was kept incarcerated in a dungeon. Throughout Elisabeth's reign, the memory of the boy Tzar Ivan had been allowed to lapse into oblivion. No one had questioned her right to reign. Even Peter's accession had passed unchallenged. But Catherine was a foreign usurper and Ivan was now a man of twenty-four, stunted in his mental development but not an idiot, ignorant but not illiterate. In his early childhood, when he was still imprisoned with his parents at Kholnogory, a kindly pastor had taught him to read and told him stories of the various saints and martyrs. The solitary boy, whose life was one long martyrdom, had gathered strength from these legends and would recount them to his jailors, the only human-beings he was ever allowed to see and who in a sense were also prisoners, for they were never allowed to leave the fortress even to visit their families and, as a result, became brutish and callous towards their innocent victim.

Ivan was removed to another prison when Schlusselburg was being prepared for a still more illustrious 'guest'. But the Emperor Peter's sudden death brought him back within a month. On his way from one prison to another, he was visited by the Empress Catherine who wished to see for herself the Romanov whose continued existence menaced her throne. Later she described him as 'stammering and unintelligible in his speech and bereft of understanding'. But had she found him a drooling idiot, she could have afforded to spare his life and thereby proclaim her magnanimity to the world. His warders reported that he was conscious of his position and, when goaded by ill-treatment, would berate them for daring to lay hands on their rightful sovereign. Throughout the years of deprivation he appears to have preserved the remnants of sanity, sufficient to alarm the cool, unscrupulous woman who felt no pity for this poor, innocent creature with the matted hair and pale, blotched skin of one who never saw the sun.

Catherine's attitude towards her royal prisoner shows her at her worst. Elisabeth had wept when she had visited Ivan in his dungeon and given orders to alleviate his treatment, which his guardians, the Shuvalovs, promptly disobeyed. Even Peter showed signs of humanity, but both of them were

Romanovs and may have felt a certain shame at seeing one of their own blood reduced to such a pathetic condition. Catherine had no such scruples. Ivan to her was no more than a threat to her throne. Preferring him to die a natural death, she gave orders that, in case of illness, he should be denied all medical attendance. But a second and more inhuman decree to which she put her signature stipulated that, should there be any attempt at rescue, the prisoner was to be instantly killed by his jailors rather than have him fall alive into the hands of his rescuers. This time she put Panin instead of the Orlovs at the head of a secret commission in charge of the royal prisoner, for with her already tarnished reputation, Catherine could not afford a second blunder.

Did Ivan die as a result of a conspiracy? Or was the wretched conspirator himself the victim of a subtle and complicated plot? Early in 1764 a young subaltern called Mirovitch was appointed to garrison duties at Schlusselburg. He was a proud and embittered young man, head over heels in debt and harbouring a grievance, having had his family estates confiscated by Peter the Great when his grandfather took part in the Mazeppa revolt. Catherine had refused to give him back his lands, but he had continued to haunt the antechambers of Panin, who must have given him some encouragement. In the spring of 1764, the minister was sharing a large country house with the Dashkofs. The Prince, who was in Poland commanding his regiment, had entrusted his family to his uncle's care, hoping that the prudent statesman might keep his wife's impetuous temperament in check. The fact that the Princess and the minister were living under the same roof and that Mirovitch was sometimes seen driving up to the house, was later interpreted by Dashkova's enemies as proof of her complicity in the plot. But uncle and niece had separate entrances and rarely saw one another's guests. In the past year, Ivan's warders had been writing pathetic letters to Panin begging to be relieved of their duties and allowed to return to their families. In December they were categorically informed by the minister that they would not have long to wait and that 'everything would be over by the summer'.

Three months later, Mirovitch was attached to the garrison at Schlusselburg where his fellow officers found him a moody and difficult companion, given to drinking bouts and visionary dreams. Somehow or other, he appears to have become aware of the identity of the nameless prisoner, and in that labyrinth of dungeons discovered the secret cell where Ivan was kept under constant guard. His tormented mind evolved a plot to rescue the rightful heir and restore a Romanov to the throne. Thereby he would emulate the glory of the Orlovs who, from obscure lieutenants, had become the most powerful men in Russia. Why should not he, the despised and persecuted Mirovitch, stage a *coup d'état* which would earn him the everlasting gratitude of the Tzar?

But there are certain strange aspects to this story. How was it that an officer, newly arrived at Schlusselburg, was able to probe its carefully guarded secrets? Or was Mirovitch in reality only the dupe of Panin who promised him the restitution of his properties and the Empress's favour if he helped him carry out a certain delicate mission? He may have been told that the compassionate Empress wanted Ivan to escape and leave the country. The truth remains obscure. But the plot was so ill-conceived, so hopelessly mishandled, that only a drunken visionary like Mirovitch can ever have believed in its success. Nevertheless, it provided an excuse for carrying out the deed which removed the last obstacle to the security of Catherine's throne. Mirovitch was only able to command the loyalty of a handful of ignorant and bewildered men. Yet he never appears to have hesitated, and on the evening of 4 July he made his tragic attempt to change the course of history.

After a brief struggle, he and his followers managed to penetrate the inner defences and reach the entrance to Ivan's cell. This again seems strange in view of the fact that the prison was considered to be impregnable. Standing at the entrance were the grim, silent figures of the two warders and at their feet the lifeless body of the young Tzar lying in a pool of blood. At the first sound of fighting, they had carried out their orders and thereby won their freedom. Mirovitch appears to have been too stunned with horror to make the slightest attempt to defend himself. Kneeling beside the body of the murdered Tzar, he reverently kissed the blood-stained hand before surrendering himself. Under interrogation, he freely confessed his guilt and behaved with a calm dignity which impressed his judges. All he asked for was that the men who had followed him should be pardoned, as they had only sinned in ignorance. His impassive behaviour throughout the trial, the indifference with which he heard the death sentence, leads one to believe that he was confident of a reprieve, counting on promises made by Panin.

The Empress was paying her first state visit to Riga when she received the news, at which she openly rejoiced without making the slightest attempt to show even a semblance of pity. She even had the effrontery to evoke the Almighty in her letter to Panin. 'The ways of God are wonderful and beyond prediction. Providence has given me a clear sign of her favour in putting an end to this undertaking.' Not a tear was shed for the young innocent who had been so cruelly murdered, nor was there a word of clemency for the obscure lieutenant who maybe knew too much to be allowed to live. But there were rich rewards for his two warders, 'our servants', who had carried out their duties so swiftly and efficiently, and congratulations for Count Panin, the subtle, prudent minister, who had been careful not to involve her by putting too many unnecessary details into writing. She must have congratulated herself on having used Panin instead of those beloved but irresponsible Orlovs. Mirovitch died on the scaffold, the first Russian to be executed for over twenty years, since Elisabeth on her accession had made a vow never to sign a death warrant. But Catherine was of sterner stuff. The life of an obscure lieutenant was of little consequence when the security of her throne was in question.

On Panin's advice, she returned at once to her capital where, to her anger, she found that Ivan's death and the first execution for nearly a quarter of a century had made a far greater impression than she had imagined. In spite of Panin's discretion, she was definitely associated with the crime, which in England won her from Horace Walpole the unenviable title of 'Tzar-slayer'. Even the French encyclopaedists, whom she was at such pains to woo, showed a certain hesitancy in accepting her largesse. Her hero, Voltaire, with whom she had lately entered into a correspondence, was beginning to have second thoughts, writing to his friend D'Alembert 'I believe we should moderate a little our enthusiasm for the north', while D'Alembert, who prided himself on having refused a very generous offer from the Empress inviting him to Russia to act as tutor to her son, was now confirmed in the wisdom of his decision not to accept an invitation to a country where 'people are apt to die so suddenly from the colic'. He wrote, 'I am getting somewhat tired of an Empress who deposes people and then says how sorry she is, but that, of course, she had nothing to do with it.' But D'Alembert was neither as vain nor as venal as Voltaire who, after his quarrel with King Frederick, was only too delighted to have another crowned head as a disciple, above all an Empress who was as lavish as the King was mean. It was not long before the generosity of Catherine's gifts had dissipated his last scruples and we find him defending her in a letter to Madame Deffand,

I am perfectly aware that people reproach her with certain little matters with regard to the treatment of her husband. But these are family affairs in which I am not concerned. Besides, it is not a bad thing to have a fault to make amends for. That gives her a motive for spurring herself to great efforts in the pursuit of public admiration.

CHAPTER FOURTEEN

'Les Philosophes'

Catherine's correspondence with Voltaire, a man thirty-five years her senior, the doyen of the *philosophes* and the most widely read writer in Europe, was inspired by a mixture of hero-worship, expediency and a passionate desire for fame. Voltaire was a name to conjure with. One mention from his pen placed one among the immortals; even his criticism was preferable to being ignored. In order to curry favour with the patriarch of Ferney, the Autocrat of all the Russias, the head of the Orthodox church, proclaimed herself in her letters as Voltairian in philosophy and a sceptic in religion. In the beginning, Voltaire showed a certain reluctance to embark on a correspondence with a woman whom he and his friends referred to in private as *la belle cateau* (the handsome wench), or simply as 'the wench'. At heart he agreed with D'Alembert 'that converts of this kind gave philosophy little cause to boast'. But Catherine was both persistent and generous, and the veteran philosopher, who had professed an admiration for the Princess Johanna, could hardly refuse the offers of friendship made by her more famous daughter. Ivan Shuvalov, the friend of Voltaire who, in Elisabeth's reign, had commissioned him to write the life of Peter the Great, was recalled from exile and forgiven by Catherine for his 'gaffe' in having extolled the heroism of the Princess Dashkof. He and his nineteen-year-old nephew, Andrei, who had completed his education at Ferney, received appointments at court and were admitted into the charmed circle of the Empress's personal friends. It is even asserted that the young Andrew, an accomplished French scholar and talented versifier, edited and corrected Catherine's letters to Voltaire. But neither he nor his uncle was in Russia in 1763 when Catherine made her first overtures through one of her French secretaries.

Voltaire had barely completed his Russian history and was still under the spell of Peter's complex character when he received a letter from the young woman who had placed herself on the throne of the Romanovs, condoned the murder of Peter's grandson, and connived at that of his great-nephew. In this letter she professed to be the patriarch's most ardent disciple, having discovered his works at a time when she was so unhappy as to be on the verge of suicide. She worshipped him as 'the divinity of gaiety', who had helped to console her in her misery and later completed her education. 'Whatever style I possess,' she wrote, 'whatever powers of reasoning, have all been acquired through the reading of Voltaire.'

The old man was touched and flattered at having another royal disciple who would spread his doctrines through northern Europe. He was impressed by the little German Princess, whom her fellow monarchs had predicted would not keep her throne for more than a few weeks, and had not only proved them wrong, but in the first year of her reign had had the courage to discard the old alliances of Russia and, by signing a treaty with the King of Prussia, had brought her former lover to the throne of Poland. She had opened out her frontiers to foreign immigration and invited German colonists to settle in the sparsely inhabited areas of the Volga basin. Barely ten years later, she was proudly announcing to Voltaire 'that her colony of Saratof had grown to twenty-seven thousand souls'.

New towns and villages were changing the face of Russia. Hospitals and schools were being built, not only in St Petersburg and Moscow but in all the provincial towns. Following the tradition of her predecessor, European architects and painters were being offered princely salaries to help in embellishing the capital. Not a *Ukaze* was passed in the Senate without having been first considered by the Empress. Yet this extraordinary young woman still found the time to dedicate several hours a day to the compiling of what was called her *Nakaz*, the most ambitious plan of legislation which had yet been introduced in Russia.

Voltaire, at first, was inclined to be a dilatory correspondent, and few of his letters survive from the first years. But by the end of 1765 he had fallen completely under the spell of the new 'Semiramis of the North'. The name was more apt for Catherine than for Elisabeth. It was almost too apt, for Semiramis, like Catherine, had murdered a husband in order to mount a throne. But the Empress was not over-sensitive. Semiramis or *cateau*, what did it matter, so long as she harnessed his genius to her chariot. The incense of Voltaire compensated for the disapproval of the Paris *salonières*, who, with the exception of Madame Geoffrin, referred to her as a 'Tzar-slayer, usurper and a whore'. The Duchess de Choiseul voiced the general opinion in a letter to Madame Deffand,

She [Catherine] has had the wit to realize that she needs the protection of men of letters. She flatters herself that their base eulogies will impenetrably conceal from the eyes of her contemporaries and from posterity the various crimes with which she has astonished the world and revolted humanity. That obscure, vile and mercenary writers lend her their abject pens I can understand – but Voltaire?

And of them all, it was Voltaire who ended by being the most sycophantic. 'The northern star', 'Semiramis', 'Sainte Catherine', were only a few of the names given to his heroine, and the most gratifying of all was when he called her 'Emperor' instead of 'Empress'. She in return showered him with rich gifts, of sable pelisses and jewelled snuff-boxes. There was no limit to her generosity. She gave diamonds to his niece and paid exorbitant sums for the watches produced by his colony of unemployed, a philanthropical experiment which Voltaire, as usual, succeeded in making highly profitable. But being a sensible, hard-headed German, Catherine could not refrain from mentioning that he had sent her twice as many watches as she had ordered – something a Russian prince would never have deigned to notice.

The Empress's purchase of Diderot's library in 1764 won her a paeon of praise from the encyclopaedists. She not only allowed it to remain in his possession for his lifetime, but appointed him librarian with a salary of a thousand livres a year to which she added another thousand 'for the pain and trouble he had taken in putting together such a fine collection'. Even D'Alembert wrote to thank her for her generosity towards his collaborator and friend, to which Catherine replied with becoming modesty 'that she never thought that buying Diderot's library would bring her so many compliments'. But she could not quite forgive D'Alembert for refusing to act as tutor to her son, and with that gentle admonishment in which she excelled, she wrote to him, 'Your philosophy, founded on the love of mankind, requires you to serve mankind. In refusing to do so, you fail in your duties.' Nevertheless, she could afford to forgive his ungraciousness now that she had Denis Diderot on her payroll.

The fifty-year-old cutler's son from the provincial town of Langres was the most celebrated and controversial figure of what was known as 'The Republic of Letters', a republic without frontiers whose citizens were trying to find a new approach to life, a new medium in which to express themselves and their ideas. Diderot was as warm-hearted as Voltaire was cynical, as rough as he was polished, as simple as he was sophisticated, retaining throughout his life the enthusiasms of adolescence and the innocence of a child, fed by the pure flame of his genius. As Catherine once described him, 'He was in certain ways a hundred, in others not yet ten.'

He rose to fame as the guiding spirit and the chief editor of the new Encyclopaedia, 'the bible of the enlightened', of which the first volume appeared in 1751. Ten more were to follow and its publication was regarded as the greatest event in civilization since the invention of printing. It revolutionized the whole concept of living, arousing curiosity and doubt in the minds of men. It defied nature, declaring that experience was only derived from sensation, that the universal aim in life was happiness through the combined exercise of intelligence and the senses. This humanistic philosophy set new standards, glorifying the dignity of labour, stressing the importance of industry and of technical knowledge, warning against superstition and 'the myths and mysteries of the Roman Church'. Within a few months of its appearance, it had already been denounced by the French government, the Jesuits and the Jansenists, and during its chequered career its printing licence was twice removed and only grudgingly restored.

The vicissitudes of its publication in France gave Catherine the opportunity to proclaim herself the protector of the arts and sciences by offering to have the remaining volumes printed in Riga. But this offer was made only a few months after her accession and the editors of the Encyclopaedia were not yet prepared to trust their future to a country 'so perilously close to Siberia'.

Ten years later, both Denis Diderot and Frederick Melchior Grimm, the news-vendor of Europe whose *Chroniques Littéraires*, written from Paris, enlivened the tedium of various German courts, were both on their way to Russia in the service of the Empress Catherine. Even Voltaire, who was by then in his late seventies, was toying with the idea of paying his personal respects to 'Sainte Catherine'. But, strangely enough, this appeared to be the last thing she wanted, and one finds her writing urgently to Grimm, 'For God's sake, try and persuade the octogenarian to stay at home. What should he do here? he would either die here or along the roadside from cold, weariness and the bad roads. Tell him that *cateau* is seen better from a distance. By the way, "*cateau*" tickled me not a little.' For once, her habitual self-confidence appears to have failed her and she was nervous of exposing herself and her country to the scrutiny of Voltaire's cold and dissecting eye. Neither 'the wench' nor the octogenarian had any wish for a closer relationship. If Voltaire ever sincerely contemplated going to Russia, it was to see for himself the Empire created by his hero, Peter, rather than to pay homage to the Princess of Anhalt-Zerbst. The last volume of the history of Russia had only just appeared and Catherine would have liked him to live long enough to chronicle the triumphs of her reign. All she wanted was his praise, above all his praise of her *Nakaz*, the legal code, or rather the instructions, which she persisted in regarding as her greatest contribution to Russia.

To clean out the Augean stables of a corrupt and inefficient administration, to put an end to the terrible abuses which occurred in provinces thousands of miles distant from the capital, and protect the poor and weak from the exactions of the landlords, was more than even the most enthusiastic and determined of Empresses could achieve. Every department was in a state of chaos. The legal code dating back to the days of Tzar Alexis in the middle of the seventeenth century was completely out of date. Peter the Great had opened the floodgates to reform, but half of his decrees had never even got into the statute books. Age-old privileges and abuses had merely been driven underground to reappear in some new and more vicious form under his weak and incompetent successors. He had attempted to curb the power of the aristocracy by obliging every nobleman to enter the service of the state. The civil, military and court hierarchy had been divided into grades extending from the humblest to the highest, from the College Registrar to the Chancellor of the Empire, from the cornet to the Field-Marshal, from the lackey to the Lord High Chamberlain. Hereditary nobility gave way to the nobility of service and every foreigner in state employ became automatically a gentleman, thereby making Russia into a happy hunting-ground for adventurers and scoundrels kicked out of their own countries. A new and prosperous middle class of bankers, tradesmen and manufacturers was established in the towns and given certain privileges on the pattern of the German guilds. Here again it was the foreigners who benefited, being permitted to acquire property and intermarry with Russians while continuing to trade under their own flag.

But the great reformer did nothing to alleviate the lot of the vast rural population. On the contrary, he degraded them, for in the old days the cultivators of the soil had been divided into three classes. There was the prosperous and free peasant proprietor; there was the farmer who worked the landlord's land on the *metayer* system, giving him a half share of the products while maintaining his personal liberty. And lastly, and by far the most numerous, was the serf attached to the land. One of the cruellest and most inhuman of Peter's decrees was to confound these three classes into one, subjecting them all to a fixed residence and a capitation tax to be collected by the landlord who had the right of determining the conditions of labour. This was not only equivalent to serfdom but it also increased the power of the aristocracy, whose abuses in other respects Peter had attempted to curb. His only philanthropic edict was to control the sale of slaves by decreeing that husbands should not be separated from their wives, nor children from their parents. But even this was suppressed, when his niece, the Empress Anna, whose cruelty and viciousness bordered on the pathological, legalized the sale of slaves by collecting dues on every sale.

No Romanov could have had a greater reverence for the reforming Tzar than the little German Princess who had usurped his descendant's throne. The adventuress in her thrilled to the magnificence of the achievements of a man to whom nothing had been impossible. He had made the country into a European power and conjured a modern Western capital out of a marshy swamp; he had built a navy, reformed the army, emancipated women, introduced religious tolerance and developed commerce. But he had died too young and his heirs, unworthy of their great inheritance, had allowed his reforms to founder into chaos. It was Catherine's task to complete his work and civilize the Empire he had created. But the cultivated, Western Princess, the pupil of a humanitarian Huguenot governess, could not yet reconcile herself to the thought that what Peter had achieved could never have been done without slave labour. The canals, the forts, the dock-yards, and above all his city on the Neva, were all the fruits of serfdom.

It was a system so utterly repellent to Catherine that one finds her writing in the first months of her reign 'serfdom is damaging to the State, for it kills initiative, industry, the arts and sciences and destroys honour and prosperity'. The famous *Nakaz* or instructions to which she devoted three hours a day for the first five years of her reign, and which was to serve as a guide for a new legal code, makes direct reference to serfdom. But it insists that even the humblest has the right to be treated as a human being and that every citizen should be subject to the same laws. Inspired by Montesquieu's *Spirit of Laws* and later by Beccaria's *Crime and Punishment* which appeared in 1764, Catherine probably intended that every Russian should enjoy the same rights as citizens. But her friends and advisers soon managed to persuade her that the illiterate peasants on the Volga and the wandering tribes of the steppe could hardly be classified as citizens. Her attempt to improve the lot of the industrial serfs was a failure and the slightest hint of the future enfranchisement of the serfs met with violent protest from the very people who prided themselves on their liberalism. Even Princess Dashkova, who regarded herself as a disciple of Montesquieu, would have been horrified at the thought of running her estates on paid labour. So convinced was she of the rights and privileges of her class, that she later succeeded in convincing a confirmed democrat like Diderot of the necessity of serfdom in Russia.

Catherine herself was never entirely convinced. When Diderot was her guest in St Petersburg and ventured to criticize the dirt and squalor of the Russian *moujik*, the Empress replied with unusual bitterness, 'why should they bother to be clean when their souls are not their own'. The opposition of her own subjects prevented her from realizing her ideals. She did not dare to defy the ruling classes on whom at first she depended for survival and who later contributed to the glory of her reign. When the *Nakaz* was published in 1767 it was shorn of all the dangerous and controversial ideas she had borrowed from Western philosophers. Prudent advisers like Nikita Panin had warned her that some of her maxims would be high explosives in the hands of immature and inexperienced legislators. To quote Montesquieu to magistrates who still abided by the advice of the early Tzars, 'look to your office and indemnify yourself', and to expect the principles of Beccaria to impress judges whose idea of punishment consisted of torture and the knout, was to demand the impossible of a people who had suffered three hundred years of Tartar domination and who valued human life by Asiatic rather than by European standards.

For all its deletions, imperfections and flagrant plagiarisms, the *Nakaz* was a sufficiently impressive document to earn Catherine the approval and admiration of *Les philosophes*, the prophets of enlightenment, of whom Voltaire was the acknowledged high-priest. Many of the maxims included in her instructions were for their benefit, rather than for the commission who from 1766 to 1768 assembled first in Moscow, then in St Petersburg, to digest and to discuss a new code of laws under the inspired guidance of their Empress. There were representatives from all parts of the Empire, beginning with the delegates from the state services, the Senate, the Holy Synod, the various Colleges and courts of Chancellory. The nobles sent a representative from every district, the merchants and tradesmen one from every city. The army, the militia, the free-born peasants and the fixed tribes, irrespective of their religion, were all allowed to choose a deputy from every province, even the *atamans* of the Cossacks were privileged to attend – all except the vast, voiceless majority of nearly ninety per cent of the population.

Five hundred and sixty-four deputies sat at the conference which opened in Moscow on 4 August 1767. Each representative was presented with a draft of instructions and a gold medal stamped with an effigy of the Empress on which was written 'For the happiness of each and all'. One suspects that the latter was the more appreciated by the majority of the delegates, but what must have been particularly disappointing for Catherine was that some of the deputies were so unworthy of their privileges that many of the medals were promptly sold. But what could a Lap, a Kalmuck or a Cossack of the Don make of a document of six hundred and fifty paragraphs compiled and arranged by a German-born Princess and largely borrowed from the most advanced thinkers of the Western world. 'The nation is not made for the sovereign, but the sovereign for the nation.' 'Liberty is the right to do all that is not forbidden by law.' 'It is better to spare ten guilty men than to put one innocent man to death,' were maxims so new and alien to the majority of the Russian people as to be almost incomprehensible. Each deputy was only concerned with his own local grievances. Minor details were discussed for hours at numberless committees and the vital questions were barely touched, but Catherine was proud of her work and with superb self-confidence declared, 'that the more people who read her instructions, the less crime there would be'.

She realized it had been no more than an experiment and later admitted it had not been entirely successful:

I summoned delegates from the whole Empire in order to learn the conditions of every section of my realm. Every part of my instructions provoked disagreement. I allowed them to cancel what they pleased and they omitted over half my draft. I begged them look upon the rest as rules upon which opinion could be based to serve as a guide in their law-making activities. They neither formed a code nor created a Parliament.

Much was started, nothing was finished. The merchants demanded the same privileges as the nobles and the right of owning serfs. The nobles demanded greater powers than they had already, and in the end very little was achieved. But Catherine's *Nakaz* was read with immense interest abroad and received the most laudatory notices. The most exaggerated in his praise was Voltaire who hailed her as a successor to Solon and Lycurgus, calling her *Nakaz* 'the most beautiful monument of the century which will bring you more glory than ten battles because it is conceived by your own genius and written by your own fair little hand'. Fortunately for Catherine, she never heard the comments of the diplomatic corps which were very different from those of *les philosophes*. The English ambassador described her *Nakaz* as a comedy, the French dismissed it as a farce, but the Prussian envoy was more careful in his comments now that the philosopher King and the philosopher Empress were going into harness to perpetrate one of the most heinous political crimes of the century.

CHAPTER FIFTEEN

A King for the Pole

Stanislaus Poniatowski was still waiting to be summoned to St Petersburg when in 1763 Catherine wrote to him of her intentions to make him King of Poland. The reigning monarch, Augustus of Saxony, was dying and it was generally assumed that his son would succeed him in Poland. His candidature was favoured by Austria, France and, in the old system of alliances, had also been approved of by the Empress Elisabeth.

But Catherine had other ideas. To give her ex-lover a crown was the kind of dramatic gesture in which she delighted. But this time her decision was dictated, not by her sense of drama, but by hard common-sense. Poland, which since the fourteenth century had been joined to the Duchy of Lithuania, was still in a sense a dual state. One of its many anomalies was that it was at once a republic and a monarchy. There was both a king and a diet. The monarchy was elected and the national Diet itself had little power. For every regional diet had the power to revoke its decisions, while any single deputy could close a session by exercising the fatal *Liberum Veto* which brought democracy very close to anarchy.

Poland was in a state of decline, but till now it had managed to survive, thanks to a few strong patriotic kings like Sobieski and the rivalries of her powerful neighbours. Its territories still encompassed the vast plains between the Dnieper and the Oder and stretched from the Baltic almost down to the Black Sea. Enclosed in these territories were large tracts of land of what had once been part of the great principality of Kiev, which every Russian Tzar from Ivan the Third to Peter the Great regarded as his natural inheritance. In the past hundred years, a series of successful wars had won them back Smolensk and Kiev and the whole of the Ukraine. But there were still parts of White and Red Russia (Galicia) in which Orthodox Slavs were being persecuted by their Catholic overlords. Catherine cherished the same ambitions as her predecessors, but she intended to secure by peaceful means what they had obtained by force. By promoting the candidature of Stanislaus Poniatowski and taking into account his gentle and submissive character, she knew it would only be a question of time before Poland was completely under Russian influence. The Czartoryski played into her hands by asking her help to ensure the succession of a native-born king. But neither Prince Michael nor Prince Augustus envisaged their nephew as a likely candidate. Stanislaus was no more than a useful liaison with the Russian court and they now hoped to benefit from a relationship which, until now, they had had very little reason to be proud of. The Dauphin was Prince Adam, son of Prince Augustus and of one of the wealthiest heiresses in Poland – a young man of exceptional talents and immense popularity. While Poniatowski had been travelling abroad, sitting in Paris at the feet of Madame Geoffrin and indulging in Russia in a dangerous and romantic adventure with an unhappy Grand Duchess, his cousin had been consolidating his position in his own country so that every Polish patriot looked upon him as their natural leader; one who would be sufficiently strong to establish a hereditary monarchy, create a standing army and do away with the abuses of the *Liberum Veto*. But the last thing the great powers, and in particular Russia, wanted was a strong Poland. Catherine wrote to her ambassador in Warsaw that Count Poniatowski was the very man they needed, 'amiable, poor and not too much of a patriot', in short the perfect puppet king. There was very little sentiment in her letters, either to the ambassador or to King Frederick of Prussia, whom she knew to be as interested as herself in maintaining Poland in what she cynically described as 'that fortunate state of anarchy'.

Exhausted and penniless, his country devastated by war and without a single friend in Europe, Frederick was only too ready to accept Catherine's offer of friendship, which coming at this moment was as welcome as it was unexpected. He assured her that he was ready to support the election of any candidate she might choose.

Poniatowski's own attitude was difficult to define. He was at once ambitious and timid and saw himself far more in the role of a prince consort, helping the Empress to civilize her Empire, than as the ruler of a country in which he had always felt himself a stranger. He had so little in common with the unruly, hard-living feudal aristocracy, who recognized no authority other than their own and would be ready to turn against their king at the first threat to their privileges. Nor, on the other hand, did he feel very much in sympathy with his family. The brilliance he had shown in early youth had in recent years been so far eclipsed by his cousin Adam that a certain element of jealousy clouded their relationship. He was conscious of having disappointed his uncles and resented their disapproval of what they called 'his incorrigible frivolity'. Catherine, who knew him so well, was aware that she had only to mention Prince Adam as her second choice for him to conquer his fears and hesitations.

His first reaction had been to refuse. 'Let me be with you in any capacity you will, only do not make me into a king. I will be able to render you far greater service as a private citizen, Sophie. I beg of you – I beg of you to listen to me – you of all women I never thought would change. Life without you is nothing but an empty shell.' This rekindling of an old passion inspired by his imagination evoked a completely erroneous picture of a lonely young Empress, coping with the problems of her enormous Empire and desperately in need of help.

But Catherine was neither lonely nor helpless. On the contrary, she was enjoying herself, venturing for the first time into the field of foreign politics in which she was far more at home than in playing the role of legislator. On King Augustus's death in the autumn of 1763, we find her writing to Panin,

'You will laugh when I tell you but I nearly jumped out of my chair at the news of the King of Poland's death.' She might not have been so jubilant had she thought that Austria and France were prepared to take up arms in support of the Elector. But the Seven Years' War had barely ended and none of the great powers were prepared to go on fighting over the Polish succession.

Meanwhile, Frederick of Prussia had shown his approval of the Empress's choice by presenting Stanislaus Poniatowski with the Order of the Black Eagle, a somewhat unsuitable decoration for the most unmilitary of men. But it pleased Catherine and was a small price to pay for the defensive alliance signed by Prussia and Russia on 31 March 1764, whereby the Empress, adhering to the northern system of Panin, exchanged the friendship of Austria for a questionable alliance with Prussia. Meanwhile, the courts of Europe were informed as to their intentions in regard to Poland.

The news took Europe by surprise. No one could believe that the young Empress would have the audacity to force her former lover on the throne against the wishes of the majority of the Polish people. Princes like the Potocki and the Radziwills, who all their lives had been sworn enemies of the Czartoryski, were prepared to resist by force. The Czartoryski were jubilant for, although they would have preferred Prince Adam, they regarded Stanislaus as being sufficiently malleable for them to rule in his name. They did not know the secret convention which had been added to the Prusso–Russian treaty in which the two powers guaranteed to the Polish republic the right to free election of their king and undertook to preserve by force of arms, if necessary, the constitutional and fundamental laws of the republic. These high-sounding phrases served as a cover to Catherine's and Frederick's secret plans. They meant that a Russian candidate would be elected in Poland, that there would be no reforms along the lines proposed by the Czartoryski and that Poland, with the blessing of Russia, would continue in her 'fortunate state of anarchy' until they were ready to intervene 'to save her from herself'.

Both in Russia and abroad, it was generally assumed that

[173]

Catherine wanted to make her lover into the King of Poland in order to marry him at a later date. Stanislaus himself was the first to believe it and, according to his memoirs, this was the only reason he accepted the crown. This view was so widely diffused that even the Orlovs believed it and Gregory Gregorievitch made one of his rare appearances in the Senate to protest against the nomination of one whom he had always regarded as a potential rival. Another voice raised in protest was that of Catherine's new War Minister, Zachary Tchernichev, one of the two brothers who, in the early days of her marriage, had suffered exile for having dared to make amorous advances. But more important than the protests of her lovers was that of the Chancellor, Prince Vorontsov, who advised the Empress to abide by her traditional alliances and support the Elector, rather than run the risk of antagonizing both Austria and France who would immediately retaliate by stirring up trouble at the 'Sublime Porte'.

As a neighbouring state, the Ottoman Empire was directly interested in the question of the Polish succession. Austria was still looked upon as enemy number one, and the Sultan had approved the Russo–Prussian agreement and the election of a native-born king so as to prevent Maria-Theresa's candidate from ascending the throne. But French diplomats at the Porte lost no time in pointing out the danger of having a young, unmarried man upon the throne of Poland, one whom the Russian Empress had already had as a lover and might very well choose as a husband if the marriage settlement brought her the lands west of the Dnieper. By June 1764 the Sultan was already raising objections to Poniatowski's candidature on the grounds that he was too young and inexperienced, and above all unmarried.

But Catherine was drunk with power. She ignored her Chancellor's advice and trampled on the susceptibilities of the gentle Poniatowski by sending a peremptory message informing him of the objections put up by the 'Sublime Porte' and telling him that it was essential to marry either before or after his election. The Czartoryski were of the same opinion and put pressure on their nephew by urging him to announce his engagement to a Polish girl. At first Stanislaus refused. No one could force him to accept the crown under these conditions. His uncles appealed to his patriotism, the Empress to his ambition and the Primate of Poland, who had been heavily bribed by Russia, appealed to his religious sentiments. Finally he succumbed, heartbroken and completely disillusioned but, for all his sensibility, sufficiently hard-headed to write to his faithless 'Sophie' that if she wanted to make him into a king, then it was up to her to provide the wherewithal to enable him to live up to his position. Catherine, who was always generous to her lovers, whether past or present, sent him a hundred thousand ducats to settle his most pressing debts.

The so-called 'free' elections took place in the summer of 1764. Dashkow was in command of the ten thousand troops whom Catherine had sent to keep the peace. The Potocki and Radziwills, who dared to raise the standard of revolt, were forced to flee the country; others succumbed to bribery and on 19 August 1864, Stanislaus Poniatowski was unanimously elected King of Poland under the shadow of Russian guns. The first act of the Polish tragedy had begun.

Three months after Poniatowski's succession, the Russian ambassador, Prince Repnin, was already informing him that the Empress would allow no reforms in Poland until he was ready to make concessions to the religious minorities by allowing them to worship in their own churches under their own bishops and take part in the public life of the community. These were impossible demands to impose on a people who were fanatically Catholic and preferred to fight rather than suffer the slightest infringement of their privileges. One's heart goes out to the young King who had dreamt of becoming Catherine's husband, instead of which he found himself her vassal at the orders of her ambassador. Repnin was a brilliant soldier-diplomat, but the soldier predominated and he was better at giving military orders than at making diplomatic suggestions. Stanislaus was proud and his uncles were even prouder. They had begun to realize the appalling mistake they had made in seeking the alliance of Russia and were now encouraging their nephew to assert his independence, the

[175]

religious question being one on which he could count on the support of the whole country.

Catherine took umbrage when Stanislaus began to defend his rights, for there was a strong element of the bully in her make-up and she was not prepared to accept the slightest show of resistance from a man whose very weakness had made her suffer so terribly in the past. She had given him money to pay his debts and these were still unpaid, while he set out to make his palace into a miniature Versailles, attracting poets and artists to his court. Even the redoubtable Madame Geoffrin was unable to resist an invitation to his capital and, regardless of age and infirmities, made the long journey across Europe to visit the King who still called her 'Bonne Maman'. His picture gallery, created on borrowed money, reflected his exquisite taste with Chardins, Lancrets, Bouchers and Fragonards. He would have been far more suited to the role of prince consort than in trying to rule a country where he always felt a stranger, having nothing in common with his unruly, half-educated nobles, many of whom were far richer and more powerful than he. He was more at home in the boudoirs of their wives who were usually cleverer and better educated. Visitors to Poland were always impressed by the obvious superiority of the women, their interest in politics and the arts. Unfortunately, this interest in politics was also dangerous, aggravating the quarrels and intrigues. There was the pro-Austrian, the pro-Prussian, and the pro-Russian party, to which the handsome Prince Repnin made many converts. Last of all, there was the King's party of whom several members were in love with the charming Stanislaus. But when their religious privileges were threatened, then the Poles of every party, men and women, remembered they were patriots and the Diet of 1766 firmly refused to consider Russian demands for further concessions for the dissident minorities.

But Catherine was in a strong position. Those she upheld were the poor and the humble. She was the loving mother protecting the persecuted and the weak, and no less a person than Voltaire supported her cause.

King Frederick was, in the meanwhile, effectively fermenting discontent in the Polish enclave of East Prussia. There was a Lutheran secession in 1766, closely followed by an Orthodox secession in White Russia. These events only served to strengthen the opposition of the Poles. Intransigent landlords, including Radziwills, Potocki and Branicki, gathered at Radom in southern Poland and launched a manifesto accusing the King and the Czartoryski of having betrayed their country to the Russians.

With half the nation in arms, the members of the Diet sullen and mutinous, the Catholic prelates fulminating against the wickedness of the dissenters, Catherine had no alternative but to send her troops into Poland. This time she sent them to Warsaw on the excuse of protecting her ambassador but in reality to coerce the puppet King into submission. The patriotic Bishop of Cracow was deported to Russia, a measure taken against the advice both of her ambassador and of Count Panin. King Stanislaus's disillusion was complete. The soft, white hand of his 'enchanting Sophie' had become a mailed fist. Shocked by the transformation, he had not the courage to resist. The thought of Russian guns bombarding his palace, destroying his pictures and making him into a penniless exile, was too terrible to contemplate, and on 7 November 1767, a Diet which abounded in absentees submitted to Russian pressure. February of the following year saw the signing of a Russian–Polish treaty of alliance, by which liberty of worship was granted to the dissenting minorities and the King was committed not to attempt any changes in the constitution without Russian consent. Disgusted by their cowardly nephew, full of animosity against Russia, the Czartoryski had nevertheless to rely on the Empress's protection to preserve them from the threats of the conservative landlords. The Confederation at Bar, a town near the Turkish frontier, gave the signal for civil war. The confederates appealed for help from Austria, Saxony and France, and Catherine replied by sending reinforcements who put the secessionists to flight and captured the old Polish capital of Cracow. The rebels had not only the Russian troops to contend with. In Polish Ukraine, the Orthodox monks encouraged their flocks to ravage the countryside until Russian troops were forced to intervene in order to restore law and order. Catherine had succeeded in making Poland into a vassal state, with the King a puppet in her hands. But she had made enemies of the Czartoryski, the only family capable of keeping order in the country. She had aroused the jealousy of Austria and the cupidity of Prussia. Frederick had not signed a treaty of alliance in order to see the whole of Poland fall under Russian influence, when two million Lutherans in East Prussia were ready to offer him their allegiance. Both Sweden and Denmark were concerned in the future of Poland, while farther west the two traditional enemies, France and England, were viewing with a growing suspicion the revival of Russia's expansionist policy.

The Grand Duchess Catherine had been in the pay of England and had rendered her useful services. The ten thousand pounds lent to her by Hanbury-Williams had never been repaid, not through any fault of her own but because the English ambassador, Lord Buckingham, had been specially instructed by the Foreign Office to prevent the Empress from repaying the money and to urge her to accept it as a gift from the King of England. Today, ten thousand pounds sounds a very trifling sum, but in those times it was considered to be sufficiently important to place the Russian Empress under permanent obligation to England. Catherine appears to have accepted the gift and forgotten her obligations. In theory, she was a sincere admirer of England and of the English constitution, and in her more sentimental moments would speak with gratitude of the country which gave her the friendship of 'the Chevalier Williams'. But the ambassador's tragic mental collapse, ending in suicide, appears to have left her curiously unmoved. His successors were always welcomed at court, invited to her intimate supper parties and chosen as her partners at cards. But her personal affability in no way reflected her political intentions. She had barely been a year upon the throne when she signed a treaty of commerce which prevented England from securing the monopoly of the Baltic trade, and later, when rebellion broke out in the American colonies, England discovered how little Russian promises could be relied upon.

Catherine's relations with France had always been strained. She had never forgiven the intrigues of the '*Cabinet noir de Versailles*', nor Baron de Breuteuil's refusal to lend her money at a time when she was in desperate need. She hated the feeling that King Louis was familiar with every detail of the *coup d'état* which had placed her on the throne. A French embassy secretary by the name of Ruhlière had recorded the events in a diary, giving certain pithy and amusing sidelights which did not always redound to her credit. This document was still unpublished but the author was often persuaded to read certain extracts aloud in the fashionable salons; the King was known to have been provided with a copy. Catherine did all in her power to get the document suppressed, but Ruhlière could never be persuaded to part with the manuscript which was only published after his death.

Catherine's principal grievance was against the King of France, that he regarded her as a usurper and refused to accord her the title of 'Imperial Majesty' which he had grudgingly given to Elisabeth. She made no attempt to hide her anger, and we find the French Foreign Minister, the Duc de Choiseul, writing,

We all know the animosity which the court of Russia harbours against France. The King has such a deep-rooted contempt for the Princess who governs that country, of her sentiments and conduct, that our intention is not to make a single step towards altering the situation. The King considers Catherine's hatred to be far preferable to her friendship. At the same time, he wishes to avoid the explosion of an open rupture.

France had always been the Sultan's traditional ally. She enjoyed greater privileges in the Levant than any other Christian power, and she now began to stir up trouble with the Turks over the Polish question with which they were directly involved. In the past hundred years the Russian Empire had expanded as far as the Pruth, the Sea of Azov and the Caucasus. Her armies in Poland were now in a position to threaten Wallachia and Moldavia and advance to the lower reaches of the Danube and the Dnieper. It did not require much effort on the part of France to convince the 'Sublime Porte' that it might be wiser to declare war on Russia before the enemy was fully prepared. And when the confederates of Bar appealed for help the Ottoman Empire was the first to reply. War broke out in October 1768, when Russian troops, pursuing some rebellious Cossacks, violated the Turkish frontier between the Dnieper and the Bug. It was a war which Catherine had not intended to embark upon for another year and where failure might well cost her the throne. But for the Russian people, war against the Turks had all the fervour of a religious crusade. After posing as the champion of the Orthodox faith in Poland, Catherine found herself being claimed as the champion of the Christians against the Infidels. 'Your Majesty', wrote Voltaire, 'has now two enemies to contend with – the Pope and the Padishah.'

CHAPTER SIXTEEN

Chesmé

Catherine found herself at war without a single ally. For all his protestations of friendship, Frederick of Prussia did not mobilize a single soldier to fight an adversary from whose defeat he had nothing to gain. The lack of preparations on both sides, the inadequate supplies and disorganization at headquarters was viewed by him with a typical Teutonic contempt, and he dismissed the Russo–Turkish war as a contest between 'the one-eyed and the blind'. Had he forgotten those heroic Russians who less than eight years ago had stormed the gates of Berlin and decimated his finest armies? Elisabeth's eaglets had grown into Catherine's eagles; Roumiantsev, Souvarov and Dolgourouki were names to conjure with in the Russian army, inspiring the ill-clothed, ill-fed soldiers with a bravery which matched their own. And the little Pomeranian Princess knew how to inspire her generals, writing them long letters to the front which were almost like lover's letters, encouraging them and cajoling them to victory. Officers on leave were entertained to sumptuous dinners at the Winter Palace, and there was not one single military parade at which the Empress did not appear in the uniform of the Colonel of the Regiment; uniforms which, as the years went by, became always a little tighter. For Catherine had begun to put on weight, which in the beginning improved her looks, making her face rounder, her features softer and effacing the aggressive thrust of the chin. Her arms and shoulders had become smooth and plump and she now had the fashionable *décolletage* she had always yearned for.

The general opinion was that she was far better looking at forty than at twenty. For all his infidelities, Orlov was still passionately in love with her and jealous of every young officer who attracted her attention. For twelve years they lived almost as man and wife, and during these years Catherine learned to think and speak as a Russian. Orlov was no longer the svelte young guardsman who had won the heart of a lonely young Duchess. He was now more of a Hercules than an Apollo, but he was still the handsomest man at court, able to take his choice of the most beautiful maids-of-honour.

His blatant infidelities were such as to shock and at times disgust the Empress's entourage. Even ambassadors complained that 'there was neither decency nor decorum in his behaviour and that he was even said to beat her'. 'He is Emperor in all but name', wrote the French envoy, 'and he takes liberties with his sovereign such as no mistress in polite society would tolerate from her lover'. There was an open scandal when Orlov seduced the wife of a high-ranking court official and Catherine had to appease the injured husband with the gift of a large estate. Any woman would have found his treatment hard to tolerate, and it was particularly wounding for someone as vain and self-confident as Catherine. Yet still she loved him with an ardour mitigated by fear, for the Orlov brothers represented a powerful faction at court and she had neither the courage nor the will to resist them.

Their intrigues had already cost her the friendship of two of her most loyal supporters – Cyril Razumovsky and Catherine Dashkova. The former lived most of the year on his estates in the Ukraine, at his splendid palace in Batourin, built for him by the Italian architect, Antonio Rinaldi, whom he first introduced at court and who, by the irony of fate, was commissioned by Catherine to build two palaces for Gregory Orlov. The latter, whose fiery and uncompromising nature made her an easy victim to intrigue, was now virtually banished, having been guilty of no other crime than that of injured vanity and careless talk. In one of his despatches, the English ambassador, Macartney, gives a fair estimate of Princess Dashkova's character:

16 Voltaire.

17 Melchior Grimm.

18 Denis Diderot.

19 Stanislas Poniatowski, King of Poland.

20 A cartoon of the great powers carving up Poland. Catherine II, the Emperor Joseph II and Frederick II point out the part of Poland that they each propose to take. The King of Poland tries to hold his crown on his head. Engraving by Le Mire after Moreau.

21 The Emperor Joseph II of Germany.

22 Count Panin.
Painted by A. Roslen.

23 Bezborodko, Catherine's most able secretary. Painted by Borovikovski.

24 Catherine as Colonel of the Guard. Painted by Schebanoff.

She is a woman of enormous strength of mind, bold beyond the most manly courage, fond of undertaking impossibilities in order to gratify a predominant passion for intrigue – a character highly dangerous in a country like this. Everyone dreaded what she might do next, and since she has left, the utmost harmony seems to be established at court.

The Princess's disgrace coincided with her husband's death in Poland. Her 'little Field-Marshal', as she called him, had been a great favourite of the Empress and played a prominent part in the entertainments of the Winter Palace which were not always of a level to be appreciated by his highbrow wife. There was nothing Catherine enjoyed so much as a good romp. She would throw herself whole-heartedly into the silliest games and laugh over the simplest jokes. Neither war nor rebellion could divest her of her irrepressible gaiety. One of her favourite entertainments, which must have been exceedingly painful to her more musical courtiers, was to sing duets with Prince Dashkof, both of them being completely tone-deaf, hitting all the wrong notes while imitating the mannerisms of the opera stars. Strangers at court were surprised to see the formidable Empress mewing like a cat, arching her back and striking out with her hand as if it were a paw. On other occasions, she would wiggle her ears, an accomplishment of which she was inordinately proud. Prince Dashkova had been the life and soul of these charades and amateur theatricals. Now he was dead, leaving his young wife to pay off his enormous debts and defend herself against her enemies. Not even Panin could save her from the Orlovs' vindictive hatred and, in the early months of her widowhood, she was informed by the Ministry of Police that she would find the climate of Moscow healthier than that of St Petersburg.

She behaved admirably, retiring to Moscow, practising the most rigid economy, acting both as her own steward and as her children's nurse and tutor, selling most of her jewels and plate rather than mortgage one hectare of her son's inheritance. The result was that five years later she had paid off every rouble of her husband's debts and was free to travel abroad with her children. Unfortunately, her tongue was still her worst enemy. Injudicious remarks had reached the Empress's ears and she was greeted with a marked coldness when she returned to St Petersburg and made a brief appearance at a ball at the Peterhof in order to request such a permission to travel. Permission was granted, and Catherine even presented her with a gift of four thousand roubles to pay towards her travelling expenses. But Dashkova wept in anger at what she considered to be a niggardly present and was only prevented from returning it by the intervention of Panin. By her departure, Catherine lost the one friend who had the courage to tell her the truth which, as the years went by, she was ever more unwilling to hear. She complained that Gregory Orlov never paid her a compliment but he would certainly never have dared to criticize a woman who was so far his superior in intellect and experience.

He made laudable attempts to educate himself and thereby assert his independence. He became the patron of the famous scientist, Lomonosov, who, having been honoured by Elisabeth, was neglected by Catherine in the same way as she had barely allowed Rastrelli to complete the Winter Palace before replacing him by other architects. The master of Russian Baroque never got a single commission from Elisabeth's successor. Orlov's patronage of Lomonosov enabled the scientist to spend his last days in comfort. After his death, his widow sold Orlov all his books and manuscripts, and a special library was built in which to house them, a noble gesture on the part of a man whom his enemies branded as illiterate. Stranger still was Orlov's patronage of Jean-Jacques Rousseau, whose doctrines were totally inimical to Catherine though she seems to have approved of her lover's generosity in offering him a home.

Orlov's letter to Rousseau was that of a plain, honest soldier, lacking in any elegance or style but going straight to the point.

You will not be surprised at my writing to you. As you know everyone has his peculiarities. You have yours, I have mine. This is natural and the motive of my letter is equally so. I see that for a long time you have been living abroad, moving about from one place to another. I also know the reasons, though perhaps I am misinformed. I believe that, at the moment, you are in England with the Duke of

Richmond, who no doubt makes you very comfortable. But I have an estate which is sixty *versts* from St Petersburg, where the air is healthy and the water good, where the hills and lakes lend themselves to meditation, the inhabitants speak neither English nor French, still less Greek or Latin. The priest is incapable of arguing or preaching, and his flock think they have 'done their duty when they have made the sign of the cross'. Should you think this place would suit you, you are welcome to live in it. You will be provided with the necessities of life and find plenty of fishing and shooting.

The postscript, which must have been added at Catherine's suggestion, was more elegantly worded. The writer mentions in it 'the pleasure he has derived from reading the master's works and looks forward to the hour of their meeting'. However opposed to the teachings of Rousseau, the Empress was delighted whenever her guardsman-lover showed any intellectual leanings. Rousseau never came to Russia and Orlov soon lost interest in philosophy. But throughout his life, Catherine persisted in regarding him as a genius, 'Nature's spoilt child, endowed with every gift, but too lazy to take advantage of them except in times of emergency'. At the Empress's instigation, Orlov founded a society which was called the 'Free Society of Economics', for the purpose of discussing the economic and commercial problems of the Empire. As president of the society, Orlov, either on his own inspiration or on Catherine's orders, produced a paper, 'On the Expediency of Peasants having the Right to Own their own Land'. A prize presented by an unknown lady, who was none other than Catherine herself, was given for the best treatise on this subject. It is interesting to note that, among the few nobles who spoke out in favour of enfranchisement, was Count Orlov, the pampered favourite who had received no less than ten thousand serfs in gifts from his grateful Empress, and Count Sheremetief, who was one of the richest men in Russia.

Catherine's judgment may not have been entirely at fault in describing her lover as an 'untutored genius'. He rarely appeared either at the Senate or at the meetings of the Grand Council of which he was a member. But on two occasions he astounded his listeners by his lucidity and eloquence. The first was on the eve of war, when he asked the Council to decide 'whether a war was really necessary, and what were its primary aims. If these aims could not be clearly defined, then it was better to negotiate in favour of peace.' Those words reflect Catherine's uneasiness and fears that defeat might cost her the throne. But once war was declared, Orlov was the first to volunteer and he was bitterly disappointed when his mistress would not let him go.

The second speech made by Orlov in the Senate referred to the famous 'Greek project' which was later associated with Potemkin, but which was first conceived by Peter the Great when he was campaigning against the Turks in the Caucasus. The revival of the Byzantine Empire by the capture of Constantinople was a dream as fascinating to a German princess as to a Romanov. Catherine, who had not a drop of Paleologue blood in her veins, already looked upon herself as the heiress to Byzantium.

Gregory Orlov now pointed out a new way to Constantinople via the eastern Mediterranean and the Greek Islands, where the inhabitants still suffered under the Turkish yoke. He maintained (and even Catherine must have wondered how he got the knowledge) that the Russian fleet had only to appear in the archipelago for every Greek to rise against his oppressor, and the flames of revolt to spread to Asia Minor, to Egypt and the Syrian desert. The boldness of the scheme staggered both the Empress and the Senate. Until now, the Russian fleet had hardly ventured beyond the Baltic. The picture of her men-of-war sailing out into the North Sea, refuelling at English ports, coasting the shores of France and Spain, penetrating the Straits of Gibraltar and flaunting the flag of the Greek Orthodox Empress in the Papal port of Civita Vecchia, was conceived on such an ambitious scale that it made even Catherine feel somewhat out of breath. The mystery as to how the Orlov brothers had got their knowledge of the Greek Islands was explained by Alexis having an ardent Greek patriot in his service, and Gregory being the friend of a young French officer who had passed into the service of Russia after fighting in the armies of the Venetian Republic. The Minister of War stood up in the

Senate to protest against this mad and dangerous plan. But the minister was none other than Catherine's old admirer, Zachary Tchernichev, who was consumed with envy and hatred of the Orlovs.

Earlier in the year, Catherine had asked the British government to loan her the services of some senior naval officers to help in rehabilitating her fleet. England had consented for, in fighting the Turks, Russia was in a sense fighting against France who was Turkey's traditional ally, and in the past years had been supplying her with technicians, and engineers. Thus Russia secured the services of outstanding naval officers such as Elphinstone and Grieg, both of whom were given the rank of Rear-Admiral and a far bigger salary than they received at home. They welcomed the chance of fighting the Turks and seconded the Orlovs' scheme with enthusiasm while the Empress, who was the greatest adventurer of them all, gave her official consent to an undertaking which was disapproved of by almost the whole of her Senate.

In 1769, two Russian squadrons under the supreme command of Alexis Orlov sailed out of the Baltic, viewed with astonishment in Europe. The fury of the French is reflected in the despatches of Sebastian de Cabres, acting *chargé d'affaires* in Russia. With a pen dipped in gall, he writes to the Duc de Choiseul:

The Empress and her entourage are suffering from swollen heads. She dreams and talks and thinks of nothing, but of capturing Constantinople. Her delirium is such that she is persuaded that the sight of her two miserable squadrons is going to strike terror throughout the Ottoman Empire, that her armies have only got to appear for the Turks to run away, that all the discontented Greeks are only awaiting the arrival of the Russians to burst into open rebellion, and that as a result of these continued efforts, she will succeed in crushing the 'Grand Signor' and overcoming his Empire which in her imagination she has already disposed of as if it were her own.

But the Frenchman made no allowances for Catherine's lucky star which protected her throughout her life from the consequences of her own rashness. Although Alexis Orlov was officially in command of the expedition, Admiral Elphinstone was virtually in charge, and he must have been a man of extraordinary talent to deal both with Alexis's egomania and the jealousy of his Russian colleagues. His ships were allowed to revictual and carry out repairs in British ports and were given all facilities in passing through the Straits of Gibraltar; the Grand Duke of Tuscany offered the Russian squadrons winter quarters at Leghorn and, had Elphinstone been solely in command, he might have succeeded in forcing his way through the Dardanelles, bombarding Constantinople, and joining up with the Russian armies on the northern shores of the Black Sea. But Alexis Orlov saw himself in the role of liberator of the Greeks without having made the necessary preparations for giving them active help. The appearance of the Russian ships in the archipelago was the signal for revolt. But the Greeks were divided among themselves and relied on the Russians for leadership and ammunition, neither of which was available. It only needed a regiment of Janissaries to crush an abortive insurrection.

After blowing up a fort at Navarino, the Russian squadron sailed north towards the Dardanelles and was met by the Turkish fleet off Lemnos. The enemy was far superior in ships and guns but the Russians went over to the attack and ended in defeating the Turks who took refuge in Chesmé Bay. But Elphinstone barred their exit with an audacity which spread panic throughout the Turkish fleet, and sent in fireships to destroy them. Eye-witnesses recall that the flames of the burning ships could be seen for miles along the Anatolian coast, while hundreds of drowned sailors were washed up on the beaches for many days to come. There were many heroes at Chesmé, both Russian and Turkish, and Alexis Orlov was foremost in the fray. But the real hero of the day was a young British lieutenant called Dugdale who led the fireships into action and himself ignited the flames.

Chesmé was a great victory, as dramatic as either Catherine or the Orlovs could wish. But it had to be a completely Russian victory. The British officers were decorated and handsomely rewarded, but there is no mention of them in the paeons of praise with which Catherine acclaimed her heroic navy. The propaganda value of Chesmé was immense. Russia had proved herself to be a naval power. The presence of her ships in the Mediterranean and the establishment of a Russian base in the archipelago spread alarm in the European courts, though one and all sent official congratulations. There was wild rejoicing in St Petersburg and *Te Deums* were sung in every church throughout the country. The Empress wasted no time in giving an account of the battle to Voltaire, writing: 'I always told you the Orlovs were capable of greatness.' And he in reply celebrated her triumphs in verse.

The Russians were masters of the Aegean, and the road to Constantinople lay open. Elphinstone's plan was to force the Dardanelles while the Turks were still suffering from shock. But Orlov again wasted precious time by celebrating his victory in the islands of the archipelago. A plan to spread insurrection in Egypt and Asia Minor was grossly mishandled, and by the time he gave orders to sail, French engineers had succeeded in making the Dardanelles impregnable. With half of its crew suffering from dysentery or wounds, the proud Russian fleet withdrew to winter quarters at Leghorn. But 1770 was a lucky year for Catherine. There was news of victory on land as well as at sea. Roumiantsev had advanced into Moldavia and captured Jassy, the capital. Dolgourouki was bombarding Turkish strongholds on the Black Sea, and Catherine boasted to Voltaire, 'at the risk of repeating myself or becoming a bore, I have nothing to report to you but victories'. From his peaceful Swiss retreat, the old philosopher hailed her as the new Empress of Byzantium. Frederick of Prussia was still more fulsome: 'I cannot keep writing to you for every victory. I shall wait till there are half a dozen.' But no one was more alarmed than Frederick over the march of events which could so easily involve France and Russia in a war with Prussia. The last thing he wanted was to be dragged into a European struggle. In 1770, the King of Prussia and the young Emperor Joseph met in secret at Neustadt and two former enemies discussed by what means they could curb the Russian Empress in her aggressive drive towards the Balkans and the lower Danube. Catherine was in her most vainglorious mood. Alexis Orlov returned in the spring of 1771 to be given a hero's welcome. A gold medal was struck in his honour to commemorate his victory and the name of Chesmé was given both to a palace and a church built on the outskirts of the city.

Had Gregory Gregorievitch been less devoted to his brother, he might have felt a twinge of jealousy to see Alexis reap the laurels he would so gladly have earned. But the Orlovs' strength lay in their loyalty towards one another, the fact that they always acted as a single unit. Alexis may have been the one whom Catherine feared and admired the most, but Gregory was the one she loved with all the tenderness and passion of a woman who was at once a sensualist and a sentimentalist. He occupied the post of Imperial favourite for nearly twelve years and, as her personal *aide-de-camp*, accompanied her wherever she went.

Catherine was one of the first European monarchs to be inoculated against smallpox, the dread disease which had just proved fatal to the King of France, and her invitation to Dr Dimsdale was made in the face of the opposition of the whole court. It was regarded as a sacrilege for a foreign heretic to inject poison into the veins of the beloved Empress. Dr Dimsdale had the somewhat unnerving experience of inoculating the Empress to the accompaniment of muttered prayers and incantations from her terrified ladies-in-waiting. Catherine maintained that her life was her own to risk as she pleased, but the risk was far greater for the Grand Duke, who was then a sickly fourteen-year-old boy and, in the case of failure, the Empress had made all the necessary arrangements for the doctor to escape from the vengeance of her subjects. Fortunately, the inoculations were successful and the whole court ended by following Her Majesty's example. The doctor was handsomely rewarded. He was given a fee of ten thousand pounds, a pension of five hundred a year, plus another two thousand for his travelling expenses. He was created a baron, a councillor of state and a member of the Academy of Science, and later he returned to Russia with his wife to organize the new hospital for 'the inoculation of the poor'. Among the gifts the Dimsdales brought back to England were portraits of the Empress and of the Grand Duke, framed in diamonds, and a pair of diamond buckles and ear-rings from the reigning favourite.

Gregory Gregorievitch had become an institution. Foreign ambassadors went out of their way to win his favour. The English in particular benefited from his Anglomania, his detestation of all that was French. And, in the first decade of the reign, it was the Orlovs and their friends who formed the nucleus of Catherine's private parties at the Hermitage.

The Empress had never felt at ease among the Rococo splendours and gilded halls of Rastrelli's Winter Palace. And in the first years of her reign, she commissioned the French architect, Vallon de la Mothe, to build her a house like a small 'French *palais*', joined to the main building by one of those vast conservatories which are to be found in so many Russian palaces. The garden of the Hermitage was one of its most delightful features, where, strolling along the gravel paths amidst orange trees and flowering shrubs, one could forget the blustering northern winds in the warmth of a tropical garden. The Hermitage was the first real home Catherine had ever had. It was a place in which to house the collections she was gathering from all over Europe, in which to place the objects she herself had chosen, and to entertain not her subjects but her friends. It was a place where the Empress could become the woman and where no one was allowed to stand on ceremony. '*Arrangez-vous où vous voudrez et venez quand il vous plaît sans qu'on le répète tout les jours*', was the invitation given to the few who were admitted into the charmed circle of the Hermitage. There were rarely more than a dozen guests. Gaiety was the order of the day and a gloomy face was ostracized for ever. 'Ten commandments' posted at the door governed the behaviour. Infringement of these rules was punished either by a forfeit or by the payment of a small sum to be placed in a box for the poor. Among the commandments, we read:

that rank and ceremony had to be set aside on entering the door, that one could sit or stand or walk about regardless of who was present, including the Empress; that anything could be discussed or argued about, but always without bitterness or temper; that one must never groan over one's own problems or inflict boredom on others; that no gossip heard must be repeated. Whatever went in by one ear must go out by the other.

But, above all, 'one must try to amuse', and because of his talent to amuse, an obscure young captain found himself one evening a guest at the Hermitage. Gregory Potemkin had already attracted the Empress's notice at the time of the *coup d'état*. He was a gay, dashing young cavalry officer, always in debt and living far above his means among the *jeunesse dorée* of the capital, where his originality and gifts of mimicry won favour with the Orlovs.

Catherine recognized Potemkin. Unknown to the Orlovs, she appears to have watched over his career from the day of their first meeting and, on occasion, recommended him for promotion. She was intrigued by this tall, good-looking man with the mocking, slanting eyes and full sensual mouth, who, when she asked him for one of his impersonations, replied by giving her an exact imitation of herself with every mannerism of speech mimicked in her guttural German accent. The guests were appalled at such lese-majesty. But Catherine laughed that clear, ringing laughter which made her seem so young. She was delighted with his audacity and from that moment Potemkin's position was assured. Later she discovered that this strange young man was not just an amusing buffoon but highly educated, a brilliant theologian and deeply religious – always torn between his worldly ambitions and a desire for a contemplative monastic life. Her pleasure in his company, at finding someone with whom she could discuss the most varied subjects, from religious dogma to the habits and customs of her Asiatic subjects, soon became so apparent as to arouse the anger of the Orlovs. Gregory was not jealous. He was far too sure of himself to fear a rival. But he was nevertheless irritated. Young Potemkin was becoming too presumptuous. It was time he was taught a lesson.

Suddenly Potemkin disappeared from circulation. He was said to have lost an eye and retired into a monastery. There were rumours of a terrible quarrel with the Orlovs, at which Alexis was presumed to have struck him so violently as to maim him for life. The truth was more prosaic. Potemkin was dirty and slovenly by nature. He caught an infection in his eye, causing an abscess which he neglected so that the poison spread and he ended by losing the eye. Horrified by his infirmity, regarding it as a divine retribution for his sins, Potemkin retired from public life and was not heard of for another two years. The Empress, who enquired after his health, was told he was in a monastery. Meanwhile, Gregory Orlov remained supreme and unchallenged in his position, still occupying the sumptuous apartments which communicated directly with those of the Empress. To give him, and perhaps herself, the illusion of liberty Catherine had commissioned Antonio Rinaldi to build her lover a country mansion twenty miles distant from the capital. And it was among the woods and lakes of Gatchina that they spent some of their happiest hours.

Catherine was a woman who, when in love, had to go on giving, and in 1770 she presented Orlov with a town house as grand and as extravagant as any of the Imperial palaces. At a time when the finest houses in St Petersburg were still built of brick and stucco, the Empress employed Rinaldi to build a palace entirely out of Finnish granite and the finest of Siberian marble. As if awed by the richness of his materials, the architect deserted the flamboyance of the Rococo for the sober elegance of the Neo-classic. And the 'Marble Palace', situated on the banks of the Neva only a few blocks distant from the Winter Palace, remains today one of the finest buildings in the city, the cool severity of its exterior contrasting with the barbaric splendour of the interior, reflecting in pillars and porticos and panels the lights and shadows of many coloured marbles. The Empress built this palace to the glory of the Orlovs and over the door she wrote the simplest of inscriptions: 'From Catherine in grateful friendship.'

But Gregory Gregorievitch never lived for more than a few months in the Marble Palace. By the time it was finished, he was satiated with luxury, bored with the toadies and hangers-on who cluttered up his antechambers and no longer in love with the woman who, till now, had dictated his life. Catherine noted the change and suffered, though at first her feminine conceit refused to admit the truth. But when the plague broke out in Moscow and the authorities lost control over the terror-stricken population, Orlov volunteered to try and restore order in the city, and the Empress, to everyone's surprise, consented to let him go.

CHAPTER SEVENTEEN

'il faut être gaie'

'*Il faut être gaie*.' The maxim that Catherine included in the rules of the Hermitage applied to her own life. No one was allowed to see her sad or despondent, no one ever heard her mention defeat. The triumphs of 1770 were followed by two years of military setbacks and private heartbreaks. But her head was held as high as ever, the eternal smile on her lips never wavered and she always had an affable word for everyone from her servants to the youngest officer on guard-duty. Her servants in particular adored her, for no mistress could have been more considerate. In the first years of her reign, we hear of her getting up at six in the morning and, in winter, often lighting her own fire and reading or writing for an hour before summoning her maid, the faithful Marie Savichina, who knew more of her mistress's secrets than any lady-in-waiting.

A bowl of hot water to rinse her mouth, some pieces of ice with which to rub her cheeks, was all Catherine needed at this early hour before she took her breakfast of five cups of strong, black coffee topped with cream, so potent a brew that it required no less than a pound of coffee every morning. There is a story told of a secretary coming to see the Empress on a particularly cold morning, and Her Majesty graciously inviting him to 'a cup of coffee'. But no sooner had he drunk it than he was seized with such violent palpitations that he had to be carried off to bed. Catherine prided herself on her digestion. It was part of her cult to be healthy as well as gay. But she was not in reality as strong as she appeared. The illnesses of her youth had left their mark and she suffered from bad headaches, cramps and colics of the stomach. Her English doctor, Rogerson, found her a difficult and careless patient who had to be coerced like a child before she would take the simplest medicine.

By nature she was hot-tempered and irascible but, by the age of forty-two, an iron self-control exercised during the eighteen years of her apprenticeship had taught her to guard her tongue and dissimulate her feelings so that she was rarely heard to utter a cross word in public. If a sentence of punishment requiring her signature arrived in a moment when she happened to be in a bad mood, the document was put away until the following day for fear that, in irritation, she might be tempted to make the sentence too severe. She had come to the throne still cherishing the liberal ideas of an enlightened Western princess. Till the end of her days, she was fond of saying that 'she was a Republican at heart and an aristocrat from duty'. But the cool reception given to her *Nakaz* had shown her that, with a few exceptions, neither the upper classes nor the peasants were ready for 'enlightenment'.

Her enthusiasm for legislation faded with the war. The Grand Commission sat for two years, indulging in wearisome and pointless debates, with the majority of the deputies only concerned with their local affairs and quite incapable of making laws for an Empire. The Empress is said to have listened in secret at one of these sessions, when a foolhardy deputy, ignoring the Imperial presence, dared to challenge the authority of the crown. There was an angry murmur from behind the screen and, with the swish of a silken skirt, Her Majesty left in displeasure. A week later, the Grand Commission came abruptly to an end. Catherine was forced to admit that 'her instructions were more appreciated in the West than in her own country' and she considered it a triumph when the publication was suppressed in France by order of the King.

Meanwhile, the war dragged on with heavy losses on both sides, with a terrible plague breaking out among the troops coming back from the front. Abortive revolts were reported from various parts of the country and, though momentarily suppressed, were ready to flare up again at the next recruiting levy.

The opposition party in the capital was growing in strength. The Grand Duke was approaching his majority and more and more people were beginning to question Catherine's right to the throne. She was fortunate in having a son who lacked the grace and ability to win the affection of her subjects. From having been a pretty, attractive child, Paul had grown into a sickly, puny adolescent, bearing a striking resemblance to his putative father. Whatever Catherine may have insinuated in her memoirs, no one who met the Grand Duke Paul could fail to be convinced that he was Peter's son. He had the same nervous tic, the staccato voice, the abrupt and clumsy movements, all of which reminded the Empress of the husband she had detested. There was a short period during Gregory Orlov's absence in Moscow when Catherine was reported to be on better terms with her son. Her correspondents were told that 'she and Paul were now on the most affectionate terms and that he really appeared to enjoy her company'. One is tempted to suspect the sincerity of these words. Paul was growing up, a pawn in the hands of Panin who still remained the most powerful of her ministers and, on more than one occasion, had tried to curb Catherine's autocratic power by suggesting some form of constitution. Paul had pledged himself to accept this plan as soon as he came to the throne. But the Empress resolutely set her face against any curtailment of Imperial power and her minister had to accept her decision.

Her most dangerous enemies were in the church. On coming to the throne, she had won favour with the clergy by revoking her husband's *Ukaze* decreeing the secularization of ecclesiastical properties. She did this for the same reason as she had annulled the Prussian alliance. Both were measures calculated to win favour with the army and the church. But, two years later, when she had consolidated her power, she was herself signing a treaty with King Frederick and was having second thoughts on the question of church property. Her rational spirit could not accept the squandering and mismanagement of so large a part of the nation's wealth.

Peter the Great tried to bring order into chaos by placing the finances of the church under civil administration, establishing the College of the Holy Synod to look after its temporal affairs. But the enormous grants and privileges given to monasteries and convents under the reign of the pious Elisabeth had strengthened the power of the provincial bishops to such an extent that they continued to administer their serfs and their estates independent of central control. Catherine had only been reigning for a year before she set up a commission to enquire into the situation. Her own mind was already made up and, in February 1764, she signed a decree secularizing all ecclesiastical property and making the church into a state institution.

Resentment was bitter and widespread. But it is the tradition of the Orthodox church to submit to the secular power and, for all their complaints, the majority of the prelates ended by obeying the Empress's decree. But there were a few outspoken bishops who dared to protest in public, and one in particular became Catherine's greatest enemy. Arsény Matiévitch, Metropolitan of Rostov, a town famed for its sanctity and the number of its holy relics, did not hesitate to denounce the Empress from the pulpit as a heretic and a despoiler of the church. Nor did he moderate his language when he was summoned to St Petersburg to the Imperial presence where, according to Catherine, 'he spoke like a madman and his language was so violent that she had to stop her ears'. 'Murderess, assassin, usurper and whore', were the mildest of the invectives which echoed down the corridors of the Winter Palace.

This time, the Empress was too frightened to be merciful. The Archbishop was divested of his rank and, in the late sixties, sent to a monastery on the White Sea where he was forced to perform the most menial tasks, chopping wood and cleaning out the cells, but even this did not break his spirit and, four years later, he was still smuggling out of the monastery pamphlets so damaging to Catherine's reputation that she had him incarcerated in the fortress of Reval where not even the guards spoke Russian and where he had no other identity than that of the peasant, 'Andrew the Liar'. Here he lived for another four years, deprived of books and writing material, but even after his death a person to be feared – one of those martyrs who, in a country like Russia, becomes sanctified with the years.

Lord Cathcart, who had succeeded Sir George Macartney as English ambassador to St Petersburg, was shocked by the general atmosphere of uneasiness in the capital. He writes:

Anyone suspected of treason is quietly put away, though none of this comes to the surface. The Empress tells her dear people that, given her maternal care, which keeps her busy all day and sleepless at night, there is no necessity for them to worry about public affairs other than to act implicitly as she directs; to save them from unnecessary labour she exhorts and actively forbids them either to speak, write or think politics.

But the situation had to be very bad before Catherine had a sleepless night. For over ten years a strong and ardent lover had left her bed at midnight, when she fell into a heavy, dreamless sleep. She was sufficiently careful of her health to realize that she required her six hours sleep a night, and there is a rather touching account of her begging Gregory Orlov always to leave her room at midnight as she would never have the strength or wish to dismiss him on her own.

Whatever Lord Cathcart might write of the troubles at home and abroad, the Empress could still write gaily to Voltaire, 'Admittedly there is a war on but it is only a comparatively short time since Russia goes to war, and at the end of each one she seems to emerge more flourishing than before.' At the same time we find her boasting in the manner of King Henry of Navarre 'that every Russian peasant has always a chicken ready for the pot, though in some provinces they prefer turkey'. Like all good publicists, she was convinced that whatever is sufficiently repeated ends by being believed, and that nothing is so good for credit as to spend with an open hand. The Treasury might be empty but Russia had limitless resources. The Siberian mines and the quarries of the Urals were only beginning to be tapped. St Petersburg was still a city in the making, and the Empress was determined to transform it into one of the greatest capitals of Europe. She had inherited the glories of Trezzini and Rastrelli, the superb churches and magnificent palaces, but the quays on the Neva were still staunched in timber and the gilded, mirrored halls of Rastrelli's palaces were practically devoid of furniture. Elisabeth had been a great builder and patron of the arts, but her nomadic life and constant peregrinations left her neither the time nor the inclination to collect furniture. Vast ballrooms for concerts and masquerades, beds and couches everywhere – for in the last years of her reign her fears of assassination made Elisabeth sleep every night in a different room – tables heaped with gastronomic delicacies, were all that she needed. Such furniture as she possessed travelled with her from one palace to another. Only her father's possessions, his collection of Dutch and Flemish pictures, were regarded as sacrosanct.

Catherine was not primarily interested in art. Literature was her dominating passion. As a young Grand Duchess some of her first debts had been incurred in acquiring books which were both rare and costly at the time. Elisabeth's lover, the brilliant Ivan Shuvalov, had taught her to appreciate Voltaire, and by the time she came to the throne she already had one of the best libraries in the country. Whatever aesthetic sense she had was inherited from her mother who, for all her flightiness, was extremely cultivated. Only a meagre income had prevented the Princess Johanna from making her little principality into a Mecca for poets and artists. Catherine's husband, the boorish and drunken Peter, had somewhat surprisingly a greater liking for paintings than his wife and his collection at Oranienbaum included a magnificent Rembrandt. During her married life, Catherine's artistic activities were confined to the laying-out of the gardens of Oranienbaum and the building of an exquisitely decorated 'solitude'. Pavilions known as 'hermitages' or 'solitudes' were then the fashion, and it was in Catherine's 'solitude' that Rinaldi displayed his most charming fantasy. Both Cyril Razumovsky and Stanislaus Poniatowski helped to complete her artistic education. One wonders whether there were moments after one of her many quarrels with Orlov when Catherine regretted not having married the charming, civilized Stanislaus who, even in the midst of a civil war, managed to make his court into a miniature Versailles.

Catherine's detractors would have us believe that she had neither love nor knowledge of art and what she really admired were large battle scenes of Russian victories. She describes herself 'not as an art lover but as an art glutton'. It was a time when every civilized man of wealth, from the English *milord* on the grand tour to the German margrave, posed as a connoisseur. Competition in the art market was keen and Catherine entered it with the superb self-confidence of a present-day millionaire who wants only the best and is ready to pay for it against all comers. Her first acquisitions were from a Polish art-dealer who had on his hands no less than two hundred and twenty-five paintings bought for King Frederick of Prussia before the depredations of the Seven Years' War had emptied his coffers, and money to pay his army became more important to him than the furnishing of 'Sans Souci'. The Empress had sufficient confidence in Frederick's taste to buy the whole collection unseen and, though not all of the two hundred and twenty-five pictures were masterpieces, they nevertheless included a superb Franz Hals, a Reubens, several Teniers and a Rembrandt – the nucleus of what later became one of the best art galleries in the world. It must have been very satisfactory for Catherine to acquire what the great Frederick was no longer able to afford. And it must have been even more satisfactory when, a few years later, the famous collection of the Saxon minister, Count Brühl, came on to the market; a collection which included twelve Wouwermans, a Watteau and one of the finest Caravaggios. There had been a time when the powerful Saxon minister had held her happiness in his hands, when, after recalling Poniatowski to Warsaw, he had allowed him to return at the request of the Russian Chancellor, Count Bestuzhev. But perhaps the most satisfactory of all was when the collection of the proud Duc de Choiseul came up for sale and Catherine's agents secured her the greater part of the spoils, when he was French Foreign Minister Choiseul had refused her the title of Empress.

Catherine was lucky in the choice of her ambassadors. Dimitri Galitzine in Paris and later in The Hague, Count Musen, Poushkin in London, were men of exceptional ability who had the entry to the artistic and social circles of the capitals to which they were accredited. But the most valuable contact in Paris was Denis Diderot, who succeeded in getting at one half of its value the cream of the great Crozat collection and persuaded his friend, the sculptor Etienne Falconet, to accept the Empress's invitation to Russia to carry out the Herculean task of producing an equestrian statue of Peter the Great.

The monument was to be on a grand scale, a fitting tribute to the founder of the city. It is curious that both Diderot and Voltaire should have suggested an artist who, for the past years, had been associated with the sculpture department of the royal porcelain works at Sèvres, and was perhaps the most chauvinistic of all French sculptors. Falconet spent twelve lonely and unhappy years at Catherine's court, but his work in St Petersburg rendered him immortal. The bronze horseman, who appears to be leaping from the gigantic block of granite found in the Karelian Marshes seven miles from the capital, reflects the very spirit of the Tzar who built his capital on the marshes of Lake Ladoga in one of the most inhospitable climates of Europe. The transportation of the granite block was in itself a feat of engineering and took over a year to achieve. When Falconet arrived in St Petersburg in 1766, the Empress Catherine was enthusiastic over his work: 'Monsieur Diderot recommends his friend to us. He has brought about my acquiring a man who has, I believe, no equal.' What must have surprised her most of all was that the sum demanded by Falconet was less than what he had been offered by her ambassador. But the proud, argumentative and touchy Frenchman was not a character to remain long in favour with a patroness who hated hearing complaints. When he showed her the first model of the statue, wanting yet, at the same time, contemptuous of her praise, Catherine appears to have guessed this sentiment and said, 'Why do you ask me? What kind of opinion can I give you when I am not even able to draw? You yourself are a far better judge of your work.'

The person she relied on most in regard to artistic matters was the Director of the Academy of Arts, Count Betskoy, with whom Falconet unfortunately quarrelled. All foreign artists had to pass through the hands of this irascible, elderly courtier who was one of the more curious figures in Catherine's entourage, retaining her affection up to the day he died as a senile old man of over ninety. Betskoy was her mother's old lover who had caused so much scandal at the time of the Princess Johanna's visit to Russia. It was rumoured that he and the Princess had known one another in Paris as early as 1728, and that there was even a possibility of Catherine being his daughter. It was noted that the Empress always rose from her chair when Betskoy came into the room and that she treated him with particular respect. Not even the Orlovs were able to oust him from power, and when his health and mental faculties deteriorated, she still allowed him to retain all his privileges and appointments. He was not as good a director as his brilliant predecessor, Ivan Shuvalov, for he was always interfering with the artists who found him a difficult patron.

His real interest lay in education and Russia owes a great deal to his influence over Catherine. He was a very rich man and many of the schools she founded were partly financed out of his own private capital. In her long and unhappy years as Grand Duchess, Catherine had had to struggle to procure what little culture she possessed. The shortage of books, the lack of educational companionship and later the appalling ignorance of her subjects made her look upon education as a priority in the long list of necessary reforms. Already in 1764, Count Betskoy was commissioned to draw up a plan for the education of children of both sexes. This document, which must have been inspired by Catherine, was bold and revolutionary, and contrary to the whole concept of Russian family life. Children were to be taken away from their parents at the age of six and, apart from a monthly visit, were to be kept apart up to the age of twenty. One must remember that her educational schemes were concentrated on the children of the upper classes who were usually left to the care of servants or of foreign tutors or governesses, most of them French and many of them low-born adventurers of doubtful morals who had come originally to Russia as valets, milliners or hairdressers. The serfs were too illiterate to count, the middle classes were too small to matter and most of the foreign merchants had already their own schools.

Later in the reign there was an attempt to establish a national school based on the Austrian system, but Catherine as usual wanted to do too much in a hurry. Teachers had to be educated before the pupils, and young men of outstanding qualifications were sent at the Empress's expense to study at foreign universities; but when they returned from Paris, Oxford or Leipzig, many of them had become infected with political ideas, not always of a nature to please even the most enlightened of autocrats. The shortage of teachers was the stumbling-block to Catherine's grandiose schemes and, like so many of her schemes, they were completely alien to the Russian mind. Principles borrowed from Locke and even from Rousseau were entirely opposed to the beliefs, customs and traditions of a Slavonic people. During her reign, schools and universities were founded all over the Empire. There were naval and military cadet schools, medical and agricultural schools, state seminaries for young priests and even an academy of drama. But the most successful of all these foundations, founded by the Empress with the collaboration of Count Betskoy, were the Foundling Hospital in Moscow and the even more famous Smolny Institute for Girls in St Petersburg.

Catherine was passionately interested in female education. Princess Dashkova hardly exaggerated when, with customary arrogance, she declared that she and the Empress were the only women in the country capable of holding an intellectual conversation. The ignorance of the finely dressed ladies and the pretty, flirtatious maids-of-honour was abysmal. The Smolny Institute, established in Rastrelli's beautiful convent and run on the lines of Madame de Maintenon's famous Institute of St Cyr, was the first serious attempt to improve female education in Russia, and proved so successful that it was still flourishing in 1916.

Catherine herself supervised every detail of the curriculum and paid continual visits to the school, looking upon the inmates as her children, encouraging them to confide in her, allowing them to embrace her as warmly and naturally as if she were their parent. She had her favourites with whom she corresponded, writing them letters as loving as those of any mother, using the charming Russian diminutives, 'my little dove', 'my little kitten'. All her frustrated maternal feelings seemed to find an outlet at Smolny. Here again, the pupils from the age of six to eighteen lived segregated from their families, who were only allowed to visit them every six weeks. This was usually on some public occasion such as a play or ballet performed by the children. Holidays were cut to a minimum, but the older pupils were sometimes invited to court and there was many an ironical remark 'on the convent which had a door open on the temptations of court life'.

There were five hundred pupils. All of them received the same education. Half of them belonged to the nobility, the rest to the bourgeoisie. All of them wore the same coloured uniform and partook of the same fare, but there was a subtle difference in their treatment. The uniforms might be of the same colour, but the dresses of the children of the aristocracy were of finer material and of a better cut, while the children of the bourgeoisie wore large aprons made for utility rather than for ornament. At table, the children of the élite were served on china and their dishes were more elaborately prepared. The education of the one was geared to the arts of pleasing, dancing a minuet with grace, speaking languages and being able to read both Shakespeare and Voltaire in the original. On his visit to Russia, Diderot was so shocked to see the charming pupils from Smolny perform what he considered to be a completely unsuitable play by Voltaire, that he offered to act as censor for all future productions. Though the fundamental education of the two classes was the same, cooking, laundering and dress-making were included in that of the bourgeoisie. Catherine was a rationalist and Smolny was run on completely rational lines. Bearded priests were welcomed to this lay convent but religious teaching was confined to a minimum. It was a convent with the Empress as the Abbess and the novices looked to terrestrial rather than to heavenly glory.

Several years after its foundation, Catherine was writing to Voltaire:

You will have heard, for nothing escapes your notice, that five hundred young ladies are being educated in a place formerly inhabited by three hundred brides of heaven. The young ladies have far surpassed our expectations. They are making astonishing progress, and everyone says they are as delightful as they are knowledgeable.

Their conduct is irreproachable, without being as straitlaced as the inmates of a cloister.

Catherine might accuse herself of being a 'beginner'. Not all her schemes came to fruition, but it was incredible what she achieved in the first decade of her reign against the background of war, pestilence and revolution. The plague in Moscow had taken toll of thousands of lives. But in the end, the boldness and decisiveness of Gregory Orlov, who had assumed supreme control, had cleared the city of the pestilence. He returned to St Petersburg as the saviour of his country. Gold medals were struck in his honour, and the Empress's gift of a palace almost as splendid as her own fell to the lot of the returning hero. But the suspicions Catherine had harboured before he left returned more insistently than before; though Orlov still paid her homage as his sovereign, he appeared to have grown indifferent to her as a woman. The ardour, the brutality and, at the same time, the tenderness of his love-making had given her the illusion of youth. Every night she had felt as if he were conquering her for the first time. But now his love-making appeared to have become a duty. He was vague, distrait and obviously bored by her attentions. Rumours she had previously refused to listen to no longer gave her peace. Gregory Gregorievitch was said to have fallen in love with his young cousin, a thirteen-year-old girl by whom he was completely infatuated. Catherine was too proud to make scenes. But when peace talks with Turkey were initiated at the suggestion of Prussia and of Austria, she appointed him to act as her representative. It was a post for which she knew him to be completely unsuited, for he was far too arrogant and impatient to come to terms with the dilatory and susceptible Turks. But she wanted to give Orlov an appointment worthy of his conduct in Moscow, and at the same time she wished to be rid of his presence. She knew he could be relied on to keep up the dignity of his country and, as a parting gesture, she presented him with a coat embroidered in diamonds which cost her a million roubles.

CHAPTER EIGHTEEN

Retreats and Reversals

The peace talks at Foksàny, a small provincial town in Moldavia, were doomed to failure from the beginning. Orlov arrived in February 1773 and the Turks kept him waiting till June before they finally made up their mind to attend the congress. By then he had lost what little patience he possessed and was in no mood to negotiate. Pride was matched by pride and neither was ready to give an inch. The Russian delegates were haughty and dictatorial, the Turks were subtle and evasive. Orlov left the meeting at the end of a fortnight with a view to frightening the Turks and retired to the Moldavian capital of Jassy. It was here he received a message from his brother, Alexis, giving him the news of the Empress having taken a new lover, a twenty-year-old Guards officer, fifteen years younger than herself. Had the message come from anyone but Alexis, he would have refused to believe it. He knew most of the outstanding young officers by name but could not place Vassilchikof, whom his brother described as 'good-looking, amiable and a complete nonentity'. It was obvious that the whole sordid affair had been cooked up by his enemies – the hypocritical Panin and Feodor Bariatinsky, the former friend whom jealousy had thrown into the arms of the opposition.

In a blind fury, he set out from Jassy without even troubling to contact the Turks or send word to army headquarters. He crossed Russia from south to north, covering three thousand miles in the space of a few weeks, travelling in a light courier's carriage so as to reach St Petersburg as soon as possible. He had already passed Moscow when a message reached him from the Empress, commanding him to go into quarantine at Gatchina; a somewhat ironic order to give a man who, barely a year ago, had stamped out a plague in Moscow and had himself decreed that all soldiers coming on leave from the front should undergo a period of quarantine. A further ironic touch was when Catherine sent him her English physician on the pretext 'that he must be ill, otherwise he would not have deserted his post without asking permission or giving an explanation'. In reality, the Empress was frightened. She was so unaccustomed to issuing commands to the Orlovs that she dreaded their reactions. They were still the most powerful faction in Russia. All five brothers enjoyed influential positions in the government and Alexis, the brain of the family, was often described as the real ruler of the country.

Desperate loneliness, combined with hurt pride, had made Catherine an easy victim to the machinations of their enemies. Gregory Gregorievitch had been both a lover and a friend with whom she could discuss her innermost thoughts, her most far-reaching ambitions. For all his shortcomings, she considered him a genius and her love and admiration made her tolerant of his faults. But she could not forgive him his passion for a thirteen-year-old cousin and Panin lost no opportunity of rubbing salt into the wound by telling her that Orlov had even gone so far as to seduce the girl. Catherine had always refused to admit the existence of middle age, but now for the first time she felt she was growing old and, in her terror of age, she went in pursuit of youth.

She frankly admitted 'she could not live one day without love'. But it was hardly a question of love with the good-looking Guardsman she chose almost at random from among the young officers who were invited to dine at her table at Tzarskoye Selo. Orlov had to have a successor. It was her only defence, the vindication of her pride. And considering the hurry in which he was chosen, the choice might have been worse, for Alexander Semeonovitch Vassilchikof came of an old Boyar family, had perfect manners and spoke excellent French. He was modest, sweet-tempered and somewhat shy and had been for seven years a cornet in the Horse Guards without distinguishing himself in any way up to the day when chance put him in command of the Empress's escort. That same night he dined at court, and Catherine noted his fine appearance, his strong muscular body, the handsome features, the soft black eyes and sensitive mouth. Panin, Bariatinsky and the Tchernichev brothers, all of whom Orlov had offended at one time or another, were quick to observe the Empress's sudden interest in the young cornet, and they arranged for his superior officers to place him in command of the personal bodyguard while they took upon themselves to instruct him on his future duties.

It was June 1772 – the month of the 'white nights', when the gardens of Tzarskoye Selo were bathed in a silvery glow and the nightingales sang in the birchwoods; it was the month for alfresco fêtes and midnight masquerades at which young Vassilchikof was the Empress's constant cavalier. He appears to have acquitted himself to her satisfaction, for the sharp eye of the Prussian minister noted 'an eagerness on the part of the Empress to distinguish the young guardsman in a crowd, her gaiety and good-humour and the corresponding discontent and ill-humour of the Orlov relatives'. These and a thousand other details had opened the courtiers' eyes. The first sign of favour was when Catherine presented the young officer with a gold snuff box, inscribed 'In thanks for the smartness of my body-guard.' Other and more expensive presents followed and Vassilchikof's reluctance to accept such lavish gifts only made the by the now infatuated Empress still more generous. By August he had become a gentleman-in-waiting, by September he was Chamberlain, moving into the post of personal *aide-de-camp*, recognized as Imperial favourite and occupying Orlov's former rooms in Tzarskoye Selo. There was general astonishment, allied to a certain uneasiness, among those who refused to believe that this nice, insignificant young man had taken the place of 'the magnificent Orlov'. The Prussian minister was again writing to his master, 'that Her Majesty's lackeys and maids-of-honour are discontented, as Orlov was liked by them and he was always a generous patron.' The general feeling was that once Orlov was back, Vassilchikof would not last a week.

Frederick of Prussia, however, who was familiar with Catherine's character, knew that her pride would never allow her to admit a mistake. For the time being, Vassilchikof would be endowed with qualities he had never possessed, for every man picked out by the Empress for purely physical attributes had at the same time to be acclaimed for his mental superiority. Therefore the King recommended his minister 'to be on good terms with the new favourite, for the first to flatter such people can be sure of winning their friendship'. It suited Frederick's schemes for the Empress to have a mediocre and unassuming lover in place of the aggressively anti-Prussian Orlov. He was in the process of wooing Catherine to consent to the dismemberment of Poland, with both Prussia and Austria taking their share of the spoils.

One is inclined to wonder whether the first partition of Poland would ever have taken place had Orlov still been in power or had Potemkin yet succeeded to his place, for both were bitterly anti-Prussian and the latter believed in a strong and stable Poland. Those twenty-two months during which Vassilchikof reigned as favourite witnessed the two most tragic events of Catherine's reign, the partition of Poland and the terrible rebellion known as the Pugachefschina which broke out in eastern Russia in May 1773.

The Empress might believe that the company of the gentle and compliant Vassilchikof offered her a harbour from the storm, but Orlov's return from Moldavia put an end to all hopes of peace.

Ivan Orlov, the eldest, the least ambitious and at the same time the most sensible of the brothers, acted as intermediary in persuading the ex-favourite to submit to the Empress's orders. Catherine herself is said to have been so frightened of his reaction that she had her bedroom locks changed for fear he might suddenly reappear, and guards posted outside Vassilchikof's apartments. But once his wild fury had abated, Gregory Gregorievitch appeared to submit to the Empress's orders. All she asked of him was to stay away from St Petersburg for a year and to resign from the appointments which gave him command of troops, for she had no intention of running the risk of another *coup d'état*. She would have liked him to travel, but at the same

time offered him the use of any of the royal palaces in Moscow
and elsewhere. She gave him a grant of one hundred thousand
roubles, a life annuity of another hundred and fifty thousand,
and authority to choose an estate as well as six thousand serfs
from any of the crown lands. These were the gifts the Empress
gave Count Orlov in gratitude for his services to the nation, but
her own personal gifts were on an even more generous scale.
They included all the furniture, paintings and other *objets d'art*
from his apartments in the Winter Palace, the superb Sèvres
dinner service for a hundred people which she had ordered for
him from Paris in the previous year, and another one in massive
silver. Yet only a few months ago she had already presented him
with a fully furnished palace.

No sovereign dismissing an ungrateful subject could have
been more generous. No word of reproach or recrimination
passed her lips. But her magnanimity may have been more
humiliating than her reproaches for a man who had always
resented the role of a 'male Pompadour'. He accepted her gifts
with grudging thanks and chose this singularly unpropitious
moment to remind her that the courtesy title of Prince of the
Holy Roman Empire, which the Emperor Joseph II had forced
his unwilling mother to confer on Catherine's lover, had never
been legalized in Russia. The letters patent were promptly
produced, but that same week Catherine asked the prince to
relinquish his most treasured possession, her portrait in miniature framed in diamonds, which he had always worn in his
buttonhole. Orlov characteristically sent back the diamonds but
kept the portrait, a gesture which touched the Empress who
was still a German sentimentalist at heart. His enemies might
question the Empress's liberality, but munificence was matched
by munificence. The following spring, on St Catherine's Day,
Prince Orlov presented his sovereign with one of the largest
diamonds in existence which had once formed part of the
Indian booty of Nadir Shah and which he had bought from an
Armenian merchant for four hundred thousand roubles. No one
could have accepted the gift more graciously than Catherine,
who mounted the diamond in her sceptre, perhaps as a reminder
that she owed the donor her crown.

Orlov disobeyed his orders. He made no attempt to travel or to move to Moscow, and stayed on at Gatchina, only twenty miles away from the capital. When the Empress suggested he was ill and needed a cure at one of the European spas, he replied that he had never felt better in his life. And on the night of 22 December 1773, he suddenly reappeared at court in the middle of a masked ball. In spite of his domino and mask, his great height made him easily recognizable, and the sycophantic courtiers did not know whether to fawn on him or to avoid him. None of the guards on duty dared to arrest him without orders from the Empress, who, with a superb self-control, remained smiling and calm, barely acknowledging his presence. Two days later, she condescended to grant him the audience he requested. But she insisted on two witnesses being present, the devoted Betskoy and her secretary, the faithful Yelaguine, both of whom unfortunately were too discreet to leave a written record of a memorable meeting.

That same evening, Prince Orlov attended mass at the palace chapel and was present at court throughout the Christmas festivities, during which the Empress made a point of appearing with her new lover at her side. Vassilchikof appeared to be somewhat overwhelmed by his position and blushed with embarrassment when, at night, the Empress gave him her arm to accompany her to her private apartments in the presence of the whole court. People were at a loss as to how to behave. No one who saw Orlov and Vassilchikof in the same room could doubt that the latter was anything more than a passing fancy. They were astounded to see the Prince chatting quite amiably with his successor, even going so far as to joke with his friends over his own downfall. His amiable behaviour, which was so completely out of character, was not entirely to Catherine's liking. At heart, she knew that the Orlov of the early days would never have accepted the situation, and that the precautions she had taken to guard Vassilchikof from his vengeance would have been all too necessary. In spite of her relief, it must have been painful for her to feel that she had hurt only his vanity. Outwardly, she remained gracious, smiling and indifferent, but before long Orlov realized that he would have to admit defeat, that the stolid, pretty-faced nonentity who had nothing to recommend him beyond his youth and his virility had come to stay. It was not a question of affection, still less of love. Catherine had taken a young lover in the same way as he had taken so many of his mistresses, merely in order to satisfy his lusts with a new experiment. Realizing that he was losing face and that his position had become untenable, he requested permission to travel and, at the farewell audience, it was noted that the Empress did not mention his return.

Those last months had been a greater strain on Catherine's nerves than she would admit. Observant diplomats reported that 'judging by what they had heard from the palace, the Empress was so taken up by the affair of Monsieur Orlov that she was unable to concentrate on anything else'. She hardly read or went out, and the general opinion was that 'it would be impossible for the Empress to settle down to work so long as she allowed herself to be intimidated by the Orlov family'.

Peace returned at the Prince's departure. But it was peace at the price of boredom. Alexander Vassilchikof was a handsome and perfectly satisfactory lover, sufficiently robust to satisfy her insatiable demands, but his intellect was so limited that it was impossible to carry on a conversation with him. She who had so much *joie de vivre* and, in her few hours of relaxation, required to be amused, found that she had introduced into the sacred precincts of the Hermitage a bore who would never have been admitted in any other circumstances. Vassilchikof was sufficiently sensitive to realize that he bored her and the sweet temper which was one of his few assets became sour and peevish. Catherine knew that she had only herself to blame in having been in too much of a hurry to find a successor to Orlov. Having made this unfortunate choice and having raised an obscure young guardsman to such an exalted position, it would be cruel to dismiss him for faults for which he was not responsible. Nor was this the moment when she wanted to expose herself to the accusations of looseness and immorality.

The Polish question on which Frederick of Prussia prided himself in acting the part of the honest broker had brought together two women who cordially detested one another. The

pious Queen-Empress Maria-Theresa, who had hitherto referred to Catherine as 'that woman', had allowed herself to be
unwillingly persuaded by her son and co-regent to be a partner
to the partition of Poland rather than risk another European
war. In the past months, both Austria and France had been
giving active help to Turkey, while officers in French and
German uniform had been fighting with the confederates in
Poland. Frederick feared that, in her insensate pride, the
Russian Empress might light the flames of a general conflagration
in which Prussia would be involved as Russia's unwilling ally.
The old war-monger had become the advocate of peace. He had
nothing to gain from a war on the lower Danube, whether
resulting in a Russian or a Turkish victory. And all his diplo-
macy was directed towards persuading the two Empresses to
slake their appetites for power at the expense of a defenceless
Poland. The one who stood most to gain by the partition was
Frederick himself, for the acquisition of Polish territories on the
Baltic coast would unite the provinces of Brandenburg and
East Prussia.

The meeting with Joseph II at Neustadt had been a success.
Joseph was a young man of inordinate ambition who longed to
make a name for himself in the world and chafed at his mother's
tutelage. Frederick, who knew so well how to fascinate and
charm, had flattered his ego and encouraged his ambitions. But
Joseph had considerable difficulty in persuading the virtuous
Maria-Theresa that it was more in Austria's interest to come to
an agreement with the two people she hated and despised most,
than to uphold the cause of the Catholic Poles. Frederick
found it easier to come to terms with Catherine, for though she
would have preferred to keep Poland as a Russian satellite,
without any interference from outside, she was nevertheless
sufficiently sensible to realize that even Russia's limitless
resources could not stand the strain of fighting a war on three
fronts and policing the whole of Poland, while at the back of her
mind was always the fear that France and Austria might enter
the war as Turkey's allies.

Her attempt to place a puppet king on the throne of Poland
had been a failure. Stanislaus had not even proved to be an

efficient viceroy. He had allowed himself to be swayed by the currents of public opinion, trying to play the role of a patriot king for which he was utterly unsuited and at the same time expecting Russia to pay his debts. Catherine had no sympathy for failures. She had no qualms in breaking up her former lover's kingdom. The King's weakness had resulted in the spread of civil war and forced her to send more troops into Poland than she could afford. To secure the neutrality of Austria was well worth the sacrifice of a mountain district in the Carpathians, hundreds of miles away from the Russian frontier. It took many months of argument, persuasion and even coercion before Maria-Theresa's trusted minister, Count Kaunitz, and her eldest son succeeded in breaking down her resistance. 'Reasons of state, a favourite formula to stifle a Hapsburg's uneasy conscience, finally drove Maria-Theresa to accept an agreement which dishonoured her reign and blemished her reputation, making her come down in history as the hypocritic, "*qui prenait en pleurant*".'

Catherine and Frederick have both been accused of having instigated the most blatant political crime of the century, but to the amazement of Europe, it was Austria who acted first by moving troops into the so-called 'Zips' territory of the Carpathians, a district largely inhabited by Swabians who, in the middle ages, had migrated down the Danube. Austria's action took place as early as January 1771, on the excuse that she was only re-occupying land which had been leased to the Jagellon kings and had never been given back. It was a dangerous precedent to assert claims which had been allowed to lapse for centuries.

These events coincided with Prince Henry of Prussia's state visit to St Petersburg, where the stiff, somewhat spartan Prince was both shocked and impressed by the sybaritic luxury of Catherine's court, the balls for five thousand guests where the tables were laden with enormous sturgeons' caviare and French champagne, grapes from the Crimea and melons from Astrakhan, where men and women vied with one another in the splendour of their jewels and the winter gardens of the Hermitage was transformed into a Sicilian orange-grove full of tropical birds.

In the middle of a gala concert at the Hermitage, the Empress and her guests received the news of Austria's move in the Carpathians, and Prince Henry is reported to have jested with the Empress in his clumsy fashion, 'In Poland, one only has to stoop down to pick up a bit of the country,' whereupon she laughed and changed the subject. According to another version, Catherine is supposed to have replied, 'Why shouldn't we both take our share?' The first is the more probable for she was in no hurry to commit herself. Even the pro-Prussian Count Panin had declared himself against partition. In March 1771, Frederick came out into the open by writing a private letter to the Russian Empress suggesting that, in view of Austrian aggression and 'the fact that she refused to give back expropriated territory without resorting to arms, would it not be best if Prussia and Russia followed her example and took what they wanted?' But Catherine still delayed in sending a reply, and it was not until the middle of May 1771 that the Prussian minister to St Petersburg was able to report in triumph to his master that the Empress had consented to partition and was waiting for the King's propositions.

The sordid haggling dragged on for another year. The Partition Treaty, which was finally signed in August 1772, met with fierce resistance in Poland. In the Carpathians, the peasants met the Austrian forces with stones and staves. In Polish East Prussia and White Russia, Catholic priests roused their flocks to march against the Lutheran and Orthodox invaders. The Poles, who were at last united among themselves, fought back with the courage of despair. Even Stanislas rose to the occasion and put himself at the head of his army. England, France and Sweden denounced the spoliation of Poland. Spaniards and Italians echoed the denunciations of the Pope. But no one was prepared to go to war for Poland. By the summer of 1773 the last attempts at resistance had been crushed, and the Poles were forced to vote for their own dismemberment in a capital policed by foreign troops. The partition deprived them of nearly two-sevenths of their territory and of nearly five million inhabitants. The King of Prussia complained that Austria had got the lion's share. And for one who had been so reluctant to dip her fingers in the Polish cauldron, Maria-Theresa had certainly shown a remarkable appetite for seizing large slices of land to which she had not the slightest right. The greater part of Galicia, with the exception of Cracow, fell to her lot. Frederick contented himself with the Baltic enclave with the exception of Danzig and some Silesian frontier towns. Russia was the only one of the three who proclaimed that her share of White Russia, including the towns of Dvinsk, Polotsk, Vitebsk and Mogilev, had originally belonged to the principality of Kiev. She was also the only one who attempted to compensate Poland for her losses by heavy bribery to individuals, enormous subsidies to the state and a constitution which, though it left them with only a shadow of their former liberties, was nevertheless more effective than any they had hitherto possessed. The crown was still elective, the fatal *Liberum Veto* was retained. But by 1775 the royal power was strengthened by the King becoming the head, or rather the president, of a permanent council of government. That Catherine intended to maintain her hold over Poland without any foreign interference was made evident by the fact that Russian troops remained quartered in the country and that the Russian ambassador had the right of entry to the Diet. However humiliating this may have been to the Poles, the permanent Council of State gave a new stability to the country and Stanislaus finally awoke to the responsibilities of his position. The princes momentarily rallied around the crown, and for the next fifteen years Poland enjoyed a brief renaissance under the rule of a scholar-king.

Outwardly, Catherine had triumphed. Even Voltaire was prepared to applaud her actions 'as the only way of restoring order to a country inhabited by Catholic fanatics, the friends of Pope and Padishah'. Catherine, however, appeared reluctant to dwell on a deed of which she may have felt secretly ashamed. She refers to it quite casually in a letter in which she expounds on the prosperity of her Empire. 'In the past months, we have raised the salary of every officer in the army, from a Marshal to an Ensign. . . . We have acquired the picture collection of the late Monsieur Crozat, and we are in possession of a diamond as large as an egg.' She adds, as a postscript, 'Also our possessions have been somewhat extended owing to an agreement we have made with the court of Vienna and of Prussia. There was no other way of guaranteeing our frontiers from incursions of so-called Polish confederates commanded by French officers.' But even Voltaire had difficulty in persuading his friends among *les philosophes* to pardon Semiramis for the partition of Poland.

CHAPTER NINETEEN

The Cossack Revolt

The peace conferences at Foksàny and Bucharest had failed. The Grand Vizer was reported to be amassing an enormous army for the spring campaign. After crossing the Danube, General Roumiantsev had been forced to beat a retreat and the number of deserters was growing at an enormous rate.

Among these deserters was a certain Don Cossack called Emelian Pugachef who, in 1773, gave his name to the first of the great social upheavals which convulsed Russia throughout the following century. It was the first mass rising of the peasants against their landlords who, freed of their obligations to the state, had developed into a useless parasitic society battening on the appalling abuses of 'serf right'. There had been many rebellions in the past – of Cossacks in revolt against the recruiting levy; of the Siberian mineworkers rising against their overseers; of the administered against their administrators. But the 'Pugachefschina' was the first explosion of class warfare in which the landlords were made aware of the hatred their abuses had bred among their slave workers, and in which the Empress was forced to recognize a situation in stark contradiction to the charming picture she had painted to Voltaire of a prosperous peasantry 'with their Sunday chicken in the pot'. The tragedy of Russia was that neither the landlords nor the Empress learned anything from the lesson.

News of a revolt on the eastern confines of the Empire took many weeks to reach St Petersburg. Orenburg, situated on the River Yaik (Ural), was a frontier town beyond which lay the unchartered steppe inhabited by the Yaik Cossacks and the nomad tribe of the Bashkirs. It was the home of the outlaw and the fugitive, and it took the deserter, Emilian Pugachef, two years to reach the Yaik from the war-front on the lower Dnieper. Military police rounding up deserters captured him on the Volga, but he succeeded in escaping down the river and in making his way hundreds of miles eastwards. In the spring of 1773 he suddenly appeared in the Orenburg district at the head of a ragged band of followers, claiming to be the Emperor Peter III who had miraculously escaped from his assassins at Ropscha. Pugachef did not bear the slightest resemblance to the late Emperor, but Peter had reigned too short a time for his features to be familiar to the masses and the impostor had no difficulty in getting both the peasants and the Cossacks to believe him. Peter's mysterious death had made him into a legend. It was said that the nobility had tried to kill him for planning to liberate the serfs. The Empress's earlier attempts to introduce reforms in the Siberian mines were accredited to her husband while she, on the contrary, was held responsible for the cruelty with which the strikes had been suppressed.

Impostors had always flourished in Russia where the simple, credulous people were only too ready to believe in miracles and mysteries. But Pugachef must have possessed a certain element of magnetism and leadership, for in a short while his motley band had grown into an army. Staves had been replaced by guns and a revolt which had begun round a camp-fire in the Urals spread with devastating swiftness across the country. Yaik Cossacks, the majority of them 'old believers' in constant opposition to the Orthodox church and the Imperial government; fugitives from the Siberian mines; nomad tribes at war with the recruiting levy who drove them into barracks like cattle into pens, were among those who enrolled under his banner. By the time that Pugachef's army reached the Volga it had grown to over fifteen thousand. Emerging out of the wilderness into the area of the great estates, they were joined by thousands of peasants who, filled with all the pent-up hatred of the oppressed, turned against their masters. Terrified landlords fled before the onslaught. Those who were unable to get away were murdered in their beds or hanged from the nearest tree. Children were raped and slaughtered in front of their parents; mansions razed to the ground. Such troops as could be spared from the Turkish front were powerless to put a halt to the wave of destruction sweeping through eastern Russia. By the spring of 1774, a small Cossack revolt had become a full-scale revolution, with the landlords fleeing to the safety of the towns, leaving their dependents at the mercy of the pillaging marauders.

Only the Empress kept her head, trying to make light of a situation which was gaining far too much publicity abroad. Writing to Voltaire in January 1774, she refers in jest to the 'Marquis de Pugachef, who is giving her a little trouble in the Urals.' Voltaire appears to have been sufficiently taken in by the lightness of her tone to inform his friend D'Alembert that '*Cateau* is not in the least embarrassed by this new husband who has turned up in the province of Orenburg'. But the man she dismissed as a Cossack highwayman was giving Catherine many a sleepless night, and by spring she was forced to admit 'that for the past six weeks I have been obliged to give my undivided attention to the affair'. One of her ablest generals was recalled from the front to put an end to the rebellion, but though Bibikof defeated the rebels on three successive occasions, Pugachef always succeeded in evading capture and escaping to the Urals to form yet another army. It was only in the late summer of 1774, when a series of massive Russian victories on the Turkish front forced the Sultan to agree to peace, that the Pugachefschina was finally suppressed.

Pugachef was about to march on Moscow when he received the news of the Turkish surrender, and for once he appears to have lost his initiative and boldness. He changed his course and struck southwards down the Volga; a fatal move, for the élite of the Russian armies under General Souvarov were advancing eastwards from the front. Panic spread among the ill-armed and ill-disciplined peasants who deserted in droves, but Pugachef fought on, braver than the man he sought to impersonate, till in the end he was betrayed by some of his own lieutenants who, in return for the promise of a free pardon, handed him over bound in chains to advance Russian units on the Yaik. The pseudo-Emperor was sent to Moscow in an iron cage where he was tried and publicly executed, and the city saw the unedifying spectacle of a nobility who regarded themselves as civilized, assisting and gloating over his execution.

Catherine displayed an admirable *sang-froid* both during and after the rebellion. Her common-sense counselled moderation and she kept urging the authorities to treat the rebels with humanity and to show clemency to all except the ring-leaders. She even went so far as to prohibit the use of torture at Pugachef's trial. Such were her wishes, but it was difficult even for an autocrat to enforce her will in towns and districts two thousand miles away. Only a small minority among the nobility shared the convictions of the Empress who, in writing to her Minister of Justice, stressed the fact that 'unless some steps are taken to alleviate a situation which is intolerable for the human race, then sooner or later they will take the step themselves'. But for all these noble sentiments, Catherine never took the first step towards the enfranchisement of her serfs. On the contrary, she allowed the abuses of the landlords to continue, making no effort to put a curb on the savagery with which they wreaked vengeance on their defenceless peasants, many of whom had never joined in the rising. Travellers to Russia in these years were sickened by the spectacle of venerable, grey-bearded men being publicly flogged and young girls openly sold in the market places, though an edict signed by the Empress Elisabeth had expressly forbidden 'the public sale of souls'.

Could Catherine have put an end to the abuses without endangering her throne is a question which to this day remains unanswered. The moment was propitious for reform. The nobility, shaken and demoralized, in fear for their future, had rallied round the crown. For once it was they who needed the Empress, rather than the Empress needing them. When visiting Moscow for the first time after the rebellion Catherine received an ovation such as she had never had before. The conclusion of a victorious war had made her the idol of the army. In Nikita Panin she had a liberal minister who, from the first day of her reign, had advocated reforms. But how many Panins were to be found in Tver or Kiev or Nishni-Novgorod? How many magistrates were sufficiently brave to defy the power of the local landlord? To see that her reforms were carried out would mean changing her whole mode of life; moving her seat of government back to Moscow, making her home in the Kremlin instead of the Winter Palace and exposing herself to the hatred and opposition of the old Boyar families if she attempted to divest them of one iota of their privileges.

She belonged to St Petersburg, Peter's city which she had made into her own, where the glories of an Imperial residence vied with the bustle of a thriving commercial port; where from her palace windows she could see the tall masts of foreign ships which carried the riches of Russia to the other side of the world. The timber and the flax, the hemp and the raw hides which, with the coming of spring, came down the great rivers, through the canals which intersected the country and out into the Neva delta, were all the produce of serf labour. And who was she to challenge the system, tolerated and accepted by Peter the Great? So the Empress evaded the issue and thereby lost her real claim to greatness. All memories of Pugachef's rebellion were stamped out. The Yaik was renamed the Ural. Many administrative reforms were carried out during Catherine's reign. There was improvement in many fields, particularly in education and hygiene, but the *Nakaz*, which embodied all the ideals and aspirations of her youth, became no more than a propaganda pamphlet to impress her liberal friends abroad. From now on she concentrated on what she believed to be Russia's more immediate interests, the interests she had always had most at heart and which were dedicated to the glory and expansion of her Empire.

The cataclysms which had convulsed the country in the past years, the wars and rebellions on the Dnieper and the Volga, had had little effect on the citizens of St Petersburg. The town had never been so crowded, nor the court so brilliant as in the summer of 1773, when it was preparing for the marriage of the nineteen-year-old Tzarevitch. Following a time-honoured tradition, the Empress had selected a suitable bride from among a list of eligible German princesses, hoping as Elisabeth had once hoped that a healthy young wife would produce a satisfactory heir for her somewhat unsatisfactory son. King Frederick was again consulted on the choice, with the result that the Dowager Princess of Hesse-Darmstadt and her three young daughters were invited to St Petersburg in the autumn of 1773. The visit was a success. The Empress professed to be delighted with her guests, in particular with the eldest daughter, the Princess Wilhelmine, a girl after her own heart, solid and healthy, not very pretty, well-educated but not too intelligent and apparently possessed of a docile character. There appeared to be no danger of the young Princess ever attempting to rival her mother-in-law and, although the family of Hesse-Darmstadt was far more illustrious than that of Anhalt-Zerbst, it was neither wealthy nor of political importance, and the young Princess's wardrobe was almost as sparse as her own had been on her first arrival in Russia. Both she and her sisters benefited from the Empress's generosity. Catherine was particularly gratified to see that her shy and moody son was attracted at first sight to his plump, spotty little bride, and for once was ready to fall in with her wishes. Princess Wilhelmine, soon to become the Grand Duchess Natalia Alexievna, appears to have had certain qualities unsuspected by her future mother-in-law, for she not only succeeded in arousing passion in her fiancé, but also in his closest friend, the handsome Andrew Razumovsky, a young naval officer who had escorted the Princesses on the boat from Lubeck. By the time she arrived in Russia, the little Princess, from whom Catherine felt there was nothing to fear, was already in the throes of a violent love-affair with Razumovsky and was displaying a remarkable talent for intrigue.

Prince Orlov was chosen to act as host to the Princesses on their first arrival in Russia, a curious choice in view of the Grand Duke's detestation of his mother's former lover. The Prince had returned to St Petersburg in the early summer where he was welcomed by Catherine as an old and valued friend and reinstated in all his former appointments. The courtiers kept wondering when he would be returning to his old quarters in the Winter Palace. But in private the Empress confided to a friend:

I have suffered for over eleven years. I now wish to live according to my fancy and inclination in complete independence. As to Prince Orlov, he can do whatever is agreeable to him. He can drink, hunt, take mistresses. He may return to his palaces, for he is entirely free to use them again. If he behaves well, he will do honour to himself. If he behaves badly, he will cover himself with shame. But I will never forget my obligation to the Orlov family and I will always protect them, for they can still be of use to me.

In this year of her son's majority, it was more vital than ever for Catherine to have loyal and devoted men around her. Panin was not loyal, but for the moment there was no one sufficiently able to replace him. And the Orlovs were the only people she could rely on to protect her from his intrigues. Both factions had to be humoured and only someone with Catherine's powers of dissimulation could have succeeded in placating them both. Vassilchikof, the creature of Panin, remained the official favourite, though by now the Empress openly admitted that 'he bored her to tears'. Her thoughts were going more and more towards Potemkin who was now a general fighting in Roumiantsev's army on the Danube. Her interest in this strange, irrational being, who on his last visit to St Petersburg had spoken of retiring to a monastery and at the same time had had the temerity openly to declare his passion for her, was gradually becoming an obsession. Sensing a danger for the future, the angry reactions of the Orlovs, Catherine went out of her way to publicly honour the Prince by asking him to act as host at Gatchina to the Landgrävine of Hesse and her daughters.

The beauty of Gatchina in the early autumn, a palace as magnificent as any of the Imperial residences, the splendour of Orlov's reception at which five hundred guests were served off Sèvres porcelain and gold plate and every female guest was presented with a jewelled favour, must have provided a curious contrast to the elegant parsimony of Berlin, where the Princesses had stopped on their way to receive their last instructions from the King. Having helped to arrange the match, Frederick exhorted his protégées always to remember their German origin, a fact which Sophia of Anhalt-Zerbst had been all too ready to forget.

On meeting the Empress for the first time, the Hessian Princesses were surprised to see her dressed in the Russian rather than the European fashion, with a long, sleeveless waistcoat worn over a pleated lawn chemise – a style which was at once dignified and becoming. On this occasion, the gown was embroidered with gold thread and pearls and the buttons were of enormous diamonds, while pearls and emeralds studded the cap she wore on her lightly powdered curls. At forty-four, Catherine could still give the illusion of a beauty she had never really possessed. In the eyes of her future daughter-in-law, she appeared in the light of a benevolent fairy godmother who held the key to a new and wonderful world. But not many months were to pass before the Grand Duchess Natalia Alexievna became aware of the steely glint behind those smiling eyes.

The nervous young bridegroom was completely overshadowed by his mother and Prince Orlov, who wore the magnificent diamond-embroidered coat which had failed to impress the Sultan's delegates, but which entranced both the Landgrävine and her daughters, none of whom had ever seen anyone so handsome. Partly in order to irritate the Empress, who had insisted on having Vassilchikof in attendance, and partly to assert his male predominance, Orlov started to flirt with the youngest of the Princesses who, according to an eye witness, responded to his advances 'with considerable vivacity'. A week later, the Prussian minister was already reporting to his master, 'the extraordinary attentions which Prince Orlov pays the Landgrävine and the freedom of manner with which he treats the Princesses, especially the youngest one, leads one to wonder whether this ambitious man has plans for a royal marriage'.

Orlov had returned to St Petersburg to find that his young cousin had left with her parents for their country estates near Moscow and that there was little hope of seeing her for several years. The Empress continued to honour him in public, but no longer showed any wish to see him in private and, in spite of no longer loving her as a woman, he missed the stimulation of her company, the charm of her conversation. He was bored, lonely and at odds with himself and may well have toyed with the idea of a brilliant marriage which would have made of him the

[226]

brother-in-law to the heir-apparent. But the Empress soon put an end to these pretensions by hurrying on the wedding and despatching the Landgrävine and her younger daughters back to Germany as soon as the festivities were over.

Travelling in the Hessian suite was a man who was destined to become Catherine's lifelong friend and correspondent, and in many ways closer to her than any of her lovers. Frederick Melchior Grimm was a gallicized German who began his career as tutor to a German princeling before he settled in Paris and won fame as the author of the celebrated *Correspondances Littéraires*, which were circulated round the various German courts. Grimm was not so much a literary figure as a delightful gossip, and his monthly letters dealt with topical subjects from politics to the arts, giving the latest news from Paris and describing the leading personalities of the day. Gradually these letters, to which his correspondents subscribed a certain sum, had become so popular that even sovereigns were eager to be included among his correspondents, the Empress Catherine paying him as much as fifteen thousand roubles a year, the King of Poland four hundred thalers and King Frederick of Prussia putting his name on the list without subscribing a pfennig.

Catherine had already been corresponding with Grimm for nearly nine years when she now met him for the first time and found him cultured, witty and urbane and, for all his snobbishness, a very endearing person. Before long, she detached him from his other allegiances and made him into her general factotum in Paris, teasing, nagging, worrying and enchanting him in turn; confounding him with the variety of her moods; her orders and counter-orders, her extravagances which alternated with sudden bouts of economy. He became what she called her '*souffre douleur*' to whom she confided whatever passed through her head, whom she made no attempt to impress in the way she tried to impress Voltaire. And the very spontaneity of her letters make them so very much better reading than the laboured wit and epigrams of her letters to the 'Sage of Ferney'. She was a prolific correspondent for she enjoyed writing and said that the sight of a new quill always made her fingers itch. Such talent as she possessed comes out in her letters, for as an author she was versatile rather than gifted. Her inspirations covered a vast field from political treatises to satirical comedies, from historical summaries to children's fairy-tales. She even attempted an epic drama called *Oleg*, a cumbersome and tedious piece of rhetoric which even ballets and transformation scenes could not prevent from being a theatrical disaster. But her letters to Grimm, 'which were not intended for the *Nachwelt*', make delightful reading. They are random thoughts and ideas jotted down on paper without any attempt at style or spelling – what Grimm, much to her amusement, described as an '*olla potride espagnole*' (a Spanish casserole).

Her letters are as vivid and uninhibited today as when they were first written, whether she is referring to her pet greyhounds or her new lover, boasting of her latest acquisition or complaining of the moods of a Falconet, the pretensions of a Clerisseau. Seeing how quickly she tired of her enthusiasms and how intolerant she was of any form of criticism, Grimm was forced to admit 'that even a Michelangelo would not have lasted a week at the Russian court'. She would haggle over the price of an exquisite Greuze, yet pay Madame Geoffrin double the price they were worth for two Van Loos. She would complain she had no more money to spend on works of art, and a few days later would be commissioning yet another palace from Rinaldi. She could not bear to hear of an important collection coming up for sale which might fall into other hands than her own, and at the eleventh hour her agent would be told to secure it at any price.

Supple and accommodating, eager to please, Grimm succeeded in winning and retaining her gratitude and esteem. But his friend, Denis Diderot, who arrived in St Petersburg in the same autumn of 1773, proved himself less accommodating and less of a courtier. It had been hard for the sexagenarian philosopher to tear himself away from Paris and a beloved circle of friends to undertake the long and arduous journey to Russia in order to pay homage to his benefactress. Referring to his departure in a letter to the Abbé Galiani, Madame D'Epinay comments 'What a curious child is our philosopher! On the day of his departure, he seemed almost astonished at having to leave and terrified of travelling further than Le Grandval. He was so unhappy when he had to pack his bags.'

The Empress, who was eagerly awaiting Diderot's arrival, did all in her power to facilitate his journey. Dimitri Galitzine, who had been transferred from Paris to the Netherlands, gave him hospitality at The Hague, where he felt so much at home among the Dutch philosophers that he stayed on for nearly three months, having apparently forgotten the object of his journey, till one of the Naryshkins on his way back to Russia offered him a place in his travelling coach. Diderot's arrival in Russia was somewhat of an anti-climax. He had hoped to lodge with his old friend Falconet. But the nervous and irascible sculptor was already put out by the unexpected and unwanted arrival of his son. His embarrassment at having to refuse hospitality to one of his oldest friends was misconstrued as coldness. Hotels and lodging-houses were crowded for the royal wedding and Diderot would have had difficulty in finding a bed, had not Alexis Naryshkin invited him to be his guest for the duration of his visit.

The Empress, who had been expecting him in the summer, was too taken up with court festivities to receive him during the first days. He was unable to attend the wedding as his baggage was still in customs; so he spent his first week in St Petersburg wandering through the streets and noting the splendours and miseries of Catherine's capital. Many of the questions and lengthy memoranda with which he was later to bombard the Empress were inspired by these walks. Autumn in St Petersburg is the most unpleasant season of the year, when the cold winds from the Baltic rip the last leaves from the trees and the rains turn the ill-paved roads into rivers of mud. Diderot's visit coincided with the first snowfall when the drosky drivers waiting for their fares huddled for warmth round the fires in the public shelters, and the docks and wharves were crowded with foreign ships, loading up their cargoes before the freezing of the Neva.

Diderot noted the curious anomalies of the town where the houses of the nobility and of the wealthy merchants, built of brick and stone, were as luxurious as any in the Faubourg St Germain, yet only a stone's throw away from these elegant façades were the miserable hovels of the original Finnish settlers. Magnificent granite quays were being built along the Neva, but nothing had been done to improve the streets so that a nobleman's coach-and-six driving along the Millonaya sent the mud-bespattered pedestrians tumbling into the gutter.

The whole town was *en fête* for the royal wedding. Church bells pealed all day and holy ikons were paraded in procession through the streets. Beer and *kvas* and hot meat pies were being distributed free to the populace; there were public fairgrounds with Punch and Judy shows, shuttle alleys and toboggan hills (the famous '*montagnes russes*') in the gardens behind the Summer Palace and on the Grand Duke's island of Kemanie Ostrov, while at night a magnificent show of fireworks blazed and spluttered above the fortress of Peter and Paul.

Diderot saw St Petersburg in the light of a stage setting rather than as a town and later complained that what he had seen was not the real Russia, 'but a confused mass of palaces and hovels, of *grands seigneurs* surrounded by peasants and purveyors'. He regretted not having visited Moscow, but he had suffered so much on the appalling journey from Mittau that he could not bear the idea of travelling another four hundred miles along roads which were no more than wooden logs laid transversely and covered with a layer of loose, wet soil. He was compensated for his colds and colics by the charm and condescension of the Empress who, once the festivities were over, gave her full attention to her illustrious guest.

Diderot had arrived at a very propitious moment when Catherine had plenty of time on hand. Vassilchikof had become a bore and Potemkin was still absent on the Turkish front. To the astonishment and jealousy of her entourage, she dedicated two hours a day to private interviews with this bourgeois Frenchman, a privilege she would never have extended to any Russian intellectual. She allowed him to question her on every imaginable subject ranging from religious toleration to the administration of her Empire. He had prepared sixty-five memoranda on political, social, legal and economic matters and one marvels at the patience with which Catherine listened to what were partly questionnaires and partly lectures, delivered in the hectoring tone of a somewhat arrogant schoolmaster. Diderot's ambition was to convert her entirely to the doctrines of enlightenment, and in the beginning she professed to be entranced by his integrity and simplicity, wishing 'that all men had hearts of his stamp'. Melchior Grimm wrote home to one of his Parisian friends, 'With the Empress, Diderot is just as odd, just as original and just as much Diderot as with you. He takes her hand as he takes yours; he shakes her arm as he shakes yours; he sits down at her side as he sits down by you, though here he has to obey sovereign orders and does not seat himself opposite Her Majesty unless so bidden.'

At times Diderot was so carried away by his eloquence that he forgot the rules of protocol, calling the Empress 'My good woman' and slapping her on the knee. We hear of Catherine complaining 'of having her thighs and arms bruised black and blue through the violence of his gesticulations and being obliged to place a table between them, so as to protect her limbs'. All went well till the French *chargé d'affaires*, Durand, tried to take advantage of Diderot's position at the Russian court by reminding him that it was his duty as a Frenchman to try and improve relations between France and Russia and, if possible, 'to efface the prejudices the Empress has against us'. Diderot did his best to resist these demands, but was finally persuaded to present the Empress with a document containing proposals for peace with Turkey in which the French government was prepared to act as mediator. He apologized to Catherine for acting in a matter completely out of his sphere and excused himself on the grounds that a refusal might land him in the Bastille on his return to France. Catherine forgave the impropriety of his behaviour on condition that he reported faithfully to Monsieur Durand the use she made of his paper, which she promptly threw into the fire.

Diderot remained in favour, his plain and somewhat shabby clothes striking an incongruous note at the court galas. He refused to accept rich brocades or sable pelisses and was indifferent to the mockery of her courtiers, saying 'I court only the favour of the lady of the house and scarcely care about the servants'. Catherine continued to praise him in public. She called him '*un homme extraordinaire*', a word which has many interpretations, but by December she was beginning to tire of his tactlessness and boorishness. She did not appreciate him telling her that he disapproved of the partition of Poland, a subject on which she was particularly sensitive. Nor did she enjoy his condemnation of despotic governments. Even his praise which was as fulsome as that of any other courtier, telling her 'that she had the soul of Brutus and the charms of Cleopatra', could not compensate for his continual criticism.

Several years later, when she was discussing Diderot with the Count de Ségur, she told the ambassador,

I frequently had long conversations with him but with more curiosity than profit. Had I placed faith in him, every institution in my Empire would have been overturned and all would have been changed for the purpose of substituting some impractical theories.

However, I listened more than I talked. Anyone being present would have supposed him to be the commanding pedagogue and myself the humble scholar. Probably he was of that opinion himself, for after some time, finding that he had not wrought in my government any of the great innovations he had advised, he exhibited his surprise by a sort of haughty discontent. Then speaking to him freely, I said: 'Monsieur Diderot, I have listened with the greatest pleasure to all that your brilliant genius has inspired you with, but all your grand principles which will make fine books, will make sad work in actual practice. You forget in all your plans for reformation the differences between our two positions. You work only upon paper which submits to everything and opposes no obstacles either to your imagination or to your pen, whereas I, poor Empress, I work upon human nature which is irascible and easily offended.' From that moment, he spoke to me only on literary subjects and politics disappeared from our conversation.

By December, the Empress had too many problems on her hands to dedicate much time to her literary conversations. Rebellion was spreading in eastern Russia, peace with Turkey was still unsigned. What she needed was not a garrulous philosopher but a virile, ambitious man who would restore her self-confidence both as an Empress and as a woman. Diderot stayed on in Russia for another three months, still treated as an honoured guest but no longer stimulated by the charm of

Catherine's company. He notes in his memorandum that the last of their discussions took place on 6 December 1773. Was it by coincidence that, on the previous day, the Empress sat down to write in her own hand a letter summoning General Potemkin back to St Petersburg?

CHAPTER TWENTY

The Cornet in the Guards

The Empress's letter was calculated to arouse the hopes of a man who had been awaiting his opportunity for over eleven years. Gregory Potemkin had been given many signs of his sovereign's growing interest. His rapid promotion in the army, rising in a few years from the grade of captain to that of lieutenant-general; the warm welcome he received whenever he appeared at court, spurred his ambition and, on his last visit to St Petersburg, he had the temerity to stake his whole future by making the Empress an open declaration of his passion. Catherine had not attempted to rebuke him. On the contrary, she had been so touched and pleased that she had given him permission to correspond with her directly, a favour which was usually only accorded to top-ranking generals or field-marshals.

Potemkin was on the Danubian front, laying siege to the town of Silistria in the last victorious campaign of 1774, when he received the Empress's letter which read:

My Lieutenant-General and Chevalier, you are probably so taken up with gazing at Silistria that you have not the time to read letters, and though I do not yet know as to whether your bombardment has been successful, I am nevertheless convinced that everything you undertake can be ascribed to your devotion to me personally and your beloved fatherland in general. But since for my part I am most anxious to preserve zealous, courageous, intelligent and skilful men, I beg of you not to expose yourself to danger. You will perhaps ask me to what purpose was this letter written, to which I would reply: 'For the purpose of the confirmation of my feelings about you', for I am always your very well-wishing, Catherine.

In spite of the ambiguity of the wording, Catherine's letter meant only one thing to Potemkin – that Vassilchikof was on the way out, and that he had been chosen as the heir-apparent. Within two weeks he was back in St Petersburg where he was disappointed to find that Vassilchikof had not yet been dismissed, though according to court gossip his fall was imminent. The Empress paid no attention to his requests, refused him all honours and decorations and, in his own words, 'treated him like a kept woman'.

Gregory Potemkin wasted no time in joining the Empress at Tzarskoye Selo and demanding a private audience, where Catherine appears to have been so carried away by his impassioned entreaties that she confessed her own feelings but begged him to be patient till 'a certain boring individual had been honourably dismissed'. Potemkin was now assured of a brilliant future and, for the next few weeks, he was constantly at court, radiating gaiety and charm, the life and soul of entertainments both at Tzarskoye Selo and the Hermitage. The Empress recovered her *joie de vivre* in the delight of his company and Vassilchikof looked even sulkier than before.

Not only Vassilchikof, but all the various factions round the throne: the Grand Duke's party headed by Panin, the Orlovs, the Tchernichevs and Vorontsovs, all of whom detested one another, viewed with a growing disquiet the meteoric rise of the young general whom the courtiers and foreign ambassadors already looked upon as the future favourite. The Orlovs were being gracious and condescending, but they had recognized a dangerous element in Potemkin from the days when he scored his first social successes at the Hermitage, and they knew there would be no dislodging him once he was installed in the palace. There is a story told how, one day, when the Prince was leaving the palace, he met Potemkin on the stairs, who asked him 'whether there was any news at court', to which he replied 'Nothing very much, except that you are coming up the stairs and I am going down', and passed on without saying another word.

Yet still the Empress hesitated as if she sensed the danger of allowing herself to fall under the spell of a man who, in a letter to Grimm, she described as being 'the greatest, the most original and the most amusing eccentric of this iron age'. Having loved the handsomest man in Russia, she had now succumbed to the fascination of a young officer on whom the loss of an eye had had such a painful effect that he completely neglected his appearance. His slim, supple figure had become so massive and disproportionate as to be almost grotesque. The face had coarsened and although the mouth was still delicate and sensual, the nose was broad and fleshy and the cavity of the left eye, over which he usually scorned to wear a patch, rendered 'his countenance far from engaging'. But he had so much animal magnetism that he had an almost hypnotic power over women; from the Empress to the youngest and most beautiful of his mistresses, all regarded him as the best looking and most seductive of men.

If Catherine hesitated, it was not because she was frightened of falling in love with him, a condition which she thrived on and which was as necessary to her as eating and drinking, but because she sensed in him a measureless ambition which would drive him on until he succeeded in dominating both her and the Empire. The Russian people had accepted the Orlovs as the corner-stone of her throne. They had even accepted Vassilchikof, who was descended from a family older than the Romanovs. But would they tolerate a succession of lovers? She was susceptible to public opinion both at home and abroad. Could she impose on the world this moody, eccentric Ukrainian whose father was a provincial noble and whose mother, upon her marriage, was discovered a bigamist? Fortunately, the lawful wife had been sufficiently obliging to retire into a convent, thereby enabling the future 'Prince of Tauris' to be born in holy wedlock. Potemkin's moods and eccentricities, his jealousy which was almost insane and did not even spare the Empress, were inherited from his father who, luckily for his family, died when his son was only seven, leaving a young wife with five children to educate.

Daria Potemkin, however, was a personality in her own right, who was loved and respected by her neighbours, and both in education and in culture her son had a far greater claim to the Empress's attention than the majority of her ignorant and superficial courtiers. Poverty prevented his mother from engaging one of those foreign tutors who, with a few notable exceptions, exercised such a pernicious influence on the young Russian nobility. He was taught to read by the village deacon, a simple and holy man with a beautiful singing voice, who awoke in him a natural love of music and to whom he showed a touching devotion in later life. At six years old, he was sent to Moscow and placed in the charge of his godfather, a high-ranking civil servant, who brought him up as his own son and encouraged an early interest in languages and theology. He was one of the most brilliant scholars at Moscow University, where he was rewarded with a gold medal for his theological treatises, and he appeared to be destined for the priesthood when his character began to betray that strange ambivalence which made of him at once the most provoking and the most tortured of human beings.

Potemkin was one of the six outstanding students whom the Director of the University, Ivan Shuvalov, took with him to St Petersburg to be presented to the Empress Elisabeth. But his first glimpse of the splendour of the court had such a demoralizing effect on the young man that he lost all interest in his studies and enlisted as a trooper in the Horse Guards – the custom of the time allowing one to be both a soldier in the Guards and a theological student. At sixteen, the young guardsman informed his mother that he would either be a minister or a bishop. 'I will start with a military career. If I am not successful, I shall take to commanding priests.' But the ambitions aroused in St Petersburg had spoiled him for the contemplative life. He neglected his work, never attended a lecture and ended by being ignominiously dismissed from the university

Back in St Petersburg, Potemkin rejoined his regiment and threw himself wholeheartedly into the dissipations of army life. But even now he was not satisfied. There were times when theology fascinated him more than military science, when he was happier discussing religious matters with the army chaplain than drinking and whoring with his fellow subalterns. Pride and lust, humility and mysticism were continually at war in his strange, complex character, and dominating all was the one fixed idea which had obsessed him from that June morning of

1762 when, as a young cornet in the Horse Guards, he had stepped out of the ranks to present the newly acclaimed Empress with a sword knot. Many years later, he charmed his royal mistress with the sentimental verses he had written on that occasion.

> As soon as I beheld you, I thought of you alone.
> Your lovely eyes captivated me, yet I trembled to say I loved.
> O Heavens! the torture to love one to whom I dare not declare it –
> One who can never be mine.
> Cruel Gods! Why did you bestow on her such charms,
> Why did you exalt her so high?
> Why did you make me love her and her alone?
> She whose sacred name can never pass my lips,
> Whose charming image will never quit my heart.

Fame did not come to him so swiftly as to the Orlovs. Twelve years had to elapse between the summer's day of 1762, when Catherine added in her own hand the name of Cornet Potemkin to the list of the young subalterns to be promoted for their services in the *coup d'état*, and the winter's morning of 1774, when her letter reached the Silistrian camp recalling Lieutenant-General Potemkin to St Petersburg. In the intervening years he had known vicissitudes, frustration and despair. The loss of his eye and the tragic deterioration of his physique convinced him that he had lost all hope of ever winning the Empress's affection. He crept into his lair like a wounded beast, shutting the door on his former friends, and was apparently forgotten by the world till the day when the Empress, driving past his house, sent in an equerry to enquire after his health and invite him back to court. Her sympathy and kindness in making no allusion to his changed appearance helped to restore his self-confidence. But she made no attempt to retain him when he volunteered for service on the eastern front, and throughout the war she let it be believed that his rapid promotion was due only to the recommendations of General Roumiantsev.

It is difficult to know when Catherine realized that she had fallen in love with Potemkin. She was at first amused, then fascinated, and finally enthralled. She found him mystifying, exasperating, insufferable and wholly delightful, and from the beginning she knew that all other encumbrances would have to be swept aside, all other attachments broken, before his over-lifesize figure would be allowed to dominate the stage. While hesitating for the last time, she ran the risk of losing him. He had had enough of her procrastinations and eternal promises and in one of his sudden, unaccountable moods, which she later learned to recognize and fear, he disappeared from court without either an excuse or an explanation. Whether it was a clever move to force her hand, or whether he was really so ardently in love that he could no longer stand the strain, and one is inclined to believe the former, his retirement to the monastery of Alexander Nevsky won the Empress's total and abject surrender. His strange behaviour at the monastery raised doubts of his sanity. Religious exultation alternated with fits of depression, when he would prostrate himself in tears before the ikon of St Catherine. The Empress doubted his sincerity, for she knew him to be as consummate an actor as herself, but she did not dare to question his motives and thereby run the risk of losing a lover who promised to be more stimulating and exciting than any she had hitherto experienced. In matters of this kind, she usually acted on the advice of her friend and confidante, Countess Prascovia Bruce, a woman of infinite tact and resource, married to a general of Scottish descent who was honourably employed as governor in the provinces while his wife rendered her mistress indispensable services in the capital.

The Countess's visit to Potemkin's cell in the monastery of Alexander Nevsky was the first of a series of confidential missions in which her discretion was tested to the utmost. The various young guardsmen who, in latter years, were to attract the Empress's attention, were all tested and approved by Prascovia Bruce before they were admitted to the royal bed. But there was no question of Potemkin ever being submitted to such a test. For Catherine, now in her forties, was as whole-heartedly and as naïvely in love as a young girl. The message transmitted by the Countess promised Potemkin 'the highest of favours' if he would only return to court, and the suitor who was said to be suffering from the pangs of unrequited love was sufficiently in control of his emotions to dictate his terms to her.

If my services justify Her Imperial Majesty's attention, and my sovereign's generosity and favours towards me are not exhausted, then I implore her to dispel all doubts of my unworthiness by appointing me as her personal Adjutant-General. *This cannot offend anybody*, and I will consider it the height of my happiness, all the more so as being under Her Majesty's special protection, I would then have the honour of receiving her wise orders and, by studying them, become more capable of serving both Her Imperial Majesty and the beloved fatherland.

It was the letter of a man in complete command of the situation who had no hesitation in asking for the appointment he wanted, and which far from giving *no offence* was bound to scandalize and infuriate both the government and the court. The post of personal adjutant was considered to be the prerogative of the reigning favourite, and Catherine gladly granted his request. It was only the first of many honours. A week later he was appointed Lieutenant-General of the Preobrajensky Regiment, of which the Empress was Colonel-in-Chief, and it became clear to all that a new favourite had arrived who would soon make them regret the amiable and modest Vassilchikof. Potemkin's energy was dynamic and before long the Empress was allowing him to transmit orders to her ministers. 'Tell Panin to make Vassilchikof go somewhere for a cure, as he greatly embarrasses me and at the same time complains of pains in the chest. After his cure, we will send him somewhere as ambassador, somewhere where there is not too much work.' But Vassilchikof showed no wish to serve his country abroad. Generously pensioned and laden with presents, he retired to Moscow, gradually turning into one of those disgruntled, elderly gentlemen who have been disgraced, forgotten or ignored by their sovereign.

Having waited so long, both the Empress and Potemkin felt they had no more time to waste. Foreign ambassadors were stunned by the rapidity of events, the manner in which the new favourite was intruding into every branch of public life. Potemkin had only been in attendance for a few weeks before the British envoy, Sir Robert Gunning, was writing to his chief at the Foreign Office:

Vassilchikof, whose understanding was too limited to admit to having any influence in affairs or of sharing his mistress's confidence, is now succeeded by a man who bids fair to possessing them both in a most surprising degree. . . . When I acquaint your Lordship that the Empress's choice is equally disapproved of by the Grand Duke's party and the Orlovs, you will not wonder that it should occasion, as it has done, a very genuine surprise and even consternation.

Gunning does not appear to have been favourably impressed either by Potemkin's appearance or his character. He reported that 'he was universally detested in the army and a notorious profligate, but nevertheless appeared to have a great knowledge of mankind and more discrimination than his countrymen generally possessed. He was a master at the art of intrigue and as supple and as cunning as the best of them.' The ambassador, who had a poor opinion of Catherine's ministers, was inclined to believe that 'Potemkin had every chance of succeeding and that, given the known inactivity of those with whom he would have to come into contact, he had every hope of rising to the heights to which his boundless ambition might aspire.'

Everyone was not so perspicacious for, when he chose, Potemkin could be as modest and unassuming as any young lieutenant. Acting on the Empress's advice, he paid court to the Grand Duke and Panin. The minister, who had begun by warning Catherine of the danger of heaping honours on such a man who had already had more than his just reward, ended in tacitly accepting a situation which was only beneficial to him in so far as it was damaging to the Orlovs. The name of the new favourite was on everybody's lips. Letters between St Petersburg and Moscow told of little else. The Empress was said to be bewitched by this sinister 'Cyclops', in spite of his dirty and unkempt appearance and repulsive habit of biting his nails to the quick. Others, and they were mostly women, wrote of his courteous manners, his delightful voice and agreeable wit. Judging by the Empress's appreciation of his talents, they advised their husbands that 'in future it might be wise to address themselves to Potemkin'.

Was the new favourite as much in love as he and his friends had led the Empress to believe? 'To think of all the years in which you sought the path which would lead to me, and that I never noticed it,' wrote Catherine in one of her first love letters. But unfortunately for her he was one of those dreamers for whom the unattainable has charms which possession can never equal. For years he had carried in his heart an image of a young woman in a green uniform and a sable bonnet crowned with oak leaves, who had turned a laughing face towards the sun as if she was challenging the world. Now that he had finally stormed the last defences and found a middle-aged woman, humbly and abjectly in love, there may have been a certain disillusion underlying the triumph, a certain satiety at having received too much. She admired him – she adored him – she idealized him – she loved him better than herself and craved him all hours of the day. We read these effusions in the letters she wrote to him during that first enchanted spring of 1774 – notes which were penned in the early hours of the morning only a short while after he had left her bed. 'Oh, Monsieur Potemkin! By what sorcery have you managed to turn a head which is generally regarded as one of the best in Europe.' The great Catherine admitted to herself that she had reverted to Sophia of Anhalt-Zerbst, the little Pomeranian Princess who was giddily and irresponsibly in love. But for the time being, she was so ecstatically happy that she was prepared to throw all pride and dignity to the winds. 'We remain together for hours on end without a shadow of boredom, and it is always with reluctance that I leave you. I forget the whole world when I am with you. There is something extraordinary that words cannot express, for the alphabet is too short and the letters are too few.'

The letters are written partly in French, partly in Russian, and her vocabulary of endearments is almost inexhaustible, ranging from the lyrically poetical to the frankly absurd. The massive giant was called 'my little pigeon', 'my golden pheasant', 'my kitten', 'my little father', 'my dear little heart'. Nothing made her laugh so much as when he teased her, for at times he could be 'as amusing as the very devil'. He would pretend that the little coat which she was knitting for her favourite greyhound was really for him and he would strut across the room stretching the tiny piece of wool across his large stomach and she literally cried with laughter. Both were born comedians, but whereas she was versed in the art of dissimulating, he delighted in exaggerating his faults. Hard years of apprenticeship had taught Catherine to control her temper and present a smiling face in public, whereas he, on the contrary, was totally undisciplined and indulged in histrionics and wild rages for the most trivial reason. He was madly jealous, not only of her present but of her past. He would accuse her of lovers she had never had and even dared to insult her as a whore.

In order to soothe this distraught lover, we find the Empress going to the trouble of annotating the list of his predecessors,

Well, my sir hero. After this confession, may I hope to be forgiven for my sins. You will see you are not one of fifteen but of one third of the number. The first of them [Saltykof] happened from compulsion and the fourth from despair which cannot be put down to indulgence. As for the other three, God knows it was not due to debauchery for which I have no inclination. If as a young woman I had had a husband I could have loved, I would have remained for ever faithful to him. My trouble is that my heart cannot rest content even for an hour without love.

This letter shows her in all her grandeur and all her weakness. It was a dangerous document to put in the hands of a man whose ambition was to dominate her entirely. He always remained conscious of the gulf which divided them, but here again he was totally inconsequential. He would stress their intimacy in front of the court to the lengths of appearing at her *levée* with naked feet, wearing a dirty dressing-gown. But there is no trace of familiarity in the notes which he addressed to his beloved sovereign, or to 'Matouchka' (little mother). The messenger who brought her letters had to deliver them on his knees and he always made the sign of the cross before opening the envelope.

For all his extravagances and dissipation, Potemkin's one purpose in life was directed to serving his Empress and his fatherland. He gave Catherine the whole-hearted devotion which she craved, and wooed her with an intensity which consumed them both. She personified for him 'the Mother of all the Russias', the 'Supreme Deity'. The woman he subjected to his will, whom he debauched and finally tired of, was only a small part of the sovereign he worshipped to the last day of his life. Many lovers were to succeed him in Catherine's bed, but eighteen years later, on receiving the news of his death, we find her writing to Grimm, 'My grief is so great that you cannot imagine it. My pupil, my friend and practically my idol, Prince Potemkin of Tauris has died. . . . Who can I rely on now?

CHAPTER TWENTY-ONE

'Un si joli paix'

1774 to 1775 was a year of triumph. The long and costly war was over and the peace signed at Kutchuk-Kainardji made Russia into a world power, with her frontiers extending along the northern shores of the Black Sea as far as the Straits of Azov. Her conquests in the Kuban and Terek districts gave her a foothold in the Caucasus and along the eastern shores of what had hitherto been a jealously guarded Turkish sea. Farther west, Russia obtained Kinburn at the mouth of the Dnieper and the steppe land lying between the Dnieper and the Bug. Even more important were her gains in the isthmus of Perekop and the independence granted to the Khanate of the Crimea, which made it only a question of time before the whole peninsula came under Russian control.

Two articles in the treaty were of concern to the Western powers. One of them was the right of Russian merchantmen to pass through the Bosphorus and the Dardanelles. The other was the Russian Empress's claim to protect all Orthodox Christians living under the Sultan's rule. Both these clauses were bitterly contested and the Treaty of Kutchuk-Kainardji took many months to ratify. In a sense, it was never more than an armistice, for Turkey had no intention of abiding by the clauses, and Russia had no intention of limiting her expanionist ambitions. Nevertheless 21 July 1774, the date of the official signing of the treaty, was a red-letter-day in European politics, for henceforth no solution of the 'Eastern Question' was conceivable without the consent of Russia.

The Western courts had now to face up to the fact that Russia was a new force to be reckoned with and that the German-born Empress knew how to play the game of power politics as well as any of their top-ranking diplomatists. Catherine had every reason to be satisfied with what she described in a letter to Voltaire as '*un si joli paix*', and she felt that she deserved to be commended by him instead of being scolded for not having taken the road to Constantinople. From his armchair at Ferney, the octogenarian philosopher had preached a crusade against the infidel and he now blamed the Empress for having left the Greeks in the lurch, as if Catherine's treatment of the liberated Greeks would have been any different from her treatment of the Poles.

The correspondence between the Empress and the philosopher had not been quite so prolific of late. The breath of criticism was sufficient to dampen the ardour of Semiramis. Voltaire made no allowances for the strain which the 'Pugachefschina' had placed on her resources, nor had he taken into account the enormous losses suffered by the Russian armies. He had even gone to the lengths of associating himself with D'Alembert in an appeal for clemency for the eighteen young French officers captured in Poland. The appeal was made in vain and the Empress was cruelly sarcastic in informing Voltaire that she intended sending these gentlemen to Siberia 'where they would be able to teach their fine French manners to the natives'.

Catherine's relations with the encyclopaedists began to decline with the advent of Potemkin. Diderot's much heralded visit had not been entirely a success. The Empress had been amused rather than instructed, and some of his questions had been too pertinent for even the most broad-minded of autocrats to enjoy. Although he left Russia laden with presents, escorted by a court official, travelling in a comfortable English carriage provided by the Empress, the largess does not appear to have been all that his needy and avaricious family had been led to expect. Catherine was graceful and liberal in her gifts, but the services of the philosopher were not paid for on the same scale as the services rendered by her lovers. The three thousand roubles

25 Lanskoy in 1782. A portrait by Levitsky.

26 Prince Potemkin of Tauris.

27 The Prince de Ligne.

LE COMTE DE SÉGUR.

28 Louis Philip, Comte de Ségur.

29 Plato Zubov, the last of Catherine's favourites.

30 Catherine in 1794.

which Diderot received for his travelling expenses sound somewhat paltry in comparison with the one hundred and fifty thousand presented to Potemkin during his first two months at the palace.

This was only a foretaste of what there was to come. The signing of the peace treaty brought him the title of Count, 'awarded to him for the assistance and good advice he had given towards it'. His bravery was recompensed by the gift of a diamond-hilted sword, while his devotion won him the most coveted of all distinctions, a portrait of the Empress set in diamonds to be worn on his heart, an honour which until now had only been bestowed on Orlov, of whose resentment Catherine appears to have been so afraid that her gift was not actually handed over to Potemkin until the following year, by which time the Prince had left the country rather than remain a witness to his rival's triumph.

Potemkin's rapid promotion met with considerable opposition. Senator Yelaguine, in whose house he stayed before moving into the palace, relates how he complained to him one day that he was not yet a member of the Grand Council where he was not wanted and where he was determined to have a seat. The Empress appears to have refused this request a second time, for a few days later the senator was dining at her table and noted that Potemkin, who was sitting beside Her Majesty, did not speak a single word throughout the meal: 'The Empress was quite beside herself and everyone else was terribly upset. The next morning, she appeared to be more cheerful, and on the same day Potemkin became a member of the Grand Council.' 'Nowhere', wrote Sir Robert Gunning, 'have favourites risen so rapidly as in this country. But there is no instance even here of so rapid a progress as that of the present one.'

Not even the beauty and prowess of an Orlov could vie with the qualifications of Potemkin. The soldier revealed himself to be a statesman who possessed a far greater knowledge of the inhabitants of the southern provinces than anyone else in the government. It was not so long ago, at a meeting of the Senate, that the Empress had asked for a map of Russia and found that their Excellencies had not even taken the trouble to acquire one.

During his years on the eastern front, Potemkin had studied the habits and languages of the various Cossack and Tartar tribes, and Catherine was not exaggerating when she wrote to Grimm, 'that he had played a far greater part than anyone else in the signing of the Treaty'. Her letters to her German *'souffre douleur'* bubble over with excitement in singing the praises of 'this extraordinary man'. It was such a new and wonderful experience to have a lover with whom she had both a physical and mental affinity, with whom she could share the delights of bed (and, in the first flush of conquest, Potemkin seems to have excelled even Orlov in his physical stamina), yet at the same time could share her working hours in helping to administer her Empire. In the past, Orlov had complained that he saw so little of her, that others had a greater claim on her time. Now it was she who craved for Potemkin at all hours of the day, who missed him if he left her for more than a few hours. She was constantly bombarding him with notes, many of them written for no other reason than to reassure him of her love. 'Can one love anyone else after having known you?' or 'My dearest darling, I wish to know whether you love me as much as I love you.' At times she was pathetically playful, 'General, do you love me? Me love General very much.' Such a demanding, possessive affection would have ended by getting on the nerves of any man, but particularly on someone as changeable and as evasive as Potemkin, who was for ever searching for the unattainable.

Yet it was he who deliberately enslaved her, who forged an intimacy so close as to break down every reticence. Their letters contained references to the most unromantic illnesses, such as colds, colic and diarrhoea. One of their favourite meeting-places was the steam bath (the Finnish sauna) and the thought of the forty-five-year-old Empress already running to fat, lying naked and perspiring in the arms of her enormous, hirsute lover does not present a very attractive picture. Nor was it the most discreet of meeting-places, for both at Peterhof and Tzarskoye Selo the bath houses were situated at some distance from the palace and were only heated on certain days. Evidently Potemkin insisted on going there at night and being served with a hot meal, for we find Catherine, who still had some regard for

public opinion, writing to him, 'My pigeon, if you want to eat
some meat, please note that everything has been prepared at
the bath. But I beg of you not to remove it from there; otherwise everyone will know that cooking is done there.' And everyone did know. That spring at Tzarskoye Selo, Alexis Orlov had
already noted the lights in the bath house and questioned
Catherine as to whether it was true that she and Potemkin met
there at night.

Alexis was one of the few men at court who would have dared
to ask her a direct question and to whom she would have replied
truthfully. There are those who assert that at one time he shared
her affections with his brother. But the devotion between the
two brothers, the way in which Alexis worked towards Gregory's
advancement, makes the supposition unlikely. Catherine's
gratitude to the Orlovs was boundless, and in particular to
Alexis, on whose loyalty she knew she could always rely and
who was ready to carry out on her behalf missions she could not
even have entrusted to Potemkin.

Alexis Orlov had returned from the Mediterranean in time
to take part in the peace celebrations in Moscow, where he
paraded as one of Catherine's 'eagles' under the gold triumphal
arches erected on the Kremlin Square. The hero of Chesmé, a
victory which had captured the imagination of the public,
received a greater ovation than any of the generals. It was
Potemkin who had insisted on the celebrations being held in
Moscow, for Moscow was the heart of Russia, the 'Holy City'
steeped in the traditions of Byzantium, and it was here that he
displayed for the first time his talents as a showman. Fireworks,
illuminations and military parades were only a part of the festivities which lasted throughout July, culminating in a great
popular entertainment at which Potemkin tried to give the
ordinary Muscovite some idea of what the army had achieved
at the cost of so much sacrifice. A large field, two miles outside
the city, was chosen as the site of the Black Sea; two roads leading to it were called the Don and the Dnieper. At the side of
these roads were built model farms, villages and inns. The field
itself was flooded and filled with boats and the surrounding hills
were scattered with pavilions, each named after a town in the

Black Sea region. Azov served as a banqueting hall, Kerch and Yenikale were ballrooms. Kinburn was a theatre and Taganrog a fairground. The whole area was transformed into one vast amusement park for the benefit of the people of Moscow.

The Empress had no longer any need to go in search of publicists abroad. Her lover had become her impresario. 'No wonder she is mad about him,' said Yelaguine, one of the few courtiers who was devoted to them both. 'They love each other, for they are exactly alike.' Their minds ran on parallel lines, their aims and ambitions were the same. Both had the same lust for power. She had the greater brain but he had the greater imagination; she had the greater strength of character, but he had the greater understanding of his fellow-men. As collaborators they were superb, with the Empress occasionally putting a curb on Potemkin's wilder flights of fancy. Nothing was left to chance. When Catherine was working twelve to fourteen hours a day, she still found the time to spread the news of her triumphs abroad. No one was too obscure to be overlooked. A friend of her Stettin childhood, now established as a *salonière* in Hamburg, where she entertained the leading politicians and writers of the day, was written long and affectionate letters, giving detailed accounts of the celebrations and enclosing a printed plan of 'The People's Festival'. 'It is impossible to describe to you the picture presented by such a multitude of people of all ranks and ages gathered together. There were about four thousand carriages, but in spite of the crowds, everything passed off without the slightest mishap amidst general merriment and delight.'

While gossiping with the *salonière* Madame Bielke and with Melchior Grimm, the Empress was working on a vast programme of administrative reform which completely revolutionized the whole system of provincial government. The country which had consisted of eleven vast, unwieldy governments, set up by Peter the Great, was now divided into fifty provinces each under a separate governor, and then subdivided into districts. Justice and finance came under separate administration. Though this system was a vast improvement on the old one, it nevertheless added to the cost of maintaining a large, expensive bureaucracy and greatly increased the power of the nobility by making them the only class eligible for the top ranks of the civil service. The extended privileges given by Catherine to members of the aristocracy were a constant bone of contention between her and Potemkin. Whereas he was at pains to discover, and if possible to correct, the causes of the underlying discontent which had exploded in the 'Pugachefschina', she continued to protect the class on which she had always relied and whose abuses she was powerless to prevent.

Potemkin belonged to Moscow rather than to St Petersburg. He had more affinity with the Oriental than with the Western mind, and he felt at home in this eastern city where Catherine had always felt an alien. She was never more aware of this than when he accompanied her on the traditional pilgrimage to the monastery of the Trinity. She had always hated what had been her predecessor's favourite retreat. It's long, echoing corridors held memories of her unhappy youth and her quarrels with Elisabeth. This time she hoped that the strength of her lover's faith would help her to overcome her fears and make her understand the mystic doctrines of a church to which, for all her efforts, she had never really belonged.

But no sooner had they arrived at the monastery than Potemkin became cold and unapproachable, shutting himself up in his cell, spending hours in prayer or engaged in long, theological arguments with the monks. There were times when he appeared to be deliberately avoiding her; other times when he spoke of renouncing the powers and vanities of the world. The Empress was in despair. Was he genuine or was this an act? Was he already bored and seeking a way of escape, or was it a kind of religious exultation which she in her rationalism could only define as madness? We find her writing to him in the tone of an angry, spoiled child. 'I shall never go on a pilgrimage again. You are so cold. I feel quite faint, you "Giaour", you Muscovite, you mixture of wolf and bird.' How different are her letters to Madame Bielke, describing the pilgrimage as 'a real picnic with not a dull moment'. In the letters both to her and to Melchior Grimm she is full of the rapturous welcome she had received in Moscow, but in her note to Potemkin the word 'Muscovite' is used as a term of abuse. According to impartial eye-witnesses, the enthusiasm of the Muscovites was reserved for the Grand Ducal couple and the cheering crowds outside their window was a deliberate insult to the Empress. The Grand Duke's former hatred of the Orlovs was now concentrated on Potemkin who no longer bothered to pay him court and openly dismissed him as a fool, while Catherine's dislike of her daughter-in-law, whom she regarded as a bad influence on her son and who, after two years of marriage, had not yet produced an heir, was exploited by all the discontented elements in Moscow. But all differences were momentarily forgotten by the autumn, for when the court returned to St Petersburg, it was officially announced that an heir to the throne of all the Russias was expected in the spring.

Catherine's happiness did not last for long. On the morning of 10 April 1776 she was summoned to her daughter-in-law's bedside where, after three days of agony, during which doctors and midwife were powerless to help, the young Grand Duchess gave birth to a dead child. The fault was not that of the doctors but of a malformation of the bone, which the Empress was told was irremediable and would prevent Natalia Alexievna from ever having a child. The labour pains were so terrible that all efforts to save her proved useless and she received the last sacraments on the evening of Thursday 13th. The Empress remained with her daughter-in-law until the end and wrote a disconsolate letter to Grimm, 'For three days I neither ate nor drank. There were moments when her sufferings made me feel that my own body was being torn apart. Then I went stony. I, who am tearful by nature, saw her die and never shed a tear. I said to myself, "If you cry, others will sob. If you sob, others will faint."'

The Grand Duke, who adored his wife, was distraught with grief and the whole court was plunged into mourning. But the Empress appeared to recover her spirits remarkably quickly. One sees this already in her long letter to Grimm, the latter part of which was written several days later when she was once more her usual gossiping self, reminding him of commissions, giving him news of her pet greyhound ('Sir Thomas Anderson'), one of a family of nine 'who has the habit of barking with joy whenever he sees anything which he finds beautiful or astonishing'. She had never liked her daughter-in-law and reproved her for her extravagances and debts, forgetting that in her youth Elisabeth had rebuked her for the same reasons. She even suspected Natalia Alexievna of having intrigued against her and recognized her hand in the lengthy memorandum which the Grand Duke had dared to present her with, accusing her of ruining the Empire by her expansionist policy and suggesting military reforms based on the Prussian model. Catherine had shown her displeasure by handing back this memorandum without a single comment. Now she was irritated to see him weeping over a wife who had betrayed him with his best friend from the first day of their marriage. Certain incriminating letters had come into her hands which she intended to make use of at the right moment. In spite of the tenderness expressed in her letter to Grimm, Catherine felt little grief over her daughter-in-law's death. A woman who could not even produce an heir was hardly worth a tear.

Certain rumours got abroad suggesting that the Grand Duchess might not have died from natural causes. There was talk of the Empress having summoned a secret council at which it was decided that, for the sake of the dynasty, Natalia Alexievna should be allowed to die. That incorrigible gossip, Sir Nathaniel Wraxall, who happened to be in Vienna at the time, tells of how certain details were related to him 'with great delicacy and reserve' by one of the Hesse-Darmstadt cousins. Whatever may have been the truth, the Empress lost no time in finding her son another German bride, for Germany was still the favourite breeding ground for eligible princesses. But Paul was far too unhappy to think of remarrying, until his mother handed him a bundle of letters which showed him that his young wife had betrayed him from the very beginning. It was a terrible blow to discover that she and Andrew Razumovsky, the only two people he had ever really loved, had blatantly deceived him. Natalia Alexievna was beyond his vengeance, but he demanded that Razumovsky be sent to Siberia. In loyalty to the father, the

Empress refused to comply and the young man was sent as her ambassador to Venice. Meanwhile, Prince Henry of Prussia was due to arrive at St Petersburg on a second state visit. As Paul resembled his father in admiring everything that was Prussian, his mother hoped that Prince Henry would exercise a happy influence in persuading him to remarry. This time, she was determined to make no mistake and her choice fell on Prince Frederick's niece, a princess of Würtemburg, who came from a large and prolific family of tall, strong men and handsome, wide-hipped women. The fact that the girl was already officially engaged to the hereditary Prince of Hesse-Darmstadt was not taken into account. Frederick, who was always ready to strengthen his ties with the Russian court, immed-iately arranged for the engagement to be broken off and, by mid-summer, the Grand Duke Paul was accompanying his friend, Prince Henry, on a state visit to Berlin where he was to encounter his future bride.

The Empress must have been glad to see him go. She had her own problems to deal with. The man who had given her the greatest happiness she had ever known was also capable of making her utterly miserable. One of the few foreigners who ever became an intimate of Potemkin has described him as 'a true favourite of Fortune, as changeable and as inconstant and as capricious as she, tired of what he possessed, envious of what he was unable to attain, wanting everything, yet disgusted with everything'. Catherine had given him everything except her crown and there were times when she felt he envied her her crown, when he could not bear the idea of being a subject. At such times, he would take a delight in humiliating her, in deny-ing her the physical satisfaction she craved, and on these occa-sions the great Empress was apt to act as foolishly as any love-sick girl. She would spend sleepless nights waiting for him to come to her room, or go to his apartments and find his doors locked against her. She would wait for him for hours in a draughty library while he was out carousing with his friends, and would write pathetic letters complaining of his behaviour. 'To hear you speak at times, one would think that I am a mon-ster, guilty of every shortcoming and, above all, of being a fool.

The causes of our quarrels are invariably trivial, the subject of our disagreements is always power and never love.'

He resented the slightest sign of favour shown to old friends and was capable of sulking for the whole day if Tchernichef or an Orlov was on duty at court. Catherine would gently upbraid him.

The one thing I beg you is not to prejudice my mind against the Orlovs, for I would consider this a great ingratitude on your part. There is no one else in the world of whom the Prince used to tell me so much good or whom he used to love so well as yourself. If the Prince has his faults, it is not for you or me to criticize them and to draw the attentions of others to them. He used to love you and, as far as I am concerned, both he and his brother are my good friends and I will never abandon them.

This is one of the rare occasions when she dared to reprimand him. Usually one finds her accepting his moods and tantrums with an amazing tolerance, grateful for any kindness, cherishing his moments of tenderness. She was always generous to her favourites, but Potemkin was the first to receive a regular income of twelve thousand roubles a year. His living expenses were charged to her personal account and cost her well over one hundred thousand. Not a feast day passed without him receiving a gift of yet another hundred thousand. On one occasion, in which she had given him a present of a jewelled belt instead, he showed his displeasure so openly that she immediately rectified her mistake by sending him the money as well. As governor of the southern provinces, he was privileged to have his own private staff, which after the acquisition of the Crimea grew into a regular court. But in spite of all this, he was so lavish and careless in his expenditure, so fantastically generous in his gifts, that he was always in debt. He would present his royal mistress with a spray of the rarest emeralds, or send a messenger two thousand miles to find her some rare plant or a bunch of the finest grapes. She in return would pay his creditors when they dared to become importunate.

What was the secret of his magic? The influence he continued to exercise long after they had ceased to be lovers? Did he succeed in obtaining what she had refused to Orlov, and were they secretly married, as the Soviet historian, Professor Barskov, maintains? According to his researches on the subject, their wedding took place at the end of the year 1774 and was celebrated in the little church of St Sampson in an unfashionable quarter of the town. Only three witnesses were present: the Empress's faithful maid, the bridegroom's nephew, Samoilov, and the Court Chamberlain, Count Tchertkov. There were two copies of the marriage certificate, one which went to the Empress's maid, the other to the bridegroom's nephew, and both appear to have been destroyed. In spite of the fact that only four people, including the priest, were present at the ceremony, rumours appear to have reached the ears both of the Emperor Joseph and the Count de Ségur, who only arrived in Russia ten years after the event.

The most convincing arguments in favour of Professor Barskov's theory are to be found in the Empress's correspondence. In letters written over the space of twenty years one finds her referring to Potemkin as 'my dearest husband', 'my tender spouse', signing herself 'Your devoted wife'. Such phrases might be used as terms of endearment between lovers, but not at a time when both were involved in other love-affairs. Nor is there any other explanation as to why the Empress should refer to Potemkin's nephew, Baron Englehardt, a young man she did not even like, as 'our nephew', while her attitude to his five pretty nieces, all of whom shared his favours at one time or another, was that of an indulgent aunt rather than of a jealous rival. Perhaps the most conclusive of all is the short note which appears to have been written at the end of 1774, immediately after the wedding, in which Catherine refers to her embarrassment at having Potemkin on duty at court, 'I think that, if you are obliged to stand behind my chair, I shall go as red as a lobster.'

Two years later, when bitter quarrels were beginning to mar their relationship, she wrote to him,

My master and tender spouse, I begin by replying on what touches me the most. Why do you want to cry? Why do you want to believe your unhealthy imagination rather than the real facts, all of which confirm the words of your wife, who is attached to you by the strongest of ties and who has never since changed her attitude towards you? Is it possible you should no longer be loved by me? Have confidence in my words. I love you and am bound to you by all possible ties.

But Potemkin was the victim of his own character – a character far more feminine and feline than that of his mistress – mean and noble at the same time, arrogant yet insecure, jealous of those he loved the most and incapable of loyalty even towards the Empress. He would criticize her in the company of his friends, who were not always hers, and expose her weaknesses to the foreign ambassadors. Naturally, his remarks were brought back to Catherine in a court so full of his enemies. At other times, he would frighten her by saying that whoever succeeded him in her affections would not be allowed to live. But, by the beginning of 1776, he was already venturing on the biggest gamble of his extraordinary career by gradually disentangling himself from a sexual relationship with a woman whose insatiable desires he could no longer satisfy. His innate fastidiousness, so curiously at odds with the grossness of his habits, recoiled before her excessive demands. The man whose physical appearance was so uncouth, for whose benefit Catherine had introduced a new set of rules at the Hermitage requesting her guests to refrain from blowing their noses on the curtains, had nevertheless the mind and soul of a poet. His love letters to his young nieces, and in particular to Varvara, whose character was as fickle, feline and capricious as his own, were ecstatically lyrical. Poor Catherine never received such letters. But throughout his life, she remained for him the incarnation of the country he adored.

What he feared most was that, by remaining her lover, he would sooner or later be dismissed in favour of some stalwart young guardsman. His jealous eyes had already noted the appraising looks she gave some of the handsome young officers on duty at the palace and the pleasure with which she received the admiration of aspiring favourites. He could not bear the idea of being pensioned off with an empty, high-sounding title. The Empress had made him into a prince at the time of the Moscow peace celebrations, but he had no intention of following in the steps of Orlov. There was still so much he could do for

Russia, so many ways in which he could serve his Empress. To rule as the viceroy of the greatest Empire in the world meant more to him than to share his sovereign's bed, and he showed both subtlety and skill in winning Catherine over to the idea that their responsibilities were too heavy, their duties too onerous to waste their time in trivial quarrels. The rules which governed the conduct of lesser men and women were none of their concern. The 'minions' who pandered to her pleasures (the contemptuous term was deliberately his own) could be chosen and changed at will. But he, Potemkin, would always be there, watching over her interests, serving her with a selfless, undying devotion. Their spiritual ties were indissoluble, their ideals were the same – to chase the infidel out of Europe and to have her crowned as Empress of Byzantium in Constantinople in the re-consecrated basilica of Hajia Sofia. What became known as the 'Greek project', a dream of Peter the Great, re-evoked by the Orlovs, and applauded by Voltaire, became a reality in the hands of Potemkin whom Catherine loved and admired because she regarded him as the reincarnation of the great Tzar.

At a time when his personal influence appeared to be on the wane, when the Empress had openly taken another lover and his enemies were gloating over his imminent downfall, Potemkin was taking an ever-increasing part in the running of the country, usurping the position of Panin in the College of Foreign Affairs, acting as host to the ambassadors at the time of the Moscow celebrations. The pro-Prussian Panin was made to take second place when the Prince entertained the King's brother during his state visit to St Petersburg, and on this occasion received the coveted decoration of the Black Eagle. A prouder man than Panin would have handed in his resignation, but the prudent old statesman maintained that he still had free access to the Empress so long as he retained his post and could help to ferment the intrigues with which the arrogant favourite had to contend, even at the height of his power.

Where Potemkin showed the greatest skill was in persuading Catherine, who was still passionately in love with him, that it was she who was guilty of infidelity. An intermittent illness from which he suffered throughout the latter part of 1775 and the early months of the following year, was of considerable assistance to his plans in enabling him to absent himself from court. We find Catherine referring in her letters to his 'spleen' which made him so sulky and suspicious, and which in all probability were acute bilious attacks, the result of his intemperate habits. His enemies called his illness by a more unpleasant name, and Potemkin appears to have deliberately fostered this rumour. Catherine had a horror of any form of venereal disease and it is significant that all her succeeding lovers who, according to the most conservative estimate, were no less than seven, had all to be examined by her English physician, Dr Rogerson, before they were admitted to the royal bed. Neither Orlov nor Potemkin, both of them notorious debauchees, was ever submitted to this humiliating ordeal or to the even more degrading experience of having their manhood tested by the enterprising Countess Bruce, who has come down to history by the name of '*l'épreuveuse*'.

Potemkin's subsequent amorous career, the eagerness with which the most sophisticated beauties, some of them bearing the greatest names in Russia, fell into his arms, proves that his illness was not so grave as his enemies made out. Nevertheless, it may have served at the time to cool a passion which he felt might end in destroying him. In the summer of 1776 he set out for a five-week tour of the central provinces, acting for the first time the role of Catherine's viceroy, for whether in Novgorod or Tver every object for his use, from furniture to the kitchen pans, was provided by the court.

Catherine's letters, and she wrote to him every day, are as tender as before. She misses him and longs for his return. 'I am burning with impatience to see you again. It seems I have not seen you for a year. I kiss you and so much wish to see you because I love you with all my heart. My beloved Falcon, you are staying away far too long.' Yet it was during his absence that she took a new lover who had every quality to make her happy but, given the jealousy of Potemkin, had not a chance of surviving for long.

The favourite's attitude to the news was characteristic. He had been straining every nerve to be free. For months he had been pressing the Empress to give him a house of his own and had chosen the so-called Anitchkov Palace which had formerly belonged to Alexis Razumovsky. The house, which overlooked the Fontanka Canal on the one side and the Nevsky Prospect on the other, had been allowed to fall into disrepair and Catherine's principal objections were based on the fact that it would cost an enormous amount to restore. But the spoiled favourite ended by having his way, and at the end of June 1776, we find the Empress signing an official document handing him over the property and a hundred thousand roubles for its repair. Potemkin hardly ever lived in the house which, within a year, was up for sale in order to pay his debts, and the long-suffering Empress bought it for him for the second time.

The new favourite was too intelligent and well-bred for his taste. In future, the Empress's lovers must be of his choosing and Zavadowsky had barely been appointed as *aide-de-camp* before he was already arousing his suspicion and dislike. Potemkin returned from Novgorod complaining that he was lonely and miserable and had no place to go, and Catherine replied with all her former tenderness and sweetness, 'My husband has written me "Where shall I go? Where shall I find my proper place?" My dear and beloved husband, come to me. You will be received with open arms.'

Small wonder if Peter Alexievitch Zavadowsky, who was deeply in love with his royal mistress, became obsessed by jealousy of Potemkin. He, too, was a Ukrainian, born of an excellent family in Little Russia and educated by the Jesuits. He had started his career on the clerical staff of Field-Marshal Roumiantsev, who combined the offices of Commander-in-Chief with that of governor of the Ukraine. The Marshal had taken him with him to the front, where his bravery on the battle-field raised him to the rank of lieutenant-colonel, and won him the reward of an estate in Little Russia.

Before leaving for the Moscow peace celebrations, the Empress wrote to the Field-Marshal asking him to provide her with two good secretaries from his Chancellory. Roumiantsev complied with her wishes and the two young men who accompanied him to Moscow were both destined to have brilliant careers. At first Zavadowsky appears to have been the one who had all the qualities necessary for success, combining a handsome figure with a courteous manner and a first-class mind. Bezborodko, on the contrary, was boorish and uncouth in his ways and vulgar in appearance, but he was to have a far more spectacular career. While Zavadowsky lived for a year in the limelight of Imperial favour, before settling down to the life of a highly respected civil servant, Bezborodko, starting from nothing, ended by becoming a prince and Chancellor of the Empire. Zavadowsky's dark good looks appealed to the Empress, who within a month had attached him to her personal staff and promoted him to the rank of major-general. But, for the time being, Bezborodko remained a clerk in the Chancellory, one of the nameless, unrecognized bureaucrats who struggled to administer the Empire.

Zavadowsky's amorous relations with Catherine were slow in maturing. She was still under the spell of Potemkin and was often lonely and unhappy, too occupied in planning the Grand Duke's second marriage to give much time to a lover. This time, her role was that of an affectionate mother only concerned with the happiness of her son. Ugly rumours had been going round the town in which both she and Potemkin were incriminated; rumours that Natalia Alexievna's midwife was bribed to let her die, and that the illness of Prince Orlov, who had in the past year been suffering from fits of the palsy, was due to poison administered by Potemkin. Nothing was too bad to be laid at the ex-favourite's door by those who believed his downfall to be imminent. But not even the charms of her new lover could make Catherine forget the man she called her 'hero' and who, on his return from Novgorod, was as powerful and as arrogant as before.

The Grand Duke's reception in Berlin had reconciled him to the idea of a second marriage. He who had always played such an insignificant part at his mother's court now found himself fêted by the great Frederick. No one was more versed in the art of flattery than the old King, and the vain and vulnerable Paul, accompanied by the victorious Field-Marshal Roumiantsev, basked in the light of success. His bride-to-be was a large, handsome girl of a sweet and amiable disposition, who had made no attempt to protest when her engagement to the good-looking Hessian Prince was suddenly broken off and her uncle produced instead the puny, unattractive Tzarevitch. The fact that he was heir to all the Russias may have helped to console her, for by the time the engaged couple left for St Petersburg, they were reported to be head over heels in love.

The Empress wanted the marriage to take place as soon as possible. The bride's conversion to the Orthodox faith was to be hurried through. This was the occasion when Catherine wrote so cynically to Grimm, 'The Princess's religious instruction should not take more than a fortnight. Conviction will come later.' But though the Grand Duchess Maria Feodorovna proved an excellent wife, presenting her husband with three stalwart sons and six lovely daughters of whom the eldest were to be the delight of their grandmother's old age, she never succeeded in endearing herself to Catherine, who was always conscious of silent disapproval on the part of a prudish and virtuous Princess.

Meanwhile, Zavadowsky, the lover but not yet the official favourite, was kept busy in helping the Empress to compile the lists for the elaborate wedding trousseau, every detail of which she supervised herself from the decorations of the bridal apartments to the lace on the bed linen, which she noted in her own handwriting 'had to be of the finest quality'. No doubt these simple tasks were rendered more congenial by the assistance of her 'little Petussia'. Catherine appears to have had a liking for diminutives whether she was addressing a giant like Potemkin or a six-foot athlete like Zavadowsky. She who was so little of a mother, either to Paul or to Bobrinskoy, her natural son by Orlov, was nevertheless curiously maternal towards her lovers. 'Petussia' was satisfactory in every way. He was warm and ardent and, unique among her favourites, coveted neither honours nor riches. It was only after the royal wedding at which Potemkin, blazing with diamonds, was the cynosure of all eyes, that Zavadowsky moved into the Winter Palace. All might have been well had it not been for his jealous, obsessive love, and loathing of Potemkin. His very adoration of Catherine was to bring about his downfall. He wanted an all-embracing intimacy and complained that the shadow of his predecessor stood between them. Catherine reasoned with him as patiently as she had reasoned with jealous lovers in the past. But it was all to no avail. He forgot that the man he had abused as a rival was also the most powerful minister in Russia and he decried him both in public and in private.

Catherine, who had been hoping for some kind of domestic peace, found she had to cope with jealous scenes from both Zavadowsky and Potemkin, who was furious at finding an open enemy installed in the palace. In the spring of 1777 he purposely absented himself from the Empress's birthday celebrations and retired to a country estate from where he appears to have issued an ultimatum, complaining of his treatment and demanding Zavadowsky's dismissal, to which Catherine replied,

You know there is nothing I would not do for you. So, in the name of God, be reasonable and compare your behaviour to mine. If I have been weak, then it is up to you to hide it, for public opinion – the stupid and the ignorant – will judge this affair by the importance you give it. You ask me to dismiss Zavadowsky, but this would only serve to damage my reputation and show up my defects. I would be committing an injustice against a man who is completely innocent. Do not make me do anything so unfair and do not lend an ear to slander.

But Potemkin was in no mood to temporize. Zavadowsky had to go, not without tears on the part of the Empress who, two months later, made a half-hearted attempt to recall him. But 1777 was a year in which politics were too absorbing, Potemkin's support too vital, to be endangered by the vicissitudes of her private life. Zavadowsky retired, bitter and disconsolate, shutting himself up on his estates in the Ukraine. But later in the reign he returned to St Petersburg, becoming a senator and a highly respected civil servant, the only one of Catherine's lovers to end his career as one of her grandson's ministers.

CHAPTER TWENTY-TWO

The Clerk and
the Pancakes

Zavadowsky's friend and colleague, Bezborodko, might never have been promoted had it not been for the incident of a dish of pancakes. It was the early winter of 1775, in the last week of the Moscow carnival, and the Empress, who had but lately arrived in the city, was working alone in her study having given her secretaries leave to attend the Shrove Tuesday fair.

She had ordered an early dinner in her room, and was served with the traditional pancakes (*bliny*), a dish of which she was particularly fond. These were perfect, oozing with caviare and dripping in cream. But there were too many for even her hearty appetite to finish, and they were far too good to waste. Someone must be found to share them, but on questioning the servants she was told that there was no one on duty except one of the Ukrainian clerks in the Chancellory. With that innate simplicity which made her so likeable, Catherine invited the clerk to share her meal, and Bezborodko, timid but not abashed, was ushered into the royal presence. She took to him at once. He was plain and unattractive to look at but engaging in his manner. There was nothing servile about him. His stockings might be rumpled, his linen none too clean, but he answered her questions with frankness and his eyes sparkled with intelligence. We can picture the scene, the small, over-heated study with the air refreshed by vinegar and scented herbs; the exotic plants in the embrasures of the double-windows giving an illusion of spring, while the snow was falling outside on a white, frozen landscape with the occasional gleam of a golden steeple shining through the mist; a little table drawn up by the fire, and two people, both of them healthy epicureans, tucking into the *bliny*, the Empress stout and comfortable in cap and morning gown, wearing the spectacles the public was never allowed to see, a napkin fastened firmly round her chin for she said herself that she was a dirty eater.

And opposite her, the little clerk, smacking his lips with pleasure, the cream oozing down the corners of his full, sensual mouth. When the meal was over, they got down to work. Catherine read him out extracts from the new 'Provinces Act' and was amazed to find he knew it by heart. But what amazed her even more was that, in discussing the Ukraine, he had the temerity to advise her to humour the Zaporavian Cossacks, whose free communities by the Dnieper Cataracts were about to be broken up by Potemkin.

The little clerk dared to criticize the decisions of the all-powerful favourite, and when Catherine asked him why he showed so much concern for the Cossacks, he replied that they were useful allies, being familiar with the regions bordering on the Crimea. She questioned him as to what the Crimea had to do with it, and he replied 'Everything. Once the Crimea belongs to Russia, there will be peace in the south and no further raids by the Crimean Tartars. The Cossacks will help in keeping the peace.'

The Empress scrutinized him sharply, for the annexation of the Crimea was a project still relegated to the future. How had he learned all this? And he replied that it was not a question of learning; he had thought of these things while at home in the Ukraine. Catherine was impressed by his political insight, his calm self-confidence. And from that day began the astonishing career which eventually made the Ukrainian clerk into one of the richest and most powerful men in Russia. Bezborodko never sought the limelight or aspired to rival Potemkin. On the contrary, he served him as faithfully as he served the Empress, helping to consolidate his schemes and harness his ambition. When the Prince was away on one of his tours of the southern provinces, we find Bezborodko watching over his interests, and warning him to return whenever his enemies appeared to be getting the upper hand or when the Empress was about to take an unsuitable lover. But he never let himself be bullied either by the Empress or by Potemkin, and on occasion had the courage to tell them unpalatable truths. He never belonged to any faction or meddled in intrigues and was scrupulously loyal to Panin, so long as the old minister remained at the head of the College of Foreign Affairs. The Empress recommended Bezborodko to Panin, and before long the Ukrainian clerk was carrying out the tiresome duties the other was too lazy to fulfil.

Panin's inertia had grown with the years. Gluttony and dissipation had destroyed his physique. He spent his time between the bed and the card-table. But so far his brain was unimpaired. He was still a loyal Prussophile and a dangerous opponent to King Frederick's enemies. For all his slothfulness (and according to the new British ambassador, he did not devote more than one hour out of twenty-four to work), he nevertheless managed in that one hour to circumvent the plans of his adversaries and prevent the Empress from adhering to any policies other than his own. Potemkin was only interested in the East, and Panin was allowed to direct Russia's relations with the West. Europe was in the throes of two political crises: the question of the Bavarian succession and the War of American Independence. For the time being, the great powers were far more concerned with the future of Bavaria than with a colonial war. Some of them, and they included Russia, were not sorry to see the arrogant English, who were usually so fond of interfering in other people's affairs, now deeply involved in their own. But the Bavarian succession, where the Elector Maximilian had recently died leaving no direct heirs, was of vital interest to all. The nearest claimant to the throne was the Duke of Zweibrücken, a Wittelsbach of a collateral branch. But the Hapsburgs had a claim through marriage and the young Emperor, Joseph II, saw in the disputed succession an excellent opportunity of extending his possessions into the heart of Germany. Here, he came in direct conflict with the old King of Prussia who, as head of the German Confederation, was determined to prevent Bavaria from becoming incorporated in the Hapsburg Empire.

War was imminent. Frederick moved his armies into Bohemia, advancing as far as the Elbe, where the Austrians were massed on the opposite bank. But neither attempted to engage the other in battle, for neither King nor Emperor really wanted to fight; nor was the rest of Europe prepared to go to war over the Bavarian succession, and the most bitterly anti-war of all was the old Empress Maria-Theresa whose son had acted directly against her wishes. She was ill and infirm and wanted to end her days in peace, whatever sacrifices that peace might entail. Nothing in her long and troubled reign must have been harder than to write a letter to the Empress of Russia asking for her intercession. Catherine was a woman she cordially disliked, whose morals had always revolted her, but she now called on her 'both as a Christian and a fellow sovereign' to use her influence with the King of Prussia in bringing about a just and honourable peace. Catherine was immensely flattered to have the virtuous Hapsburg Empress, the most respected ruler of her time, condescending to ask for her mediation over what was purely a German concern. Her personal sympathies were already veering towards Austria and the young Emperor, whom she saw as a natural ally in her Eastern projects. But she did not want that ally to become more powerful than at present, so she listened to the counsels of Panin, who maintained that it was in Russia's interest to support the German Confederation.

At the Congress of Teschen, the Empress of Russia and the young King of France, who was already involved in a costly war with England, mediated in favour of peace. By an honourable compromise, the Emperor was able to extend his dominions between the upper Danube and the Inn, thereby linking Austria proper to the Tyrol, while Bavaria remained a hereditary possession of the Wittelsbachs. The consequences of the treaty were not of themselves important, but it brought Russia for the first time to the congress tables of Europe. It was a personal triumph for Catherine, whose reputation was so enhanced that the Emperor of Austria was now determined to become her ally. Her own vanity, which was considerable, was so inflated by success that diplomats accredited to her court found it increasingly difficult to make her listen to the voice of reason and no one had a more difficult task than James Harris, the new British ambassador who arrived in St Petersburg in the first month of 1778.

Twenty years ago, as a young Grand Duchess, Catherine had been willing to spy for England in return for a loan of ten thousand pounds. Now it was England's turn to demand a loan, not of money but of men – twenty thousand soldiers 'to help her to subdue her misguided subjects in America'. It was customary in the eighteenth century for neutral countries to hire out their soldiers to fight as mercenaries in foreign wars. But in Russia, the Pugachef rebellion was too recent and the frontiers too insecure for Catherine to send her soldiers overseas, and recent ambassadors from England had received no more than evasive replies to their demands. James Harris's instructions from his government went further than the loan of a few thousand men. He was to find out whether the Russian court was disposed to enter into an offensive and defensive alliance with England. If their disposition appeared to be favourable, he was straightway to negotiate an agreement, for which purpose he was given 'extended powers and unlimited credit'.

James Harris, who ended his career as Earl of Malmesbury, was only thirty-two when he was appointed to a post where many more experienced diplomats had failed. But he had served a hard apprenticeship in Berlin, accredited to the astutest monarch of the age, and he never let himself be deceived either by the false assurances of Panin or by the Empress's flattering attentions. In spite of her personal admiration for the English, still coloured by her memories of 'Chevalier Williams', Catherine was quite pleased to have Britain and France too heavily involved in war to interfere in her projects for the Crimea. Harris arrived at a moment when England's credit on the continent was at its lowest ebb, when she was fighting a losing war against her American colonists and struggling to maintain her maritime supremacy against the combined might of France and Spain. At home her greatest statesman, Lord Chatham, was dying, her government was weak and ineffectual and the financial situation was disastrous.

It was hardly a propitious time to seek an alliance with a country whose sovereign and ministers were only impressed by success. But throughout the five years of his embassy, James Harris managed to maintain a privileged position at Catherine's court and to win the support and friendship of Potemkin. He neither obtained an alliance nor prevented the Empress from adhering to her famous declaration of 'armed neutrality', designed to protect her merchant navy and those of other neutral countries against the incursions of the belligerent powers. Though not directly aimed against England, it was nevertheless a challenge to British privateers, who regarded it as their right to search neutral ships at sea and confiscate all contraband goods destined for the enemy. The goods were usually paid for at an accepted valuation, but this high-handed attitude, which interfered in their trade with the Americas, was bitterly resented by the neutral powers. Russia's decision to protect her cargoes with armed frigates was enthusiastically welcomed by the northern states. For England it was an irritant rather than a deterrent, but the homage paid her by the neighbouring powers served to increase the Empress's already over-weening pride.

Not even the most brilliant of diplomats could have succeeded in a country whose policy was entirely dictated by expediency and changed from day to day according to the caprices of a sovereign who was convinced of her country's invincibility and her own glorious destiny. Barely a month after his arrival, the ambassador was already writing on a note of disillusion:

This country, which believes itself to be at the height of its glory and political perfection, is in one of the most dangerous crises it has ever been in. Yet the great good fortune of the Empress, joined to her resolution and other qualities, may supply the deficiencies and stand her in lieu of able generals and experienced statesmen. Her worst enemies are flattery and her own passions. She never turns a deaf ear to the first, be it ever so gross, and her inclination for gratifying the latter appears to grow upon her with age.

Harris was convinced that Turkey, supported by France and Austria, was preparing for another war. Yet the following years were to see the flowering of the Austro–Russian alliance with a Hapsburg Emperor as a guest at Catherine's court, while the year of the ambassador's departure witnessed the peaceful annexation of the Crimea, with the tacit consent of Austria. No wonder Catherine believed in her lucky star and turned a deaf ear to the voice of criticism. 'Flatter her, she cannot have enough of it,' was the advice given by Potemkin. 'You cannot be too unctuous. But flatter her for what she ought to be, not for what she is; be open and unreserved and make her feel you have full confidence in her, for she is under the impression that your nation has not got this confidence and this displeases her.' Underlying the vanity and the colossal conceit was the inferiority complex of a provincial German princess. She admired the English, but resented what she called 'their coldness and their pride'. She disliked the French but admired their culture. A French envoy reports how, at the very height of her glory, the Empress asked him in her most disarming manner whether he thought 'she would be able to hold her own with the brilliant *salonières* of Paris?'

Nowhere does Catherine's strange and contradictory character emerge more clearly than from the diaries and despatches of the young English diplomat, who has left us a detailed account of life in St Petersburg from the years 1778 to 1783, between the war of the Bavarian succession and the annexation of the Crimea. They were years in which Russian politics were concentrated on the 'Greek project' and Potemkin ruled as viceroy over Catherine's southern Empire. But these years of glory saw also the first signs of the Empress's physical and moral disintegration, when a succession of obscure young guardsmen were selected by Potemkin to satisfy the desires of a lustful, ageing woman. Zavadowsky's successor was an illiterate hussar of Serbian extraction who had nothing to recommend him other than a superb physique and a distinguished war record. Catherine had been attracted by the handsome soldier and impressed by the George Cross, the highest Russian military medal, which he wore with such panache. She even imagined herself to be in love with him, for with her, a sexual infatuation was all too often interpreted as love. But Peter Yoritz had barely been in favour for ten months when the Empress told Potemkin one morning, 'last night I was in love with him, today I cannot stand him any more'; Potemkin had made no allowance for the fact that Catherine required a companion as well as a lover, someone with a mind she could train and develop to share her tastes in art and literature. Poor Yoritz could not understand why the woman who had showered him with riches only a month before, suddenly became so distant, and he quite wrongly blamed his benefactor. There was an ugly scene one night when the Empress was on her way to a play, and Yoritz, mad with jealousy, challenged Potemkin to a duel, a challenge the arrogant Prince refused to accept.

James Harris noted every sordid quarrel and intrigue which detracted from Catherine's reputation. When he arrived in Russia, the young Serbian's star was already on the decline though the Empress did not dare to dismiss him for fear of his violence. 'He has received and spent an immense fortune,' writes Harris. 'It is probable Potemkin will be commissioned to look out for a fresh minion.' But by now the office of Imperial favourite had become a court sinecure and the various factions produced their rival candidates. Panin had a good-looking secretary whom the Empress had singled out at a ball at Peterhof and who was said to have enjoyed her favours. There was an exotic Persian prince who was supposed to be endowed 'with extraordinary physical attributes' and a nephew of the Tchernichefs, a young Prince Kantemir, reported to be as beautiful as Adonis. But Potemkin was determined to brook no rivals, and one of his young adjutants, a captain in the Horse Guards by the name of Korsak, was already waiting in the wings.

All this gossip was not very edifying, coming at a time when the Empress had just become a grandmother and St Petersburg was '*en fête*' for the birth of the Grand Duke Alexander Pavlevitch. Her loyal subjects indulged in an orgy of extravagance; money-lenders flourished and the purveyors of Parisian finery made enormous profits. A terrible flood had devastated the city the previous autumn and the damage had amounted to millions of roubles. But money continued to flow from the Royal

Mint, an expedient new to the Russian economy, and so great was the Empress's prestige that the Imperial profile stamped on the bank notes was considered to be sufficient guarantee.

The British ambassador and his young wife were caught up in a round of balls and masquerades where men and women blazed with fantastic jewellery such as was never seen at Queen Charlotte's decorous court, and where the tables groaned under golden plate piled high with delicacies from the four corners of the Empire. Prince Potemkin was said to have spent no less than five thousand roubles on one night's entertainment. But the culminating event of the social season was the ball held by the Empress in the last week of carnival, to which only the most important ambassadors and Russians of the highest rank were invited. Even the critical Mr Harris waxed eloquent over

a magnificence and good taste which surpassed anything that can be conceived. The dessert at supper was set out with jewels valued at over two million sterling and at the tables of Macao [the fashionable card-game much favoured by the Empress], a diamond of a hundred roubles in value was given by Her Imperial Majesty to each of the players who got the highest point in the game. No less than one hundred and fifty diamonds were distributed in this manner.

The ambassador confines himself to the facts, but we can envisage that night at the Winter Palace in Rastrelli's gilded halls, so sparsely furnished in Elisabeth's day but now transformed into a treasure house of art, with rare tapestries and antique statues, exquisite furniture of French and Russian manufacture, cabinets filled with Renaissance bronzes, Greek medals and Roman cameos. The Empress would take some of her more favoured guests on a tour of the Hermitage, to admire her latest acquisitions. There were no less than two thousand paintings in her collections and many of them were masterpieces. The original Hermitage had grown too small to house them and the architect, Yuri Veldten, had been commissioned to build a second and larger Hermitage purely as a picture-gallery.

The Grand Duke and Duchess received the congratulations of the guests, and Paul's ugly features glowed with pride and happiness. But it was his mother who held the centre of the stage, who in her fiftieth year could still give the illusion of beauty.

Her hair was turning grey, she had long since lost her figure, but her blue eyes were still as brilliant and her smile as enchanting as ever. She was short and stout, but her carriage was so erect and she held her head so high that those who saw her for the first time thought of her as tall. Yet in spite of her pride and courage, she had not yet dared to dismiss the black-browed Serb who was still in attendance, nor did she dare to name his successor until he was safely out of the way. For all her cynicism she was sufficiently vulnerable to suffer when Prince Orlov appeared at the ball with his young wife on his arm. The Prince had recovered from the palsy which had afflicted him two years before and, after a prolonged tour of the European capitals where he had been received with almost royal honours, had returned to Russia to marry the cousin with whom he had fallen in love when she was only thirteen.

Catherine was too much of a woman, too much of a sentimentalist, and above all too vain to accept Prince Orlov's marriage with indifference. But she behaved superbly, even going to the lengths of helping the couple to procure the necessary act of dispensation required by the Orthodox church to legalize a marriage between close relatives. The young bride was presented with a splendid gold toilet set and appointed to be a Dame d'Honneur, a title usually given to older women. Only her faithful maid and her friend Prascovia Bruce knew what it cost the Empress to receive the Prince and Princess Orlov at court. The general opinion was that the Orlov brothers had forfeited their influence by Gregory Gregorievitch's 'silly and inconsiderate marriage'.

The Empress prided herself on her tolerance, but there must have been times when she found it hard to accept the open scandal of Potemkin and his pretty nieces, three of whom were concurrently his mistresses. If she regarded him as a husband for whom all sexual desire had died, then it is difficult to explain the tender, loving letters she continued to write to him over the years, letters which suggest that there was still a physical tie between them. It is even more curious to find Potemkin acting the role of pimp in finding strong young men to satisfy her desires. She in turn accepted his nieces, the 'voluptuous

Varvara', the 'adorable Sashenka', and Catherine, the love-liest of the three. All became maids-of-honour and all made brilliant marriages. But how she must have envied them their gay and heedless youth. The twelve-year-old Princess, who had been sexually awoken by one of her Holstein uncles and married at fifteen to a backward boy, had been a mature woman of twenty-five before she had her first sad love-affair with Saltykof.

The repressions of youth go a long way to explain the restless desires of middle age. Catherine might be a fifty-year-old grandmother, but she still felt as young and ardent as a young girl, eager to love and to be loved, deluding herself in the belief that she could still arouse jealousy and passion in the beautiful young men whom she wanted to adore her not only as an Empress but also as a woman. She hated getting old. Her birth-day so publicly celebrated was to her a day of mourning, and in a pathetic letter to Baron Grimm, she writes, 'Would it not be charming if an Empress could always be fifteen.'

CHAPTER TWENTY-THREE

'Building mania is the very devil'

Potemkin lost no time in finding a successor to Yoritz. Realizing his mistake, he now chose an elegant and educated young man endowed with an almost classical beauty. Such talents as he had consisted of a pleasant singing voice and a gift for the violin; attributes which did not seem likely to attract a woman who had little understanding or appreciation of music. But when Catherine was as infatuated as she had been with Potemkin and was now with Korsakof, she was willing to sit for hours listening to their love songs.

By June 1778 the British ambassador was writing home 'Potemkin, who has more cunning than any man living, has introduced Korsakof at a critical moment, and while I am now writing, Her Imperial Majesty is at a village of Potemkin's on the confines of Finland, endeavouring to forget her own cares and those of the Empire in the society of her minion, whose vulgar name of Korsak is already changed to the better sounding one of Korsakof.' But to Catherine's doting eyes, the young man's beauty evoked the legends of ancient Greece, and in her letters to Baron Grimm, the prudish German celibate whom she regaled with her amorous confidences, she refers to her new lover as 'Pyrrhus, King of Epirus, whom every painter should paint, every sculptor should sculpt and every poet should sing'.

Grimm, who had visited St Petersburg for the first time in the suite of the unfortunate Hessian Princess, was again in attendance at the Grand Duke's second marriage and stayed on for nearly a year in Russia. Living in the Empress's entourage, he had witnessed the rise and fall of Zavadowsky and of Yoritz, observed the almost hypnotic influence of Potemkin, and learned to accept the weaknesses of his royal patroness. Unlike Diderot he never tried to lecture her or to argue with her; his flattery was discriminating; his criticism was always acceptable and he was one of the few who dared to tease her in the jolly German fashion she understood. He paid little attention to her succession of lovers and dismissed her rhapsodies on young Korsakof as just another case of sexual aberration.

His informants at the Russian court took the view that the new favourite would only last a few months, not because he lacked the necessary qualities to succeed, but because his heart was not in his job. He was expected to be constantly in attendance and was not allowed to go out of the palace or even to dance at the court balls without the Empress's permission. These restrictions only served to accentuate a longing to escape. And for once the Empress's method of testing her lovers had played her false. Countess Bruce, who was instructed to initiate them in their duties, was still a young and fascinating woman whose technique in love-making was subtle and exciting. The twenty-four-year-old Korsakof found the '*éprouveuse*' to be far more to his taste than the ever more demanding Empress. The lovers were sufficiently foolish and sure of themselves to think they could carry on an affair in the precincts of the palace, exposed to the jealousy of their enemies of which there were many, for the nature of the Countess's duties made her particularly vulnerable, there being several disappointed candidates who had failed to come up to her standards. Even Potemkin was said to be jealous of Prascovia Bruce's influence over her royal mistress.

The reign of 'Pyrrhus, King of Epirus', had lasted for little over a year, when one day in the early autumn of 1779 the Empress discovered him '*en flagrant délit*' with her lady-in-waiting. It must have been a bitter and humiliating moment for Catherine, who was still physically in love with the young man. But she behaved with immense dignity. Count Betskoy was sent to inform the ungrateful favourite that he would be generously treated if he left immediately for Moscow. At the same time

Countess Bruce was told it would be advisable for her to join her husband, who was Governor General of Moscow.

Catherine was soon to have her revenge on her disloyal friend. The Countess's love for Korsakof was entirely one-sided, she had merely helped to while away the tedium of his days. The real object of his affections was the lovely and artistic Countess Stroganov, married to one of the richest and most cultured men in Russia. The Stroganovs had been living in Paris for the last six years and had recently returned to St Petersburg, where the young Countess was just beginning to go out in society when she met and fell madly in love with the Empress's *aide-de-camp*. No one suspected the romance until the disgraced favourite left for Moscow and the Countess Stroganov followed him a few days later. Korsakof appears to have been born under a lucky star. Count Stroganov was a noble-minded man who considered it essential for the mother of his son to live in the style she was accustomed to. He presented his erring wife with a magnificent palace in Moscow and a large country estate, where she and her lover lived happily together for over thirty years, giving birth to three children and entertaining lavishly, with the whole of Moscow society flocking to their musical *soirées*.

Catherine certainly deserved the adjective of 'great' for the magnanimous fashion in which she treated her unfaithful lovers. But now at last she was to know a few years of serenity and happiness in the company of a young man who in every way deserved the riches and rewards she showered on him. Potemkin was determined not to lose the prerogative of choosing her 'minions'. It was not easy to maintain his position when some of them behaved as rashly and imprudently as Korsakof. He knew from experience that even the strongest and most virile of men could not stand up for long to the Empress's inexhaustible sexual appetites. But there was also another side to her nature, that of a frustrated mother who wanted to cherish and instruct the young men of her choice and prepare them to become high officers of state.

Alexander Lanskoy, a twenty-one-year-old guardsman who belonged to an impoverished family of the provincial nobility, possessed both looks and charm. But he lacked the robust health so necessary to Catherine's lovers. His portrait, painted by Levitsky, depicts an elegant, somewhat dandified young man with a delicate sensitive face, but does not show the superb physique which Lanskoy must have had in order to become a member of the élite Chevalier Gardes, chosen from among the tallest and handsomest men in the Russian army. A private in this privileged corps ranked as a sub-lieutenant in the ordinary army, and it was their special duty to care for the safety of the sovereign. But by the time he was twenty-four, Lanskoy found he was too poor to keep up with his brother officers living on the fringes of the court. And in the late summer of 1779 he asked to be transferred to a regiment of the line and sent to a provincial garrison. The request was turned down by the Vice-President of the College of War, who was none other than Prince Potemkin, and the bewildered Lanskoy found himself suddenly and unaccountably appointed to be the Prince's personal *aide-de-camp*.

Potemkin appears to have had an almost feminine intuition into the workings of Catherine's mind. Korsakof was still high in favour when Lanskoy was singled out as a possible candidate for the future. The Prince's knowledge of what went on in the coulisses of the palace had made him aware of Countess Bruce's infatuation for the reigning favourite, and he was taking no chances of allowing one of the most lucrative positions in the country, one which he himself had chosen to relinquish on personal grounds, to fall into the hands of a rival faction. When Catherine, lacerated in her pride and apparently broken-hearted, turned for consolation to her understanding and 'complaisant husband', she found to her delight that he had a new and handsome *aide-de-camp*, agreeable in his manners, completely unspoiled and, what was the most gratifying of all, obviously bewitched by her at first sight. But there was not only the problem of finding a new lover, there was also the problem of finding another '*éprouveuse*', someone who was more discreet and not quite so young and fascinating as Prascovia Bruce. Mademoiselle Protassof, a distant relative of the Orlovs, was chosen to fill this highly confidential post. Little is known of the lady, whose 'mystic office' was immortalized by Byron in his *Don Juan*. But many years later among the glittering figures of the Vienna Congress was a little old lady covered in diamonds whom all the Russian delegation, beginning with the Emperor Alexander, treated with the greatest deference, and who was none other than the Empress Catherine's devoted '*épreuveuse*'.

Korsakof's defection was not mourned for long. By St Catherine's day, 24 November 1779, Alexander Lanskoy had become Her Majesty's *aide-de-camp* with the rank of general. After being so poor that, according to his French teacher, he had no more than five shirts to his name, he had now a hundred thousand roubles to spend on his wardrobe, vast country estates and hundreds of serfs.

With the coming of Lanskoy began one of the happiest and most constructive periods of Catherine's private life. He did not arouse in her the wild physical passion she had felt for Orlov and Potemkin and to a lesser degree for Korsakof. But he inspired her with a quasi-maternal affection which gradually developed into a love stronger and more enduring than any that she had ever known. He for his part did everything to please her. He was by nature both intelligent and tactful and firmly refused to take an active part in public affairs or to interfere in politics. Catherine discovered to her delight that he had an excellent assimilative brain and a passionate desire to learn. He was artistic by nature with a genuine good taste and was the perfect companion for her leisure hours in helping her to lay out the gardens of Tzarskoye Selo and superintend the building of a new wing to Elisabeth's Summer Palace. In this enormous palace, with a façade stretching for over a thousand yards, Catherine had spent the first fifteen years of her reign living in squalor and discomfort. Grimm was the first to hear of her plans:

At Tzarskoye Selo there is going to be a terrible upheaval in the private apartments. The Empress has no desire to remain in two unworthy rooms. . . . She is going to pull down the main and only staircase at the end of the house; she wants to live in the midst of three gardens; she wants to enjoy from her windows the same view as from the main balcony; she will have ten rooms and for their decoration she will ransack her whole library and give her imagination free rein – and the result will be like these two pages, that is to say completely without common-sense.

The five years during which Lanskoy was her constant companion saw the fulfilment of Catherine's creative activities. Her 'building mania' was almost as costly as her *'gloutonnerie d'art'*. In 1778 she acquired the great Walpole collection from Houghton Hall. Few art sales ever caused so much furore as when Sir Robert Walpole's spendthrift heir sold his grandfather's pictures in order to pay his debts. Catherine's ambassador, Count Musin Poushkin, was first in the field, outbidding all other buyers and, after lengthy and acrimonious transactions, acquiring the whole collection for the sum of thirty-six thousand pounds. Lord Walpole's uncle, who had always coveted the pictures, commented with considerable bitterness in a letter to Sir Horace Mann, 'To be sure I would rather they were sold to the Crown of England than to that of Russia, where they will be burnt in a wooden palace at the first insurrection'. There was an outcry over the collection leaving the country. Questions were asked in Parliament. But the British government replied, as they have replied on so many subsequent occasions, that in times of crisis thirty-six thousand pounds of public money was too much to be spent on art, and two hundred pictures, including some magnificent Rubens, a *Nativity* by Murillo and a Van Dyck masterpiece, *The Virgin with a Partridge*, were added to the Hermitage collection, which by now was one of the finest in the world. Catherine wrote in triumph to Grimm: 'The Walpoles are no more to be had, because your very humble servant has placed her paws upon them and no more intends to let go than a cat would a mouse.'

Strangely enough, the British ambassador makes no mention of this either in his diary or his letters, beyond writing 'that Her Majesty has been kind enough to let my sister travel home in the frigate which has been sent to fetch the Houghton pictures'. As an art collector Catherine paid the highest prices and got the best value for her money. Like many of her kind, she appreciated most what she had paid most for. Poor Falconet who had been labouring for twelve years on his colossal statue of Peter the Great, and who had been so foolish as to ask less for his work than Catherine had been prepared to give, soon became an object of irritation rather than of admiration. His nervous and irascible temperament was not able to stand up to the Empress who wanted quick results and could not bear '*tracasseries*'. Broken in health and in spirit, he left Russia in 1778, four years before his bronze horseman was publicly unveiled on the banks of the Neva, bearing the proud and simple inscription '*Petrus Prima, Caterina Secundo*'. The Empress never invited the sculptor to return for the inauguration, neither did she express her gratitude other than by sending him a commemorative gold medal.

The Neo-classic art of Charles Louis Clerisseau roused her to the highest pitch of enthusiasm and she begged Grimm to acquire as many of his drawings as possible. Why should not Clerisseau design her a '*maison antique*' for the park at Tzarskoye Selo? Unfortunately the artist was so carried away by the importance of his commission and the affluence of his patron, that instead of designing a small pavilion, he sent her plans for a vast palace, reminiscent of Diocletian's palace at Spalato. Catherine was furious and refused to pay the exaggerated price asked for his designs. An attempt to placate her by sending her a folio of unsolicited drawings only added to her wrath. Grimm, who appears to have pleaded for the artist, was told 'liquidate Monsieur Clerisseau. Get rid of him at all costs.' But Clerisseau was not to be liquidated so easily. And a few years later the Empress was telling her '*souffre douleur*': 'Pay Clerisseau what I owe him. I do not want any more of his drawings, so see he does not send me any more.'

She would drive a harder bargain with her artists than many of her subjects, and there is more of the sensible German business woman than the extravagant Maecenas in her instructions to Grimm asking the Director of the Russian Academy in Rome,

to find her two good architects, Italian by nationality and clever by profession, whom he will engage for the service of Her Imperial Majesty of all the Russias by contract for so many years, and that he will send them from Rome to St Petersburg like a bag of tools. He is not to give them millions but a decent and sensible salary – not types like Falconet – men with their feet on the ground – not in the clouds. . . . All my architects have become too old or too blind, too slow or too lazy, too young or too idle, too stuck-up or too rich, too heavy-weight or too light-weight – in short anything you like except what I need.

Five months later two Italians landed on the banks of the Neva. One was a mediocrity called Trombara; the other was a native of Bergamo by the name of Giacomo Quarenghi, who became one of Catherine's favourite architects and helped to make St Petersburg one of the loveliest cities in the world. The French architects who had been so popular in Elisabeth's day had fallen into disrepute. Catherine declared she wanted Italians 'as we already have Frenchmen who know too much and build hideous houses both on the exterior and in the interior, just because they know too much'.

But the most original of all the architects who worked for Catherine, and who in ideas and taste was closest to his patron-ess, was a lowland Scot by the name of Charles Cameron. The Empress never professed to be a judge of pictures or of sculpture, though she was quick at detecting a fake, but she had always had exquisite taste in the decoration of her houses, combined with an infallible flair for finding the right man to execute her wishes. The frivolous taste of the gay Grand Duchess is reflected in Rinaldi's Chinese Pavilion at Oranienbaum, and the delightful folly of Katalnaya Gorka, built for no other purpose than a day's amusement, a sophisticated version of the 'icehills or toboggan slides, known to the Western world as *les montagnes russes*'. And still in middle age we find the Empress complaining to Grimm that 'her building mania is the very devil for it eats up money and the more one builds the more one wants to build. It is a disease like drunkenness, to which one becomes an addict.' Casually and in parenthesis she mentions that she has got hold 'of a Mr Cameron, Scottish by nationality, Jacobite by persuasion, a superb draughtsman, nourished on antiquities and known for a book he has written on ancient baths. We are creating together a terraced garden with baths below and a gallery above. It will be the finest of the fine.' What she does not mention is that Cameron had studied under Clerisseau in Rome and that much of their mutual inspiration was derived from the portfolio of the artist's drawings in her possession.

The Empress soon discovered that Cameron was not only an architect but an artist of subtle and completely original taste. In the first suite of rooms he designed at Tzarskoye Selo, the most enchanting results were achieved with the simplest of materials. A translucent effect was produced merely by placing coloured flannel under columns and panels of glass, while Wedgwood plaques, ordered by Cameron from England, were placed against cool green walls, and wood and stucco were painted to give the illusion of stone and marble. The Empress never allowed an architect the use of expensive materials until he had proved his worth. But by 1781 Cameron was working in agate and lapis, in malachite and bronze, giving free rein to his imagination, inspired by the recent excavations at Herculaneum and Pompeii. Catherine wrote in pride, 'People flock to see my new apartments, because nothing like them has ever been seen before, and I myself am never tired of looking at them.'

But Cameron's salary for a year did not equal what young Lanskoy spent in a week. Priding himself on being a man of culture, he became a collector of *objets de vertu*, and we hear of the doting Empress paying no less than fifty thousand roubles to present him with the Duke of Orleans's collection of Greek and Roman cameos. Yet even Lanskoy's extravagances were as nothing compared to Potemkin's reckless expenditure, which forced the printing of more and more '*assignats*'. The late seventies and early eighties saw the fulfilment of his talents as an organizer and administrator. His activities were manifold for now that they had ceased to be lovers his working association with the Empress was even closer than before. Many of Catherine's instructions to her ministers and governors were drafted and corrected in his hand. She consulted him over the most important and the most trivial things, whether it was a new tax levy or the reception of some foreign prince. But his main work lay in consolidating and expanding Russia's dominions in the south, in developing its economical and cultural life by building new ports and cities, factories and universities. Millions of roubles were spent on schemes many of which failed to materialize. Foundations of cities sank back into the steppe before they were ever built. He set himself a task before which even the greatest genius might have quailed, and instead of criticizing his failures we can only marvel at how much he managed to achieve in a comparatively short space of time. He was a man obsessed by a vision, the vision of a new Byzantium. The dream was never realized, but the Russian ports on the Black Sea survive as memorials to the man whom Catherine loved because, like Peter the Great, 'he believed nothing to be impossible'.

CHAPTER TWENTY-FOUR

'Count Falkenstein'

Maria-Theresa of Austria had never got over her dislike of the Russian Empress. Political circumstances and the fear of another war had forced her to write those fulsome and ingratiating letters which gave Catherine so much pleasure. But she was scandalized when her son accepted an invitation from one whom she regarded as 'a monster of depravity'. Joseph had no intention of listening to his mother's complaints. Both he and his Chancellor, Prince Kaunitz, were convinced that an Austrian–Russian alliance was the only way in which the Hapsburg Empire would be able to revenge itself on Prussia for blocking its way to further expansion in Germany.

The austere, reticent young man with his liberal principles and simple tastes was just as avid for glory as the extrovert Russian Empress. Both wanted to chase the Turk out of Europe. But whereas Catherine, the romantic, saw herself crowned in Constantinople, Joseph, the realist, was ready to content himself with Belgrade and the Balkans. Catherine, or rather Potemkin, dreamt of resurrecting the Roman kingdom of Dacia, with Potemkin himself as king. Joseph coveted the commerce of the lower Danube and of the Adriatic ports, for which Venice could be compensated by handing her over the Morea, Crete and Cyprus. All these chimerical plans were to be discussed, or rather hinted at, at Mogilev, for neither of the two protagonists was as yet sufficiently sure of the other to divulge the full extent of their ambitions.

Frederick of Prussia had every reason to be apprehensive over this new friendship which spelled the end of the 'northern system' and its architect, Count Panin. The old statesman, who was still officially at the head of the College of Foreign Affairs, was not invited to accompany the Empress to Mogilev. Not even Potemkin was present at the private talks between Emperor and Empress, who appeared to like one another at first sight and to have much in common. Both were children of their age, imbued with the doctrines of enlightenment, readers of Locke and of Adam Smith, advocates of religious tolerance and the right of every man to worship in his own fashion. But whereas Joseph had to battle against the bigoted orthodoxy of his mother's court, to which no heretic was ever admitted, Catherine prided herself on inviting archimandrites and Roman bishops, rabbis and mullahs to dine at the same table. The Jesuits, who were being persecuted in Catholic Europe, found a refuge in Russia. The Empress referred to them as her *'bons coquins de Jésuites'* and appreciated their contribution to the education of the country. The handsome Jesuit college at Mogilev stood out in sharp contrast to the rickety wooden buildings of what Joseph referred to as a 'vile little town', which not even the genius of Potemkin could transform into a city fit to receive two of the greatest monarchs of their time.

Joseph, who hated all ceremony, insisted on travelling *incognito* as 'Count Falkenstein', a name he adopted on his journeys abroad and which enabled him to study the people and the country he was visiting far better than if he had been surrounded by an official entourage. He had instructed his ambassador in St Petersburg 'to beg the Empress to make no alteration in her plans on his account. The object of his visit was merely in order to have the pleasure of making her acquaintance . . . all he asked was that Count Falkenstein should be allowed to move freely among the gentlemen of her court and enjoy her company whenever she could spare her time.' No flattery could have been subtler or more calculated to please. In private he wrote to Prince Kaunitz:

We have to deal with a woman who cares only for herself and no more for Russia than I do. Hence we must flatter her, for vanity is her idol. Persistent good luck, exaggerated homage and the envy of all Europe have spoilt her, therefore we must howl with the wolves and, providing one achieves some good, the means by which it is achieved matters very little.

But in spite of his cynicism, his disgust at the dirt and squalor of Mogilev, where the walls of the wooden mansion built for his reception creaked and the mud oozed through the splendid carpets with which Potemkin had covered the unpaved streets – in spite of all this, he was impressed by the obscure little German Princess who had completed the work of Peter the Great and made Russia into a European power. Her gaiety and erudition enchanted him. She, who had never met Voltaire or travelled farther west than Berlin and Hamburg, spoke of the old philosopher 'as the master whose works had formed her mind and whose recent death she had mourned as that of her dearest friend'. With the mixture of simplicity and frankness which disarmed her severest critics, Catherine told the Emperor that, when she was younger, everything she did or wrote had to pass the test of whether it would please Voltaire. She had made part of the Hermitage into a shrine to his memory. Baron Grimm was in the process of negotiating the purchase of his entire library and encountering fierce opposition from the French government. Houdon's seated figure of the philosopher cast in bronze was on the way to St Petersburg and Huber's famous caricatures were already in her possession. Catherine's enthusiasm made Joseph regret that once on his travels he had passed close to Ferney without stopping to visit the owner.

While Emperor and Empress played with the catchwords of liberty and little by little unmasked their plans for the future, the foreign envoys noted with concern that Count Falkenstein was prolonging his visit to Russia, spending a week in Moscow, while the Empress completed her tour of White Russia. He rejoined her at Tzarskoye Selo, where, respecting his desire for anonymity, Catherine had transformed one of the bath houses into an Austrian inn, with the English gardener, James Bushe, dressed up as an inn-keeper. Here Joseph was able to satisfy his wish of moving freely among Catherine's courtiers in surroundings which provided a curious contrast to the Vienna Hofburg, where no foreigner was received unless he could produce his sixteen quarterings of nobility.

Adventurers of every kind flourished in St Petersburg, appearing at the Empress's *levées* and public balls to which any well-dressed foreigner was admitted, from Casanova, who visited Russia at the beginning of the reign, to the bigamous Duchess of Kingston who in 1778 moored her yacht by the Admiralty quay. Soldiers of fortune from the penniless Prince of Nassau-Siegen, who was ready to fight in any and every war, to the American privateer, John Paul Jones, who was given the rank of a Russian admiral; from the English navigator, Lieutenant Billings, who gained enormous prestige by claiming to have accompanied Captain Cook on his last voyage to the Aleutians, to the South American revolutionary, General Miranda, who, to the fury of the Spaniards, was given financial aid by a sympathetic Empress; there was not one who did not succeed in obtaining some lucrative appointment and in leaving the country richer than when he came.

The Emperor's sombre elegance, his only order, the Golden Fleece, struck an alien note in the gilded opulence of Catherine's court, where the latest fashions from Versailles vied with the Oriental splendour of Tartar khans and Georgian princes. Nor was Joseph's cold and contemptuous manner calculated to endear him to the Russians. He disapproved of the wild extravagance, the thousands of roubles spent in one night's fireworks at Peterhof, where pyrotechnic skill depicted a temple of friendship flaming in the summer skies; he did not want to be entertained; all he wanted was to discuss politics, and even the well-disposed Catherine wished he would make a little more effort to please her courtiers. The one who disliked him most was Potemkin who was childishly jealous of the Emperor. He considered his sovereign and his country superior to the rest of the world and saw no reason for Catherine to be so flattered at having a Hapsburg as a guest. He resented being excluded from their talks and showed his displeasure so openly that Catherine had to admonish him on his surly behaviour 'which will make people wonder whether they are justified in handing out the honours and decorations I am always asking for you'.

Potemkin had a passion for orders and decorations, and all those who wished to be on good terms with the Empress had to humour this weakness. The Empress was willing to create him a 'Serene Highness', but refused him the Golden Fleece on the grounds it could not be given to non-Catholics. The Kings of Prussia, Poland and Sweden distributed their highest orders to Catherine's favourites. But when Sir James Harris hinted to the British cabinet that 'the Garter would be a good way of winning over Prince Potemkin', he was personally reprimanded by George III 'for having dared to suggest such a thing'. Potemkin's dislike of the Emperor was reciprocated. The punctilious Joseph regarded Catherine's viceroy 'as neglectful, indolent and insouciant' and deplored the fact that the Empress had no person about her 'who dared to restrain or repress her passions'. Nevertheless, Joseph was not unaware of the element of greatness in Potemkin, for he admitted 'he could understand the Empress's infatuation for the Prince. What he could not understand was her "*schwärmerei*" over a silly boy like Lanskoy.' The favourite had not accompanied his Imperial mistress on her tour of White Russia. But while she was at Moghilev, Catherine considered it quite natural for her and the Emperor to attend the magnificent banquet given by Count Yoritz, the most unworthy of all her former lovers.

The fastidious Emperor can hardly have enjoyed his evening, but he was determined to be pleasant,

to enter into the character of a woman whom he considered to be of undoubted genius, though whoever had to deal with her should never lose sight of her sex. . . . The only way to keep well with her was neither to spoil her or to affront her directly; to give way to her in matters of no importance; to render every necessary refusal as palatable as possible; to let her perceive a constant desire to please, yet at the same time a firm adherence to certain essential principles.

But in the end, it was Joseph who had to sacrifice his principles to what he called 'the Empress's Byzantine fantasies'.

The two sovereigns parted as the best of friends and their relationship was kept warm by a regular interchange of letters, some of them almost flirtatious in tone. It survived the mutual disillusion of the second Turkish war and, when the Emperor died, worn out and embittered at the early age of forty-nine, Catherine mourned him more sincerely than many of his own subjects. She described him as 'an eagle, whose greatness his ungrateful people had failed to recognize'.

As Catherine grew closer to Joseph, she became more and more hostile to King Frederick. The visit of the Prussian heir-apparent followed closely on that of the Hapsburg Emperor. But Frederick can have had little hope that his fat and unattractive nephew could counterbalance the effect made by the cultured and accomplished Joseph. The poor Prince did his best to please, even to the extent of borrowing money from his brother-in-law, the Stadtholder of Holland, in order to supplement the meagre sums allowed to him by his parsimonious uncle. But the Empress confined her attentions to the minimum, and the effusive welcome given him by the young court, the friendship which developed between him and the Grand Duke Paul was hardly calculated to win favour in Catherine's eyes, who was heard to say in public 'that after her death, her son would try to turn Russia into a Prussian province'.

No sooner had the Prussian Prince departed than the Prusso-phile Count Panin was replaced at the College of Foreign Affairs by the Austrophile Count Ostermann. But the new minister had little to do, except carry out his sovereign's orders. From now on it was Catherine who directed her own foreign policy and behind her was Bezborodko, the humble clerk now raised to the position of First Secretary – a man whom the proud Emperor despised as 'a low scribe, a mere interpreter who retains the sentiments of that class of man', but whose judgment Catherine was beginning to trust as much as she trusted that of her beloved Potemkin. Within a year of their meeting at Moghilev, the two sovereigns had signed an offensive and defensive alliance by which they mutually agreed that, in the event of a war with the Porte, they would support one another with an equal number of troops and neither would make a separate peace. Austria promised that, in the event of a Turkish attack on Russia, she would regard the aggression as 'a common cause' and come to her ally's aid. For the Emperor's wily old counsellor, Prince Kaunitz, to have permitted the insertion of this clause, showed the lengths to which he and his master were prepared to go in order to win Russia's friendship. Of the two rulers, Joseph was the more cautious and the more calculating, Catherine was the more impulsive and the more imprudent. But whereas she was the luckiest of women, he was the most unfortunate of men.

Two years after their meeting, Russia peacefully annexed the Crimea, while Joseph was still wondering whether it was worth antagonizing his brother-in-law in France 'for the sake of a strip of desert in Bosnia or in Serbia'. By failing to take him into her confidence on what she considered to be only a Russian concern, the Empress spared him the necessity of coming to any definite decision. Having won the Crimea, she was willing to wait before embarking on any further adventures. The annexation of the Crimea was largely achieved by the cunning and subtlety of Potemkin, who for the past years had been colonizing waste-lands with elements favourable to Russia and only waiting for a suitable opportunity to move his troops into the country. Plague broke out in the Crimea in the early summer of 1783 and Potemkin brought his soldiers to the borders. Still he waited, while the impetuous Catherine bombarded him with letters complaining of his unaccountable silence and begging to be informed as to what was going on in the Crimea. For two months he kept her without news, ignoring her letters. The plague decimated the population; a Georgian chieftain profited from the situation to invade the country at the head of six thousand men and, finally, Potemkin acted. Russian troops swept into the Crimea capturing the Georgian chief and forcing the surrender of his men, breaking up the last pockets of resistance among the rival khans, who all in turn swore allegiance to the great Empress from the north. On 23 July, the Crimea was officially incorporated into the Russian Empire and his grateful sovereign created Potemkin Prince of Tauris, the classical name for the Crimea. Catherine's new ally had no choice but to accept the accomplished fact and applaud her success, while making private reservations as to the compensation Austria would seek at the earliest opportunity. But the

Western powers, who had little faith in Austria's show of generosity or in Russia's desire for peace, saw with concern the approach of another war.

Potemkin's activities now extended throughout the Empire. He governed the four largest provinces in Russia, and in 1784 was appointed President of the College of War and promoted to the rank of Field-Marshal. His reforms of the army were progressive and humane. He moderated the established punishments, forbade the thrashing of recruits and issued the soldiers with comfortable and hygienic uniforms with loose tunics, wide breeches and shorter boots. The powdering and curling of hair, which was torture to the ordinary soldier, was abolished and hair was cut short so that it could be easily washed and combed. Potemkin, who was himself the dirtiest and most slovenly of men, showed an almost obsessive concern for army hygiene. The same man who would receive ambassadors wearing little more than a pair of trousers, was always immaculately groomed on the parade ground. He respected religious creeds and customs, and battalions were formed according to race and nationality. There was an Albanian battalion and a Serbian regiment made up of refugees from Turkey, but the most astonishing of all was a Jewish battalion known as the Israelovsky. The Jews, who had been persecuted under Elisabeth and were merely tolerated by Catherine, were taken under the protection of Potemkin who envisaged the day when both Constantinople and Jerusalem would be freed of the Turks, and when the Jews, who caused so much trouble in Europe, could go back to their native land. Potemkin may be said to have been a precursor of modern Zionism. Unlike the majority of his contemporaries, he believed that the Jews had a right to Palestine. More realistic than idealists like Herzl and Balfour, he foresaw that there was bitter fighting to be done before the Jews were firmly established in their own country, and the Jewish battalion was formed in order to prepare them for the future. Apprehensive tradesmen and frightened usurers who had never mounted horses in their lives were pressed into active service, to be drilled and bullied by Potemkin's sergeants into an efficient fighting force.

Was Potemkin a madman or a genius? Many were inclined to believe the former. Count Simon Vorontsov, who was nominated in the early eighties as ambassador to London, had serious doubts about his sanity when he requested him to get in touch with the British government with a view to procuring gangs of English convicts to colonize the Crimea. The discipline of the British officers serving on Russian ships and the cleanliness and the prosperity of the English colony in St Petersburg had convinced Potemkin that they would be the ideal settlers for the Crimea. His letter to Simon Vorontsov was written thirty years before the first penal station was founded in Botany Bay, but one can hardly blame the ambassador for refusing to further his request, and for soliciting the help of Bezborodko to prevent Potemkin from influencing the Empress with his mad schemes.

By the early eighties, Bezborodko was recognized to be one of the most important persons in the Empire. His influence was second only to Potemkin's and the restraint and caution which Catherine exercised in the diplomatic negotiations with England which lasted from 1780 to 1782 can be directly attributed to the secretary, whom Sir James Harris erroneously believed to be on his side. Potemkin, who was the ambassador's friend and ally, refused to admit that the Empress was at times more ready to listen to Bezborodko than to him and persuaded Harris that 'it was Catherine herself who had become weak and vacillating with age and allowed her political decisons to be entirely dictated by her passions. A slight quarrel or misunderstanding with her young lover was sufficient to throw her off balance.'

Three years' residence in St Petersburg had severely impaired the ambassador's health and temper. He had made little headway in securing the alliance so necessary to his country. Though the Empress continued to profess her friendship for England, her veneration for the late Lord Chatham and her admiration for Mr Fox, these sentiments in no way influenced her determination not to become involved in England's wars. She publicly celebrated one of Lord Rodney's naval victories by distributing money to the poor of St Petersburg and inviting the leading members of the British colony to a reception at the palace. But the following day she put her signature to the 'declaration of armed neutrality' which was a thinly veiled threat to Britain's naval power. No wonder there were times when the ambassador despaired of success and asked to be removed from 'this singular court where the policy changed from day to day according to Her Majesty's whims'. Meanwhile, Potemkin kept telling him 'to flatter the Empress's ego, by offering her a prize so glittering she would not be able to refuse'. And Harris finally succeeded in getting his government to make an offer of a nature which he thought that no one as vainglorious as the Russian Empress would have any hesitation in accepting. The offer was conditional. If Russia and England concluded an offensive and defensive pact and the Empress was able to mediate a just and honourable peace between Great Britain, France and Spain, then England would cede to Russia possession of the Balearic Islands including Minorca and the fortified Fort Mahon.

Potemkin was the first to be sounded as to the reactions of the Empress. His imagination was immediately set on fire. Already he saw Russian ships manoeuvring in the Mediterranean, the Russian Eagle flying over Fort Mahon and Greek Orthodox churches and chapels crowning every hillside on the Balearic Islands. He pleaded England's cause with eloquence and passion but the Empress, who was sorely tempted, hesitated. The prize was too glittering. Too much would be expected in return. '*La mariée est trop belle. On veut me tromper,*' was the famous phrase in which she declined an offer which would have given Russia a stake in the Mediterranean in the centuries to come. Behind Catherine, one recognizes the shrewdness and caution of her Ukrainian secretary, reminding her that Russia's interests lay nearer home.

She took many weeks before she said definitely 'no' to England's offer. Finally she drafted a declaration for Potemkin to read to the ambassador. The draft, which was written out in Russian and heavily corrected, shows that Bezborodko had a hand in it. She 'thanked the British government for its offer, expressed her gratitude and friendship, her desire to help in any way short of involving her country in a war'. Fuming with anger, Potemkin told Harris 'she has a burning desire to possess

Minorca, but she has not the courage to subscribe to the means by which it can be obtained ... her ambition disappears before the most remote probability of risk and she is sensible of nothing but the flattery of the hour, because it can be obtained without danger.' It was not Catherine's weakness but her sagacity which led her to refuse Minorca, not her cowardice but her common-sense, and it was these very qualities which gradually impressed themselves on Europe and earned her the epithet of 'great'. A year later, the Treaty of Paris gave Minorca back to Spain.

CHAPTER TWENTY-FIVE

Patroness of the Arts

England had enjoyed for centuries the privileges of the most favoured of foreign nations. Her ships had carried and handled the bulk of the Russian trade. But the departure of Sir James Harris without having successfully concluded his mission marked the beginning of the decline of English influence and the rising popularity of the French. The increasing demand for French luxury goods, the influence of *les philosophes*, the vogue for Parisian taste and culture and the growing numbers of the Russian nobility who travelled abroad and made Paris into their Mecca, all contributed to a *rapprochement* between the two countries. Even Marie-Antoinette, who had inherited all her mother, Maria-Theresa's, aversion for Catherine, was ready to welcome to Versailles women as fascinating as the Princess Dolgorouki and men as brilliant as Count Stroganov, while the legendary fame of an Orlov and a Princess Dashkova, both of whom visited Paris in the late seventies and early eighties, added to Catherine's already prestigious reputation. Russia and her Empress had become the fashion, and Baron Grimm reported from Paris that the French were suffering from an epidemic of 'Catherinitis'. The theatres were producing plays on Russian themes, every district had either a Café du Nord or a Hotel à l'Impératrice de Russie.

Tradesmen called their shops '*à l'enseigne de la Russie Galante*' and a certain tailor had made a fortune by obtaining the model of the overall that Catherine had designed for her little grandsons. The Empress was pleased, but not impressed: 'the French have taken to me as if I were a new feather to be stuck in their head-dresses and it will not last any longer than their other fashions'. Nor did she appreciate the flattering attentions paid to the Russian ladies at Versailles: 'It will only go to their heads and make them spoilt and pretentious when they get home.' What irritated her still more was the way in which Princess Dashkova had been lionized in Paris. Her self-imposed exile had made her into a European celebrity, too important to be ignored in her own country. The Princess was well received on her return to Russia. The Empress was lavish in her gifts and Potemkin went out of his way to win her to his side. Dashkova's two brothers, Alexander and Simon Vorontsov, whose loyalty to the late Emperor had excluded them from court at the beginning of the reign, were restored to favour; their sister, Elisabeth, was treated with magnanimity, for Catherine was too proud to avenge herself on someone as stupid and as vulgar as her late husband's mistress. Elisabeth Vorontsov was allowed to marry a court chamberlain and presented with a house in Moscow, but Dashkova herself was always looked upon as a potential trouble-maker. The sovereign who received the homage of the world was jealous of the presumptuous little Princess whom Paris had acclaimed as the heroine of the Russian *coup d'état*, and Dashkova, who was hurt and piqued by the Empress's lack of confidence, left Russia again in 1779 on the excuse of completing the education of her son.

In Leyden she ran into her old enemy Prince Orlov, no longer the spoilt darling of fortune but a pathetic and adoring husband, visiting every town in Europe to find a cure for his young wife who was slowly dying of consumption. Orlov managed to infuriate the Princess within the first hours of their meeting by complimenting her on the charm and good looks of her son and suggesting that he would make a perfect candidate for the post of Imperial favourite. The Empress's sexual desires were growing with the years. She was in constant need of new and younger blood. Lanskoy was already reported to be breaking under the strain. It would not be long before the post fell vacant and Orlov assured the Princess that he and his family would do all in their power to promote the chances of her son. Orlov made what he considered to be a friendly offer, but in her memoirs Dashkova professes to have been outraged by a proposition which was as insulting to her pride as it was dishonouring to the Empress. Nevertheless, on her return to Russia in 1782, we find the ambitious Princess soliciting Prince Potemkin for his help in obtaining a commission for her son. 'Serenissimus' was generally known to be the purveyor of Her Majesty's pleasures and young Dashkova's future seemed assured when he was given a commission in the Semeonovsky Guards and appointed one of the Prince's *aides-de-camp*. Before long his own indiscretions, followed by an unsuitable marriage, shattered whatever hopes his mother might have cherished of his having a brilliant career.

When the Princess returned to Russia, the unfortunate Orlov was no longer in a position to help a protégé. His wife's death in Lausanne in the spring of 1781 had completely unhinged a mind already affected by the fits of the palsy which had afflicted him in the past years. He stayed on in Switzerland, spending all day weeping beside her tomb, till finally his brothers succeeded in bringing him back to Moscow. Despair turned to dementia, and he died raving mad in the early spring of 1783.

On one occasion he managed to escape his brother's vigilance and appeared at court in St Petersburg, haggard, wild-eyed and totally inconsequential. Acting against the advice of her entourage, Catherine consented to see him, showing neither fear nor horror at his presence, speaking to him gently and kindly as to a child. It was heart-rending for her to see the magnificent Orlov reduced to this condition and she was so affected by the interview that she had to retire to her bed for several days. She had always shown loyalty and devotion to Gregory and his brothers. No bitterness or recriminations marred her memory of the man whom not even Potemkin had ever been allowed to criticize in her presence. The infidelities from which she had suffered so cruelly in the past were long since forgotten and forgiven by a woman who understood the frailties of human passion.

The letter she wrote to Baron Grimm on hearing of Orlov's death was both moving and sincere.

Although I was prepared for the event, I must confess that it has caused me the greatest pain. I have lost in him a friend and above all a man to whom I owe the deepest gratitude and who placed me under the greatest obligations. In vain I am told and say to myself all that can be said on these occasions. Fits of sobbing are my reply and I have suffered terribly since the moment when I received the fatal news. . . . Prince Orlov's genius was very great; his courage was, I believe, the *ne plus ultra* of all courage; he always knew at the crucial moment exactly what should be done for matters to be decided the way he wished; and at the right moment when it was necessary, he was gifted with an eloquence which no man was able to resist.

She admitted he was spoilt, careless and scornful of everything in which he was not directly concerned or over matters which he did not immediately grasp. But there was a certain quality about the man which no one could withstand. Unlike Potemkin, he had no lust for power, no interest in accumulating riches. The jewels and art treasures, the palaces and estates were accepted with a lazy indifference. But he never travelled abroad without being surrounded by an aura of splendour which added to her Imperial glory.

Orlov and Panin, the two men who had dominated the first years of Catherine's reign, died within a few days of one another, the one in a padded cell, the other immobilized in an invalid's chair, afflicted by a stroke which deprived him of understanding. The old statesman had remained in St Petersburg after his dismissal, 'in order to provide the Empress with a living proof of her ingratitude'. His last years were further embittered by the Grand Duke's neglect. Paul, who was a coward and feared for his own future, was frightened of attaching himself to a man who had earned his mother's displeasure.

The Empress showed little grief. Panin had always been someone to be propitiated and feared from that June morning of 1762 when he appeared on the balcony of the Summer Palace holding her son by the hand. In those early days, both he and Dashkova had plotted and intrigued to curb her powers and force her to accept a constitution. At the same time she recognized him as a patriot and an astute statesman, who had helped to consolidate her throne. Comparing Orlov and Panin, her two counsellors for many years, she writes in the same letter to Grimm:

Fire and water could not make a greater contrast yet things went on in grand style. The boldness of the one, and the qualified prudence of the other, with your very humble servant trick-riding between them, gave a touch of elegance and grace to what, in any case, is no fool's game. Count Panin was naturally lazy, but he had acquired the art of passing it off as considered caution. His nature was neither as kind nor as open as that of Prince Orlov, but he was more worldly and knew better how to conceal his faults and vices which were considerable.

It is a somewhat niggardly tribute to a statesman who had served her for over twenty years but who had also dared to contest her wishes – behaviour which even the most liberal of autocrats refused to tolerate. His last action before retirement was to oppose the Empress's plan to send her son and daughter-in-law on a grand tour of Europe. He feared she might profit by his absence to disinherit Paul in favour of her grandson, Alexander, who at three years old was the apple of her eye and whose childish sayings were fondly repeated as if they contained the wisdom of Solomon. The Grand Duchess, who longed to travel and be re-united with her family, was at first delighted at the idea but her pleasure faded when she was told that her children had to remain behind and that they were forbidden to visit Berlin.

Relations between the Empress and the Prussian monarch were at their lowest ebb. The old King could not forgive a German-born princess, the daughter of one of his former officers, for having discarded his friendship in favour of the Emperor. Frederick, who was versed in all the arts of flattery, was furious to find himself outwitted by a Hapsburg. When the Empress Maria-Theresa died only a few months after the historic meeting at Moghilev, Joseph went to the lengths of sending Catherine a frame embroidered by his mother, 'one of the objects she ordered me to distribute to her relatives and friends, among whom you are good enough to allow us to include you'. Nothing could have delighted Catherine more. The visit of the Prussian heir-apparent had been an anti-climax after the exhilarating atmosphere of Moghilev. Whatever might be his own opinion of his heir, Frederick expected a prince of Prussia to be treated with honour and respect. The breach was open and the King's vituperative tongue deliberately encouraged a defamatory campaign against 'the Messalina of the north'.

Catherine's decision to prevent her son from including Berlin in his itinerary led to bitter arguments between her and Paul, whose pro-Prussian sentiments were too well-known to be ignored. She decreed that Maria Feodorovna could meet her parents elsewhere, for the journey was to include state visits to Vienna and Versailles and to various Italian courts including the Vatican. The Empress had little sympathy for her daughter-in-law whose virtuous behaviour was in such a glaring contrast to her own. In her private letters to Grimm, she refers to husband and wife as '*das schwere bagage*' (heavy luggage). But she was ready to admit that the young Princess possessed both elegance and poise and had an excellent influence over her husband in preventing him from committing too many gaffes and indiscretions. The Empress's dislike of Paul had grown with the years. At the zenith of her power she was still so fundamentally insecure that she remained jealous of her son. Paul grew every year more and more like his father, and in Moscow the people acclaimed him as a true Romanov, while she still remained the foreign usurper. The old capital was therefore to be deliberately by-passed on the journey which the Empress had supervised down to the smallest detail. Paul regarded this as yet another of the pin-pricks and petty humiliations he had to suffer at his mother's hands.

But the journey which began under such gloomy auspices, with the Grand Duchess fainting three times before mounting the carriage, turned out to be a triumphal success. Apart from the state visits to Vienna and Paris, the voyage was one of pleasure and instruction and the young couple travelled *incognito* under the name of the Count and Countess du Nord. The Empress, who was rarely generous with her son, had on this occasion given him no less than three hundred thousand roubles for his carriages and post-horses and another hundred thousand for pocket money. Once they were out of Russia, she wrote to 'her dearest children' the most charming and affectionate of letters telling them to come straight home the moment they were home-sick and relating all the family details as to 'how Alexander had been given the map of Europe so that he could follow his parents' itinerary', and that the baby Constantine was delighted with his Greek nurse.

The poor Grand Duchess had never been told why her son had to be called Constantine and put in the charge of a Greek nurse, and she was horrified when she heard her mother-in-law discussing the possibility of having him crowned Emperor of Byzantium. It was all part and parcel of those 'Eastern fantasies' of which Paul so bitterly disapproved and was sufficiently unwise to discuss in conversation with King Stanislaus, who was the most indiscreet and garrulous of sovereigns, so that it was only a matter of days before the Grand Duke's criticism reached the Russian ambassador. Maria Feodorovna was as charmed by Stanislaus as every woman who came within his orbit. Even Catherine appears to have cherished tender memories of the lover she had admired as a man and despised as a king, and we find her asking her son 'as to whether his Polish Majesty was still such a delightful conversationalist or whether the cares of royalty had destroyed these qualities'. Somewhat ruefully she adds 'my old friend must have difficulty in tracing any resemblance between my contemporary portraits and the face he remembered from the past'.

The brilliant reception which Paul received in Poland was only a foretaste of what was still to come. The Emperor Joseph travelled to the Austrian frontier to welcome the heir of all the Russias. Vienna was *en fête* and Maria Feodorovna revelled in the understated elegance of a court and aristocracy who were supremely sure of themselves. Everything was calculated to please, and everyone from the Emperor downwards set themselves out to charm the young couple whose life in St Petersburg was one of continual frustration and neglect. The volatile and capricious Paul forgot his pro-Prussian sentiments and was completely won over by his Hapsburg host. A visit which was supposed to last a fortnight was prolonged for over a month, by which time the tired and overworked Emperor must have been delighted to see the last of his guests. But the Russian alliance was too important to be neglected. In the midst of dealing with the problems of his multi-racial Empire, with rebellion in the provinces and disturbances at home, with the reactionary aristocracy and a bigoted clergy opposing his reforms, the Emperor still found time to instruct his relatives in Tuscany, Modena and Naples as to what the Grand Duchess liked to eat. 'She prefers stewed fruit to rich desserts and neither she nor her husband touches wine. But she has a fondness for mineral water, providing it is not of the kind which purges too much.'

Taking their cue from Vienna, the Hapsburg Princes in Italy outvied one another with splendid entertainments till even the bitter and irascible Paul blossomed in the unaccustomed limelight of success. But Paris was the culmination of their journey and here again Catherine's popularity reflected on her son. Large crowds cheered the young couple whenever they appeared in public, whether at the theatre or the races; strolling through the gardens of the Tuileries or driving in a state carriage to Versailles. At court Marie-Antoinette used all her blandishments to fascinate Catherine's neglected son, while his wife was treated as a dear and cherished friend and presented with one of the loveliest and rarest of porcelain dinner sets ever to be produced by the manufacturers of Sèvres. It was so exquisite that the Grand Duchess thought it was intended either for the Queen or as a gift for her mother-in-law, and she could hardly believe her eyes when she saw the arms of Russia and of Württemberg painted on the plates.

The young couple lived in a dream world, though the tactful Grand Duchess took care not to express too much enthusiasm in her letters to the Empress, who preferred to hear of the shortcomings of the French, the bad roads, the mediocre plays; the discontented artists who looked to Russia for their benefactors. In order to please her, both son and daughter-in-law had to pretend to be bored by the frivolity and emptiness of the French court, whereas every day spent in Paris added to the enchantment of the voyage. The return to Russia came as an anti-climax. After an absence of nearly a year, their children looked upon them as strangers and clung to their grandmother's skirts. Paul was more unpopular than ever at his mother's court for the Empress had let it be known that his travels had spoilt him and put him completely out of touch with the habits and customs of his own country. For all her efforts, Maria Feodorovna had not been able to prevent some of her husband's indiscretions from reaching his mother's ears. Europe was full of Russian agents who had been trailing their footsteps and reporting every word of criticism he had uttered either against the Empress or her ministers.

But it was unworthy of Catherine to vent her indignation on the poor Grand Duchess. The money she had spent in Paris buying the latest creations of the Queen's milliner, Madame Bertin, was condemned by the Empress who appears to have forgotten her own youth. The cases from Paris had barely been unpacked before Catherine issued an edict forbidding the use of high head-dresses with feathers, and restricting frills or flounces to no more than an inch wide. Maria Feodorovna had been hoping to emulate the elegance of the French Queen, regardless of the fact that the elaborate fashions adopted by Marie-Antoinette were hardly suited to one of her tall and massive build, and she shed bitter tears when she was ordered to send Madame Bertin's creations back to Paris. Nor did it help when the stout old Empress told her with a certain complacency that large women like themselves looked far better in the simple, dignified Russian costumes than in all those Parisian fripperies.

The Grand Ducal couple returned to Russia at the time of the annexation of the Crimea and the apotheosis of Potemkin, after a year in which his influence had appeared to be on the decline. The Empress, who always expected spectacular deeds of her paladins, had been growing increasingly impatient of the Prince's delaying tactics and the fact that he rarely, if ever, troubled to answer her letters. His scandalous relations with his Englehardt nieces had reached a point when even the most tolerant of sovereigns was forced to disapprove. There was an open breach when she discovered that Catherine, the youngest and prettiest of the sisters, was pregnant by her uncle. This might have been forgiven, had she not planned to marry the fifteen-year-old Catherine to Alexis Bobrinskoy, her natural son by Orlov. The young people had been fond of one another since childhood, but Orlov had always opposed the marriage. Now Orlov was dead, having left his vast fortune to the son in whom he had shown little interest in his lifetime. Nor can Catherine be said to have been a very affectionate mother. 'Little Bo' is rarely mentioned in any of her letters and then usually on a note of irritation. After a few years spent at a military cadet school, where he was one of the wildest and most refractory of pupils, he was sent to complete his education in Paris in the charge of a dissolute and incompetent tutor. In Paris he contracted enormous debts which were only settled after his father's death. Little is known of his later life, beyond the fact that he married and settled down on one of his country estates, leaving behind him a numerous progeny. The Emperor Paul, who was capable of sudden and inexplicable acts of generosity, created him a count, perhaps out of sympathy for the half-brother whose childhood had been as lonely and neglected as his own. Still less is known of Catherine's daughter by Orlov, who was brought up as a niece of the talented Mademoiselle Protassof, who appears to have been equally competent as a foster-mother to her mistress's bastard as she was in trying out Her Majesty's lovers.

All of Catherine's maternal feelings were centred on her young lover. Alexander Lanskoy appealed to her heart, not only to her senses. 'He was a man of gold' who, as the months went by, became ever more indispensable to her happiness and well-being. Even someone as cynical as Bezborodko admitted that 'compared with the others he was a veritable angel. He had friends, he did not try to harm his neighbours and often he tried to help people.' It was a joy for Catherine to have an eager and talented pupil, who had a genuine taste and appreciation for art and who cultivated the company of men of superior intellect. He became an enthusiastic and discerning collector, and Baron Grimm was being constantly commissioned to secure some picture or piece of sculpture favoured by General Lanskoy. No one could have had a less military appearance than this charming young dilettante who, in the ordinary course of events, would never have risen above the rank of captain, and Lanskoy himself appears to have been aware of his inadequacies both as a general and as a lover, for we hear of him resorting to drugs and aphrodisiacs to enable him to cope with his mistress's insatiable demands.

Catherine did not appear to be aware of the strain she was imposing on her young lover nor of the jealousy he was arousing in Potemkin who, in spite of their mutual infidelities, considered that he had a prior claim on her affections. He had not reckoned on her falling in love with any of the pretty minions he had placed at her disposal. Now, at the height of his glory, he found he was no longer indispensable. After showering him with honours, she let him return to Kherson without shedding a single tear. On previous occasions they had never parted without both of them indulging in tears and histrionics. Now all her thoughts were concentrated on Lanskoy, whose gaiety and good humour made Tzarskoye Selo 'into the most charming and pleasant of places where the days passed so quickly one did not know what became of them'.

Catherine's happiness was of short duration. On 19 June 1784, Lanskoy complained of a sore throat which grew rapidly worse. The best doctors in the capital were summoned to his sick bed, but a malignant fever set in and in five days he died of what was said to have been diphtheria, but which, according to the Empress's English doctor, would never have proved fatal had not his constitution been already debilitated by an excessive use of aphrodisiacs.

The despair of a woman on whom fortune had smiled so constantly was terrible to witness. Her son and daughter-in-law, who came to offer their condolences, heard harsh sobbing from behind the door of the room to which they were refused admittance. Even the Empress's beloved grandchildren were kept away and we find her pouring out her grief in a heart-broken letter to Baron Grimm, telling him of the irreparable loss she had suffered from the death of her dearest friend, 'a young man whom she was bringing up; who was grateful, gentle and sincere; who profited by his studies and shared her tastes and whom she had hoped to be the support of her old age'. At the end of the letter she writes, 'I do not know what will become of me but I do know that in all my life I have never been so unhappy as now that my best and kindest friend has abandoned me like this.'

So bitter was her grief, so poignant her despair, that Bezborodko wrote to Potemkin asking him to return to court as quickly as possible. Three weeks later, the Prince was back in St Petersburg and Catherine describes him 'gliding round the palace like a great cat, howling with me in my grief and thereby making me feel more at ease'. The man who could be so cruel and heartless, so obsessed with his own ego, was now as gentle and as understanding as a woman, feigning a sorrow he was far from feeling, coaxing and gradually nursing her back to life, though two years later, the Empress was still found weeping by the Grecian urn she had put up to Lanskoy's memory in the gardens of Tzarskoye Selo, with the inscription 'from Catherine to my dearest friend'.

CHAPTER TWENTY-SIX

Serenissimus

The Empress remained all summer in seclusion at Tzarskoye Selo. It was only when the weather became damp and the apartments had to be heated that she was driven away by a smoking chimney in her room. 'Having nowhere to put my head, I ordered a carriage and came unexpectedly and with no one knowing it back to town. I disembarked to the Hermitage and yesterday for the first time I went to church, and everyone saw me and I saw everyone. But in truth it was such an effort that, on returning to my room, I felt so prostrate that anyone except myself would have fainted.' The date of this letter is 8 September 1785. From then on, Catherine led a more or less normal life, though it was February before she could face moving from her private apartments in the Hermitage back to the state rooms at the Winter Palace.

The wound caused by Lanskoy's death was by no means healed and the post of favourite was vacant for over seven months. The woman 'who found it difficult to exist one hour without love', now turned a deaf ear to all Potemkin's proposals. But he was very clever, or as she called it 'very sly'. There was no shortage of *aides-de-camp*. When one of them proved unsuitable, there was always another one at hand, and finally he succeeded in interesting her in a young man whom she had first met when he was a boy of thirteen. Alexis Yermolov was solid, safe and kind. He was lusty and handsome in a broad, rather coarse-featured way. She was in no mood for any arduous adventures, and his honest and straightforward manner, his dog-like devotion were qualities which for the moment were more appreciated than either charm or brilliance.

By the early spring of 1785, she was already confiding to Baron Grimm 'I am once more inwardly calm and serene, because with the help of our friends, we have made a great effort to control ourselves. I cannot complain of not being surrounded by people whose affection and care are all that is necessary to bring me back to life and give me relaxation. In short, I have found a friend who is very capable and very worthy of the name.' This is the only occasion on which Yermolov is mentioned in her correspondence and then it is not even by name, and in a very different tone from the extravagant praise bestowed on a Korsakof or even on a Yoritz. He appears to have acted as a sedative rather than as a cure, and the best that can be said in his favour is that he gave her sufficient serenity to work. The seventeen months in which he occupied the post of Imperial favourite were highly productive in both the artistic and the administrative fields.

These years saw the acquisition of the celebrated Baudouin collection, which Grimm had been trying to make her buy for the past five years, and the arrival in St Petersburg of Houdon's seated figure of Voltaire which, together with his bronze bust, cost the Empress no more than two thousand livres. The gallery of the Hermitage was so crowded that its contents overflowed into Catherine's summer palaces. She showed considerable discernment in her patronage of living artists, commissioning romantic ruins from Hubert Robert, a still-life from Chardin and paintings of all the basilicas in Rome from Pannini. When David Roentgen, a Moravian brother from Neuwied on the Rhine and the most celebrated cabinet-maker of the day, presented her with a secretaire, she was so overwhelmed by the perfection of his workmanship that she added another five thousand roubles to the twenty thousand he had asked. But Roentgen's visit to Russia was not an unqualified success. As in the case of Diderot and Falconet, he ended by boring his hostess, who complained to Grimm that he tried to convert the whole Hermitage to his faith, 'so he got his pay, gave us the keys and left. With him gone, tedium has gone as well.' Catherine was also a patron of music, though here she had to rely on the judgment of Potemkin who was intensely musical and kept an orchestra of Italians, conducted by the famous Sarti. Paisiello and later Cimarosa were attracted to the Russian court where they received princely salaries from a woman who bitterly regretted being tone-deaf and was ready to offer the highest reward to any doctor who could cure her of this affliction.

The early eighties saw the conciliation and literary collaboration of two old friends. Catherine Dashkova had returned to Russia for the second time in 1781 and the amiable Lanskoy, who admired the Princess's erudition, went out of his way to heal her differences with the Empress. A few months later came the surprising news that Catherine had appointed the turbulent and quarrelsome Princess to be Director of the Academy of Science – a post which above all others required both tact and discretion in dealing with a group of touchy and irascible scholars. Even Dashkova appears to have hesitated before accepting the post. But her love of notoriety, combined with a genuine desire to raise the standard of education in the country, led her to accept a task before which many might have quailed. Contrary to all prognostications, she proved to be a success – almost too successful for Catherine's entire satisfaction, for there was always a certain element of jealousy in the Empress's relations with a woman whose desire for publicity was as great as her own. She was also a born intriguer, and Catherine wrote on a flippant note to Grimm, 'I have given the Princess a job which is a mouthful and will keep her molars busy and leave her no time for intrigue'. But in reality she gave her the job because she was the only person capable of filling it. The Academy, which had been founded in Elisabeth's reign under the direction of the celebrated Lomonosov, had fallen into disrepute under the rule of incompetent young Directors, such as Feodor Orlov, the youngest and idlest of the Orlov brothers.

Dashkova was also a brilliant businesswoman and she achieved the extraordinary feat of making the Academy pay for itself, by keeping the printing presses busy with popular publications and reprints. Her greatest contribution to Russian national thought was the launching of a journal to which the leading writers of the day contributed, ranging from the satirist, Fonvizin, to the Empress herself, who supplied over half the contents of the first number. The *Sobresednik* was the first Russian journal to dispense entirely with translated material. All the articles were original and some were even controversial. The Princess professed to be a liberal and encouraged criticism. Before long, the Empress found her régime being challenged in a journal to which she was the principal contributor. Fonvizin, who was a school friend of Potemkin and the object of her particular dislike, was the author of a frank and open attack on some of her ministers, and Dashkova's championship of the dramatist resulted in the paper being suppressed after a run of only sixteen months.

The Empress's latent jealousy of the Princess's personal prestige abroad, the honours bestowed on her by foreign academies, prevented many of their schemes from coming to fruition. Dashkova was responsible for the institution of a Russian academy devoted to the study and development of the Russian language, which in the last hundred years had been debased by the introduction of foreign words, completely alien to a Slavonic people. Catherine had seconded the idea with enthusiasm and it was decided that a comprehensive dictionary and grammar would be the first task of the new Academy. But the Empress's enthusiasm was short-lived. The Princess failed to consult her over the laying out of the dictionary. And in the year which followed on Lanskoy's death, while Catherine was living at Tzarskoye Selo, she announced to the world that yet another dictionary was to be published compiled under her personal supervision. The decision to compete with her own Academy can only have been dictated by vanity and pique and was hardly worthy of a woman who was called 'Catherine le Grand', but the Empress's failings, so feminine and even childish at times, only make her the more human. Her conceit was such that she did not hesitate to tell Baron Grimm, who in turn was to inform the literary world, 'that her comparative dictionary would serve as the most usual reference work for all languages, whereas the Academy was too lacking in learning to compile a dictionary of any value'.

The first volume of the Empress's *magnum opus*, compiled by 'a most illustrious personage', only came out in 1787. Heralded by a fanfare of publicity, it was nevertheless a failure, being badly arranged, careless in construction and prohibitively expensive. The Academy's dictionary, on the other hand, which was not half so pretentious, was a success and proved another triumph for the indefatigable Princess, who this time had sufficient sense to pay tribute to the Empress's enlightened patronage.

Catherine's literary output was enormous. Yermolov appears to have made but little claim on her time for, during his seventeen months of favour, she wrote no less than six plays, most of which were intended to be satires but were totally lacking the wit and sparkle of her conversation. They were all performed at court and an invitation to assist at these private performances at the Hermitage theatre were more often an ordeal to be endured than a pleasure to be enjoyed.

Catherine's genius lay in governing. Clemency was tempered with justice. Her ministers were praised in public and admonished in private, and she took infinite pains never to hurt the pride of any of her servants. If she lost her temper, she never failed to apologize even to the youngest of her secretaries or the clumsiest of her maids, but throughout her reign she was hampered by a shortage of good administrators. The new Provinces Act, which she genuinely believed would benefit the ordinary people of Russia, was being held up by the lack of an efficient bureaucracy. Peter the Great had made the nobility act as civil servants. His successors relieved them of their duties, while allowing them to retain their privileges, so that gradually they degenerated into a completely parasitic class, and there was no 'third estate' to run the provincial tribunals.

Count Sievers, a Livonian of German extraction, who was one of the ablest of Catherine's governors, had attempted to introduce reforms in his province of Novgorod by giving the serfs more time to work on their own account and reasonable terms on which to buy their freedom. This would have created a class of free citizens of whom the country had so great a need. But the selfishness of the nobility put an end to his schemes and the Empress was powerless to support a governor who had aroused the enmity of the landlords whom she did not dare to offend. Sievers was dismissed and replaced by Potemkin who added Novgorod to the vast provinces already under his control, provinces he ruled in the manner of an Oriental satrap, equally reckless of the expenditure of money and of lives.

Foreign travellers to Russia were impressed by the rapid growth and prosperity of St Petersburg, the handsome buildings, the bustling activity of the wharves, the number of foreign ships unloading on the quays, and the quays themselves all faced with granite – an enormous work, only recently completed by the architect Yuri Veldten; the new factories, the Imperial glass and porcelain manufacturers; the exquisite furniture of Karelian birch copied from the designs of Adam. St Petersburg was a commercial port, allied to the elegance of a court where on summer nights the Neva was crowded with pleasure boats and the quality took the air on the Millonaya and drove their curricles along the Nevsky Prospect. But there was another side to the picture. The public building enterprises had attracted a large number of vagrant labourers to the town, many of them escaped serfs with neither name nor passport. Anyone working for the crown became automatically a free citizen. No questions were asked and pay was high, when either the Empress or her favourite ordered that a building should be finished at a certain time. But the men were dismissed as soon as the work was completed, and found themselves with nothing to live on and nowhere to go. The former serfs did not dare to return to their masters and ended by drifting into crime and joining the bands of highwaymen who roamed the suburbs and made it perilous to venture out at night. The last person to hear of this outbreak of lawlessness was probably the Empress, who appears to have been totally unaware of the inefficiency of her police. A diplomat accredited to her court tells of a morning visit to the Chief of Police to complain of an injury done to one of his nationals, only to find him still *en déshabillé*, playing a game of patience, and very annoyed at being disturbed.

The Empress rarely dismissed either ministers or servants, perhaps for no other reason than because she knew that there was no one better to replace them. But in Yermolov she had a lover who went out of his way to report every scandal and abuse which came to his notice. He regarded it as a holy duty to redress all wrongs and made a point of informing her of matters she would far rather not have known. He even went so far as to accuse his benefactor, Potemkin, of having diverted for his own purposes money which was intended for the deposed Khan of the Crimea. The Khan had abdicated his sovereignty on payment of a large pension which was considerably in arrears, and he naturally blamed Potemkin who was in control of the area. Yermolov heard of his complaints and handed them on to the Empress, who prided herself on treating her Moslem subjects generously and fairly and was furious with Potemkin for neglecting to carry out her orders.

He for his part was so outraged by her accusations and Yermolov's base ingratitude that he did not deign to reply to the charges and left his quarters in the palace without even asking for an audience. The Empress had built him a pavilion, or rather a house, looking out on the Millonaya, and joined to the Hermitage by a long gallery. It was here that he lived after selling the Anitchkov Palace for the second time in order to pay his debts. The scandal was made still more public by the Prince remaining in St Petersburg and lodging with one of the Empress's oldest friends, that same Leon Naryshkin, who as a young man had aided and abetted her in all her amorous escapades and in old age still remained the jolly buffoon who delighted her leisure hours. Naryshkin had a pretty daughter, who was the latest object of Potemkin's volatile affections. The Prince had now the audacity to install himself in his house and to order the servants to serve his meals at a separate table in the company of their young mistress.

This time his friends considered that 'Serenissimus' had gone too far in insulting both Naryshkin and the Empress. They begged him not to allow a presumptuous boy to blacken his character for the sake of his own vanity. Among those who dared to speak to him so frankly was the new French ambassador, who had arrived in St Petersburg only the previous year but, through his charm and brilliance, had already succeeded in becoming an intimate of the Hermitage and, what was far more difficult, in becoming a friend and intimate of Potemkin, who until now had been violently anti-French and looked upon France as the chief obstacle to Russia's plans for expansion in Turkey and the Levant.

After many failures, the French government had finally chosen the right man for the right job. Belonging to one of the most illustrious families of France, Louis Philip de Ségur combined the graces of Versailles with the valour of the soldier who had won his military laurels serving under Lafayette in the American War of Independence. The young ambassador made his first appearance at the Russian court wearing both the diamond Order of the St Esprit and the bronze oakleaves of the American Order of Cincinnatus, a gesture calculated to please a sovereign who was fond of calling herself 'an aristocrat by profession and a republican by heart'. But his greatest triumph lay in conquering Potemkin's initial distrust by treating him with an ease and familiarity no one else dared to assume.

Potemkin was first given a lesson in manners by this thirty-year-old diplomat. When Ségur visited the Prince and found him lying half-naked on a divan, exposing his hirsute torso and wearing nothing but a pair of trousers, he retaliated in kind by inviting him to dine at the embassy and receiving him in a dressing-gown. The Prince took the hint and in future received him as befitted a minister of France. Potemkin, who was always complaining of his ignorance and had a thirst for knowledge, was impressed by the Frenchman's erudition, so carefully concealed under a mask of frivolity. He was forever asking him questions about the Western world, of which he knew so little and in public affected to despise. In replying, the diplomat gradually won him over to the idea that France and Russia could still be friends in the Levant.

Ségur did not hesitate to remonstrate when he saw Potemkin committing what looked to him like political suicide, and he warned him that he was playing into the hands of his enemies by not attempting to defend himself to the Empress. But the Prince replied on a note of contempt. 'So you also say that I am working for my own destruction and that after all the services I have rendered, I should defend myself against the allegations of an ungrateful boy. But no little whipper-snapper will bring about my downfall, and I do not know of anyone who would dare to do so.' He spoke with so much pride and confidence that Ségur went away convinced that neither Catherine nor her Empire could survive without Potemkin.

His conviction was correct. A few weeks later, at the end of June 1786, on the anniversary of the Empress's accession to the throne, Potemkin staged a dramatic scene in the middle of a ball at Peterhof. No setting could have been more spectacularly beautiful than Peter's summer palace in the month of the white nights, with the terraced gardens stretching down to the silver waters of the Gulf of Finland, the statues gleaming against the sculptured hedges, the fountains tossing their plumes of gold into the pale northern sky. This year Potemkin, the impresario of all the Imperial fêtes, had played no part in the arrangements and the Empress, who seemed low-spirited and bored, had left the ballroom earlier than usual, dismissing her favourite and retiring with her ladies to her boudoir. Supper was about to be served when a whisper went around the palace that 'Serenissimus' had arrived. The crowds parted, the dancing stopped, as Potemkin's towering, massive figure, resplendent in a gold-embroidered uniform, covered in decorations and blazing with diamonds, passed through looking neither to right nor left, till he came across Yermolov seated at one of the Macao tables. Then all his pent up fury vented itself against the hapless young man. Cards were scattered, the table flung to the ground, his partners fled, as Potemkin hurled on him invective after invective: 'You cur – you white nigger – you monkey – who dare to bespatter me with the mud of the gutters from which I have raised you.'

Yermolov, who was proud and nobly born, put his hand to his sword hilt, but the full force of Potemkin's fist sent him reeling to the ground and not even a lackey dared to pick him up. The Prince passed on, bursting into the Empress's boudoir without knocking, and such was the fear he inspired that none of the guards on duty dared to stop him. The doors closed, but not before he was heard shouting as he went in, 'It's he or I. If this nonentity of nonentities is allowed to remain at court, then I quit the state's service from today.' The ladies retired in confusion and Catherine was left alone to face the uncontrolled rage of the man whom she still regarded as a 'respected consort'. However angry and however frightened she may have been, and later she confessed to her friend, Anna Naryshkin, that she was petrified with fear, she nevertheless felt the wild sexual excitement which Potemkin's scenes invariably aroused in her. Her excessive femininity, so curiously at variance with her clear masculine mind, required to be subjugated and even at times ill-treated. Now she was not so angry as she was frightened – not so frightened as she was relieved that the weeks of stony silence were over and Potemkin was making one of those scenes which were invariably followed by a tender reconciliation. She was bored with Yermolov, bored with his noble principles, his meddlesome interference into matters which were none of his concern. Potemkin had not deigned to reply to the accusations and now she was ashamed of having made them. For what did the grievances of a Tartar Khan count beside the services of a man who had won her the Crimea, and extended her Empire from the mouth of the Dnieper to the Sea of Azov. In those seventeen months which had elapsed since Lanskoy's death after he had nursed her back to health, they had worked together with a frenetic energy of which they alone were capable on projects which they alone believed to be possible.

These were the months when they completed the plan of what was to be the most spectacular event of her reign and which until now had been only briefly mentioned in her letters and rarely taken seriously by her correspondents. In 1780 she had already spoken to the Emperor of her intention to visit the southern provinces, and the sceptical Joseph had dismissed it as a figment of Potemkin's over-heated imagination. But it was a dream she had cherished long before the coming of Potemkin. As a sixteen-year-old girl, travelling in the wake of an Imperial pilgrimage to Kiev, she had looked down from the heights of the Petchersky Monastery at the great river flowing below, the wharves crowded with merchandise destined for Turkish ports, and envisaged the day when a Russian Empress would sail down the Dnieper to Russian ports on the Black Sea. Catherine cherished a dream which Potemkin was making into reality.

To lose him meant losing her dream. Hence the arrogance and confidence with which he had spoken to the Count de Ségur; the dramatic scenes which ended in total victory, the ignominious dismissal of young Yermolov; the triumphal return to the ballroom with Potemkin leading the Empress by the hand, looking as someone described on a similar occasion, 'very mellow and voluptuous'.

A month later, Catherine was already writing to her Imperial friend and ally that she was planning to visit her southern provinces in the spring, leaving for Kiev in January, where she would wait for the Dnieper to become navigable before pursuing her journey down the river as far as the cataracts and from there travelling overland to Kherson. The month of May would be spent in touring the Crimea or, as Catherine calls it, 'the Tauris', evoking classical memories of Iphigenia. A journey involving thousands of miles, across steppe and desert, parts of which were inhabited by hostile tribes and where vast areas were devoid of any form of habitation, was referred to as gaily and as casually as if she were embarking on a picnic on the Neva. Joseph wrote to Kaunitz 'that he had an uneasy feeling that this might be the preliminary to an invitation which would be very difficult to refuse but, as it was a long way ahead, there was still time to find some suitable excuse'.

CHAPTER TWENTY-SEVEN

Voyage à la Potemkin

No event was ever more publicized and dramatized than the Empress of Russia's journey to the Crimea. With the passing of years, it has turned from history to legend, acclaimed by eye-witnesses as one of the most fantastic journeys ever accomplished by a reigning sovereign; decried by Potemkin's enemies as a gigantic hoax of cardboard villages and hollow painted façades, of drafted soldiers disguised as prosperous peasants. The Empress was said to have seen nothing of the inhabitants, nor of the provinces through which she travelled, that it was nothing but a theatrical decor staged by the greatest impresario of his day. The phrase '*voyage à la Potemkin*', synonymous for sham, has passed into the international vocabulary. But those who criticized the journey were not present, while the triumph of Potemkin's organization was witnessed and praised by two shrewd and acute observers. Neither in the memoirs of the Count de Ségur or of the Prince de Ligne is there any mention of cardboard villages, though Ségur does say 'that every village, town and country house, even to the most rustic of cabins, was so decorated and disguised by triumphal arches, garlands of flowers and elegant architectural conceits, that to our eyes they gave the illusion of superb cities, of palaces raised by magic and of gardens created overnight'.

This could apply to any royal progress when the rubbish is removed, the beggars kept out of the way and the prettiest girls dressed in their Sunday finery scatter flowers in the sovereign's path. The only difference was that Potemkin's genius was able

to conjure such a variety of scenes and people as to keep the
Empress and her highly sophisticated guests interested and
amused throughout the two hundred and fifty mile journey
down the Dnieper. A Cossack fantasia staged in the middle of
the steppe; an English garden with shady trees planted where no
flowers had ever grown before; a fleet of decorated boats filled
with boys and girls chanting their native airs; a floating orchestra playing a triumphant ode composed and conducted by the
great Sarti; nothing was impossible for a man who combined
unlimited imagination with unlimited resources. Philip de
Ségur pays him a tribute which vindicates him to posterity.

Prince Potemkin knows in a fantastic way how to remove every
obstacle in his path; to discipline nature, shorten distances, disguise
misery, dissipate boredom and impart an air of life to the most sterile
deserts. He may not be a great statesman or a great general or a great
politician, but he is the greatest and subtlest of courtiers, with a
profound knowledge of his sovereign's character and an adoration
for her glory. Nor must one belittle what he has achieved in the
space of a few years. He has tripled the population of the vast territories under his control and established flourishing towns in places
where formerly were only a few nomad encampments.

The Empress's triumphal progress to the Crimea cost the
country nearly ten million roubles. It was made with a double
purpose of impressing Europe and terrifying the Turks. Her
guests included the ambassadors of Austria, France and Spain,
what she called 'her little cabinet'. The Prussian representative
was deliberately excluded, for the old King's death in the preceding year had done nothing to heal the breach between the
two countries. Some of the guests showed a certain reluctance to
embark on this adventure and it required all of Prince Kaunitz's
diplomatic skill to persuade his Imperial master to become part
of what Joseph called 'the Empress's travelling circus'.

Catherine was apt to be flippant in her letters, a quality more
admired by her inferiors than by her fellow monarchs. The
Hapsburg Emperor took umbrage at the 'cavalier' fashion in
which the official invitation was casually inserted as a postscript
at the end of a letter speaking of other matters. He told his
minister that he would sleep on the answer. 'It will be short, but

I will not omit telling the Catherinized Princess of Zerbst that she should show a little more respect.' But Kaunitz begged him to make allowances for female vanity and to take into account the advantages to be derived from this alliance. In the end, Joseph was persuaded to meet the Empress at Kherson and accompany her on her tour of the Crimea, couching his acceptance in such flattering terms as to evoke from Catherine the reply 'that she was trembling with joy at the thought of a reunion with "Count Falkenstein"'.

The Emperor's reluctance contrasted with the enthusiasm of his friend and confidant Prince Charles de Ligne, who was delighted to be invited by a sovereign whom he regarded 'as the greatest genius of her age'. He had formed this opinion on his first visit to Russia in 1780, only a few months after the Imperial meeting at Moghilev. The visit was ostensibly for family reasons as his elder son was about to marry a Polish girl whose dowry consisted largely of claims on the Russian government. But the ease with which he forgot his family duties, and the trouble he took in courting both the Empress and Prince Potemkin, makes one believe that he was deliberately sent by Joseph to help in strengthening the tenuous links of the Austro Russian alliance. No one could have been more fitted for his task than Charles Joseph de Ligne who, in spite of his effervescent gaiety and quick and witty tongue, was at the same time diplomatic and discreet. The Emperor was not a man of many friends, but he placed an implicit trust in this Belgian-born Prince, who was both a grandee of Spain and an Austrian Field-Marshal – a true cosmopolitan as much at home at Versailles as at Schönbrunn, as happy in his beautiful gardens of Beleuil as at a military camp in Germany; equally at his ease in corresponding with Marie-Antoinette or with Voltaire. His friendship with Voltaire would alone have been sufficient to admit him into the intimacy of the Hermitage. Catherine, who worshipped at the shrine of '*la divinité de la gaieté*', found his perfect disciple in the fifty-year-old Prince who never spoke of age and could laugh and frolic like a boy, yet had a profound knowledge of the world and the kindly tolerance of those who were really good at heart. They were made to be friends, for in many ways they were alike with the same humour, the same healthy zest for life, both cynical and sentimental at the same time.

The Empress received the Prince at Tzarskoye Selo, where he spent three weeks in her company, seeing her almost every day in the charming setting she had made so essentially her own; in the Cameron apartments, where the little rooms 'glowed with translucent colour like jewelled snuff-boxes'; in those parks and gardens where fantasy had had full play in building follies and pavilions, columns and triumphal arches, commemorating the victories of Roumiantsev and of Orlov. De Ligne was fascinated 'to see the conqueror of the Turks tending her flowers, the legislator of the greatest of Empires sowing her own lawns; her simplicity contrasting with the splendour of her exploits, only rendering her company all the more piquante'.

Some of the Polish landlords who had had their properties so cruelly expropriated, the free peasants of the Ukraine who had been handed over in serfdom to worthless favourites, would have had difficulty in recognizing the portrait drawn by de Ligne of a woman 'overflowing with kindness, who gave with an open hand, partly out of natural generosity, partly out of charity, partly out of compassion'.

This praise was not the sycophantic adulation of a courtier. It was written in his memoirs long after the Empress's death, and if Catherine had a fault to find with a man whom she described 'as the pleasantest company and the easiest person to live with that she had ever met', it was precisely because he did not publicize her praises as much as she would have wished. She must have dropped a hint to this effect, for we read in one of his letters 'I have seen, I have admired, I have hardly said anything. I have listened and never moved. I have not told a hundredth part of what I felt. The clarion trumpet of M. Voltaire has proclaimed your fame throughout the world. My feeble little instrument which is only heard in camps and battlefields could only repeat what has already been said.' The friendship which began in 1780 flowered in a correspondence which reads more like the letters of two young lovers than those of an elderly Empress possessed by her ambition writing to a famous Field-Marshal. The Empress's reply to the Prince's congratula-

tions on her annexation of the Crimea combines hard facts with
poetry. She asserts her triumphs:

It is I who have given White Russia and the Tauris to my country,
therefore I can dispose of these lands as I please. As you number
among the friends whom I know I can depend on, I have instructed
Field-Marshal Prince Potemkin, governor of the province, to put you
in possession of the district, where Iphigenia is said to have served in
the temple of Diana. But I do not want you to visit that beautiful
country without me. I have the intention of going there myself either
at the end of 1786 or at the beginning of 1787 and I shall take with
me several of our mutual friends. By then I hope you will have had
hammered some sense into those 'be-wigged hard-headed frogs', and
you will deserve your laurels. But come and pick them with me in
Tauris, where they grow in the open fields.

What an entrancing invitation to receive for a harassed
officer campaigning in the mud and fog of the Low Countries,
where the Dutch had flooded the fields by opening the dykes.
Hence the Empress's allusion to the 'be-wigged frogs'. But by
the end of 1786 the rebellion had been suppressed and de Ligne
was back in St Petersburg receiving the itinerary of the journey
on behalf of his Imperial Majesty. Small wonder he called himself 'Joseph's diplomatic jockey', for he was only a few weeks in
Vienna before he was back on the road, first to Warsaw to
attend his son's wedding (evidently it was Potemkin rather than
Catherine who had seen to the restitution of the confiscated
lands), and later rejoining the Empress in Kiev.

Catherine's decision to spend three months at Kiev and await
there the breaking of the ice on the Dnieper caused consternation at court. Her ministers viewed with horror the prospect of
travelling to and fro over six hundred miles of icy roads. The
ambassadors saw themselves confined to the boredom of a
provincial town, away from their chancellories, their mistresses
and clubs and completely out of touch with their families and
governments at home. But the one who regarded the journey
with the greatest apprehension of all was the Empress's new
favourite, conveniently produced by Potemkin only a few days
after Yermolov's dismissal. The twenty-six-year-old Alexander
Dimitriev Momonof, who appears to have had great charm and

fascination, had taken complete possession of Catherine's ever tender heart, and we find her describing him to Baron Grimm in the same exaggerated terms of praise to which he had had to listen so often in the past. With her weakness for nicknames, the Empress refers to her new lover as 'Redcoat', who has the kindest of hearts and an inexhaustible source of gaiety, being original in his outlook and exceptionally well informed. In the skittish tones she often assumes on these occasions, she writes 'Our whole tone is that of the best society; we write Russian and French to perfection; our features are very regular; we have two superb black eyes and eyebrows and a noble easy bearing.' If Momonof's education was above the average, it was largely due to his uncle, the erudite Count Stroganov. Otherwise he was frivolous, superficial and easily bored. Where he differed from the majority of his predecessors was in his devotion to Potemkin and a complete lack of jealousy, probably due to the fact that his heart was not involved. Catherine never let him out of her sight, and he must have dreaded the prospect of being shut up for days on end in an over-heated coach, in the company of the Empress and the sharp-eyed Mademoiselle Protassof, whose very presence recalled an embarrassing experience. Other guests invited to share the Imperial coach were the faithful Naryshkin, the Grand Chamberlain Ivan Shuvalov, an the Austrian ambassador Count Cobenzel, a light-hearted Viennese with a talent for amateur theatricals which made him *persona grata* at a court where the Empress herself was an indefatigable playwright. But Naryshkin's out-dated jokes, Shuvalov's literary conceits and Cobenzel's endless recitations were all equally boring for a young man, who complained to his Imperial mistress that he found the atmosphere in the coach 'quite stifling'.

By January 1787, Momonof had been the established favourite for nearly eighteen months and was already showing signs of lassitude. Catherine, on the other hand, was as infatuated as ever. But her sexual obsessions in no way prevented her from being a doting grandmother. She had planned on taking her two eldest grandchildren on the journey, to show them the lands she had added to their inheritance and the Black Sea fleet created by Potemkin. But to her anger and surprise, she encountered a determined resistance from the children's parents. The gentle, amenable Maria Feodorovna grew almost hysterical at the thought of exposing the delicate Alexander to the hazards of food poisoning and malarial fevers. Dr Rogerson, the only physician who had any influence over Catherine, was of the same opinion. But still the Empress persisted, pleading, with all the virtuosity at her command, that it was cruel to let a lonely old woman go off on such a long journey without a single member of her family to console her. But when the Grand Duke offered to go with her himself, the suggestion was received in a frozen silence. Providence intervened at the eleventh hour by Alexander falling ill with chicken-pox, to which six doctors had to testify before the Empress was fully satisfied.

On 18 January 1787, fourteen coaches mounted on sleighs, one hundred and twenty-four sledges, with forty more held in reserve, and five hundred and sixty horses set out from Tzarskoye Selo on a brilliant winter's day. The temperature was seventeen degrees below zero and, in order to protect them from the cold, the travellers wore bearskins over their more precious furs and bonnets of stone marten to cover their heads.

A portrait of the Empress painted by the Russian artist Shibakov shows her as she must have appeared on that last morning, before embarking on the greatest adventure of her reign. It depicts a handsome, dignified old lady in an elegant, simple travelling costume, her soft white hair crowned by a sable bonnet and a lace ruffle hiding the fleshy folds of the chin. The blue eyes are wise and tolerant, the plump cheeks look warm and firm. Only the thin line of the mouth betrays the autocrat whose will must never be opposed. Before leaving on a journey of nearly four thousand miles, she was still sufficiently resentful of the Grand Duke's opposition to her plans to deny both him and his wife admission to her last *levée*.

The Count de Ségur, who shared a coach with his English colleague, Mr Fitzherbert, a young man whose melancholy nature was in direct contrast to his own ebullience, has left us a vivid account of the journey. The eight hundred miles from St Petersburg to Kiev were accomplished in little more than eighteen days in a season when the whole of Russia from Riga to

Kamchatka lay under a pall of snow and there was barely six hours of sunlight. But the log roads, over which one bumped so painfully in summer, were excellent when covered with a coat of smooth and solid ice, and the sledges travelled at an incredible speed across the deserted plains and forests hung with icicles which glittered like crystals in the winter sunlight. 'It was a time when every animal stayed in its stable, every peasant by his stove and the only signs of human life were the convoys of sledges passing like small ships over a frozen sea.'

It was a fantastic voyage for a woman of nearly sixty years of age to undertake in winter, and shows the Empress's implicit trust in the master-mind which for three years had been planning and supervising every detail of this enormous enterprise, from the number of troops required to patrol the route to the number of candles required to light Her Majesty's bedroom.

Speaking one day to Ségur, the Empress said,

Everything was done to deter me from this journey. I was assured on all sides that my progress would be bristling with obstacles and unpleasantness. They wished to frighten me with stories of the fatigue of the journey. These people had a very poor knowledge of me. They do not know that to oppose me is to encourage me and that every difficulty they put in my way is an additional spur that they give me.

She thought nothing of travelling nearly ten hours a day, starting at nine o'clock in the morning and, after an hour's pause for dinner, driving on until seven in the evening. Even nightfall held no hazards, for all along the road were huge bonfires and blazing torches to light the royal way. The most primitive of municipal halls in the smallest of provincial towns was transformed by Potemkin into a luxurious palace to house the Empress for the night. But on one or two occasions when Her Majesty honoured the local landlord with her presence and his mansion was not large enough to accommodate her party, the young ambassadors of France and England, rivals in politics but excellent friends in private, had to bivouac in a peasant's cabin, where the stench was so unbearable as to preclude all ideas of sleep.

Philip de Ségur, the French aristocrat who had fought in the
cause of liberty, saw with a pitying eye hundreds of serfs, looking
more like animals than human-beings wrapped in their tattered,
uncured fur-skins, their long beards crackling with ice, braving
the elements to have a fleeting glimpse of the Imperial sledges,
and being driven back by guards when they pressed too closely
against the gates of the landlord's house. Yet the Empress was
fond of telling him, as she once told Voltaire, that 'the soil of the
country was so productive and the rivers so rich in fish that the
Russian peasant was happier and better fed than any other in
the world'.

Kiev, the oldest and holiest of Russian cities. welcomed the
Empress to the sound of cannon-fire and the pealing of church
bells. Marshal Roumiantsev, governor of the Ukraine, escorted
her into the town. But her smiles and favours were reserved for
Potemkin, who now appeared on the scene for the first time,
stealing the limelight from his former chief. The old Marshal
complained that he was kept without money to pay his troops
and carry out public works, while Catherine's viceroy wasted
millions on building and restoring palaces for the entertainment
of her guests. Each ambassador was provided with his own
house, furnished with every comfort, including an excellent
cellar and a large staff of servants. The delegations which arrived
from the four corners of the Empire to pay homage to the great
Tzarina all lived at her expense. The Prince de Ligne, who
joined the party at Kiev, was overwhelmed by the scene that
greeted him in the crowded city, and his description in a letter
written to Madame de Coigny reads like an Oriental fairy-tale.

Good heavens, what a riot of diamonds; gold and stars and cor-
dons, chains and ribbons, of turbans and scarlet caps, some furred,
some pointed, the last belonging to grotesque little beings called
lesghians, who have come as a deputation (as have various
other vassals) from the frontiers of China and those of Persia and
Byzantium. The sons of the king of the Caucasus' Heraclius are
here; nearly twenty archbishops, a trifle unclean with beards to their
knees. . . . Escorts of Uhlans with glittering sabres and jewelled hilts
escort the Polish *grands seigneurs*. There is something for the whole
world here; great and little politics; great and little intrigues; great

and little Poland; a few of the famous of that land, who deceive themselves or are deceived, or deceive others – all very amiable – their wives still more so, all watching for a glance from Prince Potemkin.

This letter breaks off, with the Prince being fetched to attend a display of fireworks, said to have cost forty thousand roubles. Meanwhile, Roumiantsev's troops wore old and shabby uniforms and the fortress walls were crumbling. The Empress who hated failure was irritated by the Marshal's complaints and annoyed to find the town looking more neglected than under the reign of the Empress Elisabeth who had lavished riches on the monastery and the churches.

One day Catherine asked the three ambassadors to give her their impressions of the town, to which Cobenzel, who was always the perfect courtier, replied, 'Kiev is the most fascinating city I have ever visited.' The truthful Fitzherbert said 'Faith, madam, it is nothing but a mass of ruins,' while Ségur, who was the cleverest and subtlest of the three, said 'Madame, Kiev is a city with a glorious past, which holds hopes of a glorious future.' Small wonder that the Empress was half-enamoured with this delightful young Frenchman, who had recently scored a diplomatic triumph in getting Russia to sign a commercial treaty, giving France certain trading facilities which had hitherto been monopolized by England. But there were times when Ségur's conversation was too sophisticated, his witticisms too salacious to be appreciated by a princess who, in spite of the flagrant promiscuity of her private life, maintained the highest standards of decorum in public and frowned at jokes which Ségur's virtuous young wife would have greeted with laughter.

The winter was long and severe, and the ice on the Dnieper did not begin to break up till April, by which time the entertainments had begun to pall and tempers were becoming frayed. Adventurous spirits like Ségur had hoped that, by travelling in the Empress's suite, he would see something of the sights and customs of the country through which they passed and complained that 'Court life in Kiev was as monotonous as elsewhere and that he had a surfeit of Greek masses and of public balls.' His complaints reached the Empress's ears, who told him 'That

she travelled not to see the places, but to see the people, and
above all to be seen by them, so that they could feel her living
presence among them and approach her with their petitions,
knowing that she would punish the injustices of those who had
abused their authority.' But who among the crowds in the streets
of Kiev would have dared to present her with a petition? And
how many hands would it have to pass before it ever reached her?

The whole of the Russian world was at her court. Only
Potemkin was conspicuous by his absence, having retired for the
duration of Lent to the Petchersky Monastery. Ministers and
generals had to wait for hours in unheated cloisters before he
would condescend to see them, and then he addressed them only
in monosyllables giving the impression of being in the worst of
tempers. Even Catherine warned her friends 'to avoid the
Prince when they saw him looking like an angry wolf'. For
the first time, Potemkin was showing signs of breaking under the
strain of his tremendous responsibility in having staged a
pageant which might easily lead to war. He was generally
looked upon as a war-monger, but for the moment he was
more concerned in consolidating the territory which was won
than in embarking on new conquests, and the spectacular
journey down the Dnieper was designed to intimidate the Turk
rather than to provoke him.

The leaders of the Polish opposition who flocked to Kiev to
air their grievances and steal a march on the King, who was
waiting to meet the Empress farther down the river, were coldly
received by Catherine's viceroy, for Potemkin had no intention
of fermenting a civil war so close to the Turkish frontier. Even
his adored 'Sashenka', now married to General Count Branicki,
one of the King's most implacable enemies, was publicly reprimanded and told it was her husband's duty as a Polish patriot to
make his peace with his King.

'Did the Empress want war?' was a question all Europe was
asking. Would this woman with her insatiable ambition put an
end to the few precarious years of peace and upset the whole
balance of power? The French ambassador in Constantinople
reported that his Russian colleague was making menacing
threats to the Porte, and new alliances were being made to

counteract this fresh threat from the East. England and Prussia were drawing closer. The former, who had never forgiven Catherine her declaration of 'armed neutrality', was now subsidizing Turkey and encouraging Sweden to enter into alliance with the Turks. Even the Emperor was beginning to wonder whether his country could afford the cost of Russia's friendship. Only Catherine maintained her vaunted imperturbability. Ségur describes her 'as being in perfect health and of a gaiety which not even the discomfort and gloom of Kiev can change. She plays cards for the greater part of the day, has herself painted for her favourite and never lets a cross word pass her lips. Her ministers seem to think of nothing but their amusements and long for the end of a journey they never wanted in the first place.'

It was not until the first of May that a salvo of guns announced that the Dnieper was free for navigation, and the Empress could finally embark on the red and gold painted barge which was to take her down the river to keep her assignations with a vassal King and a fellow Emperor.

The procession of seven elegant barges, each with their own band of musicians on board and seventy-three smaller craft, manned by a crew of three thousand men, provided a superb spectacle for the cheering crowds on the river banks. The Empress travelled with her young lover and the indispensable Mademoiselle Protassof, Potemkin with his two favourite nieces. Cobenzel shared his quarters with Fitzherbert, and Ségur with the Prince de Ligne, the two having become inseparable friends. The rest of the party consisted of the faithful old courtiers, Naryshkin, Shuvalov and Tchernichev, and foreign princelings like the Princes of Anhalt and of Nassau-Siegen. Doctors, hairdressers and master-cooks, engineers and artisans swelled the numbers of Cleopatra's fleet, the name given by the romantic de Ligne who writes 'If anyone on seeing us embark had asked us what we were going to do in these galleys, we would have answered "Amuse ourselves, and *en vogue la galère*"'.

CHAPTER TWENTY-EIGHT

The Royal Progress

Six days of sailing along the frontiers of Poland brought them to Kaniev where King Stanislaus had been waiting for the past two months. No one, least of all the Empress, was in a hurry to arrive, for after the long frozen winter the country had suddenly burgeoned into life. The animals came out of their lairs and the river birds sang in the rushes. As they travelled southwards, the meadows became carpeted with flowers and the trees burst into blossom. Idyllic days were spent picnicking on wooded islands, visiting each other's barges, dining with the Empress on the state barge built for sixty people, or stepping on shore to visit a local fair ground or attend a military manoeuvre, where the splendid troops in their new uniforms showed they had passed out of the old Marshal's jurisdiction and were now in the territory of Prince Potemkin. The 'angry wolf' of Kiev had become a gracious master of ceremonies, entertaining his guests with his private orchestra of a hundred and twenty musicians, with his two lovely nieces contributing to the gaiety of the evening. Spirits rose to mercurial heights and the gayest of all was the fifty-nine-year-old Empress, in amorous dalliance with her twenty-six-year-old favourite and in no way looking forward to meeting a lover of nearly thirty years ago.

Catherine was aware of how greatly she had changed, and for all her indifference to King Stanislaus was sufficiently female to dread the look of disillusion in eyes which once had been so full of admiration. Time had dealt kindly with King Stanislaus, who at fifty-six was still a strikingly handsome man who had kept the elegant figure and graceful movements which had charmed her in her youth. But Catherine's tastes had coarsened over the years. Orlov and Potemkin had accustomed her to a stronger diet. The King's beauty now struck her as insipid, his compliments long-winded and his manners too exquisite. Stanislaus was hoping that this meeting would revive old memories and rekindle old affections; hundreds and thousands of roubles, most of it borrowed from Russia, had gone to stage a reception worthy of the Empress. Thirty-five thousand men, the élite of the Polish army, were encamped on the hills above the river. Potemkin, who had had a previous meeting with the King, had been favourably impressed and ready to support his claims for a greater share of independence. But the morning began somewhat inauspiciously with thundery clouds and gusts of rain, and the King was drenched to the skin before he boarded the sloop which had been sent to bring him on board the state galley. There he was greeted by the Empress with all the honours due to a fellow sovereign. She had taken great pains with her appearance and was wearing gala dress. But her manner though courteous was distant. After presenting him her foreign guests and ministers, she retired with him for a private talk at which only Potemkin was present. Later in the day she confessed to her secretary Krapovitzky, who recorded it in his diary, that the interview had been a difficult one. Prince Potemkin, whom she had asked to be present, had not opened his mouth, and she had had to do all the talking.

The King had tried to make her prolong her visit, first by three days, then by one; he was finally reduced to asking permission to drive with her on the following day. But she had had to be firm. These few hours were the only ones she could spare for an old lover whose very weakness only made her the more intolerant. Stanislaus offered to provide her with thirty thousand picked troops in the event of a war against the Turks, and in return asked for the abolishment of the *Liberum Veto* and a new constitution for Poland. But this offer was politely and definitely refused. When they joined the rest of the party for the gala dinner, it was noted that Catherine looked embarrassed and Stanislaus looked sad. Philip de Ségur, who was sitting opposite the Empress who had the King on her right, observed: 'They spoke little but each was watching the other; we listened to an excellent orchestra and drank the King's health to a salvo of artillery fire.' The King on rising could not find his hat, which the Empress retrieved for him and handed over with a smile, whereupon he remarked with his usual gallantry that on a former occasion she had presented him with one which was far more handsome. This was an allusion to the crown of Poland which he had accepted with such reluctance and now clung to with such desperation.

The gala dinner was followed by a reception at which the atmosphere was so cold and formal that Stanislaus Augustus must have realized that no tender memories of lovers' trysts in the garden of Oranienbaum would prevent the Empress from relentlessly pursuing her policy of *real-politik*. The crowning humiliation came when Catherine refused to attend the ball he was holding in a palace specially built for the occasion. The refusal was all the more humiliating as the Empress had attended every provincial ball from St Petersburg down to Kiev.

Potemkin was furious and warned his sovereign that this public rebuff would only serve to encourage the King's enemies. He was so angry that he gave vent to his feelings by slapping the face of General Count Branicki, an insult the arrogant Pole would never have accepted from the King, but had perforce to swallow from his wife's all-powerful uncle with whom he was usually on the best of terms.

While her guests attended the King's ball and the young ambassadors flirted with the fascinating Polish ladies, the Empress watched the fireworks from the deck of her galley in the company of her young lover, who paid her the highly flattering compliment of pretending to be jealous of the King. So ended a meeting of which so much had been expected. But in the end it may have been Stanislaus who wounded Catherine more than she had wounded him. She told Potemkin that 'the King bored her', but she was probably less bored than piqued by his indifference. The coldness which transpired through the affected smile and flowery compliments showed all too clearly that the poet in Stanislaus Poniatowski could not forgive her having grown fat and old.

On the following morning the Imperial flotilla sailed at dawn. Though Catherine could afford to be rude to a vassal King, she could not keep an Emperor waiting.

Joseph of Hapsburg was a born traveller. No sooner did he escape from the pomposity of the Vienna court than he became a younger and happier person. As Count Falkenstein he travelled light with little baggage, an equerry and two servants, with the result that he always arrived ahead of the scheduled time. He had only been twenty-four hours in Kherson before his sharp eye had noted 'that Potemkin's dockyards in the Dnieper estuary had been built in the wrong place and that its commerce, which depended entirely on Poland, was of no use to Russia'. Impatient of delay, he decided to travel overland to Kaydak where the fleet of barges was approaching the first of the Dnieper cataracts. The progress down the river had been slow, impeded by the continuous appearance of sand-banks which the larger barges had difficulty in manoeuvring and on more than one occasion got stuck in the sand.

No sooner had Catherine heard of Count Falkenstein's arrival in Kherson than she insisted on disembarking and meeting him on his way. The meeting between two of the most powerful sovereigns in the world took place in a Cossack hut. Writing to his Commander-in-Chief, Count Lascy, the Emperor expatiates on the vicissitudes of a journey across the steppe. 'I got into the Empress's carriage and we returned together to Kaydak, leaving our respective staffs behind, so there was no one to prepare our dinner. The Princes Potemkin and Nassau-Siegen and Count Branicki cooked us an uneatable meal. The weather was so cold we had to wear our pelisses and light a fire in the evening.' Commenting on his hostess he writes:

The Empress is only a little thinner but in excellent health. As for the galleys they are comfortable but much too large and heavy for river travel. The confusion is unbelievable and the landings are very difficult. There are more things and people to disembark than there are carriages and horses. Prince Potemkin, who is mad on music, has no less than a hundred and twenty musicians on board, but there are hardly any doctors or medicines available. One has to resort to the local *kibitka* to transport one's belongings and one's baggage. Carriages get broken, china, linen, silver all go flying pell-mell over the steppe. There are abundant meals but all very badly cooked and usually served cold. Apart from the amiability and charm of the Empress and some of the foreigners it would really be a penance to take part in this journey. Potemkin who makes the wheels go round is in high favour, while poor Marshal Roumiantsev is very much on the decline.

Describing the Empress's entourage Joseph admits that the new favourite is good-looking but does not appear to be very brilliant and seems astonished to find himself in this position. 'The Frenchman Ségur is delightful but gives the impression he cannot stand it much longer. The Englishman Fitzherbert is very cultivated and does not attempt to hide his boredom. De Ligne is at his best and is really devoted to my interests.'

But in spite of his criticisms, Joseph ended by falling completely under Catherine's spell and confessed to his Field-Marshal that he could not resist the opportunity of accompanying the Empress to the Crimea, 'which will be very interesting'. He insisted on maintaining his *incognito*, attending the Empress's *levée* with the other gentlemen of her court, striking up a friendship with the Count de Ségur in order to sound the reactions of the French government; speaking to him freely and openly of the extraordinary woman who had become his ally. He was convinced that Catherine wanted another war and was longing to come to grips with the Turks, with or without his co-operation. Her continual good fortune had blinded her to the danger of antagonizing both France and England. The Empress struck him as being frivolous by nature, more addicted to pleasure than to serious politics, which were only discussed by fits and starts and usually in the middle of a large dinner party of over a hundred guests. Nevertheless he was fascinated by the physical vigour and vitality of a woman who, though ten years his senior, was still making plans for conquest.

Catherine found the Emperor looking worn and old, but he was still 'Caesar', to be wooed and flattered with all the blandishments at her command. After twenty-four hours at Kaydak, the two sovereigns left for Ekaterinoslav, the new town created by Potemkin, where in the presence of the local archbishop they laid the foundations of a cathedral which according to Potemkin's ambitious plans was to be even larger than St Peter's in Rome. Joseph, who appears to have had little faith in the future of this city built on the edge of the steppe, remarked with his usual sarcasm, 'that in less than an hour he and the Empress had laid the first and the last stones of the new cathedral'. Contrary to his expectations, Ekaterinoslav (Dnepropetrovsk) is today one of the most flourishing of all the cities of what was then 'New Russia'. But even Joseph was impressed, when a thousand Tartars appeared out of a cloud of dust to escort their new sovereign across the Nogai Steppe, and Catherine entrusted herself to their care as naturally as if they were the Chevalier Gardes escorting her to Tzarskoye Selo.

Meanwhile the barges had succeeded in getting through the cataracts and Emperor and Empress made their state entry into Kherson by water, but there was no salvo of cannon-fire to greet their arrival, owing to a recent storm having shown that the city was built on such fragile foundations that the whole fortress would have crumbled at the first cannon-shot. The Emperor remarked to Ségur that everything in Russia was built for show; that both Potemkin and his Imperial mistress were always embarking on projects which never got finished. Six years ago, Kherson had been no more than a few huts in a reedy marsh. Now there were six thousand houses and shops filled with merchandise from Paris and Constantinople. But there were neither quays nor warehouses and the splendid-looking ships in the dockyards were built with green wood. 'But what does this matter', said Joseph, 'in a country which exists on slave labour and where anything which crumbles can be built again. Money is limitless and lives are of no account. In Germany and France we would not dare to attempt things which they risk here every day, without encountering a single obstacle or hearing one word of complaint.'

No one dared to tell Catherine of the failings and short-comings of Kherson and in a letter to Baron Grimm she enthuses over a flourishing town, which the genius of Prince

Potemkin had raised out of the marshes of the Dnieper estuary. She ignored the fact that it was the pestilential air of these reedy marshes which made Kherson so unhealthy and took such a heavy toll of lives in the building of the town.

The Empress had intended to proceed along the coast to Kinburn, and reconnoitre on Turkish territory, a provocative and dangerous gesture from which Bezborodko, who had joined the party at Kherson, did his best to dissuade her. But the Turks had forestalled her, for no sooner did her fleet appear at the mouth of the Dnieper, than a Turkish naval squadron of four men-of-war and ten frigates appeared before the Ottoman port of Otchakov, 'a miserable little place', which according to Potemkin could be taken in a few days. 'A presage of war' said Catherine to the Prince de Ligne, but her face darkened. She had not expected this kind of gesture from the Turks. And the news that French engineers were being employed in strengthening the defences and that the English government was sending subsidies to the Sultan in no way improved her temper. Ségur and Fitzherbert were both accused of intriguing behind her back with the barbarians, and laboured for several days under the cloud of her displeasure.

But all bitterness was dispelled on arrival in the Crimea and politics were momentarily forgotten in the beauty and novelty of the scene. Even the Emperor turned to poetry, competing in elegant quatrains and pretty compliments with the rest of Catherine's court. He confessed to de Ligne:

It is not easy to hold one's own against the rest of you. There is my dear ambassador, out of kindness, gratitude, liking for the Empress and friendship for me, always swinging the incense pot, into which you add grains for the rest of us. Monsieur de Ségur pays his very witty and very French compliments, and even the Englishman lets fly from time to time some tiny shaft of flattery, so epigrammatic as to be all the more piquant.

The ten days spent in the Crimea had a magic to which the most cynical succumbed. As Queen of Tartary, escorted by the descendants of the Golden Hordes of Genghis Khan, Catherine played the leading role in a fairy-tale produced by Potemkin. Her headquarters were at Bakshiserai in the former palace of the Khans, which her architect Charles Cameron had spent the past year in restoring for her use, while preserving the Oriental atmosphere, the glowing colours on the tiled walls, the marble fountains splashing in cool, uncluttered rooms, the secret gardens enclosed in hedges of myrtle and of roses. It was evening when the Imperial coach came down the steep, rocky road leading to the old Tartar capital which lay in a wide fertile valley surrounded by mountains. The muezzins were calling the faithful to prayer and the bazaars were still teeming with life. But later in the night Potemkin took over the town, illuminating the gardens and minarets, setting the mountains ablaze with fantastic fireworks, holding an Eastern feast in the palace court-yards with singers and dancers brought from every district in the new provinces, from the Dnieper to the Don.

Writing to the Marquise de Coigny in Paris, the romantic de Ligne describes this journey out of the Arabian Nights.

After leaving Kherson, we found marvellous camps of Asiatic magnificence, prepared for us right in the middle of the desert. I no longer knew where I was, or in what age. We passed a stud of dromedaries; and a group of young princes of the Caucasus, glittering in silver, mounted on dazzling white horses. When I saw they were armed with bows and arrows, then I imagined I was back in the days of Cyrus. We met detachments of Circassians, beautiful as the day and Cossack officers wearing garments of more harmonious colouring than Madame le Brun ever put into her paintings. At Star-Krim a palace had been built in which to house us for a single night. On leaving my room I could see the Black Sea, the Caucasus and the Sea of Azov. And here I am in the harem of the last Khan of the Crimea, who made a great mistake in abandoning to the Russians the most beautiful country in the world.

Of all the Empress's guests the Prince de Ligne was the one who remained the most consistently in favour. He was privileged on their travels to share the Imperial coach and overhear pithy extracts of conversation between the two sovereigns, to which the other occupant, Alexander Momonof, was far too bored to listen.

All nations and the greatest personages were reviewed in that coach. Speaking of the King of England and the loss of his American colonies, the Empress said in her low, somewhat husky voice 'Rather than sign away the separation of thirteen states, as my brother George has done, I would have shot myself.' To which Joseph somewhat less dramatically replied, 'Rather than throw up my power, as my brother of France has done, by convoking the nation to discuss its abuses, I do not know what I should have done.'

'Has no one ever attempted your life?' asked Catherine. 'I have been threatened,' was the terse reply, upon which the Empress said 'Also I have received anonymous letters.'

There was little reserve between the two monarchs, writes de Ligne, though one suspects him of occasionally indulging in poetic licence. It was only when it came to discussing the Turks that they moved warily, feeling the ground. The Empress spoke of the sufferings endured by the Sultan's Christian subjects; of the liberation of Greece and the revival of a Greek empire. But the practical Joseph interposed, 'What the devil would we do with Constantinople?' The appearance of a Turkish squadron in the Dnieper estuary had shaken his nerve. He had noted a signpost on the outskirts of Kherson, deliberately pointing in the direction of Constantinople. Catherine intended to march with or without his help, and he refused to envisage the thought of Russian armies encamped on the lower Danube. In private he admitted to Ségur that if it was a question of having the Cossacks or the Turks on the frontiers, 'then he vastly preferred the turbans'. But this was before the arrival at Sebastopol, the most dramatic part of the journey, which, like all good showmen, Potemkin had reserved to the last.

Under cloudless summer skies, the Imperial cortège drove across the mountains to Inkerman, to dine in a pavilion erected on the slopes which dominated the Black Sea. When the meal was finished, Potemkin gave a sign and the curtains at the end of the room were drawn aside revealing a view of the great bay of Sebastopol, glittering in the sunlight, sheltered by an amphitheatre of rock, and the whole of Potemkin's Black Sea fleet, sixteen men-of-war and twenty-four frigates lined in battle formation, dipping their flags and firing their guns in a royal

[339]

salute. It was a magnificent spectacle, but to the ambassadors present, who were still hoping to keep the peace, it looked like a declaration of war. The Empress's eyes shone with joy. No words could express her gratitude to Potemkin. No honour was worthy of him. No riches were sufficient to repay her debt. She rose to her feet, her eyes looked in the direction of the Prince, but her compliments were addressed to the Emperor as she drank to the health 'of her best friend, the Emperor, whose friendship had procured her the Crimea and made possible the building of the fleet she was to review today'. Everyone present knew these words were intended for Serenissimus, the ruler of southern Russia.

Conducted by Potemkin, the two sovereigns drove down to the flower-decked port, escorted by Tartar regiments in splendid uniforms. Joseph, who had been so scathing about Kherson, was completely carried away by Sebastopol which he considered to be the most beautiful port he had ever seen. Wharfs and fortifications, naval and army barracks, an Admiralty building, churches, hospitals and even schools had all been built within the space of three years. The Empress reviewed her fleet from the deck of the Admiralty launch and publicly thanked Potemkin for having given her such a wonderful present in completing the work begun by Peter the Great, the founder of the Russian navy. This was the proudest, if not the happiest day of her life. She had impressed her Hapsburg ally and shown the ambassadors of the Western powers that Russia could defend her frontiers by sea and land; but the ambassadors saw with considerable trepidation a fleet which within thirty-six hours could bombard Constantinople.

The last days in the Crimea were devoted to visiting historical sites and sailing along the fabled shores of the Chersonese. The Empress made the charming gesture of presenting the Prince de Ligne with 'the disputed rock' of Iphigenia's sacrifice, of which the gallant Prince took possession by jumping into the water in full uniform and carving the Empress's name upon the stone. On another occasion, Prince Potemkin presented the Count de Ségur with the somewhat embarrassing gift of a beautiful Circassian girl whom the ambassador had noted owing to the extraordinary resemblance she bore to his absent wife. He had the greatest difficulty in making Serenissimus understand that the gift would not be appreciated by the Countess de Ségur if he took her back to Paris.

Gradually the magic faded. Reality intruded into fairy-land. The Empress had intended pursuing her journey as far as Taganrog on the Sea of Azov but the excessive heat, combined with the Emperor's anxiety to return to his own dominions where rebellion was reported from both Galicia and the Austrian Netherlands, forced her to change her plans. The journey back overland to Moscow was an anticlimax, in spite of the sequence of brilliant entertainments staged by Potemkin to relieve the tedium of the days. Joseph, who parted from his hostess at Kisikermann on the Dnieper, had become thoughtful and morose, and on their drives across the steppes did his best to persuade the Empress of the danger of antagonizing both France and England, insisting that a quadruple alliance of Russia, Austria, France and Spain was vital before they engaged in battle with the Turks. His gloom succeeded in affecting even Catherine's ebullient spirits, for Alleyn Fitzherbert, who was the least loquacious but the most perspicacious of the three ambassadors noted, 'that no sooner had they parted with the Emperor, than she fell into a deep and irritable depression, accompanied at times by gusts of ill-humour, and in this state remained with very little intermission till her arrival home'. He added, 'It is difficult to assign the precise reason for this sudden alteration of her temper and disposition. But I think it was occasioned in part by some domestic uneasiness.' The Empress's parting with Potemkin, who left her at Kharkov to return to the Crimea, was highly emotional and there can be little doubt that during this journey, subjected to the exotic atmosphere of the south, Catherine had fallen once more completely under his domination. The letters she wrote to Potemkin at every stage of her journey home are as tender and as loving as in the early days of their courtship. He had only to say the word, and she would have been again the most clinging and affectionate of 'wives'. But there is no hint of passion in the Prince's letters which overflow with devotion, gratitude and a filial love for the mother Empress, whom he identifies with the country he adores. He who could be so gross and carnal in his appetites was fastidious and romantic as a lover, and the stout sixty-year-old Empress, still lusting for physical satisfaction, was hardly an object of romance. Had he wanted or even been able to exercise his marital rights, and Catherine's letters throughout the years leave us in little doubt that they were married, then she might have been spared the defection of Momonof and he might not have had his last years poisoned by the advent of Plato Zoubov. But Potemkin returned to the south, leaving Catherine to pursue her journey to Moscow alone, where she was to celebrate the twenty-fifth anniversary of her accession in the depressing atmosphere of a hostile city.

The Muscovites gave her an even colder reception than usual. Not even the presence of her two grandsons who had been sent to meet her could rouse the people's enthusiasm. The town was threatened by a famine in the central provinces with which the local authorities had shown themselves unable to cope. The nobility had had to feed their serfs out of their own revenues, and there was bitter resentment over the enormous cost of the Empress's journey and bitter attacks against Potemkin for having drained the resources of the Empire to create himself a kingdom in the south. The Empress ordered all feasts and banquets to be cancelled and five million roubles to be allocated for the buying and distributing of cheap grain. But the grumbling continued and in a brief moment of candour, she admitted to the Prince de Ligne 'They do not like me here in Moscow. I am not fashionable. There may have been some misunderstandings and injustices in the past.' They were words which were curiously out of keeping with her usual pride and self-confidence, but she was tired and disillusioned and feeling the strain of being continually on the stage. She longed to be quietly at home playing with her grandchildren in the gardens of Tzarskoye Selo. But she was not allowed to remain at peace for long. At the end of August came the astounding news that the Turks had gone over to the attack and that the Russian ambassador in Constantinople had been committed to the prison of the Seven Towers.

CHAPTER TWENTY-NINE

Renewing troubles

The Turkish attack took the Empress and Potemkin completely by surprise. All their plans and projects had been concentrated on when and where they would open hostilities, or whether the Turks would be sufficiently intimidated by the presence of a Russian fleet in the Black Sea to submit to a further loss of territory beyond the Dnieper. Neither the Empress nor her advisers counted on the intrigues of Prussian and English diplomacy, working on the pride and fanaticism of the Sublime Porte.

This sudden and unexpected war found Catherine and Potemkin not only unprepared, but still exhausted by the efforts of the past year. Troops which were needed to man strategic points, were dispersed all over the steppes. There were no less than three points to cover – the most important being both banks of the Dnieper, the territory between the Dnieper and the Bug, and the long sea line from Kinburn to the straits of Perekop and the Crimean peninsula. Only a brilliant tactician of great military experience could hope to succeed. And even then it would take several months to organize equipment and food supplies and solve the various administrative problems, which had been thrown completely out of gear by the continual military pageants, staged by a man who was more of an illusionist than a general. Yet the Empress never hesitated in appointing Potemkin as supreme commander, both of her land and her sea forces, over-ruling the senior claims of Roumiantsev and the superior military talents of Souvarov.

Nor does the Empress appear to have taken into account the tremendous strain which Potemkin had been labouring under in the past year. She was always begging him to take care of himself, but she never realized that his health was already broken by recurrent bouts of malaria and the irregular life he led in an unhealthy climate such as Kherson, where sexual excesses and drunken orgies alternated with exaggerated fasting. She had always looked upon him as a tower of strength, on whom she could rely in any situation. Both she and her Grand Council so misunderstood the situation that they thought it would only be a question of days before Potemkin had captured Otchakov and moved on to fresh fields of conquest. The instructions sent to the Commander-in-Chief were of an inconceivable optimism. 'Once Otchakov had fallen the Russian forces were to establish themselves firmly in the region between the Dnieper and the Bug and from there move on to the Dniester, laying siege to Ackermann and if possible to Bender,' an important Turkish fort in Bessarabia. Potemkin's failure, or rather his delay in carrying out these instructions, changed the whole course of the war. The 'miserable little fort of Otchakov', which he had boasted to Catherine 'would surrender at the first cannon-shot', took over ten months to capture, the excuse being that he wanted to save as many lives as possible and that he counted on the Turkish garrison surrendering through attrition. But in the end Otchakov had to be taken by assault amid scenes of terrible carnage and the loss of thousands of lives.

Potemkin's behaviour in this first year was so completely out of keeping with his reputation as a heroic war-lord as to spread despondency and alarm amidst his friends and allies. He was alternately paralysed by inertia and sunk in depression at a time when he should have been at his coolest and most dynamic. Weeks, even months were wasted before he even made a plan of attack. In the light of history his military behaviour and refusal to take action before he had sufficient equipment and supplies can be interpreted as being the reasoned decision of a man more concerned with the welfare of his troops than with his own military glory. In one of the few letters to the Empress, in which he attempted to defend himself against his detractors, he writes,

Let somebody else have the courage to repair a fleet that has been severely battered by a storm; build in large quantities rowing craft that can hold the sea; form entirely anew sixteen battalions of infantry and ten thousand cavalry; create a large moving arsenal; supply the artillery with an enormous number of oxen, keep going as far as food supplies are concerned, and all this during four months in the steppes, without proper headquarters.

It was a formidable task calculated to daunt the bravest spirit, but his behaviour must have been exasperating to his young officers and an impetuous ally like the Prince de Ligne who, in his eagerness to gather laurels in a fresh field of action and the fear that it would be some time before the Austrian armies would be ready to go into battle, had asked permission of his Emperor to serve on the Russian front. Catherine had been only too willing to give him the rank of general, but the chivalrous, noble-minded Prince had not reckoned with the jealousy and duplicity of the Russian court and the preponderating influence of the young favourite who, being a devoted creature of Potemkin and probably in his pay, poisoned the Empress's mind against anyone who dared to criticize the Prince.

De Ligne arrived at Potemkin's headquarters three months after the war had begun, to find the siege of Otchakov not even started and the Commander-in-Chief sunk into a state of apathy, from which it was impossible to rouse him. All his remonstrances and appeals fell on to barren ground, and before long Potemkin's moody and suspicious nature began to suspect his loyal friend of treachery. He was already being bombarded by letters from the Empress as to why Otchakov had not been taken and what was holding him back? Was he wounded or ill? They were letters to which more often than not he did not even deign to reply. And to have de Ligne pestering him every day by suggesting some new plan of attack was more than his nerves could stand.

But Catherine's attitude to the Prince de Ligne was even more shocking than that of Potemkin. After writing herself to Joseph asking for the Prince's services and expressing her personal gratitude to an Austrian Field-Marshal who had volunteered to serve under Potemkin, she suddenly turned against him as soon as he raised his voice in criticism against her Commander-in-Chief. The intrigues of Momonof, who had always resented her intimacy with the fascinating de Ligne, led her to write Potemkin a letter which showed her to be as false and as devious as any member of her court. This letter, dated 18 October 1787, reads 'This morning de Ligne received the order from his Emperor to join you. He hoped to get an Austrian command and to capture Belgrade but instead of that they are making him into a spy. If he is in the way, I think you can send him back to Vienna on the excuse of exchanging views on the present and future plans of campaign. He himself is disappointed.'

This was not the case. No one ever went more joyously to war than the fifty-year-old Prince, whose only fear was that Otchakov might have been captured before he arrived, instead of which nothing was prepared or even planned. 'If we had provisions we would march; if we had pontoons we would cross the rivers; if we had bombs or bullets we might begin to attack. But everything is lacking. Meanwhile Prince Potemkin has gone fishing.'

Weeks and months went by and still nothing was done. De Ligne wrote in despair to his Emperor, 'of having exchanged the role of Field-Marshal for that of a nurse-maid to a strong, perverse and malicious child, whose promises and stories do not contain the element of truth'. Describing his relations with Potemkin, he writes, 'I told him to his face that I am tired of all his lies and excuses and he flew into a towering passion and asked me if I thought he was going to let me lead him by the nose. But your Majesty must be getting as bored of listening to my complaints, as I am bored of having to make them.' One of the richest and most fastidious *grands seigneurs* lived for nearly a year in a room 'where the ceiling was so low he could not stand up straight and so small that he could have closed the door from his bed, had there been any handle to close, or shut the window, had there been any window panes, or light the stove, had there been any wood'. Potemkin appears to have had no qualms over billeting an Austrian Marshal in such conditions, while he himself lived in the greatest luxury.

Eye-witnesses have described the subterranean palace with pillars of lapis-lazuli in which Serenissimus made his head-quarters during the siege of Otchakov, where he entertained a harem of beautiful women, chosen from among his officers' wives, waited on by seven hundred servants who, including his orchestra, had all to be fed at the army's expense. None of these reports can have been pleasant reading for Catherine, jealous for his renown and impatient for victories. But there was only one time, after he had left her without news for months, that she suggested him handing over his command to Marshal Roumiantsev. But the war had brought the two rival Marshals together, and it was the old war-hero who now insisted on Potemkin remaining at his post. For all his faults, his vagaries and eccentricities, the Prince appears to have possessed an element of greatness which no one could deny. From the squalor of his room near Otchakov, Charles de Ligne wrote to his friend Philip de Ségur,

of a Commander-in-Chief who looks idle but is always busy, who is constantly reclined on a couch but sleeps neither by night or day. His zeal for his Empress whom he adores keeps him always awake and uneasy, and the cannon-shot to which he himself is not exposed, disturbs him with the thought that it is costing the life of some of his soldiers. . . . Trembling for others he is brave himself, stopping under fire to give his orders – alarmed at the anticipation of danger, gay when he is in the midst of it. . . . He is suspicious but not revenge-ful, asking pardon for pain he has inflicted, quick to repair an injustice, loving God but fearing the devil more. . . . He abandons himself to distrust or to confidence, to jealousy or to gratitude, to ill-humour or to loyalty, is easily prejudiced in favour of, or against anything or anyone and as easily cured of a prejudice; talking divinity to his generals and tactics to his bishops – affecting the most attractive or the most repulsive manners – concealing under the appearance of harshness the greatest benevolence of heart. What is the secret of his magic? Genius – natural ability – an excellent memory – the art of conquering every heart in his good moments – the talent of guessing what he is ignorant of and a consummate knowledge of mankind.

This was a generous tribute from a man who had experienced all the malice and the pettiness of which this strange, unaccountable creature was capable. De Ligne accepted Potemkin in the same way as he accepted Russia, that vast mysterious country with its icy tundras and dark forests, its swiftly flowing rivers and lakes as large as seas; its mines of precious stones hidden in the Ural Mountains and the limitless steppes stretching eastwards into China. Potemkin, like Russia, was a life force of energy, of secret diamond mines alternating with deserts of emptiness. They quarrelled, they argued, their friendship was strained to the utmost. But when they parted in the summer of 1788 and de Ligne returned to serve under his Imperial master at Belgrade and share with his son in the glory of capturing the city, Potemkin was the first to send his congratulations for he was never jealous of valour. Most of the intriguing was left to Momonof and there is no better proof of Catherine's declining powers, than her growing dependence on the lover of the day. It was no longer a question of affection, as it had been in the case of Lanskoy. For Momonof had only to fall ill and he was instantly replaced by another stalwart young guardsman, a distant relation of Bezborodko. But Momonof appears to have been endowed by nature with striking physical attributes and stamina, which enabled him on recovery to regain his position. From then on he nursed a vindictive hatred for Bezborodko and lost no opportunity of undermining his influence with the Empress and making mischief with Potemkin.

Catherine's subservience to this worthless young man was rendered all the more pathetic by the fact that Momonof was betraying her with one of her maids-of-honour, the twenty-five-year-old Princess Scherbatov with whom he was passionately in love. It was not an easy courtship, for with every year the Empress was becoming more jealous and possessive. On their return from the Crimea he hit on the ingenious excuse of complaining that travelling in the well-sprung court coaches made him feel ill and that he had to have carriages made on his own design and kept in his own stables. After much arguing the Empress ended by giving way. And 'Redcoat', as she still liked to call him, thereby earned a certain amount of freedom. But

in the end love was stronger than ambition. By the spring of
1788, he was writing to Potemkin begging to be released
from a position which was becoming untenable and the Prince
replying 'that it was his duty to remain at his post for the duration of the war and that he was not to be a fool and ruin his
career'.

1788 was a year of tribulation in which the Empress's habitual
good luck appeared to have deserted her both in her private
and public life. Krapovitzky's diary abounds with references to
'scenes and tears'. The intimate evenings at the Hermitage were
lacking their usual gaiety. Catherine's entourage were growing
old. Leon Naryshkin, still trying to play the buffoon, was gouty
and asthmatic; Betskoy was in his dotage; Ivan Shuvalov was
losing his memory and the mirrored walls of Quarenghi's
enchanting theatre, a miniature copy of Palladio's theatre at
Vicenza, reflected many old and wizened faces. Notable absentees were the Grand Duke and Duchess, who lived most of the
time in retirement at Gatchina, where Paul consoled himself for
the humiliation of not having been given a command on the
southern front by drilling his own regiment in the castle-yard.

There was a general stalemate both on the military and the
political side. The quadruple alliance so earnestly desired by the
Emperor Joseph and now admitted by Catherine to be vital
to the success of the war, and the possibility of an early peace,
was hanging fire. France on the brink of revolution, bankrupt in
its finances, with a weak king and a constantly changing government, was in far too parlous a state to take on any foreign commitments. The entreaties of Philip de Ségur, who was too far
removed from the scene to realize the seriousness of the situation
at home, fell on unheeding ears. The Empress was angry and
disappointed, particularly when she learned that the defences of
Otchakov were being strengthened by French engineers, and it
required all of the ambassador's fascination and tact to retain his
privileged position at court.

Another unexpected blow came in the late summer when
Sweden suddenly invaded Russian Finland. England, who was
determined to prevent the Empress's Baltic fleet from getting to
the eastern Mediterranean and repeating the exploits of

Chesmé, had persuaded King Gustavus that this was a propitious moment to enter into an alliance with Turkey and retrieve his former Finnish provinces. The brave and impulsive Gustavus, who was longing to emulate the heroic exploits of the Wasa Kings, embarked with enthusiasm on a dangerous and costly war. The Empress, who was related to Gustavus through her Holstein mother, never thought he would have the temerity to pit an army of thirty thousand against the limitless reserves of Russia. And it must have been a terrible shock for her to learn that out of the hundred thousand men whom Potemkin had assured her he could put into the field at any time, no more than six thousand were available to protect St Petersburg and the surrounding countryside. Had the King been able to follow up his initial advantage, he might have succeeded in capturing the capital. Already there were rumours of the royal coaches standing by in readiness to take the Empress to Moscow, though this was categorically denied by Catherine herself, who declared that all the available transport, including the carriages of the Imperial stables, had been mobilized to bring up reinforcements.

St Petersburg was saved not by the Russians, but by the treachery of the Swedish nobility, who had never forgiven the King for having asserted his independence of a feudal aristocracy, by taking the side of the liberals, the so-called Hats, in their victory against the Bonnets, the party of reaction, who had tried to keep the King in a state of subjection. Many of these nobles had Russian affiliations, and they now took their revenge by laying down their arms and denouncing the war as 'aggressive and unconstitutional'. In these circumstances King Gustavus had no other alternative than to retreat. But Catherine was disappointed in her hopes of peace. Among the peasants in the north and the burghers of the cities, King Gustavus found the loyalty and support denied him by a selfish aristocracy. By the spring of 1789 he had marshalled an army and equipped a navy which were to give his haughty cousin many a sleepless night and were to cost her the life of the English Admiral Grieg, who had served her so devotedly since the early seventies.

One of his last services was to suppress a threatened mutiny

among the English officers serving on Russian ships, at the news
of the Empress having appointed the American John Paul
Jones, hero of the War of Independence, to the rank of a
Russian Vice-Admiral. Like many heroes, Jones found his
country less eager for his services in peace time than in war and
arrived in Russia in the autumn of 1787 in search of adventures
bringing rich rewards. His friendship with the French ambassador, a fellow member of the Order of Cincinnatus, obtained
him an audience with the Empress. Catherine, who had a
natural affinity with adventurers, particularly when they were
tall and handsome, gave him, according to his account, 'such a
flattering reception, treating me with so much consideration,
that I was entirely captivated and placed myself entirely in her
hands, without making any stipulations to my own advantage.
All I asked was that she would never condemn me without hearing me first.' The Empress, who was so prodigal in dispensing
titles and decorations, created him Vice-Admiral attached to the
Baltic fleet. But she had not reckoned with the resentment of the
British officers on duty at Cronstadt and Reval, and she was
furious when Admiral Grieg informed her that many of them
threatened to resign if the 'pirate' Jones was given a command.
As Autocrat of all the Russias, she refused to admit subversive-
ness and she ordered the offending officers to be put under
arrest. But Grieg brought her to reason by reminding her that
such drastic action would deprive her of over half of the
officers of her Baltic fleet.

Admiral Jones was therefore despatched to Potemkin's headquarters at Kherson, where in place of the open enmity of the
British officers, he ran into a hornet's nest of intrigue. No sooner
was he put in charge of a naval squadron of seventeen sea-going
vessels than he came into direct conflict with Potemkin's Chief
Admiral, Prince Nassau-Siegen who, in spite of his illustrious
name, was a penniless swashbuckling adventurer, jealous of
anyone who might threaten his mythical reputation for seaman-
ship. A brilliant *raconteur*, he had managed to convince not only
Catherine and Potemkin, but also his friend de Ligne, that he
had all the qualities of a first-class admiral. He reported directly
to Potemkin, and when the former gave orders that Admiral

Jones should be supplied with all the gun-boats he required, the order was deliberately sabotaged.

Yet in spite of the difficulties encountered on every side Jones managed to introduce some discipline and order into his squadron, in which most of the officers had little or no naval training and the majority of the sailors were Greeks or Genoese or Crimean fishermen. The one naval victory which lightened the gloom of the first months of the war and for which Potemkin and Nassau-Siegen claimed all the credit, was almost entirely due to the courage and initiative of the American Admiral, supported by the land forces of General Souvarov. Jones's accurate report of the battle was deliberately suppressed. When he remonstrated to Souvarov, the latter replied 'You must adapt yourself like I do. Pay homage to those in power, humble yourself to them all in turn. Then no one will be jealous of you. Be as eccentric as you like. The more people think you are mad, the less they will be frightened of you.' Such was the advice of Catherine's greatest General, whose manias were as eccentric as his courage, who would run out of his tent in his night-shirt to sound the reveille, by imitating the crowing of a cock, and prostrate himself before an ikon at the beginning of every battle, which he would fight with a savagery which shocked the civilized world. But Jones, who was a blunt, plain-spoken American, had no use for the cunning and deviousness of the Oriental mind, and he succeeded in smuggling his report through to the French ambassador who, in spite of his friendship with Nassau-Siegen, handed it on to the Empress.

But no sooner was the Admiral back in St Petersburg than he fell a victim to the lowest form of blackmail in which he was accused of having violated a child. When he called in a well-known lawyer to prove that the girl and her mother were common prostitutes, who made a career out of blackmail, but he found that the lawyer in question had been warned by certain 'prominent personages' not to take on the case. The same day he received an order from the Court Chamberlain forbidding him to approach the palace or to attempt to communicate with anyone at court. Once more it would appear as if Momonof was faithfully carrying out the orders of Potemkin. Matters would have gone badly for the gallant Admiral had it not been again for the friendship of Ségur, who took up his cause as if he had been one of his own nationals, and in the end succeeded in persuading the Empress of his innocence. But with advancing years, Catherine was growing ever more reluctant to become involved '*dans les tracasseries*' and in the end it was the inefficient Nassau-Siegen who remained at his post and John Paul Jones whose services were dispensed with.

In the last month of 1788 Otchakov was finally taken by assault after a bitter and sanguinary conflict, in which Potemkin's reputation for humanity suffered from the butchery of Souvarov. The Empress, who was hungry for victories, celebrated the capture of this miserable little fort with *Te Deums* all over the country. When Potemkin returned to St Petersburg in the early spring of 1789, he was treated as a conquering hero, though his moodiness and depression showed that he himself was far from satisfied with the military situation, while brewing troubles on the domestic front gave him additional cause for uneasiness.

Alexander Momonof was in a state of decline and warned him he could no longer perform his duties. Catherine herself was often in tears, but still deaf to the suggestion of the favourite being replaced. She consoled herself as usual in writing long letters to Melchior Grimm and beginning a new play. This time it was a heavy satire at the expense of the King of Sweden, called *The Paladin of Misfortune*. It appears to have been completely devoid of either wit or humour, and Philip de Ségur, who saw it being privately performed at the Hermitage, was saddened to think that 'such a brilliant Princess should display such a lack of taste in lampooning a heroic adversary, whose courage has earned him the admiration of Europe'. The first thing Potemkin did on his return to St Petersburg was to prevent Catherine from having the play performed in public, which would have offended every patriotic Swede and prejudiced the chances of a just and honourable peace. But the peace openly desired by Potemkin and secretly wished for by Catherine did not materialize for nearly two years and both St Petersburg and Tzarskoye Selo were several times subjected to the cannonading of the Swedish fleet. In a letter to Grimm, written in the summer of 1790, the Empress writes

You will be pleased to hear that General Zoubov and I keep calm and happy by translating Plutarch into Russian while the windows of the Tzarskoye Selo rattle to the reverberation of the Swedish cannon fire.

By the end of June 1789 Alexander Dimitriev Momonof had been officially dismissed and replaced by the twenty-two-year-old Plato Zubov. For the first time in fourteen years Potemkin had played no part in the choosing. Zubov was deliberately put forward by his enemies, seizing on the propitious moment when he had returned to the front. The young man was a protégé of Field-Marshal Count Nicholas Saltykof, who as Governor of the young Grand Dukes had considerable prestige at court, and he was aided and abetted by Anna Nikitishna Naryshkin, the friend of Catherine's youth, who had taken part in the revels of Oranienbaum and the midnight suppers with Poniatowski and with Orlov. As a member of the Roumiantsev family, Anna had never forgiven Potemkin the slights he had inflicted on the old Marshal.

Whether by accident or design, young Zubov, a lieutenant in the Horse Guards, obtained the privilege of commanding a detachment of soldiers on guard at Tzarskoye Selo. Though Momonof was the official favourite at the time, his infidelity was common knowledge to all except the Empress, who still imagined that his spleen was due to the restrictions of court life. But by the beginning of June she was forced to realize that he was bored not only with his life but also with her. Being still physically in love with him, she devised a scheme by which he could ensure his future by marrying while still remaining at court. Prascovia Bruce on dying had left her daughter in her charge and the girl was one of the richest heiresses in Russia. The Empress now offered her as a bride to Momonof and the greatest shock came when he refused the offer. In a letter full of falsehoods, excuses and professions of adoration, he confessed his love for Daria Scherbatov, giving away the fact that he had proposed marriage to her several months ago. The Empress,

who had not yet accepted the fact that she could arouse no other
feeling than a maternal love and respect, looked upon the
twenty-six-year-old girl as an unscrupulous hussy and a hated
rival. But she was at once too proud and too magnanimous to
behave as Elisabeth would have behaved in the same circumstances, either by disfiguring her rival's beauty or condemning
her to a nunnery. She had loved Alexander Dimitriev and
planned great things for his future. She had believed in his silly
stories of stifling at court, whereas he was only stifling from his
own duplicity. In Potemkin's absence she unburdened herself
to a female confidante, to her loyal old Anna Nikitishna. And in
his diary her secretary, Krapovitzky, records that in the evening
of receiving Momonof's confession, she dined alone with her old
friend and spent most of the night in tears. Three days later she
summoned Count Momonof and the Princess Scherbatov into her
presence. One glance was sufficient to realize that the girl was
heavily pregnant, and it is not surprising that Daria Scherbatov
fainted at the end of the ordeal, during which the Empress announced their betrothal and wished them happiness for the
future. The same afternoon she signed a *Ukaze* granting the
young couple a country estate and the gift of a hundred
thousand roubles. Ten days later they were married in the
palace chapel and the Empress, according to custom, dressed
her maid-of-honour's hair with a diamond coronet and blessed
her with an ikon. She even presided at the wedding supper after
which Count and Countess Momonof left for the country, where
they were to await the bride's confinement.

The Empress's dignity and generosity won universal admiration. Unfortunately her dignity deserted her when it was a
question of her passions. Count Saltykof and Madame Naryshkin
were quick to profit by the situation. Zubov was conveniently
on duty at Tzarskoye Selo. On the day after Momonof's
betrothal Anna Nikitishna and her protégé were already dining
at the palace and three days later, Krapovitzky notes in his
diary that the Empress told him to bring her some rings from
the jewel cabinet and to place ten thousand roubles under sofa
cushions in her boudoir. From then on Zubov was constantly in
attendance, and no one was surprised when, after ten days,

the twenty-two-year-old lieutenant was appointed to be Her Majesty's personal *aide-de-camp* which carried with it the rank of general. But who could have guessed that this modest young man with the soft brown eyes and quiet deferential manner, concealed beneath his pleasing exterior a rapacious ambition, which was to cast a dark cloud over the last years of a glorious reign.

CHAPTER THIRTY

Plato Zubov

Had Potemkin lived, the second and third partitions of Poland would never have taken place. The Prince had always upheld the usefulness of a buffer state between Russia and her Western neighbours. He had had only to say the word, and Catherine would have upheld his claims to become either Duke of Courland or King of Poland. But he had always supported Stanislaus Augustus, and it was the warring factions among the Poles themselves which ended in destroying their country.

In 1772 the partitioning powers had imposed on Poland a constitution, which kept it in a state of anarchy, limiting the powers of the King and increasing the privileges of an unruly and selfish aristocracy. But the shock of the partition and hatred of the occupying powers brought about a resurgence of patriotism. The enlightened elements of the country gathered round the King, and Poland's literary and political revival attracted the attention of Europe and particularly of France. One of the tragedies of history is that Poland's heroic attempt to shake off her shackles should have coincided with Potemkin's death and the outbreak of the French Revolution.

A Prussian diplomat of Italian descent, trained in the labyrinthine diplomacy of Frederick the Great, contributed to Poland's undoing. The new King of Prussia, Frederick William II, was no friend of Catherine's. He had neither forgotten or forgiven the cavalier treatment he had received at her court, and he was only waiting for a chance to show that he could be just as formidable an adversary as his famous uncle. The stalemate of the Russo–Turkish campaign of 1788 gave him the opportunity he was looking for, and the Italian Luchesini was sent as ambassador to Warsaw, to employ his wiles in inciting the Poles to assert their independence and abrogate the hated constitution. Disowning its partners in the first partition, Prussia now offered Poland a military alliance as the price of the coveted Baltic port of Danzig.

Catherine's immediate reaction on hearing that the Polish Diet had voted in favour of these measures, was to order more troops into the country. But Potemkin succeeded in dissuading her from taking an action which would bring about a war with Prussia, who was allied both with England and with Holland, whereas Russia had no other ally but Austria who was already facing the bulk of the Turkish army in the Balkans. With two wars on hand, the Empress had neither the money nor the troops available for fresh adventures. Such men as could be spared had been sent back to the land to repair the ravages caused by the failure of last year's harvest. But Catherine never forgave the Poles for abolishing the constitution she herself had drafted, nor their insolence in demanding the evacuation of her troops. From now on they were 'public enemy number one', whom she hated more bitterly than either the Swedes or the Turks, and in the future neither King Stanislaus nor his country could expect either clemency or pity. The unfortunate King, who was so much cleverer than the majority of his subjects, was the first to realize the folly of the Diet, but he had no other choice than to allow himself to be swept along on a tide of wild, exhilarating patriotism.

Meanwhile Russia's military situation was improving in the south. She and her allies were winning victories on every front. Potemkin had reached the Dniester and captured Ackermann. The Austrians had occupied Belgrade, and the allied armies in conjunction had defeated Turkish forces four times their number at Foksàny, and were driving them out of Moldavia and Wallachia. But the losses in lives were enormous and the sufferings were intense, and for the past months Potemkin had been urging the Empress to make friendly overtures to England with a view to securing peace, and to discard all plans for a quadruple alliance which, in the present state of France, would never materialize. But until the end of 1789, so long as Philip de Ségur remained in St Petersburg, that brilliant and accomplished diplomat succeeded in convincing both the Empress and Bezborodko that France was the only power with sufficient prestige to mediate a just and honourable peace. Catherine was still clinging to this illusion after the fall of the Bastille, an event whose tremendous significance she never seems to have grasped. One finds her writing to Princess Dashkova 'that the outbreak was due to the schemes of a few criminals. A little action and firmness on the part of the authorities, and these vermin will creep back into their holes.'

Yet she was in St Petersburg when the news first burst on the town, and the crowds rushed out into the streets in what Ségur described as 'one of the most extraordinary and spontaneous demonstrations of mass enthusiasm' he had ever witnessed. 'Men of every class and nationality, Russians, French, Danes, English and Germans, embracing and congratulating one another, cheering their heads off with joy, over the destruction of a fortress thousands of miles away which the philosophers had made into a symbol of tyranny.' It lasted for only a few moments before the crowds were dispersed, for Catherine's capital was no longer a place in which people could express themselves so freely. Yet it was the Empress herself who had sent these young men to study in foreign universities and who boasted of having introduced Voltaire into every Russian school; it was the Empress who had contributed to the most progressive newspapers in her country and invited artists and philosophers from the West to become members of her Academies. Long after she had lost her first enthusiasm for 'enlightenment', she was still employing a Swiss republican as tutor to the young Grand Dukes.

It was Lanskoy who first brought Frederick-Caesar LaHarpe to her notice, by engaging him as tutor to his brother, and the Empress was so impressed by the extent of his knowledge and his sound and honest principles, that in 1784 she appointed him tutor to the six-year-old Alexander. It speaks for Catherine's fairness and common sense, that LaHarpe retained his job after

Russia had become flooded with French *émigrés*, none of whom had a good word to say for the Bernese republican, whom Catherine kept in her palace throughout the worst years of the terror in France. She would tease and irritate him by calling him 'Monsieur le Jacobin' but she continued to treat and respect him 'as an honest man'. But the benefactress of Diderot, the disciple of Voltaire, who allowed her grandson to study the philosophy of Locke and Tom Paine's *The Rights of Man*, had neither sympathy nor understanding for the men who, in the first year of revolution, dreamt of making a better world and cleaning out the Augean stables of corruption and misgovernment in France. From first to last she was guided only by self-interest, the preservation of her power and of her throne, and later by her Machiavellian schemes for Poland where, by encouraging the coalition of princes to lead a crusade against the revolution, a crusade to which she did not contribute a single Russian soldier, she was 'left with sufficient elbow-room' to carry out her own plans.

By October 1789 she had realized that the 'few criminals' had become an overwhelming and dangerous force. When Philip de Ségur came to take leave of her at Tzarskoye Selo, she already regarded him as a potential enemy, even if she still loved him as a friend. The young ambassador, whose sympathies were with his cousin, General Lafayette, was returning to France after being kept for the past months almost without news, having to rely on the information supplied to him by Bezborodko, most of it many weeks out of date. The Empress was at her most charming, telling him 'I am sad to see you go. You had far better stay here with me, than to throw yourself into the eye of the storm, which may spread further than you think. Your leanings towards the new philosophy, your passion for liberty, will probably lead you to adopt the popular cause. I will be angry, for I am and shall remain an aristocrat. It is my job. You will find France very feverish and very sick.' Ségur replied: 'I am afraid so Madame, and that is what makes it my duty to return.' She made him stay to dinner, displaying so much warmth and affection as to make the parting even harder for him. There is no greater tribute to Catherine's magnetic

personality, than that Philip de Ségur, after spending five years
at her court, and in the past year having had to put up with
many scenes and recriminations, should nevertheless be sad
at having to say goodbye. 'When I went, I thought I was
only going on leave. The departure would have been still more
painful had I known I was seeing her for the last time.'

Ségur records another tribute to Catherine's fascination.
When passing through Vienna, the Emperor Joseph, who was
already a dying man, had got out of bed to receive him, and the
ambassador naturally thought that the Emperor's first thought
would be for his sister, Marie-Antoinette, and that he would
give him either a letter or a message for her. Joseph, however,
did not want to talk of Marie-Antoinette but of Catherine, and
not of Catherine the Empress, but of Catherine the woman,
asking him whether he could throw any further light on the true
nature of her relations with Prince Potemkin. It was a subject
they had often discussed on their evening walks in the Crimea,
when Ségur would compare himself to Giaffar and the Emperor
to the Caliph Haroun Al Raschid. But what was discussed in
the exotic setting of Bakshiserai seemed strangely out of place in
the sick-room of the Hofburg. Yet to the dying man, Catherine's
private life still appeared to be of vital interest, and he assured
Ségur 'that he had received certain information, which convinced him that the Empress and Potemkin were secretly
married'.

Three months later Joseph was dead and no one mourned
him more sincerely than the Empress. Their incongruous
friendship had survived an uneasy alliance and their mutual
esteem persisted to the end. Joseph died from strain and over-
work in trying to enforce his reforms at the butt of a gun on a
people who were not ready for them; Catherine had long since
discarded the liberal aspirations of a German Grand Duchess
who had dreamt of liberating the serfs; she had forgotten the
ideals of the proud young Empress, who in all the enthusiasm of
youth had tried to legislate a new code of laws, based on the
principles of Montesquieu and Beccaria, for a people who were
eighty per cent illiterate. In her later years she had dedicated
her energies to making her country great, rather than making

her people happier. If Joseph was the nobler of the two, she was infinitely the more astute.

She was never more astute than in those years of turmoil from 1790 to 1793, from when the first *émigrés* arrived in Russia, bringing tales of pillage and of murder which recalled the worst excesses of the Pugachefschina. Like every other autocrat in Europe she felt the panic of an approaching earthquake, threatening to convulse her throne. But while others vacillated, she held firm, steadying the throne with the weight of her authority, denouncing all those who dared to threaten 'The Divine Right of Kings'. No one could have expressed a greater sympathy for the unfortunate King of France; no one could have been more generous in her treatment of the impoverished aristocrats who sought her hospitality. It flattered her vanity to have some of the greatest names of France enlisted in the service of Russia and to pay the debts of the King's brother. But in her letters to Potemkin she writes of King Louis as being weak and incapable and of the Count d'Artois as being an unworthy descendant of her idol King Henry IV. 'I am re-reading the Henriade and the Bourbon Princes would do well to read it themselves.' But whether she is writing to Potemkin or to one of her marshals, the Empress makes it clear that she has no intention of joining the crusade of Princes. She was lavish in her advice and passionate in her defence of the royalist cause. But her real interests were centred nearer home. She was more concerned with what was happening on the Vistula than on the Seine. In her eyes the most dangerous of Jacobins were the Poles, the patriots who were gallantly rallying round their King to establish order in their country and put an end to anarchy in the form of the hated *Liberum Veto*.

Potential Jacobins were hunted down in Russia; the Chief of Police was despatched to Moscow to deal with the disgruntled gentlemen who till now had been free to air their grievances aloud in palaces and clubs. Young writers, whose 'misguided idealism' would have aroused no more than a tolerant smile in the Catherine of the seventies, now had their articles suppressed by the police. The well-known publicist Novikof, a friend and collaborator of Princess Dashkova, was suddenly thrown into prison for what was called the subversive nature of his writings.

But the harshest treatment of all was meted out to Alexander Radischev, an earnest young civil servant belonging to the minor nobility. Radischev was one of the young men selected from the Imperial College of Pages to finish their studies abroad. After three years at Leipzig he returned to Russia, full of the new and progressive ideas which flourished in the Western universities. Appointed as Inspector of Customs, attached to the Ministry of Commerce, he became the friend of the Minister Alexander Vorontsov, brother to Princess Dashkova. Radischev was a harmless idealist, disgusted by the injustices committed in every walk of public life, and he acquired the dangerous habit of transcribing his grievances on to paper. Dashkova, who was unimpressed by his writings, warned her brother that sooner or later his protégé would get himself into serious trouble, and in May 1790 the publication of *A Journey from St Petersburg to Moscow* proved her prophecy to be correct.

The book is a short, disjointed account of a journey across Russia, written in the manner of Sterne's *Sentimental Journey*, but with none of Sterne's wit or charm of style. On first reading it strikes one as being as harmless and as dull as it must have appeared to the Chief Censor, who in a moment of boredom or of lassitude allowed it to pass for public circulation. On closer inspection one realizes that this slim volume is charged with dynamite. It is not only an indictment of the horrors of serfdom, but every anecdote contains an accusation against the corruption and injustices of Catherine's Russia. Though no names are given, her officials, her ministers, her favourites, even to the omnipotent Potemkin, are all incriminated.

The book unfortunately came into the Empress's hands, rousing her to such a pitch of indignation that she declared its author 'to be an even more dangerous criminal than Pugachef'. Censor, publisher and printer were all placed under arrest. Radischev was committed for trial and two months later sentenced to death. When Potemkin heard of the Empress's intransigence, he sent an express messenger from Kherson, begging her not to make this insignificant book and its even more insignificant author into a *cause célèbre*. But though the

Empress made a show of clemency by transmuting the death penalty to 'hard labour in Siberia', she was too much under the influence of Plato Zubov and too frightened by the spectre of revolution to pay attention to Potemkin's plea for tolerance. She showed so little compassion for the unfortunate Radischev that he was not even allowed to take leave of his family before setting out on the long and terrible journey laden with chains like any common criminal.

The Empress had not reckoned on the reaction of public opinion. Clandestine copies of *A Journey from St Petersburg to Moscow* were selling under the counter at a hundred roubles each. Young liberals made it their bible and Alexander Vorontsov had the courage to send in his resignation and retire from public life in protest against the harshness of the sentence. Sympathy for Radischev was even expressed in the Grand Dukes' school-rooms and one of the Emperor Alexander's first actions on coming to the throne was to recall Radischev from exile. But after ten years of hard labour Radischev returned to St Petersburg an old and broken man.

Yet the Empress who condemned poor Radischev continued to patronize LaHarpe, who remained in Russia right up to the time of the Grand Duke's marriage in 1793. She made no attempt to interfere in the curriculum of studies or to prevent 'Monsieur Alexandre' from receiving what she called a progressive education. Her grandsons were taught to hoe and reap in the fields in the manner of Jean-Jacques Rousseau; to treat their elders, however humble, with respect and their young companions as their equals. They were made to sleep on hard beds with rough blankets and eat simple and healthy food. At the same time their grandmother liked them to appear at court in the finest of brocaded coats with lace ruffles and diamond buckles; every compliment paid to the good looks of Alexander was treasured by the doting Empress. Less was said of Constantine, who unfortunately bore a strong resemblance to his father.

The children led a double life between the gaiety of the Hermitage and the stern military atmosphere of Gatchina, drilling and exercising all day with the Prussian officers of their father's private regiment; Maria Feodorovna was a loving mother, but she was also a German disciplinarian, doing her best to prevent her sons from becoming contaminated by the licentiousness of the Imperial court. Her task was not an easy one, and it was only later that Alexander learned to appreciate her qualities and to criticize the weaknesses and defects of his darling '*Grand Maman*'.

The Zubovs were the closest companions of his adolescence, for Plato was still sufficiently a child to enjoy flying kites from the roof of Tzarskoye Selo, while Plato's nineteen-year-old brother Valerian, whom the Empress referred to as 'the Child' or 'the little Blackamoor', was always encouraging him to mischief and was the despair of his governor, Count Saltykof. There were many romps at the Hermitage, with the sixty-one-year-old Empress joining in a game of blindman's buff, which she still thoroughly enjoyed. We find her writing to Grimm: 'The children say it is more fun when I join in their games for I am the *Lustmacherin*' (the Merry Andrew of the party).

While encouraging her grandchildren to be friends with her young lover, the Empress insisted on the Princes being brought up in complete ignorance of the ordinary facts of life. Their tutors were expressly forbidden to give them any sexual instruction, and woe betide the enterprising maid-of-honour who tried to flirt with the handsome Alexander who remained a virgin till the time of his marriage at the age of sixteen.

Catherine's ability to throw off the cares of state in an evening of rollicking fun, or to concentrate on translating Plutarch to the sound of Swedish cannon-fire shows both enormous resilience and iron nerves. The continuation of the Swedish war and the defeat of her navy at Svenskund caused her for the first time to question the workings of providence. 'What have I done?' she said, 'that God should choose to chastize me with such a feeble instrument as the King of Sweden.' In the end common-sense got the better of pride, and by August 1790 the Peace of Verela put an end to a war of which neither Russia nor Sweden could claim to be the victors.

Meanwhile Potemkin and his generals were marching in to Bessarabia. Souvarov had laid siege to Ismail and Repnin had captured Kilia. But these victories were offset by the defection of Austria. Joseph's younger brother Leopold had barely been two months upon the throne, before he withdrew his armies from the Balkans. This was closely followed by a meeting between the Emperor and Frederick William of Prussia, in which Russia's two powerful neighbours signed a pact of friendship. Left without allies, Catherine used all her diplomatic skill to incite the Western powers to join in a crusade against the 'hydra-headed monster' of revolution. But Austria refused to move as long as the pacific Leopold occupied the Imperial throne. He had only known his sister when he was a small child, and he had no intention of dragging his country into a war on account of the King and Queen of France. It was only after his death in March 1792 that his son Francis joined in the ill-fated 'crusade of Princes' in their march towards the Rhine, and that Russia, after signing a peace treaty with Turkey, could give her undivided attention to the Poles.

Throughout 1790 St Petersburg saw little of Potemkin, though even in absence he continued to provide the principal subject of conversation. Tales of his growing eccentricities and extravagances circulated round the town – tales of his beautiful mistresses whom he covered with fantastic jewels, of the famous opera singers from Europe whom he hired for their entertainment; of the millions he spent on his palaces and gardens in the desert. No one grudged those wasted millions more than the avaricious Zubov, who did all in his power to belittle the one man whose influence he feared. But the Empress refused to listen to his back-biting. Prince Potemkin was a genius who could not be judged by the standards of other men. He had done far too much for Russia to be grudged the gratification of a few extravagances. Count Zubov must learn to love and understand a man who had so much to teach him in diplomacy and statecraft.

Basking in the glow of an Indian summer, 'reviving like a fly who had come in from the cold', Catherine was so happy with her boy lover that she felt neither jealousy nor disapproval of Prince Potemkin's amorous vagaries. Where she showed a curious lack of understanding was in the insistence with which she kept bringing Zubov to his notice. She was pathetically anxious for him to sanction her choice, as if he had had a hand in the choosing. She kept enumerating the good qualities of Plato Alexandrovitch, 'who was the most innocent soul with the kindest of hearts and the sweetest disposition in the world'. 'I know you love me – be kind to us and you will make us perfectly happy.' 'Do me a favour, show us some attention.' She was always asking him for some new appointment either for Zubov or his younger brother. 'Would you as chief of the Chevalier Gardes take on a new cornet, for the boy is very worthy of reward. Then his younger brother can succeed to his place in the Horse Guards.' The Empress appeared to be almost as fond of Valerian as of Plato, calling him 'our child' and asking Potemkin to help him to make a career. 'He is only nineteen, but is extremely fond of me and cries like a baby when he cannot be with me.' Every letter was more sentimental, more doting than the last, more calculated to irritate and annoy a man who for the past sixteen years had dominated her private and her public life. But Potemkin was sufficiently wise and cunning to concede what he could not refuse. Plato became an officer in the élite Chevalier Gardes, with the privilege of wearing a splendid blue and silver uniform. But his brother Valerian was ordered to the front, to report for active service as one of the Prince's *aides-de-camp*.

Meanwhile letters from his friends in St Petersburg kept warning Potemkin of the danger of allowing the infatuated Empress to fall completely under the spell of a young man who cared neither for his sovereign nor his country, but only for himself. Souvarov's capture of Ismail in December 1790 gave the Russians command of the whole of the Danube mouth. The fighting was virtually over and Potemkin was free to return to St Petersburg where the Empress was waiting to give him a triumphal welcome, though Zubov kept insisting that the real victor was not Potemkin but General Souvarov.

The new favourite bitterly resented the preparations which were being made for the Prince's arrival. The Neo-classic Taurida Palace built by Starov, one of the few great Russian architects employed by Catherine, was now finally completed.

An English traveller who visited St Petersburg in November 1790 described it 'as the finest skeleton' of a house he had ever seen. 'There is no end to the rooms, which are all as immense as the Prince himself. There is a winter garden, so large that there are several walks in it, with a temple in the middle in which there is a statue of the Empress. Most probably it will never be finished, as the Prince has sent for his gardener and his architect and is building a palace and laying out a garden at Jassy in Moldavia.'

But the Prince's servants were accustomed to travelling hundreds of miles, to laying out a garden in the desert, and to being recalled at a moment's notice, or to bringing him some special delicacy from the capital, which he had forgotten he had ever asked for long before it arrived. He had only to announce his return for all the Empress's architects and gardeners to be mobilized to put the finishing touches to the Taurida Palace, a last coat of paint on the daffodil-coloured walls, on the white Doric columns and green cupola, while the Prince's art treasures, the value of which made Zubov green with envy, were moved into the palace.

Meanwhile the court was waiting in suspense for the outcome of the first encounter between Serenissimus and the new favourite. The former was still the stronger of the two, for all Zubov's jealousy could not prevent the grateful Empress from sending a special delegation, headed by Bezborodko, to meet her victorious Commander-in-Chief in Moscow. Religious processions and military parades, triumphal arches and waving flags greeted him in every town. But he was a tired, sick man beset with worry, and for the first time in doubt of his own ability to stand up against the irresistible appeal of youth.

Bezborodko had nothing good to tell. Plato Zubov was far from being the harmless nonentity he had appeared to be at first. Nor was he prepared to content himself with the role of 'Emperor of the Night'. He had already asked to be instructed in affairs of state, and he was shown certain documents which should never have been allowed to leave the Imperial Chancery. But the most tragic event of all in the past months had been the mental and physical deterioration of the Empress. The Prince would find Her Majesty sadly changed both in her mind and in her appearance. The strain of the past year had affected her usual equanimity and she had become cantankerous and irritable, unable to stand the slightest opposition. She had put on an enormous amount of weight and suffered from disorders of the circulation. Her legs were so swollen that she had difficulty in walking and in climbing stairs. Cameron, her Scottish architect, had designed a colonnaded gallery at Tzarskoye Selo where she could take her exercise protected from the weather, and had now added a gentle sloping ramp from where she could pass into the garden without making any undue effort.

Potemkin listened with growing depression to Bezborodko's gloomy prognostications of what would happen if Catherine was allowed to fall still more under the influence of the insufferable Zubov. He made it quite clear that the only alternative was for the Prince to return to his old position in the palace and regain his hold over a weak and vacillating woman. It was an appalling prospect for a man who was just recovering from the second bout of malaria he had had that year. He had rather fight a hundred battles under the walls of Otchakov and Bender, bivouac for months under the blazing sun of Bessarabia, than go back to a position he had given up so gladly almost fifteen years ago. But he still loved his Empress and his country far too much to allow them to be destroyed by the ambition of a greedy boy. By the time their coach had reached the outskirts of St Petersburg he had already made up his mind to fight what was to be the most difficult battle of his career.

He nearly succeeded. Three months after his return Catherine was writing to the Prince de Ligne: 'When one looks at Prince Marshal Potemkin one must admit that his victories and his successes beautify him. He has returned to us from the army as handsome as the day, as gay as a lark, as brilliant as a star, more witty than ever and giving every day a feast more beautiful than the last.'

CHAPTER THIRTY-ONE

Finis Polonia

On what was to be his last visit to St Petersburg, Potemkin squandered no less than a quarter of a million roubles, and where Potemkin set the tone, the other courtiers followed in a wild orgy of extravagance, at a time when Russia's finances were severely depleted after the strain of a long and debilitating war. Edward Genet, who had been acting as French *chargé d'affaires* since the departure of Philip de Ségur, wrote home in a despatch that 'Money in Russia had completely vanished from circulation and it was evident that the government, under the guise of banknotes, were manufacturing veritable paper currency and the rate of exchange was falling daily.'

The peace terms were not yet settled, the Turks had not yet laid down their arms, but Prince Potemkin's return signified that the war was virtually at an end, and St Petersburg, freed after two years from the threat of Swedish guns, was given over to frivolity and dissipation. The nobility vied with one another as to who could provide the more brilliant entertainment for their beloved sovereign. The leading actresses of the Comédie Française, the most famous of the Italian castrati were attracted to Russia by enormous salaries. Count Bezborodko gave a ball at which he spent no less than five thousand roubles on building a ramp in his palace to save the Empress the exertion of climbing the stairs. Her girth was now so vast that it was becoming increasingly difficult for her to walk and she occupied two seats at the theatre of the Hermitage. But outwardly she was as gay and indefatigable as ever, and Plato Zubov, who in the past year had become both a general and a count, was in constant attendance, looking so incongruous as her lover as to provoke Bezborodko to remark: 'The Empress wears him like a decoration.' But it was noted that Potemkin's return had in no way diminished Zubov's credit and the Prince's open contempt for the favourite only made the Empress unhappy. He had informed his friends that he had returned to St Petersburg in order 'to have a tooth taken out which was hurting him', *zub* being the Russian for tooth. But not many dared to laugh at the pun, for it was generally accepted that young Zubov had come to stay and that his power was rapidly increasing.

The Empress was hopelessly enslaved by a boy who had nothing to recommend him other than his youth. For all his glory, it was too late for a fifty-two-year-old libertine to revive a passion of which even the embers had grown cold, and Potemkin had at last to realize that all his attempts to warn the Empress of the harm she was doing both to herself and to her country in allowing a mediocrity like Zubov to interfere in public affairs only ended in spoiling their relationship. Catherine kept begging her 'dearest husband, her little Grischa', to show some tolerance for her lover's youth; 'the boy was a willing pupil, who loved and admired him beyond all others'. This was hardly the case, as they mutually detested one another.

Many years later, Zubov told a friend 'the Empress feared the Prince. She treated him like a difficult and exacting husband, but it was me whom she loved.' The saddest hour in Potemkin's life was when he realized that all he had done for Russia and for his sovereign counted for nothing beside the sexual satisfaction she derived from the embraces of an immature youth. The recklessness with which he wasted his health and fortune during those spring months of 1791 give a hint of his despair. The splendid feasts, of which the Empress wrote to the Prince de Ligne, were merely screens to hide the bleakness of the future. The most brilliant of these feasts, and the one which has come down in history, was the masked ball held in the Taurida Palace to celebrate the Empress's sixty-second birthday on the night of 28 April 1791. It was the last gesture of a great showman out to dazzle and astonish the town, which his over life-size personality had dominated for so long; a last tribute of gratitude to the sovereign who had made of him the first subject of her Empire.

The festivities began with a fair held in the neighbouring square, in which there were swings and roundabouts and lotteries to amuse the populace. Fountains ran with wine. There were barrels full of *Kvas* and piles of roasted meats, and baskets full of sweetmeats and hot pies. That night even the humblest could feel they were taking part in Potemkin's ball when the Empress drove through the square on her way to the Taurida Palace, acknowledging their cheers with a warm, maternal smile which embraced them one and all. Three thousand people had been invited to the ball, which opened in the great colonnaded hall with a ballet led by the two Grand Dukes and composed of the most beautiful young men and women at court. Then followed a series of *tableaux* representing the various races of the Empire, each wearing their native dress and singing their native songs. Dancing took place in a ballroom lit by two hundred chandeliers, and at supper six hundred guests were served off gold and silver plate, while the rest of the company gathered round an enormous buffet placed at the entrance to the winter gardens.

Thirty years later, people in St Petersburg were still talking of the wonders of Potemkin's ball; of the beauty of the winter garden, where sandy paths meandered through groves of orange and myrtle and exotic birds flitted from branch to branch; where cascades of water flowed into marble basins and crystal aquariums reflected the shining fins of tropical fish. Mirrors cunningly devised gave the illusion of endless vistas, and in the centre of the garden surrounded by flowers was Shubin's marble statue of the Empress. Illusion followed upon illusion. At one moment the garden glittered with a thousand fireflies, the next it reflected a myriad of precious stones; an obelisk of transparent agate appeared to be on fire and the trunk of a golden elephant, studded with emeralds and fitted with a mechanical device, summoned the guests to supper.

The Empress was so enraptured by the beauty of the setting that she stayed far later than her usual hour. Her enthusiasm was so great and her farewells were so loving that Potemkin fell on his knees before her and, carried away by his emotion, bathed her hands in tears. Tears are contagious and, caught up in a surge of memories, Catherine forgot her young lover and, with moist and glistening eyes, tried to express her gratitude for the seventeen years of glory Potemkin had given to her and to their country.

The Prince remained another two months in St Petersburg, but the last meetings between him and his sovereign were clouded by misunderstandings, not only on account of Zubov but also over the question of Poland. Potemkin had always insisted on the necessity of maintaining the independence of Poland as a useful buffer state between Russia and her Western neighbours. He advised the Empress to follow the example of Prussia and of Austria in accepting the new constitution of 1791 which had abolished the *Liberum Veto* and restored the privileges of the king in making the crown hereditary, to pass after his death to the House of Saxony. But on this occasion Catherine allowed her personal vindictiveness to cloud her better judgment. Her eagerness to conclude a peace with Turkey and even to sacrifice certain claims to conquered territory were dictated by her impatience to exterminate what she called 'that nest of Jacobins in Warsaw'. Potemkin was now offered the unenviable task of carrying out the work of extermination and, given his suspicious nature, immediately recognized the hand of Zubov. Nothing would suit the favourite better than to involve him in an inglorious war a thousand miles away from the capital. The Prince's instinctive reaction was to refuse, but not even 'Serenissimus' dared to thwart the arbitrary wishes of an ageing autocrat.

His first job was to make peace. During his absence, his generals had won a succession of victories and the Turks were prepared to negotiate. But when he finally set out for Jassy on 24 July 1791, he was already so sick at heart that he had lost all interest in living. His last gamble had failed. Zubov was firmly installed in the apartments which he had once regarded as his own and to which till now he had always held the key. In spite of her tears, Catherine had been relieved to see him go. The dissipations of the past month, combined with the continual strain, had had a disastrous effect on his health. The effort of maintaining the role of a triumphant hero had been too much for his strength. Travelling in the hottest month of the year, bumping on dusty roads across the endless plains, made him suffer so much that he was unable to attend the civic receptions which awaited him in every town. Even the sound of a military band was more than his shattered nerves could stand. And all that the welcoming committees saw of him was his huge, tousled, one-eyed head leaning out of the carriage window and shouting to them to stop that infernal noise and let him have some rest. Yet he continued to ignore his physician's advice, preferring old peasant remedies, living on a diet of cabbage soup and raw turnips which only accentuated his already agonizing stomach pain. On reaching Jassy, he was so ill that he was carried half unconscious to bed with what appeared to be a fresh bout of malaria.

Couriers travelled to and fro between Jassy and Tzarskoye Selo bringing him loving gifts and messages from the Empress. But the one message which would have cheered him, the news of Zubov's dismissal, never came. And in every letter Catherine added 'loving greetings from the boy'. By the end of September, he knew that he was going to die. Countess Branicka, his beloved Sashenka, was summoned to his bedside, and in a last letter to the Empress we read: 'Matouchka! Beloved Sovereign! I have no more strength to endure my torments. My only chance is to leave this town and I have given orders to be taken to Nicolaiev. I do not know what will become of me.' He had always hated Jassy. Now he felt his only hope of survival was to get away as quickly as possible. Both niece and doctor pleaded that he was in no state to travel. But in the first days of October, he set off in his coach, accompanied by Countess Branicka, his doctor and three of his young officers. Autumn had already begun, and a thick mist hung over the plains. They had barely travelled two hours before he called on the coachman to stop, saying 'I'm dying, there is no point in going any farther. I want to die on the ground.' A mattress was laid on the roadside and Sashenka knelt down in the dust to hear his last wishes. An hour later, the mightiest man in Russia lay dead on a deserted road on the Moldavian plain.

It took a week for the news to reach the Empress, who was so overcome with grief that she had to be bled three times before she was sufficiently composed to announce Potemkin's death to the army, in a manifesto in which she extolled the Prince's virtues and called on all young officers to emulate his heroic example. She felt utterly lost and bereft, for she had never thought he could die before her, leaving her alone to grapple with the multifold problems of her Empire, and in between her tears she kept repeating 'Whom shall I rely on now?' This phrase recurs in a pitiful letter to Grimm, in which she dwells on 'the wonderful courage of the Prince's heart, the greatness of his mind and soul which set him apart from the rest of humanity'. These eulogies were repeated to everyone, even to the young lover who secretly rejoiced over the death of the only man whose authority he had never dared to challenge. Now the way was open for him to collect, by his talents in the boudoir, the honours and titles which Potemkin had earned over the years he had dedicated to the service of his country. Bezborodko, who was one of the few men of stature in the government, and also one of the few who had scorned to pay homage to Zubov's rising star, was at the favourite's suggestion sent to conclude the Peace Treaty of Jassy, and during his absence Zubov's relatives and friends were brought into the College of Foreign Affairs, of which an insignificant Count Markov was put in charge.

The Empress's hurry to get the peace treaty signed and ratified resulted in terms which would never have satisfied Potemkin, for the territory between the Dnieper and the Dniester was a poor return for all the costly victories gained in the past three years. Catherine sacrificed her dreams of Byzantium in order to wreak her vengeance on the Poles, and Bezborodko had barely returned from Jassy before he received instructions which were to destroy both King Stanislaus and his country. A group of reactionary malcontents were bribed by the Russian government to denounce the Constitution of 1791 as being contrary to the fundamental liberties of Poland, and, at the request of the so-called 'Confederation of Targovitza', eighty thousand Russians and twenty thousand Cossacks marched into the Polish Ukraine.

Now it was Prussia's turn to betray the Poles, who counted on their help. In his eagerness to secure his share of the spoils, Frederick William went back on his word and, having agreed to support the Constitution, now said that 'he had never been previously consulted and therefore considered himself absolved of all commitments'. Catherine, who would have preferred to act alone, had to accept the collaboration of her former partner in crime, no longer the great Frederick but his nephew whom she had already disliked as Crown Prince. Rather than see his capital go up in flames, his art treasures looted by Cossacks, King Stanislaus took the cowardly course of abrogating the Constitution and joining the forces of reaction. But the honour of the name of Poniatowski was retrieved by the bravery of his nephew, Joseph, who fought to the bitter end in a hopeless struggle and whom the Russian troops were to meet again in the forefront of Napoleon's legions.

Caught between two invading armies, with dissension in their own ranks, the Poles had no other choice but to submit to a further partition of their country, by which Catherine took as her share all the eastern provinces from Livonia in the north to the frontier of Moldavia, while Prussia got the coveted cities of Danzig and Thorn and a large part of 'Great Poland' up to twenty-five miles west of Warsaw. Catherine had at least the excuse of occupying lands which had once belonged to the principality of Kiev and where the majority of the inhabitants belonged to the Orthodox faith, but Prussia had no justification for seizing territory in the heart of Poland which threatened the very existence of the capital. This time Austria had no share in the spoils. Her luckless campaigns against the victorious revolutionary forces in the Netherlands and Flanders left her in no position to interfere in Poland and she was in too great a need of Prussia's alliance on the Rhine to dispute her acquisitions on the Vistula.

Catherine and Frederick William now proceeded to legalize their barefaced robbery by forcing King Stanislas to go to the

town of Grodno in Lithuania, where he had to preside over a
Diet which, under the threat of Russian guns, 'was to come to
an amiable understanding with the partitioning powers'. To
help them in their decision, the Russian ambassador, Count
Sievers, announced 'that the troops of her Imperial Majesty
would occupy the lands of any deputy who opposed the will of
the nation' and on 23 July 1793, a sullen and mutinous assembly
gave consent to the signing of the treaty with Russia. But the
Poles' hatred of the Prussians was such that they refused to ratify
the cession of their territory to the country which had betrayed
them, and for days they sat in obstinate silence till the Russian
ambassador, Count Sievers, who was himself opposed to the
aggrandizement of Prussia, had on the Empress's instructions to
declare that 'silence meant consent'. The Diet of Grodno was
formally dissolved and King Stanislaus could return to his palace
at Warsaw, where his treasures were still intact but where he
lived ignored and despised by his own subjects.

Poland was now reduced to one third of its original size, with a
population of under four million and an army of less than
fifteen thousand. But Catherine had not taken into account the
courage which is born of despair, and the rising of 1794, under
the inspired leadership of Taddeus Kosciuszko, took her completely by surprise. Kosciuszko was a brilliant young army
officer who had studied engineering in France and fought in the
American War of Independence. For the first time in Polish
history, men of every class and creed, with peasants fighting in
the front line, rallied under his banner to win back their
country's freedom. The revolt which broke out in Cracow
spread to every town in Poland. There was a gleam of hope
when the partitioning powers began quarrelling among themselves, and Austria entered the field to assert her claims. But
heroism could not survive for long before the sheer weight of
man-power. In a desperate attempt to prevent two Russian
armies from joining, Kosciuszko fought a battle at Maciejovice,
which ended in total disaster, with himself being taken prisoner and carried half dead from the battlefield. Full of hatred
for the Poles, the Russians fought like savages. An army
under Souvarov marched on to Warsaw, taking the suburb of

Praga by storm, massacring over twelve thousand of the inhabitants, including women and children, till the streets were piled high with corpses. Europe re-echoed with tales of the butchery of Praga which equalled the worst days of the Terror in France. But Catherine ignored the brutality and the bloodshed and, delighted by the capture of Warsaw, created Souvarov a Field Marshal, before proceeding to the final dismemberment of Poland in which Zubov and his friends received the greater share of the confiscated properties and thousands of Polish peasants became their serfs.

The last and final partition of Poland gave Prussia the land between the Nieman and the Vistula, including Warsaw. Austria obtained territory north of Galicia, with Cracow and Lublin, and Russia took the rest, including Courland which had hitherto been only under her protection. Catherine could write 'Finis Polonia' across the map of Europe, but she had brought the aggressive power of Prussia so many miles nearer to the Russian frontier and bred a legacy of hate among a people who were now incorporated in her Empire. All the intelligent politicians in her government were against the dismemberment of Poland, but Catherine allowed her obsessive megalomania and her hysterical fear of Jacobins both at home and abroad to dominate her actions till she ended in destroying the image of the enlightened autocrat she had been at such pains to create.

The partitioning powers each took a share of the prisoners. Those who were not imprisoned became exiles in foreign lands, spreading the anti-Catherine legend of a senile Messalina gloating over the ruins of Warsaw. Kosciuszko was taken to Russia and incarcerated in the Schlusselburg where he was visited by the Grand Duke Paul who, acting in defiance of his mother, brought with him his seventeen-year-old son Alexander, and the young Grand Duke was said to have been moved to tears by the plight of the wounded hero. King Stanislaus was confined to a palace at Grodno till the accession of the Emperor Paul, when he was brought back in state to St Petersburg and, by an irony of fate, lodged in the marble palace which Catherine had built for Orlov. The proud Czartoryskis had their properties impounded and Prince Adam's two sons were brought as hostages to Russia to pay allegiance to the Empress and by their good behaviour retrieve their father's land. It is through the eyes of the nineteen-year-old Prince Adam, in memoirs written many years later, that we see Catherine as she appeared to one who had every reason to hate her and yet ended in giving her a grudging admiration.

The young Poles were presented to the Empress at Tzarskoye Selo. Prince Adam describes her as

an old lady well advanced in years but still fresh, short rather than tall and very stout. Her gait, her demeanour and the whole of her person were marked by dignity and grace. None of her movements were quick. All in her was grave and noble. But she was like a mountain stream, which carries everything with it in its irresistible current. Her face already wrinkled, but full of expression, showed haughtiness and the spirit of domination. On her lips was a perpetual smile, but to those who remembered her actions this studied calm hid the most violent passions and inexorable will. On coming towards us her face assumed a gentler expression, and with the sweet look which has been so much praised she welcomed us to her court.

Catherine had always known how to charm and subjugate. Prince Adam and his brother had to enter the Russian service, but with that curious inconsistency which is so often apparent in Catherine's relations with her grandsons, she appointed the Polish Princes as *aides-de-camp* to the two young Grand Dukes. The friendship which sprang up between Prince Adam and the future Emperor Alexander resulted in Catherine's grandson adopting a Polish policy diametrically opposed to her own.

When Adam Czartoryski came into Alexander's life, the seventeen-year-old Grand Duke had already been married for two years. The void left by Potemkin's death, the loneliness which not even Zubov's embraces could dissipate, the reminder that even the most omnipotent on earth are not immortal, made Catherine determined to secure the future of her dynasty and establish her progeny more firmly on the throne. As time went by, her son's eccentricities were becoming more pronounced. Years of frustration and neglect had warped a character which initially was not without generous impulses. Paul's behaviour was sometimes so abnormal that even his loyal wife began to wonder if he was mad, and the Empress contemplated disinheriting Paul in favour of Alexander, much in the same way as Elisabeth had planned to disinherit Peter.

In the year of 1793, when the tumbrils were rumbling through the streets of Paris and the princes of Europe were mobilizing their armies against France, the Empress of Russia celebrated the betrothal of the fifteen-year-old Alexander to the fourteen-year-old Louise of Baden. An immature boy who had never indulged in even the most harmless of flirtations was expected by his grandmother to fall rapturously in love with a girl who was little more than a child and to whose innocent demonstrations of affection he did not know how to respond. In her impulsive fashion, Catherine wrote to Grimm that 'there was never a pair more suited to each other, as lovely as the day, full of grace and spirit, and everyone delights in smiling on their budding love'. But in private his tutors were of the opinion that the Grand Duke was not yet ripe for marriage. And though the wedding took place in October 1793, it was not till seven months later that the young couple assumed the responsibilities of marriage.

It was at this crucial period in Alexander's life that the Empress finally dismissed LaHarpe. In view of her mounting hysteria against those whom she classed as Jacobins, it is amazing she should have kept him so long. Liberals, intellectuals and, above all, her old friends *les philosophes* were now identified with 'the hydra-headed monster of revolution', whose forces were destroying the world, till there came the day when even the bust of Voltaire was removed from its place of honour in Cameron's gallery at Tzarskoye Selo and Diderot's library was consigned to the cellars. After worshipping at the shrine of French culture, Catherine turned against everything that came from France, and began even to have suspicions of the *émigrés* who had hitherto enjoyed her largesse. She even managed to find fault with the art of Madame Vigée le Brun, the most charming of the *émigrés* who came to the banks of the Neva, where she enjoyed an unprecedented success, leaving behind a whole gallery of portraits including those of the younger members of the Imperial family. But the Empress complained to Grimm that the artist has made her pretty granddaughters look 'like simpering monkeys'. And in one of her last letters to the Prince de Ligne, she admits openly 'that she is looking forward to the day when Madame le Brun can return to her own country with all the rest of her *émigrés*'.

LaHarpe's dismissal came both too late and too soon. He had already sown in his pupil's mind the incipient seeds of liberalism, but he left before the young prince's education was completed or his character fully formed. Adam Czartoryski met Alexander when he was still bitterly regretting his tutor's departure, and the young Pole supplied the need for the companionship and understanding he could not find either at Gatchina or at his grandmother's court, where he was made to cultivate the society of Zubov, who in his private opinion 'he would not have employed as a lackey'.

The most distasteful of all the tasks imposed on the young Czartoryskis was having to pay court to Plato Zubov, on whose favour depended the restitution of their father's property. He was the most powerful man in Russia, and they had to attend his *levée* once a week, where they saw the highest in the land humbling themselves before the young upstart who kept playing with his pet monkey and hardly addressed a word to anyone. Having stepped into Potemkin's shoes, Zubov now imitated his arrogance, assuming a cold and distant manner to cover up his fundamental insecurity. He was conscious that all the old courtiers disliked and despised him and lost no opportunity of showing up his ignorance. Bezborodko, who had been forced into semi-retirement, would say with his usual cynicism that 'he was only called in to regild what Zubov had defaced'.

The favourite's response to this underlying hostility was to surround himself with his own creatures, who were mostly men as unscrupulous and as ignorant as himself and only interested in enriching themselves at the expense of their country. His passion for money was almost a disease, and it is significant that very few of Catherine's purchases for the Hermitage were made after 1790, the year in which she commissioned from Sir Joshua Reynolds the allegorical painting of the young Hercules wrestling with the serpents, which was supposed to represent Russia overcoming its difficulties. Unlike his predecessors, Zubov does not appear to have had any interest in collecting drawings or cameos. All he wanted was power, and to obtain that power he was prepared to exercise every form of emotional blackmail on a woman whose sexual appetites, in spite of her age and infirmities, still remained insatiable.

There is singularly little hate in Prince Adam's picture of a young man obsessed by his ambition, pandering to his old mistress and, according to the Prince, being hopelessly in love with Alexander's beautiful bride. We hear of the favourite returning to his rooms after a visit to the Empress 'prostrate with fatigue and pitiably sad, throwing himself upon his couch and drenching his handkerchief with scent', as if he had just endured the most terrible ordeal.

But Catherine herself appears to have been devoid of shame. If anyone dared to criticize her liaisons or the choice of her intimates, she would reply 'Before I became what I am today, I was thirty-three years the same as other people. It is only thirty years since I have become what they are not, and that teaches one to live.' In her sixty-fifth year, she was writing to Grimm,

The day before yesterday, on February 9th, it was fifty years since I arrived with my mother in Moscow. I doubt if there are ten people living today in St Petersburg who remember. There is still Betskoy, blind, decrepit, gaga, asking young couples whether they remember Peter 1st. There is old Countess Matuchkine, who at seventy-eight danced yesterday at a wedding feast. There is the Grand Chamberlain, Naryshkin, and his wife. There is the Master of the Horse, who denies this because he does not want to appear so old. There is one of my old maids, who I still keep, though she forgets everything. These are all proofs of old age and I am one of them. But, in spite of this, I enjoy as much as a child of five years old to play at blindman's buff and all childish games, and I still love to laugh.

Epilogue

On 2 (13) September 1796, a ball was to be held at the Winter Palace to celebrate the betrothal of the Empress's eldest granddaughter, Alexandra, to the seventeen-year-old King of Sweden. Four years had elapsed since his father, Gustavus III, had been murdered in the middle of a masked ball in Stockholm; since when the Empress had been cherishing plans for a marriage that would bring Sweden, who had always been an independent and unruly neighbour, more directly under Russian influence. The plan had met with unexpected opposition in Sweden, for the Duke of Sudermania, the young King's uncle and Regent, was bitterly anti-Russian. But a combination of bribes and threats ended in overcoming his resistance. And, in the middle of August, both King and Regent had arrived on a state visit to St Petersburg, where the beauty and charm of the fourteen-year-old Alexandra soon succeeded in winning the heart of a young man who, at seventeen, promised to become one of the most fascinating and accomplished of monarchs.

There was only one matter to settle, which was the question of religion. With her supreme self-confidence, it never seems to have occurred to Catherine that a 'little King' of Sweden could expect a Russian Grand Duchess to change her religion. It was not a matter of conviction but of pride. As head of the Orthodox church, she insisted on inserting a clause in the marriage contract by which Alexandra should be allowed to have an Orthodox chapel with her own priests and confessor. Instead of discussing the subject with the King, Catherine left everything in the hands of Zubov, who had lately been exalted to the rank of prince and was therefore more arrogant than ever. He in turn left the negotiations to Markov, who was totally inexperienced and so careless that he never bothered to acquaint the King with the Empress's stipulations until he presented him with the marriage contract one hour before he was due at the Empress's ball.

Catherine made her entry into the throne room on the stroke of seven. Every year it was becoming more of an effort to be laced into her gala clothes, but she was still a great actress who could present to the outside world the impression of calm, unruffled majesty. Tonight she was superb, covered in diamonds, wearing the Swedish Order of the Holy Seraphim, and round her throat the famous emeralds given her by Potemkin. The whole of the Imperial family was present, including the Grand Duke Paul and his wife who had come from Gatchina to be present at their daughter's betrothal over which they had not even been consulted. In her thirty-seventh year, Maria Feodorovna had just presented her husband with a third son, which was somewhat embarrassing for her daughter-in-law who, after two years of marriage, was not even pregnant. All eyes were on Alexandra standing by her grandmother's throne, waiting for the fiancé who dared to be late for Her Imperial Majesty. The courtiers were beginning to murmur, when Markov was seen entering the room and whispering to Zubov who left in a great state of agitation.

The King had refused to sign the marriage contract presented by Markov, in which he read for the first time the clauses inserted by Catherine. The idea of a Queen of Sweden belonging to the Orthodox faith and having her own chapel in his palace was not only contrary to the laws of his country but against his own strict Lutheran principles, and he refused to agree to clauses it would be impossible to carry out. Both Markov and Zubov, and finally Bezborodko, on whom they had called in their despair, tried to prevail on Gustavus to desist from a course which might have dire consequences both for himself and for his country. Neither the Empress nor her subjects would ever forgive the affront, nor would her father and brothers forgive his heartless behaviour towards the Grand Duchess Alexandra. For three hours they threatened, argued and implored, while Catherine and her court waited in the throne room. The Empress's face was becoming dangerously red – her mouth was shut in a thin, hard line, while her granddaughter looked pathetically near to tears.

In spite of the arguments and threats, the King refused to give in. At ten o'clock he retired to his room, locking his doors and leaving the Russian ministers stunned by his audacity. Everyone blamed the Duke of Sudermania for this rigid stand on the part of a seventeen-year-old boy, who was said to be in love with his fiancée. Even some of the Swedes were shocked, and no one dared to break the news to Catherine. It was Zubov who finally had the unpleasant duty of informing his sovereign that all her cherished plans had foundered, largely owing to his own stupidity and incompetency.

Even now she could not bring herself to believe that a King of Sweden had dared to defy her in her own palace. She rose from her throne and staggered. She tried to speak but the words were unintelligible. The gentlemen in attendance came forward to support her to her room. And that night she had her first attack of apoplexy.

The attack was a slight one, for a few days later she was sufficiently recovered to appear in public and take formal leave of the King of Sweden, noting with a sombre satisfaction that he looked as pale and as unhappy as her poor little granddaughter, who had fallen ill from disappointment. But the Empress's nervous system never recovered from the shock of the first public humiliation she had ever experienced. The fury she had been at such pains to control reacted on her already failing health, though outwardly she appeared to be as 'imperturbable' as ever, still maintaining the legend of her eternal youth, writing to Grimm that 'she was feeling as merry as a lark', at the good news of allied victories, of the French armies having had to re-cross the Rhine. On the evening of 4 November, she celebrated the victory with a small party of her intimates at the Hermitage, including the Austrian minister, Count Cobenzel, and her old friend Leon Naryshkin who, at seventy, still played the role of court jester. Though she appeared to be in the best of spirits, it was noted that she retired earlier than usual, on the excuse that 'she was suffering from a colic after laughing too much'.

On the following morning she rose at the usual hour, and after being visited for a few moments by Prince Zubov, was settling down to work with one of her secretaries, when she asked him to retire for a moment into the antechamber. There he waited for an hour and, when no call came, began to be anxious. He summoned the maids and valets, one of whom opened the door of the dressing room, where to their horror they saw the Empress lying on the floor. She had fallen from the commode and was straddled between the two doors leading from the closet to the dressing room. Her face was livid, her body completely inert. With difficulty they dragged her on a mattress back to her room, where she lived on for two days without recovering consciousness. It was a sad end for a sovereign who had earned the title of 'the Great'.

Bibliography

Unpublished Documents
Correspondence of the Prince de Ligne from the family archives.
Public Record Office Folios 6513–14–15–17.
Archives of the Quai d'Orsay, Paris, Vol. Russia 120 1785–1787–1788.

Main Sources
Alexander Bruckner: *Katherine die Zweite* (Berlin 1863).
The Cambridge Modern History Vol. IV: The Eighteenth Century (Cambridge 1970).
F. Gooch: *Catherine the Great and Other Studies* (London 1954).
Correspondance artistique de Melchior Grimm avec Catherine II (Paris 1932).
V. O. Kluchersky: *A History of Russia*, Vols 4 and 5, trans. Hogarth (London 1931).
C. F. Masson: *Mémoires Secrets sur la Russie à la fin du XVIII Siècle* (Amsterdam 1800).
Albert Rambaud: *The History of Russia from the Earliest Times*, Vol. 2, trans. Leonora Laing (London 1879).
George Soloveytchik: *Potemkin, a picture of Catherine's Russia* (London 1938).
Le Roman d'une Impératrice, Catherine de Russie d'après ses Mémoires, sa Correspondance et les Documents Inédits des Archives d'Etat (Paris 1893).
Autour d'un Trône (Paris 1894).
Mémoires de Catherine II écrits par elle-même, preface de Herzen (London 1859).

Other sources
E. M. Almedingen: *Catherine the Great, a portrait* (London 1963).

Katherine Antony: *Catherine the Great*, Life and Letters series, Vol. 13 (London 1913).

Joseph II, Katherine von Russland. Ihre Brief Weschel, ed. A. Ritter von Arneth (Vienna 1869).

Nisbet Bain: *The Last King of Poland and his Contemporaries* (London 1909).

Augustus Burell: *Paul Jones, Founder of the American Navy*, Vol. 2 (London 1900).

Memoirs of the Princess Dashkov, 2 vols, ed. Mrs Bradford (London 1840).

Madame Vigée le Brun: Memoirs, trans. Lionel Strachey (London 1904).

Catherine II, sa cour et la Russie en 1772 par le Chargé d'affaires français, Sebastien de Cabres (Paris 1862).

Cambridge History of Poland Vol. ii 1697–1935 (Cambridge 1950).

History of Catherine II, Empress of Russia, by Castéra, trans. Henry Hunter (London 1806).

Un diplomat français à la cour de Catherine II 1775–1786. Journal intime du Chevalier de Corberon, Vol. 2 (Paris 1901).

Arthur Coxe: *Travels into Poland, Russia, Sweden and Denmark*, (5 vols) Vol. 2, Vol. 3 (London 1792).

Diderot correspondance 1773–1774 (Paris 1967).

Paul Dukes: *Catherine the Great and the Russian Nobility* (Cambridge 1967).

Comte de Langeron Mémoires (Paris 1902).

Pierre Gaxotte: *Frederick the Great*, trans. R. A. Bell (London 1941).

Memoirs of Prince Adam Czartoryski, 2 vols, Vol. 1, ed. Adam Gielgud (London 1888).

Ian Grey: *Catherine the Great, Autocrat and Empress of all Russia* (London 1961).

Francis Gribble: *The Comedy of Catherine the Great* (London 1911).

Correspondance de Catherine Alexievna, Grande Duchesse de Russie et Sir Charles Hanbury-Williams, ambassadeur d'Angleterre (Paris 1946).

James Harris, Earl of Malmesbury: *Memoirs, Diaries and Correspondence* (London 1844).

D. B. Horn: *Sir Charles Hanbury-Williams and European Diplomacy* (London 1930).

H. Montgomery Hyde: *Empress Catherine and Prince Dashkov* (London 1935).

Correspondence of Catherine the Great when Grand Duchess with Sir Charles Hanbury-Williams, and letters from Count Poniatowski, ed. the Earl of Ilchester (London 1928).

Audrey and Victor Kennet: *The Palaces of Leningrad* (London 1973).

Memoirs and letters of the Prince de Ligne, trans. Katherine Prescott, with introduction by Saint Beuve from 'Causeries de Lundi' (London 1899).

Lettres au Prince de Ligne, ed. Princess Charles de Ligne (Brussels 1924).

Philip Longworth: *The Three Empresses. Catherine I, Anne, Elisabeth of Russia* (London 1972).

Archivio del General Miranda, Viajes Diarios 1785–1789, Vol. 2, (Caracas 1929).

George Loukomski: *Charles Cameron*, adapted and edited in English by Nicholas de Gren (London 1943).

Fitzgerald Molloy: *The Russian Court in the Eighteenth Century*, Vol. 16 (London 1905).

Paul Morane: *Paul Ier de Russie avent l'avènement 1754–1796* (Paris 1907).

Zoé Oldenbourg: *Catherine the Great*, trans. Anne Carter (London 1965).

Daria Olivier: *Les Romanoffs* (Lausanne 1968).

Daria Olivier: *Elisabeth de Russie* (Paris 1967).

Lettres d'amour de Catherine II à Potemkin (correspondance inédite), introduction by George Oudard (Paris 1934).

Jean Orieux: *Voltaire* (Paris 1967).

Saul K. Padover: *The Revolutionary Emperor Joseph II of Austria* (London 1967).

Jean Palewski: *Stanislas August Poniatowski, Dernier Roi de Pologne* (Paris 1946).

Alan Palmer: *Alexander II* (London 1975).

Charles Pearce: *The Amazing Duchess*, the romantic history of Elisabeth Chudleigh, maid-of-honour, the Hon. Mrs. Hervey, Duchess of Kingston, Countess of Bristol. Vol. 2 (London 1911).

Alexander Polotsoff: *The Favourites of Catherine the Great* (London 1948).

Louis Reau: *L'art français dans les pays du nord et de l'est de l'Europe au dixhuitième et dixneuvième siècles* (Paris 1932).

Documents of Catherine the Great. Correspondence with Voltaire, ed. W. Reddaway (Cambridge 1931).

Charles de la Rivière: *Catherine II et la Révolution Française* (Paris 1895).

Michael Roberts: *Macartney in Russia* (English Historical Review 1974).

William Spence Robertson: *The Life of Miranda* (N. Carolina 1929).

Frederic de Schmitt: *Frederick II, Catherine II et le Partage de Pologne* (Paris-Berlin 1861).

Gladys Scott-Thomson: *Catherine the Great and the Expansion of Russia* (London 1947).

Mémoires ou souvenirs et anecdotes par le Comte de Ségur, Vol. 2–3, (Paris 1806).

Mémoires de Casanova de Seingalt écrits par lui-meme, Vol. 7 (Paris 1912).

Picture of St Petersburg, trans. from the German of Henry Storch (London 1801).

Letters of Horace Walpole, Vol. 10, ed. Mrs Paget Toynbee 1777–9 (Oxford 1903–5).

Fernand Vallon: *Falconet* (Paris 1927).

Ernest Vizetelly: *The true story of the Chevalier d'Eon with the aid of state and secret papers* (London 1895).

Voyage de deux Francais Vol. 3–4 (Paris 1796).

Arthur Wilson: *Diderot* (New York 1972).

Index

Catherine II—*cont.*

67–9, 70–3, 78, 79–80, 96; relationship with Bestuzhev, 73, 76, 78–9; ambition to become Empress, 73–4, 76, 79–80, 105; relationship with Frederick II, 81, 300–1; love of Russia, 81; birth of Grand Duchess Anne, 82–3; confrontation with Elisabeth, 86–95; relationship with her children, 96; disassociates herself from Peter III's treachery during Seven Years War, 98; and Panin, 98–9; and Princess Dashkov, 99–100; relationship with Gregory Orlov, 101–2, 105, 129–30, 146–7, 149, 151–4, 182, 184–5, 190, 191, 193–4, 199, 206; and Elisabeth's death, 102, 103–4, 106–8, 109–10; financial problems, 104–5; and Peter III's accession to the throne, 109; birth of Bobrinskoy, 113; conspiracy against Peter III, 114–16; becomes Empress, 117–25; imprisons Peter III, 125, 126–8; state entry into St Petersburg, 128–9; and Peter III's death, 133–6; first years as Empress, 137–47; rewards the conspirators in the *coup d'état*, 139–40; and serfdom, 140–2, 166–9; coronation, 142–3; secures her position on the throne, 149–50; discovers plot against Orlov family, 152–3; and Ivan VI's death, 154–9; and government of Russia, 161–2, 312–14; and the encyclopaedists, 162–4; reforms Russian legal code, 164–5, 166–9, 196, 223; makes Poniatowski King of Poland, 170–8; relations with France, 179; first war with Turkey, 180, 181; 'Greek project', 186–9, 258; smallpox innoculation, 190–1; builds the Hermitage, 191–2; relationship with Potemkin, 192–3, 225, 233, 234–6, 238–44, 247–51, 254–60, 341–2; ill-health, 195–6; church reforms, 197–8; opposition to her reign, 197–9; and St Petersburg, 199; artistic interests, 200–3, 280–3, 309–10; educational reforms, 203–6; affair with Vassilchikof, 207–10, 212–13, 235; dismisses Gregory Orlov, 210–13; and partition of Poland, 214–18; Pugachefschina, 219–22, 246; neglects social reforms, 222–3; arranges marriage for Grand Duke Paul, 223–4, 225–7; meets Diderot, 230–3; administrative reforms, 250–1; relations with Muscovites, 252, 342; and Natalia Alexievna's death, 252–3; possible marriage to Potemkin, 255–6, 361; affair with Zavadowsky, 260–1, 262–3; and Grand Duke Paul's second marriage, 261–2; and Bezborodko, 264–6; and Bavarian succession, 267; England seeks defensive alliance with, 268–9; later affairs, 270–1, 275–80; celebrates the birth of Grand Duke Alexander, 271–2; appearance in later life, 272–3, 379; disturbed by Gregory Orlov's marriage, 273; and Baron Grimm, 275–6; affair with Lanskoy, 279–80, 289, 297, 305–7; Austria seeks alliance with, 286–91; foreign policy, 290; refuses England's offer of Balearic Islands, 294–5; dislikes French interest in Russian culture, 296–7; and Orlov's death, 298–9, 300; relationship with Grand Duke Paul, 301–2; affair with Yermolov, 308–9; compiles dictionary of Russian language, 311–12; writes plays, 312, 353; quarrels with Potemkin, 316–17; journey to the Crimea, 317–18, 319–21, 323–30, 331–42; friendship with de Ligne, 321–3; affair with Momonof, 323–4; second Turkish war, 343–7, 349, 358–9; affair with Zoubov, 354, 355–6, 366–9, 370–1, 382; relations with Joseph II, 361–2; suppresses *A Journey from St Petersburg to Moscow*, 363–4; physical and mental decline in later life, 368–9; and Potemkin's death, 374–5; second and third partitions of Poland, 375–9; arranges marriage of Grand Duchess Alexandra, 383–5; death, 385–6; correspondence with Grimm, 227–8, 235–6, 244, 248, 251–3, 262, 274, 279–80, 282, 299, 300, 301, 306–7, 309, 310, 311, 324, 336–7, 353, 354, 365, 375, 380–1, 382, 385; correspondence with Poniatowski,